Teacher Preparation

See a demo at
www.prenhall.com/teacherprep/demo

D0066552

Your Class. Their Careers. Our Future. Will your students be prepared?

We invite you to explore our new, innovative and engaging website and all that it has to offer you, your course, and tomorrow's educators! Preview this site today at www.prenhall.com/teacherprep/demo. Just click on "go" on the login page to begin your exploration.

Organized around the major courses pre-service teachers take, the Teacher Preparation site provides media, student/teacher artifacts, strategies, research articles, and other resources to equip your students with the quality tools needed to excel in their courses and prepare them for their first classroom.

This ultimate on-line education resource will provide you and your students access to:

Online Video Library. More than 250 video clips—each tied to a course topic and framed by learning goals and Praxis-type questions—capture real teachers and students working in real classrooms.

Student and Teacher Artifacts. More than 200 student and teacher classroom artifacts—each tied to a course topic and framed by learning goals and application questions—provide a wealth of materials and experiences to help your students observe children's developmental learning.

Lesson Plan Builder. Step-by-step guidelines and lesson plan examples to support students as they learn to build high-quality lesson plans.

Articles and Readings. Over 500 articles from ASCD's renowned journal *Educational Leadership* are available. The site also includes *Research Navigator,* a searchable database of additional educational journals.

Strategies and Lessons. Over 500 research-supported instructional strategies appropriate for a wide range of grade levels and content areas.

Licensure and Career Tools. Resources devoted to helping your students pass their licensure exam; learn standards, law, and public policies; plan a teaching portfolio; and succeed in their first year of teaching.

How to ORDER *Teacher Prep* for you and your students:

◆ For students to receive a *Teacher Prep* Access Code with this text, please provide your bookstore with ISBN 0-13-223799-7 when you **place** your textbook order. The bookstore **must** order the text with this ISBN to be eligible for this offer.

Upon ordering *Teacher Prep* for their students, instructors will be given a lifetime *Teacher Prep* Access Code. To receive your access code, please email: **Merrill.marketing@pearsoned.com** and provide the following information:

◆ Name and Affiliation
◆ Author/Title/Edition of Merrill text

Meaningful Assessments of the Young Child

Celebrating Development and Learning

THIRD EDITION

MARGARET B. PUCKETT
Texas Wesleyan University

JANET K. BLACK
Texas A&M International University

PEARSON

Merrill
Prentice Hall

Upper Saddle River, New Jersey
Columbus, Ohio

KH

Library of Congress Cataloging-in-Publication Data

Puckett, Margaret B.
  Meaningful assessments of the young child : celebrating development and learning/Margaret B. Puckett, Janet K. Black.—3rd ed.
    p. cm.
  Rev. ed. of: Authentic assessment of the young child. 2000.
  Includes bibliographical references and index.
  ISBN-13: 978-0-13-223759-8
  ISBN-10: 0-13-223759-8
  1. Educational tests and measurements. 2. Early childhood education—Evaluation. 3. Child development—Evaluation. I. Black, Janet K.
II. Puckett, Margaret B. Authentic assessment of the young child. III. Title.
  LB3051.P69 2008
  372.126—dc22

2006103493

Vice President and Executive Publisher: Jeffery W. Johnston
Publisher: Kevin M. Davis
Acquisitions Editor: Julie Peters
Editorial Assistant: Tiffany Bitzel
Production Editor: Linda Hillis Bayma
Production Coordination: Kelly Ricci/ Techbooks

Design Coordinator: Diane C. Lorenzo
Photo Coordinator: Lori Whitley
Cover Designer: Terry Rohrbach
Cover image: Corbis
Production Manager: Laura Messerly
Director of Marketing: David Gesell
Marketing Manager: Amy Judd
Marketing Coordinator: Brian Mounts

This book was set in Zapf Calligraphic by Techbooks. It was printed and bound by Hamilton Printing Company. The cover was printed by Phoenix Color Corp.

Photo Credits for Chapter Openers: Getty Images, Inc.–PhotoDisc, p. 2; Paige Killian, pp. 26, 88; Anne Vega/Merrill, p. 54; Scott Cunningham/Merrill, p. 116; Barbara Schwartz/Merrill, p. 140; Lori Whitley/Merrill, p. 168; Sargent N. Hill, p. 218; Margaret B. Puckett, p. 258.

Pearson Education Ltd.
Pearson Education Singapore Pte. Ltd.
Pearson Education Canada, Ltd.
Pearson Education—Japan

Pearson Education Australia Pty. Limited
Pearson Education North Asia Ltd.
Pearson Educación de Mexico, S.A. de C.V.
Pearson Education Malaysia Pte. Ltd.

10 9 8 7 6 5 4 3 2 1
ISBN-13: 978-0-13-223759-8
ISBN-10:   0-13-223759-8

7/29/08

To early childhood educators everywhere who, on a daily basis,
find precious moments to celebrate the uniqueness of each learner

and

To our children and grandchildren, whose growth, development,
and learning have always been a source of joy and enlightenment to us.

◇ ◇

About the Authors

Margaret B. Puckett is Retired Professor of Education and Chair of the Elementary and Early Childhood Education department at Texas Wesleyan University in Fort Worth, Texas. She has taught courses in Child Development, Early Childhood Education, Elementary Education, and Day Care Administration at the University of North Texas, Texas Tech University, and Tarrant County College. She has taught children two years old through grade three and has worked in school administration.

Dr. Puckett received a B.S. from the University of Texas at Austin, an M.S. in Child Development from Texas Women's University, and a Doctorate from the University of North Texas. Through funds for faculty enrichment provided by the Richardson Foundation, Dr. Puckett has studied child care and education in Israel and England.

She is a past president of the Southern Early Childhood Association, the Texas Association for the Education of Young Children, and the Fort Worth Area Association for the Education of Young Children.

She has been honored with the Outstanding Alumnus in Early Childhood Education Award by the University of North Texas, and the Texas Wesleyan University Faculty Recognition Award for excellence in teaching, research, and professional outreach. She is coauthor of *The Young Child: Development from Prebirth Through Age Eight,* published by Merrill/Prentice Hall, and *Teaching Young Children: Introduction to the Early Childhood Profession,* published by Thomson/Delmar Learning.

Janet K. Black has twelve years of experience teaching young children from ages three through eight in public schools in Ohio and Illinois. She has also taught preservice and inservice teachers for twenty years at universities in Ohio and Texas. Currently she is Executive Director of the San Antonio office of the Vice Chancellor for Academic and Student Affairs of the Texas A&M University System.

Dr. Black received a Ph.D. in Early and Middle Childhood Education from The Ohio State University, where she was recipient of the Outstanding Graduate Student Award for Research and Creativity from the College of Education. She also was named a Promising Researcher by the National Council of Teachers of English. Dr. Black has published in such journals as *Young Children, Dimensions, Language Arts,* and *Research in the Teaching of English.* She is coauthor of *The Young Child: Development from Prebirth Through Age Eight,* published by Merrill/Prentice Hall.

She is Past President of the Texas Association for the Education of Young Children and has served on committees for the National Association for the Education of Young Children and the Southern Early Childhood Association. Dr. Black was an invited participant in the 2001 White House Conference on Early Childhood Cognitive Development hosted by First Lady Laura Bush.

Preface

Is it possible to merge formal testing requirements with informal assessment practices, such as *authentic assessment* or *performance assessment,* to achieve a coherent assessment system? We think so. Thus, we have retitled this third edition as *Meaningful Assessments of the Young Child,* from the previous *Authentic Assessment of the Young Child.* Based on the premise that curriculum, assessment, and teaching are inextricably intertwined, this text is designed to help educators of young children develop a complementary and comprehensive assessment system by drawing information from both formal and informal assessment strategies. This meaningful assessment system then uses data from varied sources to inform educators, learners, parents, administrators, and other groups who are accountable for student progress and achievement. Comprehensive, reliable, and valid assessment data pave the way for meaningful, relevant, and engaging learning opportunities for children.

FOCUS ON UNDERSTANDING FORMAL AND INFORMAL ASSESSMENTS

This text invites you to revisit the concept of authentic assessment as introduced in previous editions, but with a new caveat. Education is now characterized by what some refer to as a "culture of testing." This culture of testing summons our best thinking and concerted efforts to explore both the opportunities and challenges in assessing development and learning in young children.

From many classrooms to the home and spread throughout the populace through the media is the message that large-scale standardized testing is an essential element in educating the nation's children. From preschool through college, students are being tested in schools for a multiplicity of purposes, primary among them is to hold institutions accountable for learning outcomes.

In this social/political/educational context, attention is often diverted from developmentally appropriate, authentically derived assessments of individual child development and learning. Yet, it is appropriate to expect educational programs to be accountable to those whom they serve and those from whom their financial support comes. Inherent in this accountability is the expectation that programs serving young children and their families do so in a manner that serves their best interests. Therefore, our text shows prospective teachers how to create an assessment system that incorporates both formal testing and informal, more authentic, performance-based assessments without compromising developmentally appropriate practices.

The text provides:

◆ extensive guidelines for obtaining and using information derived from both formal and informal assessments.

◆ techniques for observing and documenting growth, development, and learning.

◆ guidelines for drawing valid inferences from observations and assessment procedures.

◆ suggestions for collaborating with individual learners to support and guide their performance and progress.

◆ suggestions for engaging families in a collaborative assessment model.

◆ suggestions for developing a tiered portfolio system that meets both needs for assessment *of* and assessment *for* learning.

◆ guidance for including program assessment in a comprehensive and meaningful assessment system.

ORGANIZATION AND CONTENTS OF THIS TEXT

This text is divided into three sections. Part I provides a contemporary portrait of the social, educational, and political expectations driving curriculum and assessment practices. Illustrated in **Chapter 1** are the "languages" applied to assessment and the purposes of assessment embedded in an exploration of underlying early childhood development and education theories. Also emphasized are the ethical practices in evaluating young children's development and learning. In **Chapter 2,** a "big picture" paradigm demonstrates the concept of a comprehensive assessment system. Such a meaningful system incorporates principles of (1) whole child development, (2) multicultural perspectives, and (3) meeting the needs of children with developmental challenges. In addition, this chapter includes the developmentally appropriate practices aligned with curriculum content and outcomes standards.

Part II provides a framework for integrating formal and informal assessments into a meaningful assessment system. **Chapter 3** places emphasis on the appropriate uses of formal assessments, including large-scale standardized testing, and discusses how formal assessments might contribute to a meaningful assessment system. How to interpret and use scores and information from standardized tests and other formal instruments is addressed. **Chapter 4** emphasizes the importance of ongoing, in-context assessment practices and describes many types of informal assessment procedures. The chapter describes the development and uses of meaningful rubric systems. Chapters 3 and 4 provide sample observation and assessment forms, graphs, and anecdotal illustrations to help the student construct a meaningful assessment system that utilizes reliable formal and informal assessments. **Chapter 5** describes the development, use, and potential accountability function of portfolios. Additionally, **Chapters 6 and 7** describe procedures for collaborating with child learners and their families to inform and support learning and assessment processes. **Chapter 6** explores the notion that children themselves can become engaged in setting goals and assessing their own progress. It also describes techniques for collaborating with individual learners in an assessment process. **Chapter 7** extends the collaborative model to include families in the assessment process. It also discusses guidelines for understanding and working with diverse families, along with specific suggestions on engaging families in the process as essential to the development of a comprehensive and meaningful assessment system.

Part III engages the student in a number of child-development issues associated with the implementation of meaningful assessment practices. Because many states have or are developing programs to promote and assess school readiness, **Chapter 8** focuses on the indicators of readiness in all developmental domains. The need for early screening and intervention is described through the early childhood educator's role in promoting, assessing, and responding to individual readiness characteristics. Further, this chapter elucidates the proposal that readiness does not rest solely with the child, but with families, schools, and communities. **Chapter 9** highlights the fact that a meaningful assessment system necessitates an evaluation of early childhood programs through licensing, other mandates, and professional accreditation programs.

UNIQUE FEATURES OF THIS TEXT

Each chapter includes thought-provoking, theme-supporting quotations, chapter objectives, teacher anecdotes and case examples, review strategies and activities, and suggested related literature and resources. The end-of-chapter pedagogy poses *Vexing Questions,* framed to invoke spirited discussion and debate. Appendices include a rich array of relevant and useful resources that augment information throughout the text.

Supplementary Materials

Online Instructor's Manual: A new manual is provided for download from Prentice Hall's website at www.prenhall.com at the Instructor's Resource Center. Adopting professors may register for a password and have access within 24 hours or less.

Online Test Bank: A new test bank, with multiple choice and short answer items, is also available for download at www.prenhall.com.

ACKNOWLEDGMENTS

We are particularly grateful to our students and colleagues who have read and critiqued this text. From the numerous classroom teachers who have shared their experiences in applying the concepts proposed in this text, we have found both affirmation and challenges. Their daily encounters with young children steady our focus and motivate our continuing explorations into this critical area of research.

We also extend profound appreciation to those who reviewed the revised manuscript for this edition: Jacqueline Coffman, California State University, Fullerton;

Delisa Dismukes, Jacksonville State University; Jill E. Fox, Virginia Commonwealth University; and Robert Harrington, University of Kansas.

Finally, special appreciation is extended to our editor, Julie Peters, who has shepherded this revision project with insights, skill, and patience. To other friends at Merrill/Prentice Hall, whose interest, skill, and diligence has made this text possible, we extend our profound appreciation.

Brief Contents

Contents

PART II   COMPONENTS OF A MEANINGFUL ASSESSMENT SYSTEM   53

Note: Every effort has been made to provide accurate and current Internet information in this book. However, the Internet and information posted on it are constantly changing, so it is inevitable that some of the Internet addresses listed in this textbook will change.

Overview of Assessments of Young Children

1

Assessments of Young Children
Striving for Meaningful Practices

These are the children of promise—preschoolers, whose boundless energy is matched only by their curiosity and creativity, whose agility is the envy of their parents and teachers, whose openness and expressiveness are always remarkable and occasionally breathtaking. Watching them, it is easy to believe that they can do anything they want to do, be anyone they want to be; it is easy to summon the optimism that yet a new generation is rising to fuel this nation's historical belief in endless possibility.

Years of Promise, Carnegie Corporation of New York (1996)

After reading this chapter, you will demonstrate comprehension by being able to:

❑ discuss the current emphasis on assessments in education and its implications for practices in early childhood education.

❑ distinguish among the various languages of assessment and their intended audiences.

❑ elucidate the different purposes of assessment.

❑ describe sociopolitical trends associated with contemporary assessment practices.

❑ discuss ethical considerations and responsibilities in assessment practices with young children.

CONTEMPORARY SOCIAL AND EDUCATION REALITIES

Today's education is characterized by reliance on more and more testing and assessment. Education is in an age of accountability. This age of accountability, brought about by the standards movement of the 1990s, has yielded increasing emphasis in every grade (including the early childhood grades) on test scores that are purported to assure that schools, teachers, and students are meeting society's expectations. A testing culture has evolved that has markedly altered the types of education experiences children are offered as they progress through the grades of their formal schooling.

Professionals in education, psychology, sociology, and political science share the view that schooling today is an entirely different enterprise in many aspects than it was in years past, even the recent past. Schools are educating a greater percentage of the total population, in which there is enormous diversity in culture, ethnicity, first language, and socioeconomic status. Increasing numbers of immigrants continuously change school population profiles. Families bring diverse values, goals, and expectations to the dynamics of educating their children. Moreover, political pressure to hold schools accountable for student achievement continues to increase, along with increasing emphasis on *academic standards* and *learning benchmarks*. Grade-level expectations continue to push curriculum downward, subjecting younger children to content and teaching strategies previously offered to older children.

The information explosion, driven by evolving and revolutionizing computer technology and spectacular advances in the sciences, profoundly widens our knowledge universe and continually alters the content of subjects to be taught. Additionally, the biological sciences have brought new insights into brain growth and neurological development, particularly in the earliest months and years, changing our views of how children learn and how intelligence is defined. Child-development research and changing knowledge about the long-term effects of early experiences is focusing, in an unprecedented way, public and policy-maker attention on very young children. This emphasis has brought about renewed interest in educating very young children (ages birth to five years), as well as more focused emphasis on the primary grades (grades one through three). Heightened interest in the earliest developmental years has helped to blend the goals of the child-care sector and formal school settings. *Universal prekindergarten* is a topic addressed in many legislatures today as policy makers respond to the much touted potential for learning during the early years. The terms *school readiness* and *learning readiness* have taken on renewed importance as states and localities attempt to delineate child *readiness indicators*.

The information explosion has also had an impact on curriculum content and teaching methodology at all levels of education. Some experts suggest that the knowledge generated during the twentieth century exceeded that accumulated from all previous centuries! In this era, popularly referred to as the *information age*, individuals must be able to collect, analyze, synthesize, structure, store, and retrieve information in a selective and discerning manner. Preparing today's students for a future in a highly technological world, a diminishing globe, and a "loaded" information age requires thoughtful consideration of how best to prepare students for *their* future. Curriculum content and teaching strategies must be continuously scrutinized for the potential to provide both broad and deep

Information Blitz

It is estimated that the amount of new words, sounds, pictures, and numbers produced and stored on paper, film, or electronic formats almost doubles in three years. The Library of Congress is the world's largest collection of books and papers, yet the amount of new material (electronically) saved during the year 2002, if converted to print, is reported to be enough to fill half a million book collections the size of the book collection in the Library of Congress. Most of this material (86 percent) is produced and stored in business offices; the remainder is produced by news and magazines, books, and scholarly organizations (Lyman & Varian, 2002).

coverage of essential knowledge, skills, and responsible citizenship. At the same time, there is a profound need for meaningful methods of determining what students know and are able to do and how best to use this information to assure relevant and meaningful educational experiences for them.

Although educators do not forecast the future, they must be cognizant of what futurists predict. Those who forecast the future generally address changes expected in political structures; economics; immigration and population trends; social welfare and family life; education; and science, health, and medicine. Hence, educators are challenged to consider what life will be like for their students in the coming decades and what demands for knowledge and skills await them. Educators are challenged to consider how best to help today's children become tomorrow's constructive, productive citizens. For today's children, whose lives will span the twenty-first century, the following essential skills and characteristics are most frequently identified:

◆ basic reading, writing, and computation skills and the disposition to use these skills as tools to communicate effectively through oral, written, and technological means and to efficiently manage their personal lives

◆ the ability to access and select wisely from vast amounts of rapidly emerging new information

◆ the ability to think critically and efficiently

◆ creative problem-solving ability and the confidence to pursue the unknown

◆ a broad knowledge base that includes knowledge and skills in many and varied content areas

◆ the ability to relate to others in positive and productive ways, which includes the interpersonal skills of perspective taking, empathy, and altruism

◆ the ability to function productively in group contexts that require cooperation, collaboration, negotiation, and conflict resolution

◆ positive self-regard complemented by worthy personal goals and self-determination

◆ a sense of shared democracy in a global society that is growing increasingly smaller, yet more and more interdependent and complex

The premise of this text is that curriculum, assessment, and teaching should be uniquely designed to address these projected essential capabilities in the context of a very complex and changing world society. This design intertwines curriculum, assessment, and teaching. In this perspective, curriculum, assessment, and teaching are interdependent and inseparable. Figure 1.1 illustrates this point of view by contrasting it with traditional assessment practices. We will attempt to lay out an assessment gestalt that facilitates, at least in part, progress toward achieving these essential knowledge, skills, and characteristics.

We begin to discuss the development of an assessment gestalt by providing an overview of the languages of assessment that are so often commingled in popular press and casual conversation and are often confusing, if not misleading.

Figure 1.1
Meaningful Assessment, Representing
Teaching, Learning, and Assessing as
Ongoing and Interwined

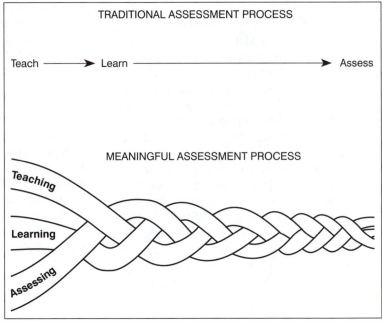

THE LANGUAGES OF ASSESSMENT

Throughout the professional literature and popular press, the phrase *best practice* in education is frequently used. Its meaning is nebulous, having many connotations, depending on who is applying it and the context in which it is being applied. We posit that best practices evolve from knowledge of children's growth, development, and learning and information derived from meaningful assessments of children that take place over time and in many contexts. When it comes to assessment of young children, the effort to define and implement best practices can be confused by the language used to describe it. Let's begin our exploration of meaningful methods of determining what children know and are able to do with a preliminary discussion of the "languages of assessment."

It is midsummer and the local newspaper tantalizes the public with news of soon-to-be published state and local test scores and school ratings. When reported, these data will compare student, school, and district performances on *state-mandated* tests that have been administered on a designated date (or dates) and to selected grades on particular subjects. *Large-scale testing* is intended to provide comparative data that portray *student achievement* in individual classrooms and schools within individual school districts. Student test-score data can be compared with that of districts across the state, in other states, and even on international scales. Popular references to the data often provide very generalized descriptions such as *high-performing* and *low-performing schools*. Some descriptions are more disquieting, with terms such as *succeeding schools* and *failing schools*. The readership is told that it can expect school ratings after their release from the *state education agency* later in the week.

A few days later in the local newspaper, on television, and through the Internet, the data are shared with the public. Area schools are listed and ranked or rated according to terms such as *exemplary, recognized, academically acceptable, academically unacceptable*, or *low performing*. These and similar ranking or rating terms are used throughout the states. The intent of such reporting is to assure the taxpaying public that the schools in their state or locale are being held *accountable* to high *academic standards* and that tax dollars are focused on *improving schools* and/or *student performance*.*

This type of reporting is addressed to a variety of audiences: local governments seeking to entice businesses to the community; local businesses seeking to employ a well-educated workforce; realtors seeking to find homes for families near the "best" schools, and politicians and policy makers seeking to demonstrate their interest in the schooling of America's children. Parents may use this information to compare their child's school's reported test performance with that of other schools in their town or district.

Such reporting is based on the assumption that students will be praised for good efforts and performance and continue their good work or, as indicated by the data, be motivated to improve test scores. Further, it is assumed that teachers and school personnel will likewise be inspired to reach peak performance. Often such reports either intentionally or unintentionally serve the purpose of putting administrators of school districts on notice, exerting pressure to demonstrate that their's are *high-performing schools*. This charge to raise test scores and to show *adequate yearly progress* is then communicated to individual school principals, classroom teachers, and pupils and their families.

In news reports and the media, in speeches before Congress and state legislatures, and in literature generated by the professions, we encounter terms such as *world-class standards, academic benchmarks, high-stakes testing, curriculum alignment*, and *school readiness*. These and many related popular terms represent a major focus in assessment of student learning and accomplishments. They are representative of one of the languages of assessment—a form of assessment that we describe more fully as we proceed.

But there is another language of assessment, not quite so familiar to the general public and seldom described in the popular press or media reports. In this language we hear terms such as *performance-based assessment, authentic assessment, student-centered classrooms, hands-on curriculum, integrated learning*, and *portfolio development*. The assessments implied by these terms take place on a day-to-day basis (as opposed to once or twice a year in selected grades) and are generally associated with individual student performance, as opposed to school district, teacher, or school performance. Unlike the language of large-scale testing, which is directed to many audiences, this language is more germane to student, teacher, and parent communication and is focused on a multiplicity of factors, both ecological and developmental, affecting successful learning outcomes for individuals. Because of their day-to-day, ongoing nature, these types of assessments are useful in planning, implementing, evaluating, and modifying daily activities, curricula, and expectations to address individual student capabilities, challenges, and aspirations.

A third language of assessment is that of *screening, identification*, and *intervention* with children who have *developmental challenges* and *special needs*. In this language

---

*Italics are used for emphasis in this chapter. A complete glossary is included following the appendices to define and amplify important terms, which appear in boldface throughout the text.

In a testing culture, parents are often concerned about publicly reported school test results.

EyeWire Collection/Getty Images, Inc.—PhotoDisc

we read and hear terms such as *developmental* and/or *academic risk, risk factors,* and *eligibility for special services.* This language of assessment addresses highly individualistic needs and is generally guided by professionals in the health-care, psychological, and psychiatric professions, along with *licensed education diagnosticians* and classroom teachers with academic backgrounds in *special education.* This language includes terms most recognizable to individuals who have specialized training in screening, assessing, and diagnosing and is communicated according to *professional and legal standards of student privacy* as a *team of professionals* develops *individualized education and family-service plans.* These plans are structured to meet specific individual developmental and education needs and are monitored frequently for expected *student outcomes.**

At this point we make a distinction very nicely articulated by Richard Stiggins (2002). It is the difference between assessment *of* learning and assessment *for* learning. The language of large-scale student testing is about assessment *of* learning. The language of day-to-day assessment is for the most part about assessment *for* learning. The language of screening and diagnosis is about assessment for the delivery of essential services or prescriptive supports for development and learning.

---

*Although a comprehensive discussion of this area of assessment is beyond the scope of this text, as with the other languages, we will attempt to address important aspects of it in the context of an assessment gestalt.

In the current context of education in America—with its federal and state mandates and the influence of scholarly research that is expanding the body of knowledge associated with human growth, development, and learning—each language must speak clearly and accurately to its audience(s). More importantly, educators are best informed when they distinguish between and employ both assessment *of* and assessment *for* learning. Tantamount to that is the need for—indeed, the responsibility of—educators to be knowledgeable and skilled in the selection, administration, and uses of many forms of classroom assessment (Stiggins, 2002).

A fourth language of assessment is related to school or program effectiveness, as measured not by how children score on selected tests, but by how the teaching and learning settings meet expectations associated with certain ecological and psychological attributes. This language may include concepts associated with *long-term effects* of certain types of *teaching strategies, curriculum models, assessment models, interactive climates,* and *teacher qualifications.* Further, this language includes references to *availability of resources;* nuances and ambiances of the *physical settings* for learning and teaching; the types and rhythms of *daily schedules;* and attention *to extracurricular opportunities.* It is the language of school or program quality and standards for *licensure* and *accreditation.*

Regardless of the language and the context in which various terminology is used, everyone—policy makers, federal, state, and local reporting agencies, journalists, educators, and others associated with student assessment—has a responsibility to obtain and portray assessment information in ways that are intellectually honest, meaningful, and useful in education contexts. The integrity of assessment systems depends on that. Assessment information is only as good as its ability to serve, in equitable ways, the learning needs of all students in all education settings. This topic is further addressed later in this chapter in our discussion of ethics in student assessment.

THE PURPOSES OF ASSESSMENTS IN EARLY-CHILDHOOD EDUCATION

Assessment is broadly defined as a process of collecting information about individuals and groups for the purpose of making decisions (Salvia & Ysseldyke, 1998). From the foregoing discussion of the languages of assessment, we can extrapolate the following purposes of assessment:

◆ identify, diagnose, and provide essential services to selected child and family populations

◆ determine individual developmental needs, strengths, and aspirations

◆ determine individual growth, development, and learning progress and academic achievements and challenges

◆ communicate with and assist learners in reflecting on their own progress and setting learning and achievement goals

◆ communicate individual student progress and needs with parents or guardians

◆ analyze curriculum content and teaching strategies and make needed adjustments to assure student success

◆ meet state and national licensing and accreditation requirements

◆ meet local, state, and federal mandates and accountability requirements

This book is about the selection and utilization of meaningful and relevant assessments of young children. Although the emphasis is on what has come to be known as "authentic assessment," a secondary emphasis will be on the search for that place where all assessments can be compatible with prevailing philosophy in early childhood education. The philosophy behind the search for a meaningful assessment gestalt includes a focus not only on cognitive and academic achievements, but also on growth, development, and functioning in other domains: physical/motor, language, social, emotional, and moral (Comer, 2006). This has historically been referred to as the *whole child perspective*. It is an essential perspective if early childhood education is to fulfill its obligation to assure wholesome, healthy childhood experiences. Indeed, the overall integrity of the growing and developing human organism depends on this perspective (Shonkoff & Phillips, 2000).

The whole child perspective is sensitive to human diversity and takes into consideration knowledge of the various contexts in which individual children grow, develop, and learn. Implicit in a whole child perspective is an understanding of and sensitivity to the needs of children with disabilities and of children from diverse cultural, language, and socioeconomic backgrounds. Curricula and assessments must be interwoven and carefully crafted to be age and individually appropriate, as well as relevant, meaningful, and useful to the learner both in and out of school contexts. Further, the preparation for and administration of mandated assessments must be sensitive to the dynamics of *developmentally appropriate practices* in education. This dictates that both the psychological and educational impact on children who are assessed must be considered. This, then, brings us to a very cursory review of some of the major theories that lie behind education and assessment practices in early childhood education.

THEORIES EMBEDDED IN INSTRUCTIONAL AND ASSESSMENT PRACTICES

Each language of assessment suggests different foci and, often, dissimilar assumptions about children, learners, teachers, and teaching. A look at underlying theoretic perspectives should foretell the intentions and expected outcomes of the varying assessment and testing practices.

Behavioral Theory

Large-scale testing practices are based primarily on behavioral theories. Such theories are based on assumptions that learning is a process in which the learner acquires knowledge incrementally in a linear fashion. Curricula (and assessments) are thought to be most effective when broken into sequential parts that address very specific skills and selected units of knowledge. Success and/or failure on a particular task or test is thought to motivate learning through the negative or positive reinforcement such an outcome or its attendant reward or negative consequence provides. Proponents of behavioral theory attend to overt, observable, and measurable behaviors.

Traditional behaviorists place more emphasis on learned behaviors than on innate attributes and developmental stages or time lines. Experience is considered an overriding factor in explaining behavior and learning. Behaviorists do not attempt to infer internal processes that may be responsible for an individual's particular response or behavior. Instead, attribution is given to reinforcement systems that include strategic use of negative or positive reinforcements for shaping behaviors and advancing learning. Positive reinforcements include both tangible (stickers, gold stars, candy, popcorn party) and intangible (praise, applause, special privilege) rewards. Negative reinforcers may be used strategically to encourage appropriate behaviors by removal of aversive or threatening stimuli. Punishment is the imposition of something aversive (time out, reprimand, loss of privilege) to bring about appropriate responses or behaviors.

In similar fashion, large-scale test-score reports for individuals, schools, or districts are not designed to consider such influencing factors as the type of physical or psychological environment in which tests are administered or the internal physiological or psychological state(s) of the test takers. Detractors of this point of view cite circumstances that can impede students' best efforts. Examples of extenuating circumstances abound: dilapidated school building with drafts and whistling windows versus a warm and cozy classroom with comfortable seating, lighting, and a relaxed ambiance; a test taker who has a fever, suggesting an impending illness; a learner who is overcome with stress or fear of failure; the competitive culture of parents whose pressures on their children to succeed impose on both children and teachers; a teacher whose employment is threatened on the outcomes of the test; and families whose efforts to put food on the table override their interest in their child's test performance. Nonetheless, the scores reflect only how accurately students answered questions posed by a particular test. Even so, they then are thought to represent the skills and units of knowledge that ostensibly were adequately taught and to what extent students learned these particular skills and units of knowledge, thus reflecting positively or negatively on the student, teacher, school, and school district. Scores are then used to reward, reinforce, and/or punish learners, teachers, schools, and school districts. One could conjecture that the *voucher system,* in which parents are provided financial assistance or other incentives to move their children to a higher-performing school, is a type of "punishment" intended to motivate low-performing schools to improve.

Aspects of behaviorists' approaches exist in classroom practices on a daily basis and facilitate some (though, certainly, not all) teaching/learning situations. As a rule, behaviorist classrooms are teacher centered, and curricula are usually predetermined. Lessons follow a prescribed sequence, and positive and negative reinforcing strategies are used to encourage appropriate student behaviors and achievements. Learning tasks are segmented into manageable parts that are intended to eventually become meaningful in a larger (or whole) context.

This *part-to-whole* process works well for many, but not all, learners. Some learners move from part-to-whole learning, whereas others benefit from whole-to-part perspectives. Further, this process works well for some, but not all, curricular topics and tasks. A cooking experience with young children, for example, is best broken into small, manageable parts and a sequence followed to assure safety, selected concept and/or skill development, and the best "product." On the other hand, the development of a class mural depicting a recent field trip to a bakery is best pursued in a wholistic, more free-flowing manner that encourages language, creativity, and social and intellectual interaction. When it comes to assessment, behaviorists adhere to curriculums and instructional practices that are focused primarily on the content and outcomes of structured tests. Hence, the curricula and instructional strategies tend to be more narrow and restricted, paralleling the content of the test. Test content most often follows the part-to-whole model.

Cognitive-Interactionist Theory

Performance assessments are best derived in settings where learners are engaged in interactions with concrete learning materials, other learners, and adults whose interactions with children facilitate learning and on-the-spot informal assessment. These interactions may occur spontaneously through play behaviors or be elicited through planned instructional strategies and strategic selection of curriculum themes and supporting learning materials. Assessment of learning is focused on how children pursue and use skills and new information. This approach to assessment of learning has roots in Piagetian and neo-Piagetian theory, commonly referred to as cognitive-interactionist theory. Based primarily on the research of Swiss biologist and psychologist Jean Piaget (1926, 1952, 1963), educators recognize that young children construct meaning from their interactions with objects and people.

Piaget proposed a cognitive-interactionist theory in which both inherited traits and environmental opportunities together influence cognitive development. Meaning occurs as young children engage all their sensory and motor capabilities, hear and employ language in many contexts, experience real events, explore concrete materials, and interact socially with others. This theory explains the very design and nature of the early childhood classroom, with its learning centers, concrete hands-on materials, manipulatives, varied art and construction media, realia, sociodramatic props, picture books, and many interactive opportunities. (It is interesting to note that this methodology has in recent years found its way into upper grades and, as we shall explore later, is reflected in academic standards proposed by subject-area specialists.) In these settings, learning occurs through both spontaneous and facilitated discovery, through interaction, inquiry, and dialogue, and through use of information and emerging skills. Through these experiences, children construct knowledge and understanding—hence, the concept of *constructivism* and the paradigm for constructivist pedagogy and curricula.

Assessment of learning is focused on how children pursue and use new information.

University Christian Church Weekday School, Fort Worth, TX

Constructivism

In the constructivist approach, a curriculum starts with the interests of the learner, building new information and experiences on the learner's prior knowledge and experience. It capitalizes on the child's immediate curiosity and initiative. As Kamii (1990, p. 24) emphasizes, when curiosity and initiative are present, we know that mental activity is taking place. "The overriding cognitive goal in the constructivist framework is that children *think*." Here we contrast Kamii's reference to the need for curricula that engage thought processes in learners with curricula that present incremental sets of facts to be memorized and demonstrated through simple recall or rote recitations. The former is a cognitive-interactionist point of view; the latter is more akin to a behaviorist point of view.

Building on children's interests and prior experiences, constructivist curricula strive for meaningful and relevant activities specifically designed to encourage thoughtful exploration, inquiry, invention, solutions to problems and dilemmas, new discoveries, and expanding interests and curiosities. Constructivist educators value the interactive process, in which children explore and use materials to gain knowledge and understanding and interact with their classmates and teachers who both facilitate and challenge the learning process. Constructivist classrooms are generally arranged in working centers or minilaboratories in which children engage in firsthand experiences with a variety of tools for learning. Activities and materials in each of the centers are strategically selected to facilitate learning in all content areas and to promote self-directed and autonomous thinkers. Educators are trained to observe and facilitate learning by providing appropriate instruction and scaffolding to further each child's learning experience.

Constructivism, the notion that meaning is constructed within the mind of the doer/learner, finds further amplification in the works of Russian psychologist Lev Vygotsky (1934/1962, 1978). Whereas Piaget portrayed learners as constructing, meaning primarily through their own actions on the environment, Vygotsky emphasized the importance of the child's culture and social contexts as sources of guidance and support for learning. Others, adults and children, provide assistance or scaffolding for the learner, which encourages and supports new learning. Vygotsky also emphasized the importance of language to cognitive development, demonstrating that when children are provided words and labels, they form concepts more readily. He believed that thought and language converge into meaningful concepts and assist the thinking process. Vygotsky advanced the concept of the *zone of proximal development* (ZPD), which refers to the point at which children are on the verge of understanding or being able to do something, so that all they need is a clue or other assistance to follow through on their own. This theory is demonstrated in classrooms in which social interaction is encouraged, where teachers converse with children and use language to mediate their learning, where children are encouraged to express themselves both orally and in writing, and where conversation among members of the group is encouraged and valued.

Psychosocial Theory

In addition to cognitive theory, the classic psychosocial theory of Erik Erikson (1963) prevails today. In Erikson's theory of healthy personality development, the individual experiences eight stages from birth to maturity, in which the resolution of certain psychosocial oppositional crises is expected to occur. The first four stages are of particular relevance to our focus on the development, education, and assessment of infants and young children.

Beginning at birth with the oppositional crises of *trust versus mistrust*, the human personality is confronted with forces within the family, culture, and society that support or impede development. It is hoped that the scales are tipped toward a healthy sense of trust, which occurs when infants experience warm, nurturing, supportive, predictable, and trustworthy environments and relationships. The child who learns to trust others during infancy can more successfully grow in self-trust. In later childhood, having resolved successfully subsequent oppositional crises, the child grows in the ability to successfully "mistrust" through discerning choices and decision making. Successful resolution of trust-versus-mistrust crises lays the foundation for later psychosocial development, particularly the second crisis. This crisis arises at about age two, that of opposition between *autonomy and shame or doubt*.

Autonomy is the desire to be self-directing or self-governed. This stage is characterized by attempts on the part of children to do more and more for themselves, such as choosing what clothing to wear, dressing themselves, resisting transitions from family time to bedtime, fastening seat belts, self-feeding and choosing certain foods over others, and learning to manage toileting as neurological control over bowel and bladder emerges. The successful resolution of this crisis depends on adult-child relationships that encourage rather than discourage or punish these early attempts at self-government. Erikson's theory suggests that adults need to find that important balance between meeting the child's ambivalent needs for both dependence and independence and control and freedom without leading the child toward feelings of inadequacy, shame, or doubt.

Building on the foundations of trust and autonomy, the third of Erikson's psychosocial stages is that of *initiative versus guilt,* which emerges between three and six years of age. During this psychosocial crisis, children are attempting to undertake and pursue ideas of their own making; planning and carrying out a variety of tasks and play themes; and enlisting others through conversation, questions, sociodramatic play, and idea exchanges. Play with others, particularly sociodramatic play, is especially important during this period as children become less egocentric and more socially interactive with their age-mates. The opposite of initiative is a sense of guilt, which emerges when children are unsuccessful in their initiations or when adults fail to recognize the significance and importance of children's efforts or respond to their efforts in disparaging or nonsupportive ways.

The fourth stage that is important to teachers of young children is that of *industry versus inferiority*. During this period, from about ages six to eleven, children are seeking to be engaged in what they perceive to be "real" tasks, as opposed to make-believe and pretend. Interest in how things work, constructing and creating from a variety of media, writing to communicate, reading for information and other school-skills development, and carrying out helpful and meaningful chores and tasks and a need for a sense of accomplishment mark this psychosocial stage. Children who experience frequent or embarrassing frustrations and failures during their early attempts to grow more proficient at home, in school, or in social interactions develop a sense of inferiority. Tipping the scales toward the positive side of these psychosocial oppositional crises is a major goal of developmentally appropriate practices in the education of young children.

Addressing the psychosocial dimensions of early development and learning is an important focus in authentic or performance-based assessments. Such assessments consider not only academic achievements and progress, but also the emotional and social dimensions of healthy personality development within the context of schooling and its expectations. Such assessment recognizes the influence of emotional states on learning and the impact that the social and emotional climate of the classroom and school can have on individual performance. Further, contemporary emphases on *school readiness* focus not only on cognitive abilities, but quite importantly on the emotional and social development of children prior to kindergarten and first-grade entry (Kaufman Early Education Exchange, 2002; Peisner-Feinberg et al., 2001; Raver & Knitzer, 2002).

Ecological or Contextualistic Theories

Emphasis in recent literature on the contexts in which children grow and develop has led early childhood educators to pay closer attention to the social, cultural, and economic aspects of children's lives (Bronfenbrenner, 1979, 1986, 1989, 2004; Bronfenbrenner & Morris, 1998; Cole & Cole, 1993). The contexts of children's lives affect not only cognitive development and academic achievement, but all other developmental domains as well. Bronfenbrenner's ecological (or contextualistic) theory is of particular interest to early childhood educators. This theory proposes ever-widening circles of influence on children, expanding out from parents and family to neighborhood, school, faith-based institutions, and community agencies, to the media, local governments, and the dominant beliefs and ideologies of a society. Children's experiences in these various contexts and their subsequent development and behaviors are shaped by the reciprocal interaction of the child and the environmental contexts. Bronfenbrenner's ecological theory helps us recognize that there are numerous and diverse pathways by which children grow, develop, and learn. Recognizing that child development and learning is influenced variously on many fronts, resulting in wide differences in background experiences, abilities, aspirations, achievements, needs, and challenges among children and their families, the search for fair and unbiased assessment practices becomes an important responsibility in early childhood settings. An ecological point of view reminds us that a one-size-fits-all paradigm in either teaching strategies or assessment practices will inevitably fail some children.

Developmentally Appropriate Practices in Early Childhood Education

Although the concept of developmentally appropriate practices is not a theory in the strictest sense of the word, it is a construct by which we examine and explain what we do and why. The concept of developmentally appropriate practices in early childhood education was forwarded by the National Association for the Education of Young Children through its position statement, first published in 1987, subsequently revised in 1997 (Bredekamp, 1987; Bredekamp & Copple, 1997), and further amplified in 2006 (Copple & Bredekamp, 2006). The concept of developmentally appropriate practices has served to focus early childhood educators on a common goal for planning and implementing programs for young children. The positive influences of high-quality programs and developmentally appropriate practices on child development has been extensively documented (Barnett, & Boocock, 1998; Barnett, Young, & Schweinhart, 1998; Campbell, Ramey, Pungello, Sparling, & Miller-Johnson, 2002; Dunn & Kontos, 1997; Huffman & Speer, 2000; NICHD, 2002; Peisner-Feinberg et al., 2001; Schweinhart, 1997; Schweinhart & Weikart, 1998). As we shall see, developmentally appropriate practices have critical implications for the manner in which child growth, development, and learning are assessed.

The National Association for the Education of Young Children, in its publication *Developmentally Appropriate Practice in Early Childhood Programs* (Bredekamp & Copple, 1997, pp. 8–9), defines developmentally appropriate practice as resulting:

> . . . from the process of professionals making decisions about the well-being and education of children based on at least three important kinds of information or knowledge:
>
> 1. what is known about child development and learning-knowledge of age-related human characteristics that permits general predictions within an age range about what activities, materials, interactions, or experiences will be safe, healthy, interesting, achievable, and also challenging to children;
> 2. what is known about the strengths, interests, and needs of each individual child in the group to be able to adapt for and be responsible to inevitable individual variations; and
> 3. knowledge of the social and cultural contexts in which children live to ensure that learning experiences are meaningful, relevant, and respectful for the participating children and their families.

Developmentally appropriate practices take into consideration the wide ranges of needs and developmental characteristics of young children, including children with special needs and developmental challenges. Developmentally appropriate practices are inclusive and sensitive to the capabilities and strengths of each child. They also are sensitive to cultural and linguistic diversity and promote cultural understandings and mutual respect among all members of the community of learners. *Antibias* curricula are employed in developmentally appropriate classrooms (Brown & Conroy, 1997; Derman-Sparks, 1989; Roach, Ascroft, Stamp, & Kysilko, 1995; Van Ausdale & Feagin, 2001).

An antibias approach to early childhood education goes beyond simply teaching about different cultures. Rather, antibias programs provide environments that reflect sensitivity to and respect for all members of the group, regardless of gender,

Figure 1.2
Criteria for Good Assessment
Note: From *Developmentally Appropriate Assessment: A Position Paper by the Southern Early Childhood Association,* 1998, Little Rock, AR: Author. Copyright 1998 by the Southern Early Childhood Association. Reprinted by permission.

- Assessment must be *valid*. It must provide information related to the goals and objectives of each program.

- Assessment must deal with the whole child. Programs must have goals and assessment processes which relate to children's physical, social, emotional, and mental development.

- Assessment must involve observations across time and in a variety of settings. This helps teachers find patterns of behavior and avoid quick decisions which may be based on one-time behavior by children.

- Assessment must be continuous and ongoing. Children should be compared to their own individual course of development over time rather than to average behavior for a group.

- Assessment must use a variety of methods and sources. Gathering a wide variety of information from different sources enables informed and professional decisions.

- Assessments must be used to modify the curriculum to meet the individual needs of children in the program.

- Assessment must involve parents. Parents and extended family members provide information that is both accurate and beneficial in program planning.

Meaningful assessments of young children celebrate growth, development, and learning in all developmental domains: physical/motor, social/emotional, and cognitive.

Lisa A. Witkowski

race, ethnicity, or ableness. Such environments include materials, books, puzzles, dolls, sociodramatic play props, bulletin boards, and other tools of learning that reflect diversity among children and adults and avoid stereotyping about race, gender, or ability. Interactions with and among children and their families promotes understanding and mutual respect. Antibias curricula are intellectually honest and teach children how to resist bias. It follows that antibias assessment practices take into consideration the cultural backgrounds of each child and his or her family and are particularly sensitive to the challenges that language differences pose (Barrera & Corso, with MacPherson, 2003; Garcia, 2005).

These prevailing theories undergird the philosophy and pedagogy suggested in this text. Each is further elaborated throughout the text. Assessment practices are based on our best understandings about how young children grow, develop, and learn. The practices suggested in this book are compatible with constructivism, healthy psychosocial development, and developmentally appropriate practices. In addition, practices suggested in this book are discerning and responsive to new insights regarding child development and learning.

ETHICAL ISSUES ASSOCIATED WITH ASSESSING YOUNG CHILDREN

Consider the following dilemmas:

Ms. Madison is sharing lunch in the teacher's lounge with some of her colleagues. She is the only kindergarten teacher in her school, and the two first-grade teachers take an interest in the children who will be in their classes next school year. They ask questions of Ms. Madison, such as, "Are you going to have your students ready for next year's first grade?" and "I am teaching Jamie's sister this year.

How is little brother doing in kindergarten?" "When we are on the playground, I notice that Marcy cries easily. Do you think she is going to outgrow that behavior by first grade?" Ms. Madison also encounters a parent in the grocery store one afternoon after school and is queried about the progress of the child of a friend. How should Ms. Madison respond to such inquiries?

Mr. Jacobs, the first-grade teacher, is a creative and avid advocate of student portfolios, which he develops to help students and parents track progress. Each portfolio contains students' school work, assessment data, and teacher notes. Mr. Jacobs stores the portfolios in open shelves in the classroom for easy access. A fellow teacher from another grade, curious about the progress of a particular student, asks to review the student's portfolio. How should Mr. Jacobs respond?

In preparing for the school's fall open house, Miss Jamison displays examples of student work throughout her third-grade classroom and on the adjacent hallway walls. Many items with grades and teacher comments on them appear in whole class groupings. During the open house, as parents peruse the classroom, admiring student products and visiting with one another and Miss Jamison, a parent is noticed comparing the grades of various children enrolled in the class with her own child's performance and grades. What should Miss Jamison do?

It is standardized testing week for the third-grade. Mr. Vegas, who has spent hours of instructional time coaching and preparing his students for the test, is concerned about the ability of one student to do well on the test. Further, the student is stressed and fearful; he is nauseated and asks to go to the nurse's office during practice exercises. Mr. Vegas suggests to the student's parents that because the child is not coping well with the situation, they should simply keep the child home the day the group test is administered. What issues arise from such a strategy? How much and what types of test preparation are necessary or appropriate in classrooms where all children must be tested on state- or district-mandated tests? If this is a state-mandated accountability test, how are group or class scores affected?

An item on a prekindergarten test asks the color of an apple. One child answers that an apple is white and sometimes brown. The scoring directions for this particular test instruct that only an answer of red (or green) can be counted as correct. Mrs. Juarez knows that the child is referring to the colors of a peeled apple. How should Mrs. Juarez score this child's answer to the question?

Situations such as these are frequently encountered by classroom teachers. Such situations require tact, good judgment, and ethical behaviors.

Ethics refers to the honesty and integrity with which individuals conduct their personal and professional responsibilities. Professionals in all fields are called upon to adhere to a set of principles or a code of conduct that defines the profession and assures everyone of the honesty and accuracy with which members of the profession conduct themselves and carry out the tasks and responsibilities of the profession.

The teaching profession has always adhered to a code of ethics quite clearly defined by such organizations as the National Education Association (1929; 1975) and the National Association for the Education of Young Children with the Association for Childhood Education International (current revision 2005), Scholars and researchers in child development and psychology are also guided by strict rules of conduct set forth by such organizations as the Society for Research in Child Development (1990) and the American Psychological Association (2003). Education psychometricians and diagnosticians also meet ethical standards set forth by such organizations as the Division for Early Childhood of the Council for Exceptional

Children (2002), the National Association of School Psychologists (1997), and the joint statement of the American Educational Research Association, the American Psychological Association, and the National Council on Measurement in Education (1999).* Where questions of impropriety or legal rights arise, courts are influenced by the extent to which an individual within the profession has adhered to such codes of ethical conduct.

Classroom assessments, whether formal or informal, require the highest levels of ethical practice. The psychological, social, and cognitive impact on children of assessment procedures and outcomes is of paramount concern, and the margin for error is exceedingly thin. All students are entitled to fair, unbiased, and accurate assessments. Assessment errors such as those associated with misdiagnosis of physical, emotional, social, or learning issues; errors associated with school or class placement, delayed school entry, or in-grade retention; errors associated with provision of, or lack of provision of, special services or specific instructional procedures; and other important developmental or academic decisions can have not only immediate deleterious effects on children and families, but lifelong negative consequences for an individual.

Professionals in early childhood education embrace a set of core values and moral obligations widely accepted in the profession and well defined by the National Association for the Education of Young Children (NAEYC) and endorsed by the Association for Childhood Education International. These values and obligations include a personal commitment to the following (NAEYC, 2005a):

◆ Appreciate childhood as a unique and valuable stage of the human life cycle.
◆ Base our work on knowledge of how children develop and learn.
◆ Appreciate and support the bond between the child and family.
◆ Recognize that children are best understood and supported in the context of family, culture, community, and society.
◆ Respect the dignity, worth, and uniqueness of each individual (child, family member, and colleague).
◆ Respect diversity in children, families, and colleagues.
◆ Recognize that children and adults achieve their full potential in the context of relationships that are based on trust and respect.

The NAEYC Statement of Commitment is shown in Figure 1.3.

The first and foremost principle in most of the aforementioned codes of ethics is similar to the following, set forth by NAEYC and ACEI:

> Above all, we shall not harm children. We shall not participate in practices that are emotionally damaging, physically harmful, disrespectful, degrading, dangerous, exploitative, or intimidating to children. This principle has precedence over all others in this Code. (p. 3)

To this end, there are some important considerations associated with the assessment of children.

---

*Each professional organization's code of ethics can be accessed in its entirety through the organization's Web address, included in Appendix C.

Statement of Commitment*

As an individual who works with young children, I commit myself to furthering the values of early childhood education as they are reflected in the ideals and principles of the NAEYC Code of Ethical Conduct. To the best of my ability I will

- Never harm children.
- Ensure that programs for young children are based on current knowledge and research of child development and early childhood education.
- Respect and support families in their task of nurturing children.
- Respect colleagues in early childhood care and education and support them in maintaining the NAEYC Code of Ethical Conduct.
- Serve as an advocate for children, their families, and their teachers in community and society.
- Stay informed of and maintain high standards of professional conduct.
- Engage in an ongoing process of self-reflection, realizing that personal characteristics, biases, and beliefs have an impact on children and families.
- Be open to new ideas and be willing to learn from the suggestions of others.
- Continue to learn, grow, and contribute as a professional.
- Honor the ideals and principles of the NAEYC Code of Ethical Conduct.

*This Statement of Commitment is not part of the Code but is a personal acknowledgment of the individual's willingness to embrace the distinctive values and moral obligations of the field of early childhood care and education. It is recognition of the moral obligations that lead to an individual becoming part of the profession.

Fair and Unbiased Assessment

Each and every child is entitled to unbiased, fair, and age- and situation-appropriate assessments utilized only as necessary and for the purposes of promoting the child's well-being. Assessors have a responsibility to self-examine for bias and pre-conceived notions about what children of a particular age, ethnicity, gender, or socioeconomic status should or could know and be able to do. This reflection on one's own thinking and assumptions is necessary to prevent potentially damaging stereotyping and assessment error.

Assessors have a responsibility to select and use appropriate assessment measures and to use these measures only for the purposes for which they are designed. Decisions associated with test or assessment outcomes are based on sound principles of measurement, knowledge of child growth, development, and learning, and full consideration of the long-term developmental consequences of the uses of the assessment information.

Recognizing the Limits of One's Expertise

Those who assess growth, development, and learning of young children should know the limits of their knowledge and expertise and recuse themselves from assessment procedures for which they are untrained and unqualified to carry out. By the same token, the educator who recognizes his or her limitations continually engages in professional development in order to maintain highest standards in assessment practices.

The accuracy of assessments and the appropriateness of education decisions regarding children that are derived from assessments depend on a thorough knowledge of how children grow, develop, and learn. Knowledge of child growth, development, and learning is an ethical responsibility. Professional educators continuously study and stay abreast of the knowledge base in child development.

Confidentiality

Assessments provide a considerable amount of particular and personal information about individual children and, in some cases, their families. Assessors are obligated to treat this information with utmost confidentiality. Sharing information about a student, individual or group test scores, or examples of student work products from which assessments have been obtained occurs only with individuals who have a legitimate right to know, such as the child's parent(s), a resource counseling, or tutoring professional, or a member of the health care profession so designated by the child's parent or guardian as someone with whom assessment information may be shared. Test data, records, reports, and portfolios (written or electronic) must be stored, accessed, transferred, and disposed of in a manner that protects each student's right to privacy.

Test Security

Where formal testing instruments are mandated by local school districts or by state or federal policy, test content or specific test items are never revealed to others. Test booklets and all other artifacts of the formal testing procedures are kept in the most secure place inaccessible to anyone other than those officially designated to distribute, administer, and score them.

The assessment of growth, development, and learning of young children can be a challenging endeavor given the variability among children in their rates of growth and background experiences. Rapid growth during the early years yields a moving target for assessors. Day-to-day participation and performance in learning opportunities can vary. Assessments necessarily need to be varied, ongoing in many contexts, and cognizant of both advances and regressions in children's behaviors. As we shall see in later chapters, young children are not good test takers. Behavior or accomplishment one day may suggest the emergence of a skill or understanding that is not quite so discernable another day. An understanding of this variability is particularly important when mandated tests constitute part of the early childhood assessment system.

BASIC ASSUMPTIONS UNDERLYING MEANINGFUL CURRICULA AND ASSESSMENTS

Our quest for meaningful assessments is based on assumptions relating to several aspects of the education process: (1) early childhood education (birth through age eight), (2) learning, (3) knowledge, (4) teaching, and (5) assessment, all of which are projected in the following lists. You will see the assumptions played out throughout this text as we examine the construct of meaningful assessments and propose assessment strategies.

Assumptions About Early Childhood Education

◆ Young children have an innate need to know and, therefore, are competent, eager to learn, and trustworthy learners.

◆ Within a supportive and enriched setting, young children can initiate and direct their own learnings.

◆ Young children construct knowledge while interacting with adults, one another, and with meaningful materials and realia.

◆ Young children develop physically, emotionally, socially, and intellectually at different rates.

◆ The first eight years are important foundational years for growth, development, and learning.

Assumptions About Learning

◆ Learning proceeds from the concrete to the abstract through (1) active exploration and inquiry, (2) enriched learning environments, (3) social contexts that encourage interaction among learners, and (4) adult or older-child supports and scaffolding.

◆ The mind must be engaged if learning is to occur.

◆ There are different intelligences involved in learning: linguistic, logical-mathematical, spatial, musical, bodily-kinesthetic, interpersonal, intrapersonal, naturalistic, and others (Gardner, 1983, 1999).

◆ All learning has its foundations in early childhood.

Assumptions About Knowledge

◆ Knowledge is rooted in the language, beliefs, and customs of different cultures.

◆ Different kinds of knowledge exist: physical, logical-mathematical, and social-conventional (Piaget, 1952).

◆ Both products and processes are important to the acquisition of knowledge.

◆ Problem solving supersedes rote memory of facts if knowledge is to be meaningful and sustained.

◆ New knowledge builds on prior knowledge and experience and is influenced by the individual's perceptions.

◆ Knowledge is more efficiently acquired in meaningful contexts.

◆ The acquisition of knowledge is a lifelong process.

◆ It is impossible to define a particular body of knowledge that is essential for everyone to acquire.

Assumptions About Teaching

◆ Specialized training and skills are essential to teaching young children.

◆ Effective teaching is child centered and views curriculum and assessment as tools that facilitate and enhance growth, development, and learning in all developmental domains.

◆ Effective teaching occurs in individualized and small-group situations.

◆ Teachers are cognizant of and responsive to emerging research and new knowledge about child growth, development, and learning.

◆ Teachers are cognizant of and responsive to the ever-changing knowledge pool in curriculum and content areas.

◆ Teaching strategies acknowledge and are sensitive to diverse cultures, languages, and unique learning styles.

◆ Teaching and assessing are both ongoing and interconnected.

Assumptions About Assessment

◆ Comparing assessment results across populations is of little value to individual learners.

◆ Assessments are not reflective of inherent capacities; rather, they are reflective of emerging capabilities and an individuals' interactions with the environment.

◆ Meaningful assessments are rooted in scientific evidence from the developmental, cognitive, and neural sciences.

◆ Meaningful assessments in context provide valid information about the learner and the education process.

◆ Meaningful assessments consider different intelligences, diverse learning styles, and varying contexts in which learning occurs and reflect our best understanding of human variability.

◆ Assessments that are rooted in knowledge of child growth and development can make valid predictions of later performance.

◆ Both quantitative and qualitative forms of assessment provide objective and reliable data about the learner.

◆ Developmentally appropriate assessments are derived from developmentally appropriate curricula, and vice versa.

◆ Meaningful assessments provide opportunities for both the learner and the teacher to reflect on goals and ways to achieve them.

◆ Assessment must involve parents. Parents and extended family members provide information that is both accurate and beneficial in program planning.

REVIEW STRATEGIES AND ACTIVITIES

1. Review the position statements on assessment of various professional education and psychology associations. Compare their concerns and their suggestions for assessing the progress of young children in school. Most professional organizations post their position statements on their Web sites (e.g., NAEYC, ACEI, AAP, SECA, and many others).

2. Select a number of current child-development or early childhood education journals, and locate and read articles that discuss new insights in child development and learning, sociopolitical influences on early childhood education, curriculum and assessment alignment, and contemporary assessment practices. Discuss the information in these articles with your classmates. How do practices differ today from those of your schooling experiences?

3. Discuss with your instructor and classmates how the languages of assessment foretell the purposes and uses of assessment information. Consider how and for what purpose(s) assessment information can or should be used.

4. Revisit the ethical dilemmas noted in the section on ethics in this chapter. Write a brief essay on the ethical issues and potential consequences for all parties involved of failure to adhere to a professional code of ethics in each of these situations. Consider ways to prevent such situations from occurring.

SUGGESTED LITERATURE AND RESOURCES

Bracey, G. B. (2003). *On the death of childhood and the destruction of public education: The folly of today's education policies and practices.* Portsmouth, NY: Heinemann.

Bredekamp, S., & Copple, C. (1997). *Developmentally appropriate practice in early childhood programs* (Rev. ed.). Washington, DC: National Association for the Education of Young Children.

Copple, C., & Bredekamp, S. (2006). *Basics of developmentally appropriate practice: An introduction for teachers of children 3 to 6.* Washington, DC: National Association for the Education of Young Children.

Cosby, A. G., Greenberg, R. E., Southward, L. H., & Weitzman, M. (Eds.). (2005). *About children: An authoritative resource on the state of childhood today.* Elk Grove Village, IL: American Academy of Pediatrics.

Fosnot, C. T. (2005). *Constructivism: Theory, perspectives, and practice* (2nd ed.). New York: Teachers College Press.

Garcia, E. E. (2005). *Teaching and learning in two languages: Bilingualism and schooling in the United States.* New York: Teachers College Press.

Kohn, A. (1999). *The schools our children deserve: Moving beyond traditional classrooms and "tougher standards."* Washington, DC: Teaching for Change.

Reeves, D. B. (2004). *Accountability for learning: How teachers and school leaders can take charge.* Alexandria, VA: Association for Supervision and Curriculum Development.

Reynolds, A. J., Wang, M. C., & Walberg, H. J. (Eds.). (2003). *Early childhood programs for a new century.* Washington, DC: National Association for the Education of Young Children.

Seefeldt, C., & Wasik, B. A. (2006). *Early education: Three, four, and five year olds go to school* (2nd ed.). Upper Saddle River, NJ: Merrill/Prentice Hall.

2

The Big Picture
Development, Diversity, and Standards

All assessments, and particularly assessments for accountability, must be used carefully and appropriately if they are to resolve, and not create educatonal problems. Assessment of young children poses greater challenges than people generally realize. The first five years of life are a time of incredible growth and learning, but the course of development is uneven and sporadic. The status of a child's development as of any given day can change very rapidly. Consequently, assessment results—in particular, standardized test scores that reflect a given point in time—can easily misrepresent children's learning.

  Bowman, Donovan, & Burns (2000)

Although assessments used in various contexts and for differing purposes often look quite different, they share certain common principles. One such principle is that assessment is always a process of reasoning from evidence. By its very nature, moreover, assessment is imprecise to some degree. Assessment results are only estimates of what a person knows and can do.

  Pellegrino, Chudowsky, & Glaser (2001)

If our goals and objectives are not based on sound, scientific theory about how children learn in depth, demonstrating progress toward them is of little value.

  Kamii (1990)

◇ ◇

After reading and studying this chapter, you will demonstrate comprehension by being able to:

❑ discuss the types of knowledge needed to implement a fair and useful assessment system.

❑ describe the effect of the standards movement on the goals and pedagogy of early childhood education.

❑ discuss the implications of the standards movement for special populations of children.

❑ explain the importance of alignment of goals, standards, curriculum content, and assessment practices.

A "grand plan" for the assessment of young children is multifaceted and requires continuing and advancing knowledge in child growth, development, and learning, cultural and developmental diversity, subject matter and content area disciplines, and the characteristics of valid assessments. Additionally, federal and state legislation prescribes specific types of tests and assessments at certain intervals during the schooling years. Understanding the basis for these assessment policies and requirements helps educators to make appropriate interpretation and use of data generated by them.

KNOWLEDGE ABOUT CHILDREN'S DEVELOPMENT AND LEARNING

developmentally appropriate Expectations and practices based on what is known about child growth and development.

age appropriate Behaviors and expectations for behavior or learning that can reasonably be expected at a given age.

individually appropriate Experiences and expectations that are responsive to and respectful of the uniqueness of the individual.

In Chapter 1, we introduced the concept of **developmentally appropriate** practices in early childhood education. Such practices depend on the teacher's knowledge and understanding of both the common and individualistic characteristics of children at each age period. This understanding assists teachers in designing those early education experiences from which children will derive the greatest benefit and that will serve children's best interests in the long run. To be developmentally appropriate, assessment of young children must also recognize and be based on **age-** and **individually appropriate** expectations. Such expectations are cognizant of many factors in human development that contribute to the uniqueness of each individual and of the diversity and wide range of capabilities and interests among members of a grade or classroom group.

Whole-Child Perspective

Too often when we think of young children in a school or early education setting, we think primarily about their cognitive development or what knowledge and skills they will be learning that will prepare them for later schooling experiences. Many parents and teachers focus on school (or academic) knowledge and skills as indicators of maturity or achievement. "My child knows his ABCs and can count to 20," boasts the proud parent of a four-year-old. "The children in my class are doing so well at learning rhyming sounds and even some of the letter sounds," reports a preschool teacher. Both are acceptable accomplishments during the early childhood years, but they do not begin to represent the vast array or amount of learning or the impressive growth and development that has taken and is taking place. They may represent an overemphasis on scholastics to the detriment of other important growth and developmental needs.

Growth and development occurs unevenly, yet concurrently, in several developmental domains: physical/motor, psychosocial, cognitive, and language. Inherent within much of this growth and development is the acquisition of knowledge and skills related to the subject matter domains of literacy, math, science, social studies, and the arts. In all these areas, growth, development, and learning varies from child to child, with wide variations occurring among children in the same age group. Recognizing this, professional early childhood educators take a whole-child perspective that observes and facilitates growth, development, and learning in all these domains.

All growth and development is interrelated and interdependent; so, for example, although a child may "know" certain rhyming sounds, as indicated by a kindergarten teacher, the ability to recognize those sounds is as dependent on health, individual auditory acuity, past experience with language (i.e., home-language conversation, songs, verses, and stories), and current engagement in activities that promote such discrimination as it is on cognitive development or pedagogy. Hence, experience (past and present), physical development (health, sensory, and motor integrity), language development (experienced, oral, written, shared), cognitive development (prior experience and existing mental structures), and current level of engagement are all involved in the child's ability or inability to demonstrate knowledge and skills. Assessment of the young child takes into consideration many developmental determinants.

Children with Special Needs and Talents

at risk Children whose prenatal or early environments, experiences, or health conditions presuppose less than optimal physical/motor, psychosocial, cognitive, language development, or academic success.

Recognizing and responding appropriately to the educational and assessment needs of children who have developmental challenges and/or talents is an important responsibility (Figure 2.1). Children with special needs present various developmental challenges associated with health, physical abilities, emotional and social development, and cognitive development. Many of the children are **at risk** for

Figure 2.1

Position Statement on Inclusion of the Division for Early Childhood of the Council for Exceptional Children. Denver, CO: DEC/CEC. Reproduced by permission; www.dec-sped.org.

Position Statement on Inclusion

Inclusion, as a value, supports the right of all children, regardless of abilities, to participate actively in natural settings within their communities. Natural settings are those in which the child would spend time had he or she not had a disability. These settings include, but are not limited to home, preschool, nursery schools, Head Start programs, kindergartens, neighborhood school classrooms, child care, places of worship, recreational (such as community playgrounds and community events) and other settings that all children and families enjoy.

DEC supports and advocates that young children and their families have full and successful access to health, social, educational, and other support services that promote full participation in family and community life. DEC values the cultural, economic, and educational diversity of families and supports a family-guided process for identifying a program of service.

As young children participate in group settings (such as preschool, play groups, child care, kindergarten) their active participation should be guided by developmentally and individually appropriate curriculum. Access to and participation in the age appropriate general curriculum becomes central to the identification and provision of specialized support services.

To implement inclusive practices DEC supports: (a) the continued development, implementation, evaluation, and dissemination of full inclusion supports, services, and systems that are of high quality for all children; (b) the development of preservice and inservice training programs that prepare families, service providers, and administrators to develop and work within inclusive settings; (c) collaboration among key stakeholders to implement flexible fiscal and administrative procedures in support of inclusion; (d) research that contributes to our knowledge of recommended practice; and (e) the restructuring and unification of social, educational, health, and intervention supports and services to make them more responsive to the needs of all children and families. Ultimately, the implementation of inclusive practice must lead to optimal developmental benefit for each individual child and family.

Figure 2.2
Serving Children with Disabilities.

Children with disabilities are entitled to the following:

- early screening and identification
- a free and appropriate public education
- parent or parent surrogate consultation
- an impartial due process hearing if the student or his or her parents disagree with the school's decisions
- an individualized education plan (IEP)
- fair and nondiscriminatory evaluation
- confidentiality
- teachers and other professional personnel who have been provided in-service training to help them serve the best interest of the child (PL 94-142).

---

screening A first step in identifying, through tests, examinations, or other procedures, children who may need professional diagnostic evaluation and/or intervention.

intervention Strategies or activities (such as medical or psychological treatment, speech-language therapy, providing adaptive equipment, modifying the physical environment, and accessing and advocating for appropriate resources and policies) designed to facilitate optimal development in children with special needs.

inclusion Providing education for students with disabilities in general education settings.

learning difficulties in school settings. The passage of Public Law 94-142 in 1975 (now known as Part B of the *Individuals with Disabilities Education Act* (IDEA) and its subsequent amendments and reauthorizations have expanded special services for young children with special needs to include, in addition to school-age children, children ages three to five, and, in some instances, children birth through age two and provided the philosophical and legal impetus for **screening** for early identification, **intervention** with appropriate medical, psychological, and educational services, and **inclusion** practices (Figure 2.2).

In 2004, the *Individuals with Disabilities Education Improvement Act* (PL 108-446) was signed into law. Included in this revision of the Individuals with Disabilities Education Act (IDEA) is a requirement that limits but does not prohibit the use of IQ tests:

> . . . a local education agency shall not be required to take into consideration whether a child has a severe discrepancy between achievement and intellectual ability in oral expression, listening comprehension, written expression, basic reading skill, reading comprehension, mathematical calculation, or mathematical reasoning. (PL 108-446)

Children with disabilities benefit from inclusion as they benefit from interactions and role models within the class.

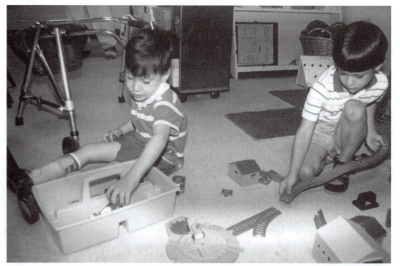

Nancy P. Alexander

underachievement The discrepancy between what a student is perceived to know and be able to do and his or her lower level of achievement.

learning styles Individual variations in preferred, or most efficient, modalities and contexts for learning.

learning disability A disorder in one or more of the basic psychological processeses involved in attending to, understanding, or using spoken or written language; suspected when a student persistently displays inabilities to listen, think, speak, read, write, spell, or do mathematical calculations.

This is a change from previous requirements in which learning disability was identified in part by a severe discrepancy between the child's apparent potential for learning, usually measured on IQ tests, and his or her low level of achievement. The descriptor often used in such a case is **underachievement.** This is an important change in the law because it limits the potential misuse of IQ test results. The law does not prohibit the use of IQ tests for identifying children with learning disabilities, but it discourages the sole use of one test score. Instead, the law encourages the placement of IQ test scores within a larger context of assessments of the child's individuality. This revision to the law also encourages practices that distinguish between children who have different **learning styles** and children who have **learning disabilities,** thus discouraging the over referral of children for special education services.

Although there are other very important revisions to the IDEA,* this revision supports the need for a multifaceted assessment system that includes both formal and performance based assessments.

Children of Diverse Cultural and Linguistic Backgrounds

If assessment practices are to serve the best interests of all children in a fair and equitable manner, they must take into consideration the wide ranges of background experiences and opportunities and the unique characteristics that are represented in any group of students. In this regard, the concept of developmental appropriateness becomes quite applicable because such practices support the unique qualities and strengths of each child and engender curriculums, classroom interactions, and assessment practices that facilitate growth, development, and learning in individual children.

Cultural Diversity

cultural diversity Refers to the amalgam of beliefs, value systems, attitudes, traditions, and family practices that are held by different groups of people.

ethnicity A particular group's shared heritage, which generally includes a common history with distinctive traditions and celebrations. Ethnic groups generally speak a common language and often share common religious beliefs.

microcultural group Groups to which all individuals belong, such as gender, social class, race, ethnicity, ableness, religion, and region.

Cultural diversity refers to the amalgam of beliefs, value systems, attitudes, traditions, and family practices that are held by different groups of people. **Ethnicity** refers to a particular group's shared heritage, which usually includes a common history with distinctive traditions and celebrations. Ethnic groups generally speak a common language and often share common religious beliefs. Whether European American, Jamaican, Latino, African, Korean, or other ethnicity, all groups experience and interpret life events such as marriage, procreation, child rearing, education, work and recreation, health issues, and death according to unique cultural points of view.

From infancy, individuals internalize these standards and role expectations of their ethnic and cultural groups. Hence, all children come to school with culturally derived identities and both conscious and unconscious cultural ways of thinking and behaving. These unique ways of thinking and interacting with others are derived from experiences in various separate but often interactive subgroups within the culture that Banks and Banks (2001) refers to as **microcultural groups.**

The microcultural groups to which all individuals belong include gender, social class, race, ethnicity, ableness, religion, and region. Each of these subgroups functions in unique ways, both interactively and singularly, to influence an individual's sense of identity, self-concept, attitudes, dispositions, and intra- and interpersonal behaviors (Banks and Banks, 2001). This has implications for assessment, in that assessors must—in an unbiased manner—draw inferences from children's culturally

*A comparison of the IDEA 1997 and the IDEA 2004 requirements can be accessed at www.nasdse.org.

unique behaviors, performance, and products. Accuracy of inferences about what a student knows and is able to do can be compromised when assessors have limited knowledge about culturally derived behaviors.

In this regard, today's classroom populations are as diverse in culture and language as they have ever been. A significant challenge in planning a fair and equitable assessment system is this changing profile of school populations. The United States contains hundreds of distinct cultural groups. Of these groups, five major ones exist: Native Americans and individuals of African, Latin, Asian, and European decent. Immigration to the United States from around the world continually alters the demographic profile of the U.S. population from that of predominantly white Americans of European descent to one that is more eclectic and global. Continuing observation, interaction with, and formal study of diverse cultures is becoming increasingly necessary for today's educators and is particularly important for individuals who are in the position of assessing student performance and achievement and subsequently making important education decisions for them.

long-term immigrant An individual who has immigrated to the United States and remains with or without permanent residency status or having applied for citizenship. May be a first, second, or later generation immigrant.

Children in Immigrant Families

legal immigrants Individuals who have been admitted into the United States with valid visa and have been approved for temporary or permanent residence.

undocumented immigrant Individuals who have entered the United States illegally, overstayed a valid visa, such as a tourist or student visa, or otherwise violated the terms of their immigration status.

Over the years, the United States has taken in more immigrants than any other country. During the colonial days, immigrants arrived mainly from the British Isles and Ireland, but soon others began to arrive from Germany, France, Switzerland, Hungary, and the Netherlands. During the mid-1800s, immigrants from China settled on the West Coast; during this same period, the United States, at war with Mexico over boundary disputes, was annexing large regions of land already inhabited by Mexicans. During the early part of the twentieth century, Italians, Russians, Poles, and other Europeans (many of whom were Jewish) settled in the United States. Since the late 1960s, a major wave of new immigrants has included mostly people from Latin America and Asia. The United States contains basically three distinct immigrant groups: **long-term immigrants,** recent **legal immigrants** (including refugees), and **undocumented immigrants.**

Assessment systems need to be culturally and linguistically sensitive and responsive.

Superstock Royalty Free

Many Languages

The children and families served by Head Start are diverse in culture and language. A survey of programs in 1999 listed over 140 languages spoken by Head Start children. This language diversity has continued to increase. Among Head Start children Spanish is the most common language spoken other than English.

Administration for Children & Families, Health & Human Resources, Head Start Bureau (July, 2003). Head Start Bulletin, p. 20.

We are a nation of immigrants. Statistics reveal that between fourteen and sixteen million immigrants entered the United States during the 1990s, which was up from ten million during the 1980s. During the years from 2000 to 2004, the foreign-born population in the United States increased by more than one million a year. This high rate of immigration is thus rapidly changing the student population profile of America's schools. One child in five under the age of eighteen is a member of an immigrant family. Furthermore, children of immigrants represent one in four of all school-age children who were low income, as defined by eligibility for the National School Lunch Program. In 2004 there were more children of immigrant families in the lower grades, with the highest number in kindergarten. However, children of immigrant families tend to be underenrolled in prekindergarten programs. These low rates of prekindergarten and earlier preschool enrollment tend to be among children from lower-income families and those whose parents have less formal education and more limited English skills (Capps et al., 2005).

This diversity in the U.S. school population has implications for assessment practices in early childhood programs because English language proficiency and prior learning experiences (in the home and/or preschool/prekindergarten) must be considered when designing an assessment system that best describes the attributes, progress, and educational needs of children whose families are newcomers to the United States.

Responding to the need for linguistically responsive ways of teaching non-English-speaking children, the National Association for the Education of Young Children published a position statement entitled *Screening and Assessment of Young English-Language Learners* (NAEYC, 2005b); see Figure 2.3.

KNOWLEDGE OF CURRICULUM CONTENT AND OUTCOMES STANDARDS

Today, most states have set content area standards and expected student outcomes for most, if not all, subjects taught and for each grade level. These subject area standards and learning outcomes have evolved in recent years into an assessment culture that dominates the focus of dialogue regarding American schooling and its perceived successes or failures.

Curriculum Content Standards

Many state standards have been modeled after national standards, which emerged from discipline-related professional organizations during the standards movement of the 1990s, but with modifications deemed appropriate for individual states. The National Council of Teachers of Mathematics led the way by developing what are considered exemplary standards for K–12 mathematics, *Curriculum and Evaluation Standards for School Mathematics* (NCTM, 1989; 1991; 1994; 2000).* These

---

*Content area standards can be accessed through the Web sites for the professional associations that publish them. These associations are listed in Appendix B.

NAEYC Recommendations on Screening and Assessment of Young English-Language Learners

Adopted Summer 2005

1. **Using Screening and Assessment for Appropriate Purposes.** *As with assessment of all young children, assessment of young English-language learners should be guided by specific, beneficial purposes, with appropriate adaptations to meet the needs of children whose home language is not English.*

1a. Screening: Young English-language learners are regularly screened using linguistically and culturally appropriate screening tools. Results of screenings are used to determine what further supports and services are needed.

1b. Assessment to promote learning: Assessments of young English-language learners are used primarily to understand and improve children's learning; to track, monitor, and support development in all areas, including language development; and to identify disabilities or other special needs.

1c. Program evaluation and accountability: Young English-language learners are included in program evaluation and accountability systems, and culturally and linguistically appropriate assessment instruments and procedures are used. Inclusion of English-language learners in account-ability systems never acts as a disincentive for programs to serve English-language learners.

2. **Culturally and Linguistically Appropriate Assessments.** *In assessing young English-language learners, great emphasis should be given to the alignment of assessment tools and procedures with the specific cultural and linguistic characteristics of the children being assessed.*

2a. All screenings and assessments used with young English-language learners are culturally appropriate.

2b. All screenings and assessments used with young English-language learners are linguistically appropriate.

2c. Translations of English-language instruments are carefully reviewed for linguistic and cultural

appropriateness by native speakers well versed in the complex issues of assessment and translation.

3. **Characteristics of Assessments Used to Improve Instruction.** *The primary purpose of assessing young English-language learners should be to help programs support their learning and development; classroom-based assessment should maximize the value of the results for teachers' curriculum planning and teaching strategies.*

3a. Programs rely on systematic observational assessments, using culturally and linguistically appropriate tools as the primary source of guidance to inform instruction and to improve outcomes for young English-language learners.

3b. Assessments for young English-language learners are based on multiple methods and measures.

3c. Assessments for young English-language learners are ongoing; special attention is given to repeated assessments of language development over time.

3d. Assessments for young English-language learners involve two or more people.

3e. Assessments for young English-language learners are age appropriate.

4. **Using Standardized Formal Assessments.** *The development of state and other accountability systems has led to increased use of standardized formal assessments of young children. Specific considerations about the development and interpretation of these assessments should guide their use with young English-language learners.*

4a. It is appropriate to use standardized formal assessments to identify disabilities or other special needs, and for program evaluation and accountability purposes. They may also contribute to monitoring and improving learning at an individual level as part of a more comprehensive approach to the assessment of young English-language learners.

Figure 2.3   NAEYC Position Statement: Screening and Assessment of Young English-Language Learners

4b. Decision makers and those conducting assessments are aware of the concerns and cautions associated with using standardized formal assessments with young English-language learners.

4c. Decision makers and test developers carefully attend to test development issues, including equivalence and norming.

4d. Decision makers and those conducting assessments know appropriate conditions for using and interpreting standardized formal assessments with young English-language learners.

5. **Characteristics of Those Conducting Assessments.** *Whatever the purpose of the assessment, those conducting assessments of young English-language learners should have cultural and linguistic competence, knowledge of the children being assessed, and specific assessment-related knowledge and skills.*

5a. It is primarily teachers who assess young English-language learners, but paraprofessionals, assessment assistants, and specialized consultants also play an important role.

5b. Those assessing young English-language learners are bilingual and bicultural.

5c. Those assessing young English-language learners know the child.

5d. Those assessing young English-language learners are knowledgeable about language acquisition, including second-language acquisition.

5e. Those assessing young English-language learners are trained in and knowledgeable about assessment in general and about considerations in the assessment of young English-language learners in particular.

6. **The Role of Family in the Assessment of Young English-Language Learners.** *Families of young English-language learners should play* critical roles in the assessment process, being closely involved in a variety of appropriate ways.

6a. Professionals involved in the assessment of young English-language learners seek information and insight from family members in selecting, conducting, and interpreting assessments.

6b. Programs refrain from using family members to conduct formal assessments, interpret during formal assessments, or draw assessment conclusions.

6c. Professionals involved in assessment regularly inform and update families on their child's assessment results in a way that is easily understood and meaningful.

7. **Needs in the Field.** *Resources should be invested to ensure rapid progress on several fronts: expanding the knowledge base; developing more and better assessments; increasing the number of bilingual and bicultural professionals; and creating professional development opportunities for administrators, supervisors, practitioners, and other stakeholders in effective assessment of young English-language learners.*

7a. Scholars provide an expanded knowledge base about second-language acquisition and the development of young English-language learners.

7b. More and better assessments are developed to meet the most pressing needs.

7c. Policy makers, institutions of higher education, and programs adopt policies and practices to recruit and retain a diverse early childhood workforce, with a focus on increasing the number of bilingual and bicultural early childhood professionals.

7d. Early childhood professionals, including program administrators, receive ongoing opportunities for professional development and support in the area of assessing young English-language learners. ◆

Figure 2.3 *(continued)*
Excerpted, with permission, from National Association for the Education of Young Children (NAEYC), Screening and Assessment of Young English-Language Learners. Supplement to the NAEYC and NAECS/SDE Joint Position Statement Early Childhood Curriculum, Assessment, and Program Evaluation: Building an Effective, Accountable System in Programs for Children Birth through Age 8. Copyright © 2005 NAEYC. All rights reserved. Online: www.naeyc.org/about/positions/pdf/ELL_Supplement_Shorter_Version.pdf.

standards, along with expected outcomes, provided a model for the development of standards in other disciplines, which soon followed. These standards included, for example, the *National Science Education Standards* (National Research Council, 1996), the *National Standards for History* (National Center for History in the Schools, 1996), *Standards for the English Language* (National Council of Teachers of English and the International Reading Association (2003), and *Dance, Music, Theatre, Visual Arts: What Every Young American Should Know and Be Able to Do in the Arts* (Consortium of National Arts Education Associations, 1994).

Through various sponsorships, federal and state agencies, scholarly and professional associations, and private foundations, discipline-specific standards in virtually every subject taught in public schools were developed during the first half of the 1990s. By 2001, forty-eight states were well on their way to implementing standards-based education policy (National Council of State Legislatures, 2005). Emphasis on standards-driven curriculum and assessment continues today under federal legislative mandates.

The standards movement found congressional support through the *No Child Left Behind Act of 2001* (No Child Left Behind Act of 2001. PL 107-110).* This law attempted to incorporate many of the state standards into a single federal policy, leading to what some consider to be a troubling expansion of the role of the federal government in the administration of elementary and secondary education, usurping much of the autonomy of states and local districts to establish their own policies (National Conference of State Legislatures, 2005).

The law's stated goal is to narrow the achievement differences among students that cross lines of skin color, ethnicity, immigrant status, and wealth. Among the requirements of this legislation are that each state:

content standards Descriptions of what a student should know and be able to do within a particular subject matter or content area.

achievement standards Descriptions of what knowledge and/or skills students are expected to achieve over a particular time period or academic year.

adequate yearly progress A term used in the No Child Left Behind Act that refers to expected achievements in reading and math beginning in third grade and refers to a predetermined percentage of students scoring at or above "proficiency" on statewide standardized tests.

◆ must demonstrate that challenging academic **content standards** and challenging student academic **achievement standards** have been adopted.

Challenging refers to academic standards that:

1. specify what children are expected to know and be able to do;
2. contain coherent and rigorous content;
3. encourage the teaching of advanced skills.

◆ must apply the same standards to all schools and all children in the state.
◆ must have standards in mathematics, reading or language arts, and science, as well as other subjects determined by the state.
◆ must develop a statewide accountability system to assure that all schools are making **adequate yearly progress,** including significant yearly improvement in certain subgroups:

a. economically disadvantaged students
b. students from major racial and ethnic groups
c. students with disabilities
d. students with limited English proficiency

The application of standards to early childhood education curricula can be challenging. Published standards for content areas should be critiqued for reasonable expectations for age and variablility among children. In developing curricula for young children, what is taught in the content areas must be easily related to prior

*This discussion includes excerpts only. The No Child Left Behind Act of 2001 is quite lengthy, and there is no attempt in this text to include all its standards and accountability requirements.

learning and experiences, relevant to the learning needs and capabilities of young children, and engaging. The joint position statement of the National Association for the Education of Young Children and the National Association of Early Childhood Specialists in State Departments of Education addresses this important concern (Appendix H).

Achievement Goals and Learning Outcomes

learning outcomes A predetermined body of knowledge or skills expected to have been achieved over a certain period of time and as a result of a particular education strategy.

The school-reform movement of the 1980s and the standards-development movement during the 1990s spurred many states to take a more active role in determining what students should know and be able to do and establishing measurable achievement goals, or **learning outcomes,** for each of the content areas taught in public schools. Many states developed and implemented statewide testing programs for selected grades.

Today, however, federal legislation makes this role mandatory for all states and carries with it sanctions when low test scores persist over a period of two or more years.* Sanctions include requiring low-performing schools to provide tutors and/or allowing students to choose to attend a higher-peforming school; and in persistently low-performing schools, the school's governance is restructured.

The No Child Left Behind Act requires states to:

◆ assess "not less than once" student achievement in reading/language arts, mathematics, and science during grades three through eight.

◆ use multiple up-to-date measures of student academic achievment, including measures that assess higher-order thinking skills and understanding.

◆ provide for reasonable adaptations and accommodations for students with disabilites (as defined by the Individual with Disabilities Education Act) necessary to measure their academic achievement.

◆ include limited-English-proficient students and provide for them reasonable accommodations for the language and form most likely to yield accurate data.

◆ produce individual student interpretive, descriptive, and diagnostic reports that allow parents, teachers, and principals to understand and address the academic needs of students and to do so as soon as is practicably possible after the assessment is given.

◆ use assessments that are consistent with widely accepted professional testing standards and objectively measure academic achievement, knowledge, and skills, and avoid tests that evaluate or assess personal or family beliefs and attitudes or publicly disclose personally identifiable information.

◆ provide a yearly assessment of English proficiency that measures oral language, reading, and writing in English skills of all students with limited English proficiency.

In addition, assessment practices are required to be aligned with the state's academic content standards, include two levels of high achievement—*proficient* and *advanced*—and a level described as *basic* to denote progress of the lower-achieving children toward mastering the proficient and adanced levels of achievement.

*It is this aspect of the NCLB Act that has caused considerable consternation among educators and child psychologists because it has changed the emphasis from enriching instructional practices to raising test scores. Curricula in many instances have been narrowed to cover the expected content of the test while foregoing broad and deep coverage of other significant and relevant content.

It is imperative that accountability systems be designed to protect the learning process as well as to measure it.

Anne Vega/Merrill

Standards and Young Children

Although it is reasonable to expect schooling at all levels to meet society's expectations that students get a "good" education and that the dollars spent on education are appropriately used to further that goal, it is imperative that accountability systems be designed to protect the learning process as well as to measure it. This is a particularly compelling concern when it comes to the establishment of standards and outcomes measures that are applied to the assessment of young children.

Professionals in early childhood care and education are increasingly concerned that the emphasis on academic accountability in third grade and above will have an adverse effect on the way younger children are taught and assessed (Hatch, 2002; Kauerz & McMaken, 2004; NAECS/SDE & NAEYC, 2002; Wien, 2004). The trend that models kindergarten pedagogy on upper-grade practices is already in place. Today's kindergarten mimics yesterday's first grade. The long-term effects of this pushdown trend may deter student learning and achievement rather than facilitate and enrich it (Zigler, Finn-Stevenson, & Hall, 2002; Zigler & Styfco, 1997; Graue, 1993; Kagan, 1999).

National Education Goals and School Readiness

The focus on early childhood and school readiness has its origins in goals set forth by the nation's governors in 1989 at an Education Summit Conference in Charlottesville, Virginia. This summit meeting was convened in response to a report of the National Commission on Excellence in Education entitled *A Nation at Risk* (1983, p. 5), in which the nation was told that

> The foundations of our society are presently being eroded by a rising tide of mediocrity that threatens our very future as a nation and a people. . . . We have, in effect been committing an act of unthinking, unilateral educational disarmament.

As a result of this summit meeting, the National Governors Association proposed eight national education goals for improving education in the United States, listed in Figure 2.4. At the same time, a National Education Goals Panel was formed to develop methods by which progress toward these goals might be measured, and the U.S. Department of Education launched its America 2000 project to urge all states and communities to formally adopt these goals. In 1994, Congress passed the Goals 2000: Educate America Act, requiring states to develop education reform plans and set voluntary standards for student performance, curricula, teacher preparation, and appropriate and sufficient resources to assure that all children have the opportunity to learn.

Figure 2.4

The National Education Goals.

Note: From *The National Education Goals Report,* 1997, Washington, DC: Author.

THE NATIONAL EDUCATION GOALS

Goal 1: Ready to Learn

By the year 2000, all children in America will start school ready to learn.

Did you know...that between 1993 and 1996, the percentage of 3- to 5-year-olds whose parents read to them or told them stories regularly increased from 66% to 72%?

Goal 2: School Completion

By the year 2000, the high school graduation rate will increase to at least 90 percent.

Did you know...that 3,356 students drop out of school each day, and that within two years high school graduates can expect to earn 25% more than dropouts?

Goal 3: Student Achievement and Citizenship

By the year 2000, all students will leave grades 4, 8, and 12 having demonstrated competency over challenging subject matter including English, mathematics, science, foreign languages, civics and government, economics, arts, history, and geography, and every school in America will ensure that all students learn to use their minds well, so they may be prepared for responsible citizenship, further learning, and productive employment in our Nation's modern economy.

Did you know...that in 27 states the percentage of 8th graders who scored at the Proficient or Advanced levels on the National Assessment of Educational Progress (NAEP) mathematics assessment increased?

Goal 4: Teacher Education and Professional Development

By the year 2000, the Nation's teaching force will have access to programs for the continued improvement of their professional skills and the opportunity to acquire the knowledge and skills needed to instruct and prepare all American students for the next century.

Did you know...that between 1991 and 1994, the percentage of secondary school teachers who held an undergraduate or graduate degree in their main teaching assignment decreased from 66% to 63%?

(continued)

Figure 2.4   *(continued)*

Goal 5: Mathematics and Science

By the year 2000, United States students will be first in the world in mathematics and science achievement.

Did you know...that only Korea outperformed the U.S. in 4th grade science in a recent international assessment?

Goal 6: Adult Literacy and Lifelong Learning

By the year 2000, every adult American will be literate and will possess the knowledge and skills necessary to compete in a global economy and exercise the rights and responsibilities of citizenship.

Did you know...that fewer adults with a high school diploma or less are participating in adult education, compared to those who have postsecondary education?

Goal 7: Safe, Disciplined, and Alcohol- and Drug-free Schools

By the year 2000, every school in the United States will be free of drugs, violence, and the unauthorized presence of firearms and alcohol and will offer a disciplined environment conducive to learning.

Did you know...that threats and injuries to students at school decreased over a 5-year period?

Goal 8: Parental Participation

By the year 2000, every school will promote partnerships that will increase parental involvement and participation in promoting the social, emotional, and academic growth of children.

Did you know...that parental involvement in school declines as children get older?

The first national goal stated, "By the year 2000, all children in America would start school ready to learn" (National Education Goals Panel, 1991). Three objectives accompany this first goal:

1. All disadvantaged and children with disabilities will have access to high quality and developmentally appropriate preschool programs that help prepare children for school.

2. Every parent in America will be a child's first teacher and devote time each day to helping his or her preschool child learn; parents will have access to the training and support they need.

3. Children will receive the nutrition and health care needed to arrive at school with healthy minds and bodies and the number of low-birth-weight babies will be significantly reduced through enhanced prenatal health systems.

This goal became known as the "readiness goal" and is further defined by the National Task Force on School Readiness and the National Association of State Boards of Education (1991, p. 10):

[A child's] readiness for school requires an emerging facility to experience and shape one's environment, rather than the mastery of discrete facts and skills. Professional opinion and common sense agree that a child's readiness for school is enhanced by good physical health, ability to speak and listen, a degree of emotional stability and independence, and social skill.

In 2001, a national survey revealed that twenty-five states had developed specific child-based outcome standards for children younger than kindergarten age (Bowman et al., Burns, 2001).*This trend continues today. Additionally, the Head Start Bureau has established the *Head Start Child Outcomes Framework* (Appendix D), which describes learning expectations in each of eight domains: language development, literacy, mathematics, science, creative arts, social and emotional development, approaches to learning, and physical health and development (U.S. Dept. of Health & Human Services, Head Start Task Force, 2002–2006).

Today, many local school districts, in collaboration with the child-care communities, are developing school **readiness indicators,** which attempt to delineate expectations for a child's outcomes in early childhood settings in both public and nonpublic schools. Such readiness indicators are believed to predict a child's ability to benefit optimally from his or her ensuing prekindergarten, kindergarten, and/or primary grade educations (Child Trends, 2001; Kaufman Early Education Exchange, 2002; National Governors Association, 2005b).

To the extent that proposed readiness indicators represent reasonable expectations for age and circumstance, they can provide the impetus for improved home and preschool learning envrionments. Such indicators can serve as guidelines for the provision of specific types of experiences and interactions that support earliest growth, development, and learning (Shonkoff & Phillips, 2000). We revisit the topic of readiness in Chapter 8.

Traditionally, most professional early childhood educators have not had to deal with predetermined, formalized early education requirements such as those that occur with standards-based curriculums and assessments. Rather, they have approached teaching young children with the assumption that curricula most effectively emerge from observing and responding to the needs, capabilities, and interests of the young learner. The term **emergent curriculum** is derived from this perspective (Jones & Nimmo, 1994). Such curriculum development depends on focused observation, ongoing assessment of student achievements and needs, and the teacher's ability to provide rich, varied, mind-engaging content and appropriate materials based on their observations. Such curricula are said to be dynamic and child centered (as opposed to scripted and predetermined) (Bredekamp & Copple, 1997; Copple & Bredekamp, 2006; Hart, Burts, & Charlesworth, 1997; L. Katz, 2003; L. G. Katz & Chard, 2000; Seefeldt & Wasik, 2002).

However, policies surrounding accountability have led to the formulation of specific currriculum content requirements and learning outcomes for children in prekindergarten and kindergarten. To respond to state mandates and to provide curricular support for teachers in meeting these standards, prescribed curricula have become more commonplace in early childhood classrooms than in the past. These changes carry the risk of **developmentally inappropriate** practices such as overreliance on whole-group lessons, teacher-centered/teacher-directed instruction, drill-and-skill activities, and tedious paper-and-pencil

readiness indicators A set of characteristics or attributes thought to be indicative of a child's ability to benefit from and succeed with a particular learning requirement.

emergent curriculum A dynamic instructional strategy that adjusts and enriches the curriculum as child development and interests emerge.

developmentally inappropriate Expectations and practices that fail to acknowledge the unique growth and developmental characteristics associated with age and individuality.

---

*Standards, outcomes requirements, and testing policies can be accessed through an individual state's education agency Web site.

tasks. Assessment practices may also mimic those designed for older children and later grades.

Responding to the fact that early childhood education has become a part of the standards-based accountability movement, the National Association for the Education of Young Children (NAEYC), with the National Association of Early Childhood Specialists in State Departments of Education (NAECS/SDE), published a position statement regarding the development of standards relevant to young children with or without disabilities and regardless of education or child-care setting (NAEYC and NAECS/SDE [2002]). The position statement begins with these words:

> The first years of life are critical for later outcomes. Young children have an innate desire to learn. That desire can be supported or undermined by early experiences. High-quality early childhood education can promote intellectual, language, physical, social, and emotional development, creating school readiness and building a foundation for later academic and social competence. By defining the desired content and outcomes of young children's education, early learning standards can lead to greater opportunities for positive development and learning in these early years. NAEYC and NAECS/SDE take the position that early learning standards can be a valuable part of a comprehensive high-quality system of services for young children, contributing to young children's educational experiences and to their future success. But these results can be achieved only if early learning standards:
>
> 1. emphasize significant, developmentally appropriate content and outcomes;
> 2. are developed and reviewed through informed, inclusive processes;
> 3. use implementation and assessment strategies that are ethical and appropriate for young children; and
> 4. are accompanied by strong supports for early childhood programs, professionals and families.

Although the focus on standards has the potential to derail developmentally appropriate practices, the development of subject matter and content standards can focus the professional educator's curriculum planning in ways that can enhance learning experiences for young children. For instance, the National Association for the Education of Young Children identified the following potential benefits of standards-based planning.

Standards can serve as a frame of reference for the development of curriculum by providing:

◆ **Important content,** by helping both content area specialists and early childhood education specialists to identify the "truly important content of each discipline."

◆ **Conceptual frameworks,** or ways of organizing large amounts of complex information to support communication and understanding among and across professional disciplines.

◆ **Coherence,** which is an essential aspect if standards are to be appropriately translated into learning goals for very young children and understood by all users—early childhood educators, parents, students, and administrators.

◆ **Consistency,** which assures that children and families encounter similar grade-level goals, experiences, and expectations when and if they move from one school to another (Bredekamp & Rosegrant, 1995, pp. 8–10).

◆ **High expectations,** which recognize that although children are capable of far more intellectually interesting and challenging study than is often recognized (Katz & Chard, 2000), they do not succeed with watered-down versions of curricula meant for older children.

University Christian Church Weekday School, Fort Worth, TX

There is a need to dispel the notion that early childhood education can successfully mimic upper grade models of curriculum and assessment.

There is a need to counteract the emerging view of early childhood education as a downward extension of elementary school curriculum and assessment practices. To this end, grass roots collaborations are beginning to occur, wherein dialogue among teachers, parents, communities, businesses, and coalitions at local, state, and national levels seek to promote more consensus regarding the framework for curricular goals, content, and assessment in early childhood education (Child Trends, 2001; Halliburton & Thornburg, 2004; National Center for Children in Poverty, 2002).

ALIGNMENT AMONG GOALS, CURRICULUM CONTENT, AND ASSESSMENT

Developmental and education goals, curriculum content, and assessment procedures should be developed in tandem with one another if the student experience is to be coherent and meaningful. Because many schools have yet to make a transition from primary (even sole) reliance on traditional forms of assessment to more eclectic systems that include performance-based strategies, incongruence between classroom instruction and assessment procedures can be problematic. By the same token, practices that rely heavily on performance-based assessments also create incongruence for the learners and ambiguity for teachers when mandated formal testing must take place.

For example, Megan is a third-grade student in a school that has been purposely designed to exemplify developmentally appropriate practices in all grade levels. All personnel have been especially trained to provide curricula that are pursued in depth and cover a broad range of topics. The faculty hold weekly meetings to colaborate on goals and processes and plan educational opportunities that involve hands-on and applied learning activities, multiage and multigrade projects, and strategies to identify and support special talents, interests, and modes of learning. Students are encouraged to work cooperatively, to peer-tutor, and to be generally supportive of one another in a spirit of shared responsibility. School policy encourages committed parent/guardian participation and holds portfolio conferencing (in lieu of traditional report cards). The school climate is learner centered, and the physical envronment is child and family friendly, not only in the classrooms but in all areas of the school building. Traditional textbook/workbook types of pedagogy are purposely kept to a minimum, although lesson plans and grade-level achievement expectations are aligned with those of the district and the state.

As a third-grade student and as required by state policy, Megan will be tested on her achievements in reading and mathematics in a few weeks. The pressure on school personnel in this almost utopian setting has altered the instructional format temporarily because all students in her grade are prepared through daily practice sessions to take the state-mandated test. Megan has complained of boredom and expressed her wish that they ". . . didn't have to sit for so long every day doing the same things over and over. It is so, sooo, boring, and Miss Paterson isn't very happy either, and the principal won't let us talk in the hallway or even in the cafeteria."

At dismissal on the third day of test preparation, Megan throws her book bag over her shoulder and trudges to the car, where her mother is waiting. She sluggishly crawls into the car, forcefully drops her book bag, buckles up, takes a deep breath, crosses her arms over her chest, and angrily proclaims, "Well, I had to cheat on a test today."

Having been confronted with a question during the practice test that she could not answer, she asked a nearby classmate (a practice otherwise encouraged through the school's cooperative learning philosophy). The classmate responded, and the two were reprimanded and sent to the principal's office for further discussion.

Morality aside (actually, it could be argued that Megan is an unusually honest child!), one has to consider the incongruence in the philosophy and daily practices to which students in the school have become accustomed and the very different mode of thinking and behaving imposed on them in the context of preparing for and taking mandated tests, on which their achievement and that of the teacher's will be judged.

Attempting to assess and document achievement using strategies that are not in alignment with school philosophy, goals, and daily practices places students in a vulnerable situation. Teachers, as well, find themselves playing roles that contradict their daily practices. Parents can also find it confusing when they notice incongruence between children's day-to-day learning experiences and information about testing procedures and performance reports. Most troubling however, is that this misalignment can lead to assessment results that are incomplete and quite likely inaccurate.

Of particular concern with regard to alignment is that of accurately reflecting the accomplishments of at-risk students and students with disabilities. Education goals, curriculum content, and assessment procedures that are too rigidly defined, particularly along traditional testing and letter-grade paradigms, can place these students in the position of never fully measuring up, leading them to feel defeated and incompetent. Indeed, Munk and Bursuck (1998) report that research suggests that 60 to 70 percent of students with disabilities in inclusion classrooms receive below-average grades. For this reason many schools are providing alternative grading systems (Bursuck et al., 1996; Munk & Bursuck, 1998). Such systems adapt grading procedures to more accurately reflect individual student progress. Common strategies used with these adaptations include basing grades on student improvement, giving multiple grades (e.g., a grade for a particular piece of work or a test and a grade for effort), assigning weighted grades for specific types of work, basing grades on meeting the objectives of an **individual education program** (**IEP**), and assigning separate grades for process and products (Bursuck et al., 1996). It is important, however, that when these adaptations are used, teachers deem them acceptable and fair and provide positive rationale for their use.

individual education program (IEP) A written plan for the education of a student with disabilities that follows procedures for development and implementation that have been set forth by federal legislation.

When goals have been clarified, decisions about the development or selection of specific content are made on the basis of current scholarship and identified best practices in early childhood education. Early childhood education curricular guidelines serve as standards that professionals can use to judge the appropriateness of certain content in the early childhood curriculum. Figures 2.5 and 2.6 contain frequently asked questions about curriculum and assessment that apply to all programs for children ages three through eight. Curricula can be analyzed according to these questions.

Specific goals and curriculum content must be appropriate to the students' age, individuality, and cultural and linguistic background. Obviously, taking into account age-related characteristics, prior experiences, and opportunities to learn, a curriculum for three-year-olds will be quite different from curriculum for six-year-olds. However, the range of developmental characteristics represented even within a particular age group requires that teachers understand children's different ways of pursuing and demonstrating their knowledge and skills and the continuum they may follow in each of the content areas. See, for example, the Continuum of Children's Development in Early Reading and Writing in Appendix E.

Assessment, then, is truly an intertwined process that influences and is influenced by curricula and pedagogy, teaching, and learning. At the heart of any assessment system should be the concerted effort to facilitate and enrich the learning process. Assessments should never be used in a manner that undermines a child's natural desire to grow up, to learn to do many things, and to acquire knowledge about lots of topics. After all, learning is what children do. The National Forum on Assessment (1995, p. 1), a coalition of education and civil rights organizations, proposed the following set of *Principles and Indicators for Student Assessment Systems.*

The assessments supported by the National Forum's principles are:

grounded in solid knowledge of how people learn;
connected to clear statements of what is important for students to learn;
flexible enough to meet the needs of a diverse student body; and
able to provide students with the opportunity to actively produce work and demonstrate their learning.

Early Childhood CURRICULUM: Frequently asked questions

1. What are curriculum goals?

The goals of a curriculum state the essential desired outcomes for children. When adopting a curriculum, it is important to analyze whether its goals are consistent with other goals of the early childhood program or with state or other early learning standards, and with program standards. Curriculum goals should support and be consistent with expectations for young children's development and learning.

2. What is the connection between curriculum and activities for children?

Whether for toddlers or second graders, a good curriculum is more than a collection of activities. The goals and framework of the curriculum do suggest a coherent set of activities and teaching practices linked to standards or expectations—although not in a simple fashion: Good activities support multiple goals. Together and over time, these activities and practices will be likely to help all children develop and learn the curriculum content. Standards and curriculum can give greater focus to activities, helping staff decide how these activities may fit together to benefit children's growth. Appropriate curriculum also promotes a balance between planned experiences—based on helping children progress toward meeting defined goals—and experiences that emerge as outgrowths of children's interests or from unexpected happenings (for example, a new building is being built in the neighborhood). While these experiences are not planned, they are incorporated into the program in ways that comply with standards and curriculum goals.

3. What are the most important things to consider in making a decision about adopting or developing a curriculum?

It is important to consider whether the curriculum (as it is or as it might be adapted) fits well with (a) broader goals, standards, and program values (assuming that those have been thoughtfully developed), (b) what research suggests are the significant predictors of positive development and learning, (c) the sociocultural, linguistic, and individual characteristics of the children for whom the curriculum is intended, and (d) the values and wishes of the families and community served by the program. While sometimes it seems that a pro-

gram's decision to develop its own curriculum would ensure the right fit, caution is needed regarding a program's ability to align its curriculum with the features of a high-quality curriculum (that is, to address the recommendation and indicators of effectiveness of the position statement). Considerable expertise is needed to develop an effective curriculum—one that incorporates important outcomes and significant content and conforms with research on early development and learning and other indicators noted in the position statement—and not merely a collection of activities or lesson plans (see also FAQ #7 in this section).

4. What should be the connection between curriculum for younger children and curriculum they will encounter as they get older?

Early childhood curriculum is much more than a scaled-back version of curriculum for older children. As emphasized in Early Learning Standards (NAEYC & NAECS/SDE 2002), earlier versions of a skill may look very different from later versions. For example, one might think that knowing the names of two U.S. states at age four in preschool is an important predictor of knowing all 50 states in fourth grade. However, knowing two state names is a less important predictor than gaining fundamental spatial and geographic concepts. Resources, including those listed at the end of this document, can help teachers and administrators become more aware of the curriculum in later years. With this knowledge, they can think and collaborate about ways for earlier and later learning to connect. Communication about these connections can also support children and parents as they negotiate the difficult transitions from birth–three to preschool programs and then to kindergarten and the primary grades.

5. Is there such a thing as curriculum for babies and toddlers?

Indeed there is, but as the developmental chart about curriculum suggests, curriculum for babies and toddlers looks very different from curriculum for preschoolers or first-grade children. High-quality infant/toddler programs have clear goals, and they base their curriculum on knowledge of very early development. Thus a curriculum for children in the first years of life is focused on relation-

Figure 2.5

Early Childhood CURRICULUM: FAQ (cont'd)

ships, communicative competencies, and exploration of the physical world, each of which is embedded in daily routines and experiences. High-quality infant/toddler curriculum intentionally develops language, focusing on and building on the home language; promotes security and social competence; and encourages understanding of essential concepts about the world. This lays the foundation for mathematics, science, social studies, literacy, and creative expression without emphasizing disconnected learning experiences or formal lessons (Lally et al. 1995; Lally 2000; Semlak 2000).

6. When should the early childhood curriculum begin to emphasize academics?

There is no clear dividing line between "academics" and other parts of a high-quality curriculum for young children (Hyson 2003a). Children are learning academics from the time they are born. Even infants and toddlers are beginning—through play, relationships, and informal opportunities—to develop the basis of later knowledge in areas such as mathematics, visual and performing arts, social studies, science, and other areas of learning. As children transition into K–3 education, however, it is appropriate for the curriculum to pay focused attention to these and other subject matter areas, while still emphasizing physical social, emotional, cognitive, and language development, connections across domains, and active involvement in learning.

7. Should programs use published curricula, or is it better for teachers to develop their own curriculum?

The quality of the curriculum—including its appropriateness for the children who will be experiencing it—should be the important question. If a published, commercially available curriculum—either a curriculum for one area such as literacy or mathematics or a comprehensive curriculum—is consistent with the position statement's recommendations and the program's goals and values, appears well suited to the children and families served by the program, and can be implemented effectively by staff, then it may be worth considering, especially as a support for inexperienced teachers. To make a well-

informed choice, staff (and other stakeholders) need to identify their program's mission and value, consider the research and other evidence about high-quality programs and curricula, and select a curriculum based on these understandings. Some programs may determine that in their situation the best curriculum would be one developed specifically for that program and the children and families it serves. In that case—if staff have the interest, expertise, and resources to develop a curriculum that includes clearly defined goals, a system for ensuring that these goals are shared by stakeholders, a system for determining the beneficial effects of the curriculum, and other indicators of effectiveness—then the program may conclude that it should take that route.

8. Is it all right to use one curriculum for mathematics, another for science, another for language and literacy, another for social skills, and still another for music?

If curricula are adopted or developed for distinct subject matter areas such as literature or mathematics, coherence and consistency are especially important. Are the goals and underlying philosophy of each curriculum consistent? What will it feel like for a child in the program? Will staff need to behave differently as they implement each curriculum? What professional development will staff need to make these judgments?

9. What's needed to implement a curriculum effectively?

Extended professional development, often with coaching or mentoring, is a key to effective curriculum implementation (National Research Council 2001). Well-qualified teachers who understand and support the curriculum goals and methods are more likely to implement curriculum effectively. So-called scripted or teacher-proof curricula tend to be narrow, conceptually weak, or intellectually shallow. Another key to success is assessment. Ongoing assessment of children's progress in relation to the curriculum goals gives staff a sense of how their approach may need to be altered for the whole group or for individual children.

Figure 2.5   *(continued)*

CHILD ASSESSMENT: Frequently asked questions

1. What is the connection between curriculum and assessment?

Curriculum and assessment are closely tied. Classroom- or home-based assessment tells teachers what children are like and allows them to modify curriculum and teaching practices to best meet the children's needs. Curriculum also influences what is assessed and how; for example, a curriculum that emphasizes the development of self-regulation should be accompanied by assessments of the children's ability to regulate their attention, manage strong emotions, and work productively without a great deal of external control.

2. What should teachers be assessing in their classrooms? When and why?

The answers to these questions depend, again, on the program's goals and on the curriculum being used. But all teachers need certain information in order to understand children's individual, cultural, linguistic, and developmental characteristics and to begin to recognize and respond to any special needs or concerns. The most important thing is to work with other staff and administrators to develop a systematic plan for assessment over time, using authentic measures (those that reflect children's real-world activities and challenges) and focusing on outcomes that have been identified as important. The primary goal in every case is to make the program (curriculum, teaching practices, and so on) as effective as possible so that every child benefits.

3. How is assessment different for children of varying ages, cultures, languages, and abilities?

The younger the child, the more difficult it is to use assessment methods that rely on verbal ability, on focused attention and cooperation, or on paper-and-pencil methods. The selection of assessments should include careful attention to the ages for which the assessment was developed. Even with older children (kindergarten-primary age), the results of single assessments are often unreliable for individuals,

since children may not understand the importance of "doing their best" or may be greatly influenced by fatigue, temporary poor health, or other distractions. Furthermore, in some cultures competition and individual accomplishment are discouraged, making it difficult to validly assess young children's skills. For young children whose home language is not English, assessments conducted in English produce invalid, misleading results. Finally, children with disabilities benefit from in-depth and ongoing assessment, including play-based assessment, to ensure that their individual needs are being met. When children with disabilities participate in assessments used for typically developing classmates, the assessments need adaptation in order for all children to demonstrate their competence (Meisels & Atkins-Burnett 2000; Sandall, McLean, & Smith 2000; McLean, Bailey, & Wolery 2004).

4. How should specific assessment tools or measures be selected? Is it better to develop one's own assessments or to purchase them?

Thorough discussion of early learning standards, program goals and standards, and the curriculum that the program is using will guide selection of specific assessment measures. In a number of cases, curriculum models are already linked to related assessments. It is important to think systemically so that assessments address all important areas of development and learning. This may seem overwhelming, but the same assessment tool or strategy often gives helpful information about multiple aspects of children's development. Other important considerations are whether a particular assessment tool or system will create undue burdens on staff or whether it will actually contribute to their teaching effectiveness. Issues of technical adequacy are also important to examine, especially for assessments used for accountability purposes. Special attention should be given to whether an assessment was developed for and tested with children from similar backgrounds, languages, and cultures as

Figure 2.6

CHILD ASSESSMENT: FAQ (cont'd)

those for whom the assessment will be used. When selecting assessments for children whose home language is not English, additional questions arise; for example, are the assessment instruments available in the primary languages of the children who are to be assessed? Given these challenges, it seems tempting to develop an assessment tailored to the unique context of a particular program. However, beyond informal documentation, the difficulty of designing good assessments multiplies. Those who plan to develop their own assessment tools need to be fully aware of the challenges of standardizing and validating these assessments.

5. What is screening and how should it be used?

Screening is a quickly administered assessment used to identify children who may benefit from more in-depth assessment. Although screening tools are brief and appear simple, they must meet strict technical standards for test construction and be culturally and linguistically relevant. Only staff with sufficient training should conduct screening; families should be involved as important sources of information about the child; and, when needed, there should always be referrals to further specialized assessment and intervention. Screening is only a first step. Screening may be used to identify children who should be observed further for a possible delay or problem. However, screening should not be used to diagnose children as having special needs, to prevent children from entering a program, or to assign children to a specific intervention solely on the basis of the screening results. Additionally, screening results should not be used as indicators of program effectiveness.

6. What kind of training do teachers and other staff need to conduct assessments well?

Professional development is key to effective child assessment. Positive attitudes about assessment and "assessment literacy" (knowledge of assessment principles, issues, and tools) are developed through collaboration and teamwork, in which all members of an early childhood program come to agree on desired goals, methods, and processes for assessing children's progress. In addition, preservice programs in two- and four-year higher education institutions should provide students with research-based information and opportunities to learn and practice observation, documentation, and other forms of classroom-level assessment (Hyson 2003b). Understanding the purposes and limitations of early childhood norm-referenced tests, including their use with children with disabilities, is also part of assessment literacy, even for those not trained to administer such tests.

7. How should families be involved in assessment?

Ethically, families have a right to be informed about the assessment of their children. Families' own perspectives about their child are an important resource for staff. Additionally, families of young children with disabilities have a legal right to be involved in assessment decisions (IDEA 1997). Early childhood program staff and administrators share the results of assessments—whether informal observations or more formal test results—with families in ways that are clear, respectful, culturally responsive, constructive, and use the language that families are most comfortable with.

Figure 2.6   *(continued)*

Excerpted, with permission, from National Association for the Education of Young Children (NAEYC) and National Association of Early Childhood Specialists in State Departments of Education (NAECS/SDE), "Early Childhood Curriculum, Assessment, and Program Evaluation: Building an Effective, Accountable System in Programs for Children Birth through Age 8. Position Statement with Expanded Resources," pages 12–13. Copyright © 2003 NAEYC. All rights reserved. The full position statement is available at www.naeyc.org/about/positions/pdf/CAPEexpand.pdf.

Figure 2.7

Principles for Student
Assessment Systems

Note: From *Principles and
Indicators for Student Assessment Systems,* by M. Neill and
R. Mitchell, Eds., 1995, Cambridge, MA: National Forum
on Assessment. Copyright
1995 by National Forum on
Assessment 342 Broadway,
Cambridge, MA 02139; 617-
864-4810; email:
fairtest@aol.com; http://
www.fairtest.org. Reprinted
with permission.

1. Assessment systems, including classroom and large-scale assessment, are organized around the primary purpose of improving student learning.
2. Assessment systems report on and certify student learning and provide information for school improvement and accountability by using practices that support important learning.
3. Assessment systems, including policies, practices, instruments, and uses, are fair to all students.
4. Knowledgeable and fair educators are essential to high quality assessment systems and practices.
5. Assessment systems draw on the community's knowledge and ensure support by including parents, community members, and students, together with educators and professionals with particular expertise, in the development of the system.
6. Educators, schools, districts, and states clearly and regularly discuss assessment system practices and student and program progress with students, families and the community.
7. Assessment systems are regularly reviewed and improved to ensure that the systems are educationally beneficial to all students.

The seven principles are listed in Figure 2.7. Principle 3 is particularly germane to the discussions in this chapter. The National Forum on Assessment lists the following indicators that accompany Principle 3:

1. Every student has the opportunity to perform on a variety of high-quality assessments during the school year.
2. Schools prepare all students to perform well on assessments which meet these principles.
3. Assessment practices recognize and incorporate the variety of cultural backgrounds of students who are assessed.
4. Assessment practices incorporate the variety of different student learning styles.
5. Assessments, particularly for young children, are developmentally appropriate.
6. Assessments are created or adapted to meet the needs of students who are learning English.
7. Assessments are created or adapted and accommodations made to meet the needs of students who have a disability.
8. All students are knowledgeable and experienced in the assessment methods used to evaluate their work.
9. The group which designs or validates an assessment reflects, has experience with, and understands the particular needs and backgrounds of the student population, including race, culture, gender, socio-economic, language, age, and disability status.
10. Committees of persons knowledgeable about the diverse student population review large-scale assessments for bias and are able to modify, remove, or replace items, tasks, rubrics, or other elements of the assessment, if they find them biased or offensive.
11. Teacher education and continuing professional development prepare teachers to assess all students fairly.
12. Technical standards are developed and used to ensure the assessments do not have harmful consequences for student learning or teaching.

13. States and districts report their assessment data by racial, ethnic, gender, linguistic, disability, and socio-economic status groups for analysis of school, district, and state results, provided that doing so does not infringe upon student privacy rights.

14. Schools do not use assessments to track or place students in ways that narrow curriculum options or foreclose educational opportunities (National Forum on Assessment, 1995, p. 11).

If assessment is to truly inform instruction (which, of course, is the premise of this text), then the recommendations of the National Forum on Assessment continue to make very good sense.

SUMMARY

In this chapter we have attempted to establish a frame of mind for planning a meaningful, fair, and unbiased assessment system. Assessment is not only a process for determining what students know and are able to do, but it is a powerful medium by which educators learn about child development, children's special needs and talents, and cultural and linguistic diversity. Further, the accountability culture of modern education requires educators to stay abreast of changing political and policy issues surrounding mandated large-scale assessments and to remain committed to assessment systems that facilitate and enrich learning. To the extent that educators recognize their limitations and are willing to pursue further expertise in the variety of topics associated with student assessment and are open to the knowledge that can be gained from their own assessment practices with children, assessment has the potential to truly enhance the learning and teaching process.

REVIEW STRATEGIES AND ACTIVITIES

Vexing Questions

1. Vexing questions are puzzlements that need time and dialogue to bring into perspective. Sometimes, indeed most of the time, there is no absolute way to answer them. Begin a journal of "vexing questions" associated with the assessment of young children that arise during your studies. Reflect on these questions; discuss them with classmates, your instructor, and practicing early childhood educators. Do some research through your library or electronically: Has anyone conducted research on this issue? Perhaps you will be inspired to write an essay on the topic. Here are some examples of vexing questions relating to this chapter.

   a. Can test scores on mandated school accountability tests influence the manner in which teachers subsequently grade student performance and products?

   b. What do students learn from large-scale, high-stakes tests?

   c. Should all teachers learn to speak additional languages in order to respond to the growing number of non-English-speaking students in American schools?

    d. If you were Megan's parent, how would you have responded to her? If you were Megan's teacher, how would you have responded? If you were the principal, how would you have responded?

    e. How can individual teachers ensure that accountability requirements protect as well as measure the learning process?

2. Invite a school principal to dialogue with your class about how teachers can be held accountable without compromising the principles of developmentally appropriate practices.

3. The subject of accountability through whole-group, large-scale testing is addressed in a number of books and essays. Some authors find the practice aversive, whereas others believe it serves worthwhile educational purposes. The suggested readings at the end of each chapter in this book include literature that represents varying and sometimes contradictory points of view on many topics relating to assessment practices. Structure a class debate on opposing points of view derived from one or more of these suggested readings.

SUGGESTED LITERATURE AND RESOURCES

Amrein, A. L., & Berlines, D. C. (2002, March 28). High-stakes testing, uncertainty and student learning. *Education Policy Analysis Archives, 10*(18). Retrieved 1-5-06 from http://epaa.asu.edu/epaa/v10n18/.

Bigger, H., & Pizzolongo, P. J. (2004). School readiness: More than ABCs. *Young Children, 59*(3), 64–66.

Copple, C., & Bredekamp, S. (2006). *Basics of developmentally appropriate practice: An introduction for teachers of children 3 to 6.* Washington, DC: National Association for the Education of Young Children.

Derman-Sparks, L., & Ramsey, P. G. (2005). What if all the children in my class are white? Anti-bias multicultural education with white children. *Young Children, 60* (6), 20–27.

Griffin, P., Smith, P. B., & Martin, L. (2004). *Profiles in English as a second language.* Portsmouth, NH: Heinemann.

Grisham-Brown, J., Jemmeter, M. L., & Pretti-Frontezak, K. (2005). *Blended practices for teaching young children in inclusive settings.* Baltimore: Brookes.

Jalongo, M. R. (1999). *Resisting the pendulum swing: Informed perspectives on education controversies.* Olney, MD: Association for Childhood Education, International.

Kohn, A. (2004). *What does it mean to be well educated?: And more essays on standards, grading, and other follies.* Boston: Beacon Press.

National Academy of Science. (2004). *Assessment in support of instruction and learning: Bridging the gap between large-scale and classroom assessment.* Washington, DC: National Academy Press. Available from http:www.nap.edu/catalog.

National Conference of State Legislatures. (February 2005). *Task Force on No Child Left Behind: Final Report.* Denver, CO: Author. Download from http://www.ncsl.org.

Pellegrino, J. W. Chudowsky, N., & Glaser, R. (Eds.). (2001). *Knowing what students know: The science and design of educational assessment.* Washington, DC: National Academy Press.

Seefeldt, C. (2005). *How to work with standards in the early childhood classroom.* New York: Teachers College Press.

Wien, C. A. (2004). *Negotiating standards in the primary classroom: The teacher's dilemma.* New York: Teachers College Press.

Components of a Meaningful Assessment System

3

A Planning Format for Meaningful Assessments I

Formal Assessments of Young Children

Why do educators believe that intelligence is measurable?

Anonymous

Because such a measurement would be so useful to know! And maybe because educators are idealists at heart—an endearing quality to be found in those so close to our children. Speaking for myself, I think trying to measure intelligence is like trying to measure beauty. Most of us will agree that some people are more attractive than others, but there are many different kinds of wonderful.

Marilyn vos Savant

Reprinted with permission from *Parade*, copyright © 1997.

After reading and studying this chapter, you will demonstrate comprehension by being able to:

❏ describe a planning format for a meaningful assessment system.
❏ identify developmental domains in which assessment is focused.
❏ distinguish between formal and informal assessment strategies.
❏ discuss the appropriate uses of formal testing of young children.

A PLANNING FORMAT FOR MEANINGFUL ASSESSMENTS I: FORMAL ASSESSMENTS

Determining what to assess, how to assess it, and what to do with assessment information can be daunting. Developing a blueprint (or overall plan) for assessment is a good way to identify the individual parts of the process, beginning with desired outcomes and working through each of the components that are needed to comprise a coherent assessment system. A blueprint describes the sequence of steps for planning and delineates areas that need to be carefully thought through: expected student accomplishments, how often and in what contexts progress toward these expected accomplishments will be assessed, and the curriculum content and pedagogy required to support the desired accomplishments. This blueprint may also include a plan for aligning curricula and assessments with age or grade guidelines or content standards. The goal in planning is a system for assessments that is realistic and developmentally appropriate, relies on intellectually honest instruments and interpretations, and effectively integrates curriculum, instruction, and assessments practices.

A PLANNING FORMAT FOR MEANINGFUL ASSESSMENTS OF YOUNG CHILDREN

Assessing development and learning in young children is difficult. From birth to age eight, growth, development, and learning are very rapid in each of the developmental domains—physical/motor, psychosocial, language, cognition, and literacy. Growth, development, and learning do not necessarily occur at the same pace in each of these domains. Rather, developmental changes occur in episodic fashion and are highly influenced by many environmental characteristics and the quality of parenting and early care and education practices.

Young children learn through active participation and interaction with objects and people—they learn by doing. Their active involvement in hands-on activities engages thought processes by which they come to conceptualize and understand the world around them. A young child is more likely to reveal what he or she knows and is able to do by showing rather than by listening, explaining, or writing, as is required by many forms of assessments.

emergent development The concept that growth, development, and learning are continually changing and progressing toward more mature or sophisticated forms.

Ideally, early childhood assessments focus primarily on **emerging development** in multiple developmental and curriculum content domains and on children's capabilities, as demonstrated by what they do and how they do it. Such assessments are concerned with *performance* (what a child demonstrates he or she can do); *processes* (how the child pursues or carries out a task); and *products* (the physical items produced by the child during the learning process or activity). These types of assessments are described as **formative evaluation** in that they take place during the teaching/learning process and thus provide immediate feedback to the learner and teacher about the learner's knowledge and skills and the effectiveness of instructional procedures. Formative assessments usually utilize (but are not limited to) informal assessment procedures.

formative evaluation Assessment of student learning that takes place as learning occurs and is used to inform current instructional practices.

Figure 3.1 provides an example of a blueprint for planning an early childhood assessment program. Notice that its parts are arranged in a circular fashion to show

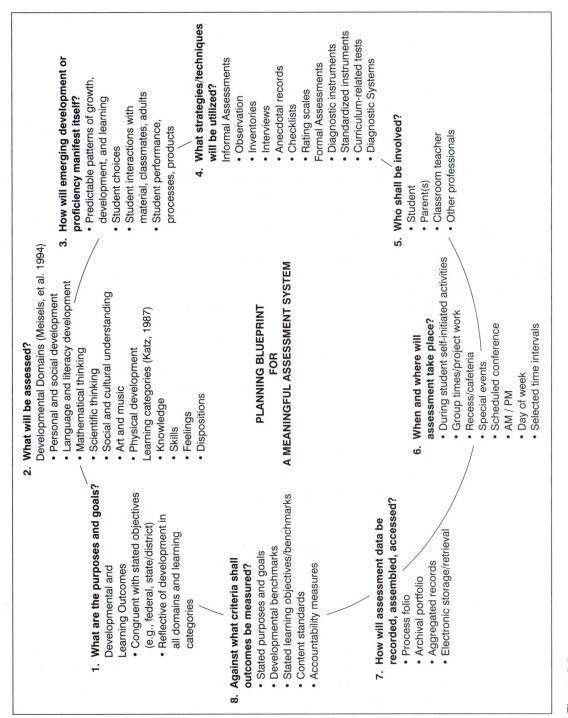

Figure 3.1
Planning Blueprint for Meaningful Assessments

that if the process is valid (that is, it assesses what it purports to assess), it fulfills the stated purposes laid out in the first step. Each step has its own set of considerations. An assessment plan begins with a holistic view, in which goals and objectives are stated. One begins by focusing on the following:

1. purposes assessments will serve
2. domains that will be assessed
3. strategies and techniques that will be used
4. information obtained and how it will be interpreted and communicated
5. how the artifacts of assessment (tests, test score reports, and student work products) will be assembled and stored

summative Summary information concerned with broad outcomes attained over time and usually compiled three times during the school year for use in collaborating with students and parents and providing summary reports for school or district evaluations.

This blueprint also depicts when and for what purposes mandated assessments will take place. Mandated assessments associated with classroom or large-scale testing are typically **summative,** although less formal types of assessments can also serve summative purposes. Summative assessments occur at specified intervals throughout the school year and are intended to provide a cumulative picture of student achievements over time. Summative assessments typically utilize (but are not limited to) formal, standardized instruments and are most frequently applied to a grade or program to determine if school, district, or state learning outcome goals are being met. Summative assessments may also be applied to individual student assessments.

Individual student summative assessments generally take place no more than three times a year, typically once every three months. Individual student summative assessment includes a review of all informal and formal assessments collected during the period since the last summative review and can be compared with previous reviews. The purposes of these individual summative assessments are to:

1. identify individual student strengths and challenges.
2. document evidence of progress in each developmental and academic domain.
3. identify areas of concern or in need of further assessment.
4. determine any need for modified curriculum content and/or instructional practices.
5. celebrate accomplishments with the child and parent(s).
6. determine next steps for continued development and learning.

Once the blueprint (or *gestalt*) is drafted, we can look more specifically at its components for day-to-day planning. Figure 3.2 provides a graphic for conceptualizing the categories of assessment information. It can be used in several mutually supportive ways. In this design, a section is provided for each developmental or content domain, and each domain can be treated as a separate planning chart. At any one time, the assessor can choose to focus on one or more domains (physical/motor development, language development, personal/social development, cognition, and literacy) and one or more indicators (performance behaviors, student products, or the learning processes a student follows in pursuing knowledge or skills). This design can be used to plan for either group or individual assessments

Developmental Domain		Knowledge	Skills	Feelings	Dispositions	Possible Portfolio Entries
Mathematical Learning	Performance					
	Products					
	Processes					
Personal/Social Development	Performance					
	Products					
	Processes					

Figure 3.2
Assessment Planning Matrix

What are Dispositions?

The term *disposition* as applied to the education of young children has been defined by Dr. Lilian Katz as:

> . . . a pattern of behavior exhibited frequently and in the absence of coercion, and constituting a habit of mind under some conscious and voluntary control, and that is intentional and oriented to broad goals" (Katz, 1995, p. 63).

> Dr. Katz asserts that ". . . the most important disposition included in educational goals is the disposition to go on learning. Any educational approach that undermines that disposition is miseducation" (p.66).

Katz, L. G. (1995). *Talks with teachers of young children: A collection.* Norwood, NJ: Ablex, 647–69.

and curriculum and instructional supports. The chart may include a stated goal or expectation and how it will be assessed. A companion chart may include information about what is expected (a particular learning outcome, benchmark statement, or skill development) and what is actually observed or demonstrated by an individual being assessed. This paradigm may also be used to plan the types of curricular and instructional supports to help children achieve the stated learning outcomes.

It is important to observe and assess feelings and dispositions as well as knowledge and skills. Often referred to as *approaches to learning,* this information provides important clues as to individual interests, motivations, and learning styles. This topic is discussed later in this chapter under the heading " Determining What Will Be Assessed."

THE PURPOSES AND GOALS OF ASSESSMENT

Meaningful assessments are carried out to provide ongoing data on student performance in such a manner as to enhance learning experiences, to ensure student progress and increasing competence, and to inform and enrich both instruction and curriculum. Effective assessments provide information for planning curriculum that is responsive to standards and curriculum goals while focusing on individual student developmental needs and capabilities. Baseline information obtained through initial assessments helps teachers set goals for individual learners and curriculum and align both with professional or state-mandated standards.

DETERMINING WHAT WILL BE ASSESSED

benchmark
a. A standard, based on research evidence, by which changes in children's development and learning are noted or marked, thereby providing teachers with direction in facilitating the next step in children's learning.
b. When referring to policies associated with accountability, defined more narrowly: "specific description of knowledge or skill that students should acquire by a particular point in their schooling" (Kendall/McREL, 2001).

As discussed in prior chapters, emphasis in early childhood education is on whole child development perspectives. As such, assessments in early childhood education focus on development and learning in physical/motor, psychosocial, cognitive, language, and literacy domains. In addition, assessments focus on the acquisition of knowledge and skills in the content areas of language arts, mathematics, science, social studies, the arts (art, music, dance, drama), and physical education. These are among the content areas for which national standards have been published. Content area standards provide a frame of reference for establishing goals and **benchmarks** for each grade.

Meisels et al. (1994) suggest the following domains that are compatible with both national standards and developmentally appropriate practices in early childhood and primary education. These domains are identified in the widely used *Work Sampling System* (Dichtelmiller, Jablon, Marsden, & Meisels, 2001; Meisels, 1993;

Meisels et al., 1994) and follow the typical content areas included in early child-hood and primary education. Although there are other well-researched assessment systems (Appendix F), the authors of this text have chosen the Work Sampling System to illustrate a developmentally appropriate, child-development-focused approach. The domains suggested by the authors of this system are frequently addressed in other contexts, such as state readiness indicators and preschool curriculum guidelines. We will refer to these domains to guide our discussions and suggest strategies throughout this text:

- personal and social development
- language and literacy
- mathematical thinking
- scientific thinking
- social studies
- the arts
- physical development

In plotting these or similar domains on a planning matrix, we must consider the classroom goals for the children and the interconnectedness of development and learning across developmental domains and curricular areas. We also consider the learning sequence that children follow, from *awareness* to *exploration* to *inquiry* to *utilization* (Bredekamp & Rosegrant, 1992; Rosegrant, 1989). In planning, the following learning categories (Katz, 1995), mentioned earlier, serve as *target behaviors* within each domain:

- **Knowledge**—facts, concepts, ideas, vocabulary, stories, and specific subject matter and content area information
- **Skills and processes**—physical, social, verbal, and mathematical skills and processes that use thinking, reasoning, problem solving, communicating, decision making, and representational strategies such as constructing, drawing, painting, and writing
- **Feelings**—security, self-efficacy, self-confidence, belonging, self-respect, and feelings about and toward others (i.e., classmates, teachers, and other school personnel)
- **Dispositions, sometimes referred to as** *habits of mind*—curiosity, friendliness, creativity, initiative, cooperation, social responsibility, and persistence or inclination to continue to explore, inquire, and use new knowledge and skills

These categories help to sort and classify the types of behaviors that children exhibit and help the assessor to focus more specifically on how a child pursues knowledge and skills and on what a child knows and is able to do.

HOW EMERGING DEVELOPMENT OR PROFICIENCY MANIFESTS ITSELF

It is essential that the assessor be well grounded in knowledge of child growth and development. The ability to recognize expected growth and accomplishments for age as well as behaviors and characteristics suggestive of a need for further evaluation are critical teacher skills. Setting developmentally appropriate goals and expectations for the class and for individual students within the class, including children with special needs and talents and children with limited English proficiency, depends on this knowledge. Tables 3.1 through 3.5, in the appendix to this chapter, although by no means exhaustive, can be a helpful starting point for learning about developmental trends and provides a frame of reference for the age ranges from early childhood through the elementary grades. With such a frame of reference, observation of children becomes more focused, and assessment of their "performance, processes, and products" is more accurately related to widely held expectations for growth, development, and learning.

Emerging development, knowledge, and skill proficiency are revealed to the focused observer through:

- the *choices* children make during self-initiated learning activities.
- the *nature and content of children's play* and sociodramatic themes.
- the *language(s)* children use to explore, inquire, and interact with classmates, teachers, family members, and others.
- the *strategies* children use to *solve problems* (e.g., trial and error, seeking help from a classmate or an adult, or accessing resources such as manipulatives, books, visuals, or other media).
- *personal accounts* of experiences and current understandings (spoken, written, or depicted in art or written work).
- *information-gathering strategies* (e.g., observing others; focused or engaged listening; role playing and imitation in pretend play; asking questions of classmates, adults, or parents; attending to environmental stimuli such as print media, signs, and symbols; exploring books, pictures, classroom visuals, or other media; experimenting with objects; and exploring realia and other teaching materials).
- the manner in which children use their *motor coordinations* for both gross and fine motor movements and manipulations, particularly for locomotion and play, to self-help, or to explore and manipulate objects, toys, and classroom materials.
- the *interests and hobbies* that are purposefully pursued and are engaging.
- the *social skills* displayed in interacting with others.
- the *manner in which a child participates* as a member of a play group and community of learners.
- the *cognitive processes* that are exhibited (e.g., recalling, reciting, comparing, contrasting, grouping, classifying, ordering, conserving, sequencing, counting, adding, subtracting, and others).
- the *problems they pose,* the *hypotheses they generate, and* the *solutions they conceptualize* and carry out.
- *performance* in the various developmental and content area domains (tasks performed, skills exhibited, or levels of mastery).
- *products* or representations of their work (drawings, writings, and constructions).

Clearly, students exhibit their emerging development, knowledge, skills, and dispositions in numerous ways. The opportunities to know each learner well is a valuable result of observing and paying focused attention to and appreciating what children do, say, and produce. The potential for enriched curriculums that can emerge from this knowledge challenges and quickens the imagination.

Knowledge about children's development and learning is critical to accurate assessments.

Nancy P. Alexander

The task of the assessor is to plan for focused observation while taking advantage of all the incidental observations that occur "on the run" during the course of the school day. Of all the skills required of the professional educator, knowing how to observe and respond appropriately to observed behaviors is among the most critical.

CHOOSING STRATEGIES AND TECHNIQUES

Assessment techniques generally fall into two categories: **formal** and **informal assessments.** Each type plays a different role in early childhood education. As we shall see, some forms of each are more successful with young children (third grade and under) than others.

Formal Assessments of Young Children

A plethora of professionally developed and published tests and measurements are used to assess growth, development, and learning in young children. Most of them meet specific criteria and standards for construction, administration, and scoring.

Standardized Tests

formal assessments
Assessments that utilize predeveloped tests that are related to specific developmental or curriculum content and are standardized and scored according to specific psychometric guidelines.

Standardized tests are developed, administered, and scored under specific guidelines that require them to meet important statistical and psychometric standards (American Educational Research Association, American Psychological Association, & National Council on Measurement in Education, 1999). Prescribed conditions for administration of a standardized test detail time limits; how, when, and by whom the test is to be given; and the manner in which the test is distributed, retrieved, and scored. As such, each test-taker is given the same question(s), framed and communicated in a precise manner that is the same for each participant and scored in a manner that protects the integrity of the test and the performance of its test-taker.

informal assessments
Assessments of child development and learning that are ongoing, in many contexts; usually designed and carried out by the classroom teacher.

normative group The sample of test-takers whose scores are used to establish the "norms" with which subsequent test-takers' scores are compared.

criterion A predetermined standard or level of performance to be achieved.

norm-referenced test A test in which the test-taker's score is compared with the scores of a normative group or reference population.

criterion-referenced test Tests or other assessments that measure success or failure to meet a predetermined objective.

age norms Normative information based on age, to which an individual's test score can be compared.

age-equivalent score A score derived by comparing a student's test performance with that of a representative sample of children at each age.

grade norm The average score for a representative sample of test-takers in the same grade to which a student's individual score is compared.

grade-equivalent score A score that is compared to an average score of a reference group of test-takers in the same grade.

percentile rank A score that reflects an individual's position relative to others; one where the score is placed on a scale where the percentage of scores that are *at or below* it are shown; not the same as a percentage of correct answers.

stanine score A nine-point scale that indicates average, below-average, and above-average ranks.

raw score The actual number of correct answers on a test.

A student's performance on a standardized test is compared with the scores of a **normative group** or a predetermined **criterion.** The former is referred to as a **norm-referenced test,** and the latter is called a **criterion-referenced test.**

A norm-referenced test is constructed to provide information about how a test-taker performs in relation to the performance of a particular population, referred to as a normative, or reference, group. There are several categories of norms used in education and psychological testing. The most commonly used norms are **age norms,** where a student's score is compared to the average age-related scores of a selected population taking the same test. Average scores are obtained by testing representative samples of children at each age; these are used to render **age-equivalent scores.** Age-equivalent scores are expressed in years and months, that is, 4–9 means four years and nine months. (*Note:* This designation uses a dash between the numerals.)

Another common norm that is used is the **grade norm,** where a student's score is compared to an average score of a reference group of test-takers in the same grade, providing a **grade-equivalent score.** Grade-equivalent scores are expressed in grades and tenth of grades; that is, 3.2 means third grade and two-tenths of a school year. (*Note:* This designation uses a decimal between the numerals.) Age- and grade-equivalent scores are both interpreted as performance that is equal to the average for that age or grade.

A third type of norm is that of the **percentile rank,** which indicates the percentage of scores in a group that are *at or above* the test-taker's score. Another way of expressing student standing in comparison to others is with the use of a **stanine score.** Stanine scores range from a low of 1 to a high of 9. Stanines 1 to 3 denote a below-average score, 4, 5, and 6, average, and 7, 8, and 9, above average.

To illustrate these types of scores, consider Jeremy. It is October and Jeremy has just completed a third-grade standardized reading test. His test-score report may include several bits of information. It may show the number of items on the test, along with the number of items Jeremy answered correctly, providing a **raw score.** The scoring process converts Jeremy's raw score into a grade-equivalent score by comparing it to the scores of a comparable population of third-grade children, the group from which the test-makers identified typical score distributions. Jeremy's score of 80 out of 100 items reveals that he is within the range of *average* for his grade. His grade-equivalent score is calculated and reveals a 3.4 grade equivalent. Jeremy's test performance does not reflect mastery or nonmastery of curriculum content, but rather his relative standing as average, above average, or below average on certain tested reading skills, as indicated by comparing his score to a reference group's score distribution on the same test.

Jeremy's score might be reported in terms of a percentile rank and stanine, in which case his score of 7 on a 10-item mathematics test gave him a percentile rank of 75. This means that Jeremy's score is equal to or higher than 75 percent of those taking the same test. His stanine score is 7, indicating that his score on this test was above average.

Now, let's look at another interesting score report. Dorsey was in kindergarten; on the test-administration date in May, she was six years and two months old. Being near the end of the school year, her class was given an achievement test. Her total reading score report revealed the following figures:

AE: 6–11

PR-S: 99–9

GE: 3.2

Dorsey's report revealed an age-equivalent score of six years and eleven months and a grade equivalent of third grade and two-tenths of a school year. Her percentile rank was 99 (only 1 percent of the population on which the test was normed would score higher), and her stanine score of 9 was the highest stanine score. Based on this test performance, Dorsey was placed in the gifted and talented program at her school. However, as she made her way through this program in first, second, and third grades, her reading scores began a downward trend, although she remained a conscientious and ambitious student and fared well in other subjects. In second grade, her total reading percentile rank was 68; by fourth grade, Dorsey's total reading percentile rank was 60.

This scenario raises a number of issues with standardized tests and their use. We know that the standardized test used in kindergarten is a widely used test with strong reliability and validity features. What we do not know is the comparability of the tests administered in subsequent grades with the test administered in kindergarten. This could explain the downward score trend because different tests tap different concepts and skills, with varying degrees of emphasis on each. Items on the kindergarten test tapped what Dorsey knew and could do. Could it be that items on different tests in later grades tapped what Dorsey did not know? This is one of the issues with testing—each test can address only a limited universe and cannot tell us *what else* a child knows and can do.

If we assume the tests are comparable, there are other questions to be asked. As a kindergarten pupil, Dorsey loved to read and write. In first grade she enthusiastically accepted the challenge to read a total of twenty books in a six-week period. She was a rapid reader and took pride in how fast she could read—153 words per minute. (By the end of first grade the standard for this school is that students will read sixty words per minute.) By third grade, Dorsey's teacher reported that Dorsey was reading on level, but she was not excelling as expected, nor did Dorsey seem to find the required reading material very interesting. Further, her teacher reported that Dorsey created a bit of a class disturbance with her talking and giggling with friends. By fourth grade, Dorsey's teacher reported that Dorsey's comprehension skills were not what they should be. Why did Dorsey's reading performance decline in these early grades? Could there be something relating to her placement, its challenges and expectations, or the nature of its requirements? The daily curriculum and pedagogy? Her relationship(s) with her teachers? Or, the availability and opportunity to read the types of books she enjoyed? Perhaps there is something in her personal or social life that has changed. Certainly, we must go beyond standardized test scores to identify and plan for the needs of individual students. Keep Dorsey in mind as we go through other forms of assessment. Perhaps we will find some answers.

As with all assessments, quality control is important. Although some state- and local school district–mandated tests are developed by committees of content area experts, the extent to which such test development meets the AERA/APA/ NCME guidelines may not be known. Standardized tests are usually published and marketed by commercial companies. However, it is important to know that not all commercially available tests have met rigorous standards in their development and standardization. A test manual or other documenting evidence typically accompanies the test and describes its purpose, construction, and the manner in which the scoring system was established. Most importantly, the manual includes the characteristics of the population of test-takers from which a "standard" distribution of scores or a criterion for performance was established and information regarding the test's **reliability** and **validity.** This information particularly reliability and validity information reveals the extent to which a test is a good test.

reliability The consistency with which various tests or assessment strategies produce the same or similar results for an individual from one administration to the next.

validity The degree to which a procedure or test measures what it purports to measure.

Reliability.   Reliability refers to the consistency with which an assessment (formal or informal) produces the same or similar results for the same individual from one administration of the assessment to the next.

Reliability can be influenced by many factors, such as distractions during the testing procedure (extraneous noises, interruptions, room temperature, or other environmental distractions), the physical state of the test-taker (fatigue, sleepiness, hunger, thirst, illness, or need for a restroom break), or the psychological state of the test-taker (anxious, stressed, fearful, inattentive, disinterested, or bored). Events preceding the test, such as parent pressure to succeed, a conflict with a friend or sibling, a reprimand from a teacher, an unfortunate accident, or witnessing a disturbing event, can also render unreliable scores. A child's score on a test under these conditions may be quite different from his or her score on the same test under more optimal conditions.

This is particularly true of young test-takers. Young children have short attention spans, are easily distracted, fatigue quickly, and have physiological and psychological needs that can be quite pressing. Further, because young children are growing and changing at a rapid pace, few assessments used with young children, whether formal or informal, can claim high reliability. For this reason, assessments of young children must be continually compared to prior ones in order to determine if assessment information accurately reflects lasting rather than temporary characteristics.

Validity.   Validity refers to the degree to which an assessment or test measures that which it claims to measure. Validity is generally determined by comparing or contrasting scores with some stated criterion or construct. There are three main categories of validity:

content validity The extent to which the content of a test samples the type of behavior it is designed to measure.

Content validity assures us that the content of the test actually samples the type of behavior (traits, knowledge, abilities, or skills) that it is designed to measure; for example, a test designed to measure reading comprehension should not have items that measure phonemic awareness, nor should inferences be drawn from the student's score regarding his or her phonemic awareness.

criterion-related validity The extent to which scores on the test can be correlated with a stated criterion.

Criterion-related validity refers to the extent to which scores on the test can be correlated with a stated criterion; for example, a test designed to assess reading readiness correlates with prior established and valid reading readiness indicators.

construct validity A test of validity based on the relationship between the test and a related theory; concerned with the psychological meaningfulness of the test.

Construct validity refers to the extent to which a test measures, in a psychologically meaningful way, a theoretical trait or characteristic; for example, based on the theory that certain readiness traits in young children presuppose successful learning upon school entry, a test designed to assess school readiness should, if it has construct validity, predict school achievement.

Standardized tests tend to fall within the following categories:

◆ *Achievement tests* measure what children have learned or what skills they have acquired from instruction. For accountability purposes, many states have developed their own within-state achievement tests—for example, the *Colorado Student Assessment Performance Test,* the *New York Regents Exams,* and the *Texas Assessment of Knowledge and Skills.* Other more widely used examples include the *Iowa Test of Basic Skills*, the *Peabody Individual Achievement Test, Revised*, the *Stanford Achievement Test*, and the *Metropolitan Achievement Test*.

◆ *Readiness tests* assess prerequisite skills, knowledge, attitudes, or behaviors believed necessary for the learner to succeed in school. Some examples of tests frequently used to determine readiness are the *Boehm Test of Basic Concepts, Dynamic Indicators of Basic Early Literacy Skills* (DIEBELS), *Metropolitan Readiness Test, Naglieri Nonverbal Ability Test (NNAT), Peabody Picture Vocabulary Test (PPVT)*, and the *Social Skills Rating System* (SSRS).

◆ *Developmental screening tests* are procedures designed to identify children who may be at risk for developmental or learning problems and who might benefit from further diagnostic assessment and intervention. Examples of screening tests include the *Ages and Stages Questionnaires: A Parent-Completed Child Monitoring System, AGS Early Screening Profiles, Early Screening Inventory, Revised, Denver II* revision of the *Denver Developmental Screening Inventory, Developmental Indicators for the Assessment of Learning–Revised* (DIAL-3), and the *Preschool Individual Growth and Development Indicators* (IGDIs).

◆ *Diagnostic tests* and *intelligence tests* are used to identify children with special needs or talents, analyze their strengths and challenges, and prescribe intervention services and/or specialized education procedures and programs. Examples of diagnostic tests are the *Assessment, Evaluation, and Programming System for Infants and Children* (AEPS), *Kaufman Assessment Battery for Children, Purdue Perceptual-Motor Survey*, and the *Southern California Sensory Integration Test*. Examples of tests of intelligence and cognitive development include the *Stanford-Binet Intelligence Scale*, the *Wechsler Intelligence Scale for Children, Revised*, and the *Wechsler Preschool and Primary Scale of Intelligence*.

Although some of these tests can be administered by the classroom teacher, most of them require specialized training and specific certifications or other professional credentials in order to administer and interpret. Many of the tests are administered individually under prescribed conditions (e.g., one-on-one in a separate, quiet room) and, therefore, are not practical for classroom assessments.

Using Standardized Tests to Inform Instruction

Standardized tests have some advantages. When the test has met rigorous standards for development, as described before, has been appropriately chosen for the purpose and population for which it is intended, and has been uniformly administered and scored, we can expect the information obtained from it to be trustworthy. (See Figure 3.3.) When scores are provided in a timely fashion, the data provided may be helpful to the teacher in instructional planning.

An examination of group test scores can reveal areas in which children in the class excelled and areas in which children were challenged. Results from group-administered standardized tests can provide group profiles from which curriculum and informal assessment planning might evolve. Thus, group scores provide a holistic perspective. Taking a holistic view of class test scores can guide the structure and focus of the curriculum until more specific information about individual developmental and knowledge levels is ascertained and corroborated through other forms of assessment.

Individual student scores can help the teacher identify a child's strengths or challenges, as portrayed by the particular testing instrument. Individual scores can

Figure 3.3
Selecting the Appropriate
Standardized Test

The wise selection of a standardized test involves consideration of the following questions:

1. What is the purpose of the test?
2. What does the reliability and validity data reveal about the test?
3. Is the test designed for individual or group administration?
4. For what age or grade is the test intended?
5. Who will administer and score the test?
6. How will the scores be interpreted and by whom?
7. How much time does the test take to administer? To score?
8. What is the time lapse between test administration and reporting scores to teachers, students, and parents or guardians?
9. How will test results be used?
10. What is the total cost per test per pupil (test materials, scoring, reporting)?
11. How does the learner benefit from taking this test?
12. How does curriculum and instruction benefit from this test?
13. What happens to students who "fail" the test?

be combined with other assessment data to provide a more comprehensive assessment and to develop individualized enrichment plans that meet identified learner characteristics. Individualized scores can signal areas of the curriculum that need review, modification, or reteaching with individual students.

However, test results must be used cautiously with full knowledge of the young child's inconsistent performance. The potential for misidentifying a child's abilities and challenges is always a concern. By the same token, it is advantageous to identify children with developmental and learning challenges early so that appropriate curriculum and procedures can be put in place to help them. Careful examination of scores derived from group tests that are compared with other observations and assessments may reveal a need for diagnostic evaluation of those students for whom intervention is necessary. Likewise, when children who have special talents are identified early, their unique needs can be addressed in a timely fashion.

Diagnostic evaluations are administered by a qualified professional who selects the appropriate test(s) to determine the specific developmental or learning issues confronting a child. Based on the results of diagnostic testing, specific recommendations are made for the types of intervention services and educational supports from which the child will benefit.

Cautions in the Use of Standardized Tests

There are a number of cautions and concerns associated with the use of standardized tests, particularly with children eight years old and under. No child should be classified, labeled, grouped, tracked, or subjected to intensive remediation on the basis of one assessment procedure. Student assessments provide more reliable and valid information when based on a variety of sources obtained over a period of time.

Further, some children are simply good test-takers; others are not. The standardized test scores can augment other information about what children know and are able to do, but they must not constitute the only information upon which instructional decisions are made.

In the use of standardized test information, teachers should avoid some of the following common mistakes:

◆ The well-known *halo effect,* in which high-scoring students are thought to be more knowledgeable, skilled, or competent than they may actually be able to demonstrate in other contexts.

◆ The *deficit effect,* in which low-scoring students are thought to be less capable than is true when they are assessed in other contexts.

◆ The *subject-success effect,* in which a content area is thought to have been sufficiently covered in the curriculum and, hence, mastered by the students.

◆ The *skill/drill effect,* in which it is thought that students will improve through repeated practice and drill over the same material or skill areas covered by the test.

Each of these mistakes leads to distorted student assessment and misguided expectations. As the use of large-group standardized testing becomes widespread, it is essential that educators strive to maintain developmentally appropriate classrooms and curricula and avoid limiting young children's experiences to preparation for tests.

Many critics of widespread testing for the purpose of holding schools accountable cite as possible alternatives random sample testing for student outcomes at selected grade levels. This makes sense given the exorbitant costs in dollars and lost instructional time of routine testing. In Chapter 4, we describe the *aggregated* portfolio, which might also serve the purposes of evaluating school and classroom performance outcomes while providing important information for improving curriculum and teaching.

Standardized Tests in Early Childhood Classrooms

In addition to ethics relating to appropriate choice and use of tests and qualifications of test administrators, use of standardized tests with young children presents another set of issues. Large-scale use of standardized tests with young children is risky. Because of the dynamic nature of early growth and development, test performance may vary appreciably from one day to the next, yielding interpretations that are less than accurate and potentially misleading. Also, trends in school placement, retention, and extra-year programs for young children have often resulted in labeling, questionable student-grouping practices, and unnecessary placement into remedial programs. Such practices inherent in the use of mass standardized testing of young children cause what Meisels (1992) has called *iatrogenic effects,* that is, unintended negative consequences with lifelong harmful outcomes. There are compelling reasons to consider alternative approaches to assessing young children:

◆ Young children may not have the auditory perception and auditory memory to follow test instructions, particularly group-administered test instructions.

◆ Young children lack well-developed receptive and expressive verbal skills.

◆ Young children are still struggling with a variety of psychosocial issues, including separation anxiety, group membership and participation, self-concept self-esteem, a sense of self-efficacy, and regulation of emotions.

◆ Young children have short attention spans and are easily distracted.

Young children form concepts and process information through concrete experiences.

University Christian Church Weekday School, Fort Worth, TX

◆ Young children may not have the motor skills to handle test materials and artifacts, particularly paper-and-pencil tests and those involving "bubble-in" answer pages or assessments that involve the use of small manipulatives.

◆ Young children form concepts and process information through concrete experiences. Most traditional standardized tests for young children require the ability to interpret and respond appropriately to pictures and symbols. Some require early reading ability.

Moreover, because of the rapid development occurring during the years from birth to age eight, we must be particularly cognizant of the fact that behaviors and test results that are diagnostic of problems of older children might actually be typical (or "normal") for a young child. For example, awkward use of scissors or writing tools is expected in young children and represents typical patterns of gross and fine motor development. Letter reversals are also quite common among young writers but are atypical at a later age.

Limitations such as these and concerns over retention, labeling, tracking, and other potentially harmful decisions based on test results suggest that reliance on standardized measures alone (or, perhaps, at all) should be curtailed. Meisels (1992, p. 170) states that "standardized, whole-group, objectively scored achievement tests are of little utility for young children. Unless their effectiveness can be demonstrated, they should be curtailed or eliminated at least before third grade." Figure 3.3 poses important questions that should be asked when considering the use of standardized measures.

Nonstandardized Tests

The preceding discussion focused primarily on standardized tests. However, there are other types of "formal" tests (as distinguished from performance-based assessments) that are sometimes administered in early childhood education, usually during the primary grades. These tests are created by teachers or are included with textbooks or curriculum materials that are adopted by a school or grade. Such tests are not standardized, seldom meet validity and reliability measures, and—unless carefully crafted—can render incomplete, perhaps inaccurate, information about what a child has learned. The purpose of these tests is to ascertain if the learner grasped the concepts or information just recently taught. Hence, many of these types of tests rely on the child's ability to recall or recognize discrete bits of information, and preparation for the test necessarily elicits the child's ability to memorize small segments of information.

For nonreaders and beginning readers, such assessments typically include paper-and-pencil exercises in which simple pictures of familiar objects or situations are used to pose questions while verbal instructions on when and how to mark certain items on the page are provided by the teacher. Figure 3.4 illustrates this type of exercise. With readers and writers, formal strategies typically include working with graphics and pictures and true-false, fill-in-the-blank, matching columns, and multiple-choice questions.

These types of tests and review exercises render information about a particular concept or skill and are usually graded in the tradition of numerical or letter grades. What children learn from this exercise is that they either "got it" or "didn't." Or, maybe they got it, but the test questions limited their opportunity to demonstrate what they had learned or what else they knew about the topic. Obviously, the use of these tests should be limited and augmented with performance-based measures if a complete picture of the child's understandings and accomplishments is to be obtained. Further, numerical and letter grades do little to help learners know what to do next. The use of grades to motivate corrective learning has been extensively researched over many years and shown to be of dubious value (Bloom, Madaus, & Hastings, 1981; Graham & Golan, 1991; Harter, 1978: Kohn, 1993, 1994; Wien, 2004). Instead, such markings tend to elicit peer-self comparisons, along with feelings that can range from self-aggrandizing to self-demeaning. How test grades and scores are conveyed and their effects on the learner and the learning process are worth considering.

Concerns Surrounding Widespread Use of Standardized Tests

Finally, persistent and mounting concerns over the increasing use of large-scale testing in schools are compelling (Amrein & Berliner, 2002; Chase, 2001; Dever & Barta, 2001; Howard, et al. 2003; Kohn, 2000; 2004; Madaus & Clark, 2001; Public Education Network, 2006; Quindlen, 2005; Sacks, 2001; Swope & Minor, 2002; Volger, 2002). It is important to reflect upon the many issues that have been raised with regard to the widespread use of formal testing procedures, particularly with young children. It is appropriate—indeed, some believe it is a "moral imperative" (Hastings, 1992)—to move away from testing, labeling, grouping, and tracking systems that sort and classify children, often leaving them with labels they can never shed. Nonetheless, federal, state, and local mandates continue to impose large-scale testing programs, often with high-stakes consequences for individual students and for individual schools. Concerns about widespread use of standardized tests center on the following themes:

1. Narrowed curricula that focus on smaller and smaller units of knowledge and isolated academic skills, often centering on that which is tested.

2. Increasing emphasis on test preparation, both in and out of the classroom.

3. Decreasing teacher autonomy to develop creative and innovative curricula.

4. Lowered expectations for some students as test scores are used to group or classify individuals rather than identifying individual challenges, talents, and learning styles.

Name *Isabelle*   Date 3-28-05

Unit 8 Checking Progress (cont.)

Write the number shown by the base-10 blocks.

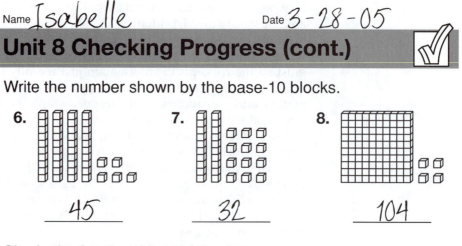

6.   **7.**   **8.**

_____45_____   _____32_____   _____104_____

Shade the fractional part of the figure.

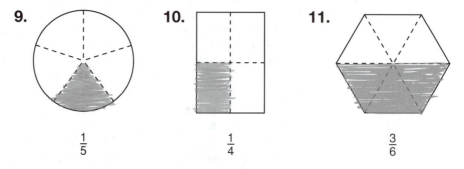

9.   **10.**   **11.**

$\frac{1}{5}$ $\frac{1}{4}$ $\frac{3}{6}$

12. Three people share 12 pennies equally. Circle each person's share. Use your tool-kit coins.

How many pennies does each person get? ___4___

Figure 3.4
Typical Review Work Sheet or Concept Test

5. Escalating academic demands in preschools, kindergarten, and first grade as preparation—or "readiness"—for academically oriented, developmentally *in*appropriate curricula.

6. Policy decision making based on test-score results that affect all levels, from placement and retention of young learners to allocation of resources to school

A comfortable, non-threatening situation helps children to do their best when tests are administered.

Nancy P. Alexander

high-stakes tests
Tests for which significant (life-influencing) decisions, such as group or grade placement, assignment to special programs, promotion, and retention are made based on an individual's score. Sometimes scores on high-stakes tests are used to rank schools, teachers, and school districts, and allocation of public funds are tied to rankings.

districts, causing a high-stakes value to be placed on tests and test results. (Tests used in this way are referred to as **high-stakes tests.**

7. Failure of widespread testing to show concomitant widespread improvement in student learning and performance.

8. Inability to predict how well students will do later.

9. Misuses of tests designed for one purpose but used for another (e.g., the scores of a standardized test designed to ascertain student achievement are used to rank teachers, school, or school districts).

10. Inappropriateness of use with young children third grade and below.

11. Failure to consider the full range of developmental, cultural, linguistic, and socioeconomic diversity of students.

12. Misappropriation of limited resources required to develop, purchase, implement, score, and publish the results of millions of tests yearly.

13. Delay in receipt of timely information about individual students in order to inform curriculum and instructional practices.

14. Scoring information that is confusing to parents and to students.

15. Misdirected focus on raising test scores, leading to counterproductive levels of anxiety among many educators, parents, and students.

Because many scholars and practitioners in early childhood education share these concerns, the need exists to identify the most meaningful and useful ways to assess young children. In schools where group standardized tests are imposed on young children (ages eight and younger), it is imperative that they are wisely selected and used only for the purposes for which they were written.

Special attention and consideration must be given to the procedures and expectations imposed on young children during the testing event. Creating a comfortable and nonthreatening context for children who must be tested is necessary if children are to be able to do their best. Children with special needs and children with limited English proficiency should be provided appropriate assistance and supports. Children's physiological needs for movement, restroom breaks, nutrition, and

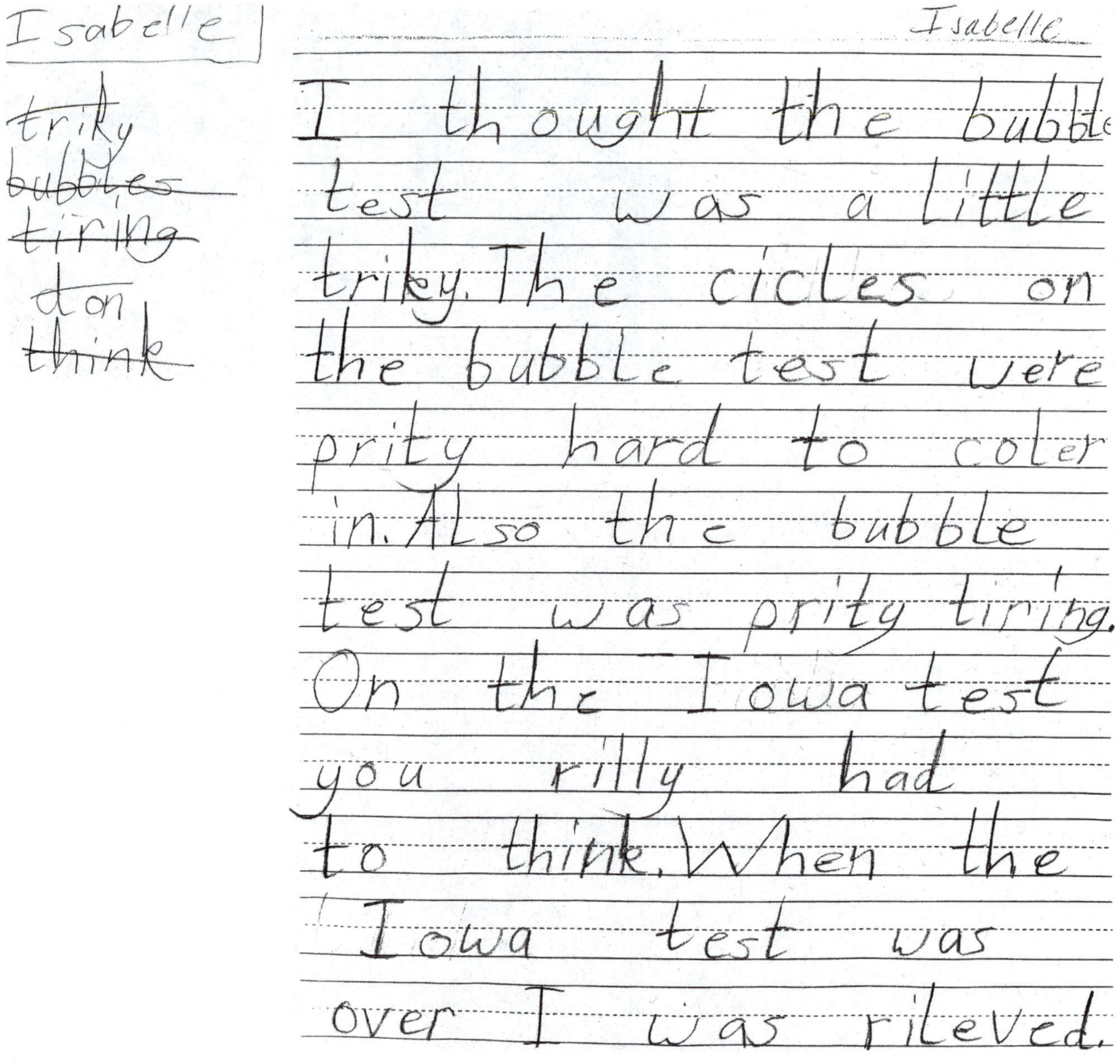

Isabelle

triky
bubbles
tiring
don
think

Isabelle

I thought the bubble
test was a little
triky. The cicles on
the bubble test were
prity hard to coler
in. Also the bubble
test was prity tiring.
On the Iowa test
you rilly had
to think. When the
Iowa test was
over I was rileved.

Figure 3.5
Isabelle Reflects on Taking a Test

hydration must be figured into the schedule and procedures of the testing situation. Helping young children view the testing situation in a positive way—one in which they get to show what they know and can do, rather than in a way that evokes anxiety—is important. (In Figure 3.5, Isabelle organizes her thoughts and writes a short essay about her experience with a standardized test.) It is also important to help parents understand the purposes of the test, how the results will be used, and how they can be supportive rather than anxious about their child's performance.

Informal Assessments of Young Children

Informal strategies for assessment provide the types of information needed to determine specific developmental characteristics of individual children. This information can be used quite readily to create or modify curricula to meet individual capabilities, needs, and interests. Informal strategies include skilled observations and valid inferences drawn from them, anecdotal records, checklists, descriptive inventories, rating scales, time and event sampling, and student interviews. All these processes lend themselves to the development of student portfolios in which a variety of representations of student products and processes can be assembled and traced for progress over time. As the title of this text suggests, assessment done well celebrates student achievement.

authentic assessment
Assessment derived from learning processes and student products emerging from meaningful, relevant, and developmentally appropriate curricula.

What has come to be known as **authentic assessment** relies heavily on informal strategies. The term *authentic* suggests the desire to obtain information that most truly reflects how a child pursues knowledge and skills and the outcomes of the child's efforts. The characteristics discussed in Chapter 4 suggest that assessment is teacher mediated, child centered, embedded in the curriculum, ongoing and cumulative, and based on multiple theories and knowledge about child growth and development.

SUMMARY

In this chapter we have begun the first phases of developing a blueprint for a meaningful assessment system: determining purposes and goals and exploring what will be assessed with a reminder that child development knowledge and whole child perspectives are essential if assessments are to be accurate and useful. With this background knowledge, educators are prepared to recognize emerging development and learning. The distinction between formal and informal assessments is made with an elaboration on the appropriate and helpful uses of formal strategies, along with precautions and concerns associated with widespread use of formal assessments with young children.

In the next chapter, we describe informal strategies for assessment as an essential part of a meaningful assessment system. We attempt to illustrate the complementary aspects of both formal and informal assessments, along with the final phases of the development of an assessment system.

REVIEW STRATEGIES AND ACTIVITIES

Vexing Questions

1. A mounting number of psychologists and educators decry the increasing use of large-scale, high-stakes testing in public education. How can classroom teachers influence policy and practices relating to the widespread use of standardized tests?

2. How can teachers help parents prepare their children for formal assessments without engendering an overemphasis on scores or anxiety about their child's performance?

3. Think about Dorsey. Can a child be gifted one year and not gifted the next?

Activities

1. Select a standardized test used in many schools or districts in your state. (Consult current volumes of Buros's *Tests in Print*.) Discuss the test with a classroom teacher or principal who is well acquainted with it. Determine the following:

   a. description and purpose of test

   b. how the test was developed and by whom

   c. validity and reliability of the test

   d. under what circumstances the test should be used

   e. how difficult or easy the test is to administer

   f. cost of administering and scoring

   g. legal considerations in the use of the test (e.g., test security, score reporting, student privacy, and who should administer)

2. Interview an elementary school principal to ascertain how school administrators view and use data from large scale test administrations.

3. Isabelle described her feelings about the group test she had just taken. Could insights be gained from engaging children in a conversation or writing project relating to their experiences with tests? Try it. What do children's words, drawings, writing, and pretend play tell us about their perspectives on the test experience?

SUGGESTED LITERATURE AND RESOURCES

Hehir, T. (2005). *New directions in special education: Eliminating ableism in policy and practice.* Cambridge, MA: Harvard Education Publishing Group.

Helmer, S., & Eddy, C. (2003). *Look at me when I talk to you: ESL learners in non-ESL classrooms.* Portsmouth, NH: Heinemann.

Howard, J., Langer, J. A., Levenson, M. R., Popham, W. J., & Sadowski, M. (2003). *High-stakes testing.* Cambridge, MA: Harvard Education Publishing Group.

Howard, V. F., Williams, B. F., & Lepper, C. E. (2005). *Very young children with special needs: A formative approach to today's children* (3rd ed.). Upper Saddle River, NJ: Merrill/Prentice Hall.

Kohn, A. (2000). *The case against standardized testing: Raising the scores, ruining the schools.* Portsmouth, NH: Heinemann.

Lopez, E. J., Salas, L. & Flores, J. P. (2005). Hispanic preschool children: What about assessment and intervention? *Young Children 60*(6), 48–57, 59.

Meisels, S. J., & Atkins-Burnett, S. (2005). *Developmental screening in early childhood: A guide* (5th ed.). Washington, DC: National Association for the Education of Young Children.

Ohanian, S. (1999). *One size fits few: The folly of educational standards.* Portsmouth, NH: Heinemann.

Pellegrino, J. W., Chudowsky, N., & Glasser, R. (Eds.). (2001). *Knowing what students know: The science and design of educational assessment.* Washington, DC: National Academy Press.

Public Education Network (2006). *Open to the public: The public speaks out on No Child Left Behind: A summary of nine hearings (September 2005–January 2006).* Retrieve from: www.publiceducation.org.

Seefeldt, C. (2005). *How to work with standards in the early childhood classroom*. New York: Teachers College Press.

Swanson, H. L., Harris, K. R., & Graham, S. (2003). *Handbook of learning disabilities*. New York: Guilford Press.

Wilde, S. (2002). *Testing and standards: A brief encyclopedia*. Portsmouth, NH: Heine-mann.

ELECTRONIC RESOURCES

National Center for Fair and Open Testing, http://www.fairtest.org

Appendix

Table 3.1
Widely Held Expectations in Aesthetic and Artistic Development

Birth–3 years	3–5 years	5–7 years
Children… • may try to grasp writing tools with whole hand.	• may learn to hold writing tools between fingers and thumb.	• continue to develop the ability to hold and use large-size writing and drawing tools.
• may draw randomly and look away while drawing or making marks on a paper or a board. • may begin to make scribbles for pleasure of seeing the results of their actions. • use scribbles, lines, and circles for expression.	• may make marks, draw, paint, and build spontaneously to express self. • may begin to name a person, place, thing, or an action in the drawing. • gradually try making lines and circles repeatedly and with more control.	• may show first attempts at drawing, painting, and building "things." • continue to name what has been drawn, painted, or constructed. • may strive for more detail and realism in artwork. • gradually include more detail and will add more body parts when drawing people.
• may begin to express pleasure or displeasure (laughing, anxiety) when listening to sounds, voices and music.	• may respond to music, art, nature through body movement that is rhythmic, such as rocking, clapping, jumping, or shaking.	• continue to expand and refine responses to a variety of sounds, voices and music.
• may begin to move body to sounds and music. • may make sounds to music without using words ("la, la," "ba, ba,") and may enjoy hearing own sounds.	• use movements that are generally spontaneous, unrehearsed, and inventive. • may be relatively uninhibited about singing and playing musical instruments. • may use both a speaking voice and a singing voice when singing alone, with a tape or with others, and may or may not be able to sing a melody in tune.	• may show imaginative and creative ways of moving and dancing. • are increasingly able to initiate and repeat movement patterns (walk like a lion, slither like a snake). • may engage in "acting out" stories spontaneously. • often continue to be relatively uninhibited about singing and playing musical instruments. • are developing a singing voice but the range will differ; may or may not be able to sing a melody in tune.
• may enjoy pretend games. • may look at, talk to (babble), grasp, bang, or drop toys.	• often engage in pretend play easily and naturally. • may talk to and play with pretend friends, television characters, stuffed and other toys.	• often continue to show lots of imagination and interest in make-believe. • continue to talk to imaginary friends and may greet an imaginary friend or call someone with a striking sense of reality.

Source: Adapted from Supporting learning: Understanding and assessing the progress of children in the primary grades (1991), pp. 20–29. By permission of the Ministry of Education of the Province of British Columbia.

Table 3.1, *continued*

7–9 years	9–11 years	11–13 years
Children ….		
• may continue to develop and refine their ability to use a variety of writing and drawing tools.	• may begin to show an interest in developing a skill and may want to know "how" to use a tool to create a special effect.	• continue to explore and refine use of various tools to create special effects in artwork.
• may begin to show interest in making their artwork realistic. • increasingly develop forms, such as a human form, and repeat it over and over.	• may want and need to see the object or scene as they are drawing and want to make artwork an exact copy of reality. • may become very self-critical of own work (may want hair to "look like" hair).	• may begin to show an interest in perspective or drawing according to scale or to create similar effects. • may focus on the whole effect of a picture or on detail work. • may appear to have little confidence and become self-critical of own artwork.
• expand and refine responses to and express personal preferences for a variety of sounds, voice and music.	• continue to expand and refine responses to sounds, voice and music and are becoming aware of cultural characteristics and of personal preferences of friends.	• may begin to develop particular choices in sounds, voice and music.
• generally like to express ideas and feeling through music and movement. • may begin to show more refined movements as coordination develops. • continue to be able to initiate and repeat movement patterns and may like to move or dance in front of a mirror. • may begin to sing in tune and generally like to contribute to musical activities. • may become better at interpreting musical sounds as being low, high, or related to certain instruments.	• may become somewhat inhibited in music and movement; may show interest in own musical activities such as lip-synch, band, and mime. • continue to develop their sense of coordination, may continue to increase ability to interpret, produce, and reproduce musical sounds.	• are developing more control over singing voice and breathing and may show an interest in joining a group activity such as band, chorus, or musical production—often with friends. • may seem self-conscious at efforts to move or dance and may appear somewhat awkward or uncoordinated because of rapid physical growth. • may continue to be able to interpret and produce musical sounds if encouraged and supported to do so.
• often continue to show their imagination through make-believe, either alone or with a variety or props. • may play the part of a parent or significant other (when playing house or school) and may show signs of cooperative play.	• continue to engage in make-believe and often have a vivid imagination. • may continue to show an interest in making up and performing their own stories, plays, or dances based on reality. • generally like to play and perform, but may prefer playing in groups rather than alone.	• may want to play but at times feel this is no longer proper or "grown-up." • may continue to develop imagination and may be less willing to share ideas publicly.

Table 3.2
Widely Held Expectations in Emotional and Social Development

Birth–3 years	3–5 years	5–7 years
Children… • may demonstrate visible expressions of emotion (temper tantrums).	• may display their emotions easily and appear very sensitive and impulsive (crying fits, "No!").	• may continue to show intense emotions (one moment will say "I love you," and the next, "You are mean.").
• actively show affection for familiar people. • may show anxiety when separated from familiar people and places.	• begin to feel more comfortable when separated from familiar people, places, and things (visiting a neighbor, nursery school, babysitters).	• may appear anxious once again when separated from familiar people and places (beginning school, sleepovers).
• are naturally very curious about other children and may watch and imitate others. • generally play alone, and may or may not attempt to interact with others.	• may play alone or beside others but are becoming more aware of the feelings of others. May be frustrated at attempts to socialize but hold no grudges.	• are learning to cooperate with others for longer periods of time, and friendships may change frequently.
• strive toward independence with support and affection (sitting up, crawling, walking, dressing, feeding, toileting).	• begin to assert independence by saying "No" or "I can do it myself!" May dump a cupful of water onto the floor while looking directly at you. • see selves as family members and as boy or girl in the family.	• continue to develop feelings of independence by becoming able to do certain things (making a simple breakfast or riding a bicycle). • may begin to talk about self and to define self in terms of what they have or own. • may feel they are being treated unfairly if others get something they do not.
• begin to see themselves as people and appear self-centered. • begin to see themselves as strong through directing others: "Sit down."	• see themselves as powerful and creative doers. If the child can't reach something, he or she will get a stool.	• begin to see themselves as bad, good, clever, and may seem very hard on themselves.
• may become possessive of belongings (special people, toys, special times).	• may continue to appear possessive. • may feel if something is shared for a brief period it is gone forever.	• begin to develop the ability to share possessions and take turns.

Table 3.2, *continued*

7–9 years	9–11 years	11–13 years
Children …		
• may continue to show bursts of emotion and impatience less frequently. • may show emotions that are both judgmental and critical of themselves and others.	• may appear relatively calm and at peace with themselves and occasionally become angry, sad, or depressed, but these moments are usually short-lived.	• may begin to show intense emotions, bouts of anxiety, moodiness. Emotions may come close to the surface (cry and anger easily).
• continue to feel some anxiety within the larger community when separated from familiar people, places, things (going to camp, sleepovers, shopping malls).	• often hide feelings of anxiety when introduced to new experiences by appearing overconfident.	• continue to hide feelings of anxiety with friends and family, often appearing overconfident with a know-it-all attitude.
• are becoming more outgoing. • are developing closer friendships with others and may begin to play mainly with children of the same sex.	• continue to be very sociable and spend time with parents, friends of the same sex, and often have a "special" friend.	• generally get along well with their friends and continue to show an interest in having a "best" friend, but fights and arguments may occur from time to time. • start to question adult authority.
• show a generally increased sense of self-confidence. • will eagerly take on tasks and activities likely to be successful but usually will not take risks. • may define self as a particular name, age, size, hair color, or other characteristics ("I'm Elizabeth Anne and I'm seven years old!").	• are generally positive about themselves and begin to understand what they are good at doing; may comment easily, "I can do that" or "I can't do that." • often define self by physical characteristics and possessions as well as likes and dislikes. • often vary between the sexes in their view of what is important in dress and physical appearance.	• sometimes engage in self put-downs—in conversations with others may say, "I can't do anything right!" • may begin to define self in terms of opinions, beliefs, values, and expand sense of self by attempting to copy the culture of current fads (clothes, music, sports).
• are sensitive to criticism and display feelings of success or failure depending on how adults respond to them.	• are sensitive to criticism and display feelings of success or failure depending on how adults and peers respond to them.	• gradually are gaining independence from parental influence. • are sensitive to criticism and display feelings of success or failure depending on reactions of others. • may become self-critical.
• continue to develop the ability to share possessions and to take turns if they understand something is not always "lost" by doing so.	• continue to develop the ability to work and play with others. • may not want to be disturbed when involved in an activity or a game.	• may appear to become possessive with own belongings, especially with younger brothers and sisters. • may view younger brothers and sisters as a bother or a nuisance when involved with peers and feel discriminated against in family situations.

Table 3.3
Widely Held Expectations in Intellectual Development

Birth–3 years	3–5 years	5–7 years
Children...		
• make direct contact with their environment to the best of their ability—doing, seeing, hearing, tasting, touching, and smelling (put objects in mouth).	• continue to explore the world around them by object manipulation and direct experience (playing). • begin to understand cause and effect ("I fall—I cried—I hurt.").	• continue to learn from direct experience (playing). • expand and refine knowledge with increasing understanding of cause and effect ("I can go to my friend's house if I call home when I get there.").
• are beginning to develop an understanding of language and how it works (imitating sounds, saying words, putting words together). • are learning to name objects and may use the same word for two or more objects (all vehicles called "cars").	• begin to use language to name objects and their own direct experiences of them ("Stove—hot."). • name objects and may find that two objects are alike in some way (cats and dogs are animals).	• continue to expand their understanding and use of language to clarify thinking and learning.
• express themselves through scribbles, lines, and circles. • "read" pictures for meaning; begin to recognize that writing has meaning (writing is intended for communication).	• are developing a sense of how writing and reading work. • combine drawing and "writing"—drawing conveys most of meaning. • play at reading—"read" pictures (telling story from pictures). • begin to read commercial and traffic signs (STOP). • continue to develop an understanding that writing conveys a message.	• are continuing to develop a sense of how writing and reading work. • combine drawing and writing to convey ideas. • understand that print "tells" the story. • develop a basic vocabulary of personal words. • read slowly and deliberately. • will substitute words that make sense when reading.
• are likely to think about time in the "here and now."	• may think of tomorrow as "after my sleep" and use words like "tomorrow" and "yesterday" though not always correctly.	• are developing an understanding of words like "tomorrow" or "yesterday." but may still be unsure about length of time ("Is it ready?" "Are we there yet?").
• are increasingly able to identify familiar faces, toys, places, and activities. • are developing personal choice (a favorite blanket or toy).	• may learn nursery rhymes, songs, and addresses, but without really trying to remember. • begin to assert personal choice in decision-making ("No broccoli!").	• may begin to organize information to remember it (own telephone number, sound-symbol relations). • continue to assert personal choice in decision-making (what to wear to school).
• may be interested in group objects (putting all the large animals to bed and leaving the small ones to play).	• are developing an interest in the number of things. • are increasingly interested in counting although the number may not match the number of objects.	• begin to understand that the number of objects does not change when grouped in different ways. • are developing the ability to match counting 1, 2, 3 with the number of objects.

Table 3.3, *continued*

7–9 years	9–11 years	11–13 years
Children …		
• may begin to do multi-step problems using objects to manipulate and count (blocks, fingers, buttons). • continue to deepen understanding of cause and effect ("If I don't go right home after school my parents will worry.").	• continue to use direct experience, objects, and visual aids to help understanding. • continue to expand and design understanding of cause and effect ("I can have a pet, if I take care of it.").	• begin to develop ability to "manipulate" thoughts and ideas but still need hands-on experiences. • do some abstract reasoning. • continue to refine understanding of cause and effect ("If I don't get my chores done I can't go out with my friends.").
• continue to expand their understanding and use of language to clarify thinking and learning. • may work with simple metaphors ("My horse runs like the wind.").	• continue to broaden understanding of language and its use to clarify thinking and learning. • may begin to use puns ("A cow is a lawn mooer.").	• continue to broaden knowledge, understanding and use of language to clarify thinking and learning. • often like jokes and words that have double meanings.
• begin to understand and use writing and reading for specific purposes. • may combine drawing and writing, but writing can stand alone to convey meaning. • develop a rapidly increasing vocabulary of sight words. • begin to self-correct errors. • develop the ability to read silently. • increase ability to read aloud fluently and with expression.	• can expand thinking more readily through writing and reading. • continue to increase reading vocabulary. • continue to self-correct errors. • read silently with increased speed and comprehension. (Silent reading speed greater than oral speed may result in oral reading difficulties.) • adjust reading rate to suit purpose (scanning). • expand reading skills to gather information from a variety of sources. • make personal choices in reading for pleasure.	• continue to expand thinking more readily through writing and reading. • continue to increase silent reading rate and time spent at reading. • continue to increase ability to adjust rate and reading to suit purpose (skim, scan, select, study). • continue to broaden their interests in a variety of fiction and nonfiction. • begin to understand that people may interpret the same material in different ways.
• may be learning to tell time and becoming more adept at understanding the meaning of "before," "soon," "later."	• continue to develop understanding of time—year in terms of important events—but may forget dates and responsibilities.	• may be able to talk about recent events, plans for the future, and career aspirations.
• are increasingly able to organize and rehearse information in order to remember, but may still forget. • continue to develop a need for increased ownership in decision-making (games, projects).	• continue to develop the ability to purposefully organize and remember information. • continue to need increased ownership in decision-making (clothing, friends, activities).	• may begin to develop more complex schemes to aid memory. • need ownership in decision-making with the continued guidance of responsible person.
• are developing ideas about lengths and quantities through experiences with blocks, building, drawing, and cooking. • may begin to compare all types of lengths and amounts.	• may use ideas of length to develop an understanding of area and its measurement through artwork, constructing, carpentry, and simple map-making.	• develop ideas about real objects and their properties—length, area, mass, capacity, and volume—through direct experiences and by thinking about those experiences.

Table 3.4
Widely Held Expectations in Physical Development

Birth–3 years	3–5 years	5–7 years
Children… • may experience a period of extremely rapid growth. • develop the ability to move about and to manipulate objects to the best of their ability.	• are experiencing a period of rapid growth. • have a slower rate of small muscle development (hands) than growth and coordination of large muscles (legs).	• may or may not experience a slower rate of physical growth. Large muscles (legs and arms) may be more developed than small muscles (hands and feet). • may increase fine motor skills (handling writing tools, using scissors).
• begin to develop vision by following slowly moving objects with their eyes.	• are usually naturally farsighted.	• usually continue to show farsightedness.
• begin to develop hand-eye coordination—reaching, grasping objects, feeding, dressing.	• continue to develop hand-eye coordination and a preference for left- or right-handedness.	• continue to develop hand-eye coordination. A preference for left- or right-handedness may still be developing.
• begin to recognize concepts of place and direction—up, down, in.	• begin to understand and use concepts of place and direction—up, down, under, beside.	• continue to develop an understanding of direction and place although may confuse right and left, up and down when playing games.
• begin to move about—sit, stand, crawl, walk, climb stairs, walk backwards—to the best of their ability.	• are developing the ability to climb, balance, run, gallop, jump, push, and pull, and take stairs one at a time.	• continue to develop climbing, balancing, running, galloping, and jumping abilities. May have trouble skipping.
• are beginning to identify their own body parts, often through nursery rhymes and games.	• are beginning to identify body parts and words used in movement—jump, wave, hop.	• are growing in their ability to know what and where their body parts are, and how they can be moved and coordinated.
• are unaware of physical strengths and limitations so may attempt activities that could be difficult or dangerous.	• seem unaware of their own physical strengths and limitations and may try potentially difficult or dangerous activities.	• continue vigorous activity, tiring easily, recovering quickly. • tire from sitting rather than running. • develop an awareness of safety with guidance.
• may often change activities. • will move about at own pace, always near a trusted adult.	• may change activities often, although sometimes concentrate on one thing for a long time if interested.	• usually show enthusiasm for most physical activities, and are sometimes called noisy or aggressive.
• are likely to play alone or beside another. • begin to play games like peek-a-boo and hide-and-seek.	• are beginning to take part in group situations, but still play side-by-side rather than "with" others. • may invent their own games and change the roles to suit needs.	• are developing the ability to take part in small group games, and usually begin to play in groups of children of same sex.

Table 3.4, *continued*

7–9 years	9–11 years	11–13 years
Children … • continue to refine fine motor development and may have slower rate of physical growth.	• may experience a spurt of growth before puberty.	• may experience rapid and uneven growth but this occurs at different rates for individual children. Arms and legs may grow rapidly.
• may experience some visual difficulties (eye testing and corrective lenses).	• may experience some visual difficulties (eye testing and corrective lenses).	• may continue to experience changes to eyesight.
• are continuing to develop hand-eye coordination, and may accomplish more complex tasks.	• are continuing to develop hand-eye coordination, and skill level for physical activities may depend on this increase in coordination.	• continue to develop and refine hand-eye skills and integrate them with whole body efforts in sports and games.
• are developing ability to coordinate left and right sides by showing a preference for batting, kicking or throwing, with one side or the other.	• are continuing to develop ability to use either the right side or left side for batting, kicking or throwing.	• continue to refine left/right preference, and may show increasing strength with one hand/arm/foot.
• are gradually increasing in speed and accuracy during running, climbing, throwing, kicking, and catching activities.	• show increased coordination, but growth spurts may begin to interfere. • develop the ability to hit a ball (softball bat, tennis racquet, golf club).	• may show periods of relatively poor coordination and awkwardness. May show some poor posture because of rapid growth.
• are continuing to understand body parts and uses. • are beginning to understand basic ideas of nutrition.	• are developing a more sophisticated understanding of body parts and function as well as basic ideas of nutrition and growth.	• may continue to develop more sophisticated understanding of body parts and functions and begin to get the idea of a simple body system.
• may show more daring, exploring behavior that could lead to accidents. • show times of high energy; become easily tired. • continue to develop awareness of safety with guidance.	• are beginning to develop the ability to pace themselves during high energy activities. • understand safety rules but sometimes take risks.	• continue to enjoy sports and group games. • learn more complex body movements. • continue to develop the ability to pace themselves during high energy activities. • understand safety rules but sometimes take risks.
• continue to show enthusiasm for most physical activities.	• may begin to show a preference for some physical activities over others.	• often vary between the sexes in their interest in physical activities.
• may be interested in playing in groups although the group and the activity probably change often.	• may appear to enjoy more complex group games and simple sports. • may show a strong sense of loyalty to a group or team.	• continue to play in same-sex groups, often engage in more formal team activities, and continue to show great loyalty to group or team.

Table 3.5
Widely Held Expectations in Social Responsibility

Birth–3 years	3–5 years	5–7 years
Children… • appear insensitive to the views of others, yet show interest in them.	• are becoming aware of others and beginning to take part in social play groups. • may play "beside" rather than "with" others.	• are developing the ability to take part in social play groups, and for longer periods of time, increasing awareness of others. • may prefer to play alone at times or with others.
• are generally self-centered in their views. • look at the world mostly from their own viewpoint (may think the sun sets because they go to bed).	• are beginning to see that their views differ from those of others but remain self-centered. • may show aggressive feelings towards others when something does not go their way.	• are developing the ability to see that others have feelings and different views than their own.
• may cry when they see or hear another child crying.	• are beginning to sense when another person is sad, angry, happy.	• may begin to respond to others in times of distress if they are supported and encouraged to do so.
• physically explore the environment to the best of their abilities using their senses (seeing, hearing, tasting, smelling, and feeling). • are natural explorers, eager for new experiences.	• become interested in exploring the environment outside the immediate home. May be interested in growing seeds, weather, seasons, the moon, and sun. • continue to eagerly explore the world around them.	• are developing an interest in the community and the world outside their own. • may begin to show an awareness of basic necessities (food, clothing, shelter). • are beginning to develop an interest in specific issues pertaining to their world (recycling).
• are beginning to distinguish between familiar and unfamiliar faces.	• are becoming more aware of family and social relationships.	• may begin to notice how people are similar and different from one another.
• are becoming aware of their own feelings and respond to others' expressions (become upset if caregiver is also upset).	• may sense another person's unhappiness (such as another child crying) and not know how to help.	• are developing the ability to respond sympathetically to others if they are hurt, upset, or crying.
• begin to recognize consequences follow actions.	• become aware of consequences of own behavior.	• begin to understand consequences of own and others' behavior.

Table 3.5, *continued*

7–9 years	9–11 years	11–13 years
Children …		
• are learning to work in groups and are developing the ability to get along with others. • can lead sometimes, and can follow others.	• continue to learn to work in groups if this activity is supported. • may become upset or distressed if they have problems with friends. • begin to understand the idea of the differing contributions of group members to a common goal.	• may show that their relations with friends are increasingly important. • continue to develop the ability to work cooperatively and collaboratively with others.
• are developing the ability to see how others act and what they expect in certain situations. • may be developing close friendships that are helping them learn to understand how others think and feel.	• are developing the ability to take a third-person view, in which they see situations, themselves, and others as if they were spectators, but still do not coordinate these views. • may be developing the ability to see others have different viewpoints but still do not coordinate these views with their own.	• are developing the ability to understand that there are several sides to an issue but are just beginning to show evidence of being able to take others' views into account. Still consider own point of view the right one. • continue to develop the ability to see the worth of others' viewpoints if this is supported.
• continue to develop the ability to respond sympathetically to others if they are supported and encouraged to do so.	• continue to try to develop the ability to respond sympathetically to others but still have difficulty in taking any point of view but their own.	• continue to develop the ability to respond sympathetically to others and may begin to consider other points of view.
• continue to be curious about the world around them and may show interest in learning about other people (food, clothing, shelter). • are developing an interest in and enthusiasm for specific issues pertaining to their world and can define simple actions to help (returning aluminum cans for recycling).	• continue to develop an awareness of how own family meets basic needs. • are developing personal views of important issues and values pertaining to their world and act upon their beliefs (making posters).	• continue to develop an awareness of how family needs affect others. • are becoming more committed to their beliefs and personal views of the world around them (writing letters to newspapers).
• are developing an appreciation for their own and other cultural heritages through special events, festivals, foods, folk songs, and other concrete experiences.	• are continuing to develop an appreciation of their own and other cultural heritages. Can talk about similarities and differences.	• may begin to appreciate the rich multicultural heritage of their own country while cherishing family culture in relation to the whole.
• continue to develop the ability to respond sympathetically to others if this is supported.	• continue to develop the ability to respond sympathetically to others and may try to help them.	• may begin developing the ability to empathize with another's feelings in understandable situations.
• continue to understand consequences of own and others' behavior.	• begin to "weigh" consequences of own actions.	• begin to "test" consequences of own and others' actions.

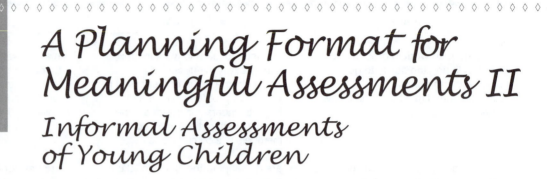

4

A Planning Format for Meaningful Assessments II

Informal Assessments of Young Children

In truth, it is normal to be different.
   Mel Levine (2002)

Extraordinary claims require extraordinary evidence.
   Charles M. Wynn & Arthur W. Wiggins (2001)

◇ ◇

After reading and studying this chapter, you will demonstrate comprehension by being able to:

❑ describe a completed blueprint for a meaningful assessment system in early childhood education.

❑ describe various types of informal assessment procedures.

❑ define and develop effective rubric systems for assessing student performance, products, and processes.

In the best of plans, information about students gained from both formal and informal assessments is used in a complementary or augmenting manner. Unlike standardized testing, informal assessments occur on a daily basis. Indeed, informal assessment is integral to the teaching process and occurs often on an unconscious level throughout each teaching day. Its conscious-level refinement is essential if it is to support and facilitate the learning process. Hence, much is written today about how to plan and implement an authentic assessment system.

Informal strategies emphasize the four "P's" of authentic assessment: *performance, process, products,* and *portfolios.* Although the term *informal* may denote less rigor in design, implementation, and scoring than is associated with formal testing, informal assessments nevertheless do not escape rigorous criteria that ensure ethical use and accurate and fair interpretation. Effective use of informal assessment strategies requires careful planning, as laid out in Figure 4.1. Given the limitations associated with formal testing of young children, informal assessments provide a viable alternative, but such assessments must:

- be embedded in high-quality, *authentic curriculum* (Figure 4.2) and congruent with its goals and objectives.
- be guided by knowledge of child growth, development, and learning and, therefore, be physically and psychologically safe for the student.
- provide representative data about all learning domains and content areas.
- be beneficial to the students and the programs that serve them.
- be ongoing and cumulative, based on many observations of relevant behaviors and examples of student products.
- demonstrate sensitivity to cultural, linguistic, socioeconomic, and gender diversity and cognizant of learning styles and dispositions.
- preserve the trust and integrity of all parties who collaborate in the assessment, particularly of the students and their families.

Authentic Assessment:
- is performance based.
- focuses on the strengths of the learner.
- is based on real-life events.
- emphasizes emerging skills.
- focuses on purposeful learning.
- relates to instruction.
- is ongoing in many contexts.
- provides a broad and general picture of student learning and capabilities.
- is based on high-quality, authentic curriculums.
- celebrates, supports, and facilitates development and learning.

Figure 4.1
What Is Authentic Assessment?

Figure 4.2

What Is High-Quality Curriculum?

From: Tomlinson, C. A. (May, 2004). How do I teach them all?: Academic diversity in today's science and math classrooms. *Eisenhower National Clearinghouse for Mathematics and Science Education Focus* (pp. 2–6). Washington, DC: U.S. Department of Education.

High-quality curriculum *engages students* and:

- is fresh and surprising to the student.
- seems "real" and purposeful to a learner.
- connects with the student's life.
- allows choice.
- requires active learning.
- is pleasurable—or at least satisfying—for the student.
- is focused on products that matter to the student.
- taps personal interest.
- allows the student to make a contribution to something greater than self.
- challenges and provides support for student success.

High-quality curriculum *promotes understanding* and:

- is clearly focused on the essential knowledge, understanding, and skills a professional in the field would value.
- is coherent (organized, unified, sensible) to the student.
- attends to student misconceptions.
- deals with profound ideas that endure across years of student learning.
- enables a student to use what he or she learns in important ways.
- requires cognition and metacognition.
- causes students to grapple with significant problems.
- causes students to raise useful questions; and
- necessitates that students generate (vs. reproduce) knowledge.

RELIABILITY AND VALIDITY OF INFORMAL ASSESSMENT STRATEGIES

Concern arises over the objectivity—and, hence, the reliability and validity—of informal assessment strategies. Recall that reliability refers to the consistency with which various tests or assessment strategies produce the same or similar results for an individual from one administration to the next. Recognizing that a young child's performance on tests is quite variable from day to day and situation to situation, few, if any, formal tests can claim high reliability. To claim the same for informal or performance-based assessment would also be spurious. Grant Wiggins advises the teacher to know what behavior to look for and to have enough evidence (about the individual student's behaviors) to feel confident that the score given is representative (Brandt, 1992). Further, one must make sure there is enough information collected over time on similar tasks and must continually observe and compare current observations with previous ones in order to draw accurate and unbiased inferences. In doing so, the teacher is better able to draw valid inferences and develop and refine a scoring process.

Wiggins also suggests using multiple judges, where possible, to strive for the highest **interrater reliability** (i.e., reliability that is derived from similar findings by different raters). Reliability is also enhanced in informal assessments by skillfully monitoring progress from task to task and giving full consideration to the contexts in which the child's performance occurs. The context includes time, setting, situation, extenuating circumstances, relationships or feelings associated with the individuals involved, physical and psychological well-being, distractions, and so on. By providing

interrater reliability The degree to which two or more observers are in agreement with what was observed. The higher the agreement between observers' accounts, judgments, and inferences, the higher the interrater reliability.

Skilled observation inherent in informal assessments reveals behaviors, skills, and interests not always captured through formal or standardized approaches.

University Christian Church Weekday School, Fort Worth, TX

many opportunities for the student to demonstrate emerging capabilities and sampling performance in many contexts over time, teachers can ensure reliable and defensible assessment data. The goal in establishing reliability is to ensure that the outcomes of the assessment effort truly reflect lasting characteristics of the student and are not attributable to bias, temporary circumstance, or chance.

Validity, on the other hand, addresses the degree to which a procedure measures what it purports to measure and is determined by comparing or contrasting an outcome with some stated criterion or construct. The goal of valid assessments is to ensure that inferences drawn from assessment outcomes are accurate and meaningful. For this to occur in informal assessments, one must relate student performance, processes, and products to established criteria and to the goals or benchmarks of a particular learning event or to the broader program or grade-related goals and benchmarks. When student performances, products, and processes are assessed over time, valid assumptions can emerge. It may take as many as six examples of similar types of student work to draw inferences about the student's ability or mastery of a particular task (Brandt, 1992). Brandt reminds us of the concept of the *novice,* whose early attempts or performance in any endeavor cannot be judged as indicative of general ability. Such performance will be inconsistent, whether by a novice artist, athlete, or writer, but it can improve with further growth and development and additional opportunities to learn and practice. Thus, sampling student performance over time is crucial to ensuring validity.

Objectivity refers to the ability of the assessor to derive data and information about a student that is free of personal feelings or biases. Skilled assessment requires an understanding of the need for objectivity and of observer characteristics that can enhance objectivity or work against it. Bentzen (1997) identifies the following characteristics that can either enhance or militate against objective observations and the inferences that are drawn from them:

◆ sensitivity and awareness (about children and emerging development, based on the observer's training and experience)

◆ fatigue, illness, discomfort, or environmental distractions [health problems or personal psychological disturbances, such as anxieties, fears, and distractions in the physical surroundings that can distort perceptions, such as lighting, crowding, noise, temperature (and, we might add, reactions of other observers)

◆ influence of self or personality (imposing or projecting one's attitudes, needs, and values onto the child being observed; or liking or disliking a child based on one's personal views of acceptability)

◆ biases (in which behaviors, e.g., aggression, anxiety, dependence, become prevailing characterizations of an individual rather than behavior commensurate with or provoked by a specific incident or context)

◆ setting or situation (size and arrangement of physical space, equipment, and materials available and in use, characteristic skills and personalities of the children, and the means by which these are evidenced)

An *inference* is an attempt to provide a logical explanation for observed behaviors. Because inferences are based on judgments, the teacher must confront his or her own biases and be cognizant of possible factors that militate against objectivity. Accurate inference depends on the observer's ability to apply sound principles of growth and development and unbiased perspectives when assessing individual children. Because inferences are constructed by the observer, if they are to be valid the observer must exercise the highest level of objectivity. One question the observer can ask when attempting to draw an inference is; Would other observers in this same time and context agree with my inference? For example: Amy throws a block from the block center. All observers can agree that Amy threw a block. But can all observers agree that Amy was angry, frustrated, being playful, or trying to get attention? Or is there another inference to be drawn? Obviously, we would have to have astutely observed and listened to all events (verbal and physical) preceding the throwing of the block and those that followed. Further, we would need more knowledge about Amy: patterns of social interaction, typical behaviors associated with fatigue, hunger, boredom, and what types of events provoke excitement, frustration, anger, playfulness, and so on. Inferences then, cannot easily be drawn from one event but must be extrapolated from information derived from observations over time in all developmental domains and in many contexts.

As with formal assessment, a good plan for the use of informal assessment strategies with young children must meet standards for reliability, validity, and objectivity. We begin the discussion of informal assessment by exploring its most important element, that of skilled observation.

Skilled Observation

Most teachers agree that observing children is an integral part of their teaching. Through observation, or *kid watching*, as Goodman (1978) called it, a conscious effort is made to focus on specific behaviors of individuals or on the interactions among small groups of children to expose and reflect on their emerging capabilities—their knowledge, skills, feelings, and dispositions, if you will. Understanding children begins with conscientiously observing them. Indeed, much of what is known about children's growth and development has been derived from observational studies and the inferences that have been drawn from them. Classroom teachers engage in both incidental and focused observations.

Incidental Observations

Incidental observations occur quite frequently as the teacher circulates among students who are engaged in classroom tasks and activities. During story time, for example, the teacher visually scans the listeners for facial expressions and body language and listens for verbal responses indicative of enjoyment, language development, and comprehension. The teacher observes children as they move about, attending to their posture, gait, coordination, agility, endurance, persistence, use of materials and equipment, and the choices they make. The children are also observed as they interact with one another and with adults. There are innumerable incidental observations inherent in day-to-day interactions with children. These incidental observations provide valuable information about what individual students *feel, think, understand, and can do* and guide the responsive teacher in setting appropriate expectations and experiences for them.

In discussing the difference between *looking* and *seeing,* Leonard (1997) cautions observers about the "visibility trap," in which the observer's attention easily gravitates toward certain highly visible children or children whose behaviors, looks, activity preferences, level of dependency, and social skills, for example, are valued by the observer, whereas other children in the group become relatively "invisible." Taking notes (Figure 4.3) and keeping organized records on all children helps to prevent this type of selective observation from occurring. Skill in observing and recognizing significant behaviors and emerging capabilities is necessary for both teaching and assessing, and, as discussed before, skilled observation enhances the reliability and validity of inferences that are drawn. Consider the following example and each teacher's observations and inferences:

Event	Teacher A	Teacher B
Christi arrives at kindergarten late. The class is assembled around the teacher who is previewing the day's schedule.	Christi is "always" late.	Christi's eyes are red and she looks tired, sad, or mad; I can't tell for sure.
Christi shoves her lunch box into her cubby. Rather than joining the group, she goes to a table to sit, leans forward, and buries her face in her arms.	Christi is in a bad mood.	Christi is obviously disturbed about something. I noticed she "shoved" her lunch box into her cubby and practically "fell" into the chair before burying her face in her arms.
Christi remains in this posture throughout the group time and well into center time.	Obviously, Christi does not wish to participate this morning.	Christi's behavior may be a call for help. I will ask.
After the teacher questions her, Christi reveals a very upsetting argument her parents had the evening before and some of the words that were exchanged.	It is sad when parents don't get along; no wonder Christi is in a bad mood.	Christi does not yet separate fantasy and reality and does not understand idioms, so she is frightened by what she heard.
The most disturbing to her was the idiom her mother used in reprimanding her father for throwing a book across the room: "You are going to kill somebody." Christi thus repeated to the teacher, "My daddy is going to kill somebody."	Christi gets frightened when her parents argue.	Most likely her sleep was disturbed, explaining the red eyes and disinterest in joining the group.

Figure 4.3
Convenient Sticky Notes Facilitate On-the-Spot
Recording of Observations.

Child's name   Jeremy Benton

Monday 11 - 2 - 07
          date
Jeremy B.
context: Block Center
observation: Aware
of concept of gravity
with trucks on ramp.

Tuesday 11 - 3 - 07
           date
Jeremy B.
context: Block Center
observation: J. explains
gravity to Juan G. and
Maria, who attempt.

Wednesday 11 - 4 - 07
             date
Jeremy B.
context:
observation:

Thursday 11 - 5 - 07
            date

Friday   11 - 6 - 07
          date

Although each teacher's observations are "correct," Teacher B has exercised more skilled observation based on a knowledge of child development. Because Teacher B's observations are more detailed, the teacher is able to explore three possible avenues for enabling Christi to learn and to cope: (1) provide opportunities to experience in positive ways the differences between fantasy and reality; (2) introduce the concept of idioms through stories, games, or by explaining many other such expressions, focusing on the more comforting ones; and (3) provide some unencumbered time for Christi to collect herself and perhaps to rest from a sleepless night. In addition, Teacher B is able to infer from his observations and thus derive a plan for future observations of Christi, being alert to other behaviors indicative of continuing discord in the family. The teacher may determine that a parent conference could help.

Teacher A established that Christi was in a "bad mood" but did not observe her physical appearance, posture, body language, or facial expression. The teacher inferred that Christi did not wish to participate without having adequate data to verify the inference or explain the behavior. The inference that Christi had been frightened was correct, but the teacher failed to connect Christi's fears with her levels of cognitive and psychosocial development. There is also evidence of teacher bias. Teacher A has observed little to be of much help to Christi or to supply any information of consequence about Christi that might inform teacher-child interactions and instructional planning.

Figure 4.4
Behaviors to Observe
in Children

talking	playing	listening	interacting
singing	pretending	rapping	building
reading	writing	drawing	painting
sorting	classifying	graphing	seriating
computing	mapping	constructing	debating
problem solving	dramatizing	empathizing	persisting
role playing	questioning	bragging	explaining
manipulating	balancing	lifting	helping
disassembling	sculpturing	climbing	running
organizing	sharing	making choices	negotiating

Skilled observation enables a teacher to attend to a variety of cues or signals that children exhibit, as listed in Figure 4.4. Teacher B responded to Christi's refusal to join the group as a signal for attention—a cry for help. Wisely, the teacher allowed Christi to verbalize her experience and thus reveal her level of understanding, which, in turn, provided Teacher B with valuable insights into Christi's current (and possibly future) behaviors. The teacher might also have gained insight from observation of Christi's pretend play behaviors. From this example, we can extrapolate the following characteristics of a skilled observer:

◆ is informed by knowledge of child growth and development

◆ avoids jumping to conclusions

◆ is empathic and holds no bias and preconceived ideas

◆ attends to details

◆ forms hypotheses and observes further for verification

◆ draws valid inferences

◆ generates a plan for further observation

◆ informs instruction and adult/child interactions

Focused Observation

Focused observation entails using a prepared format such as a checklist, rating strategy, anecdotal record, or other instrument for systematically recording observational data. Incidental observations may find their way into these formats as well because there is a need to record and assemble significant information gained from all observations. Focused observations are usually predetermined with elements of time, place, and activity controlled in some manner. Focused observations may be carried out by the classroom teacher during the course of the school day or may involve one or more other persons, such as another teacher, a parent, a classroom aide, a diagnostician, the school principal, or another appropriate observer, depending on the purpose and goals of the observation. When two or more individuals observe the same children and event, observations can be compared to determine areas of agreement and disagreement. Interrater reliability evolves from this type of process, making the inferences drawn more reliable. When in doubt

Multiple dimensions of growth, development, and learning (e.g., in this image: fine motor control, eye-hand coordination, problem-solving strategies, and perseverance) can be observed when children are presented with interesting and challenging materials.

about a particular observation, this strategy can be helpful. Good focused observations have these qualities:

◆ clearly stated purpose and goals for the observation

◆ clearly defined target behaviors to be observed

◆ well-designed instruments to focus observations specifically on the identified target behaviors

◆ observer familiarity with the purpose and goals, target behaviors, expected behaviors (or a developmental frame of reference), and the assessment instrument and how it will be used and scored

◆ adequate time to conduct the observation(s)

◆ clearly elaborated and developmentally sensitive scoring procedures

◆ professionalism and ethics in recording, evaluating, and interpreting the observation data

In addition, observers must be aware of the context in which observing is taking place and events preceding and following the observation; they should also be as unobtrusive and inconspicuous as possible during observations. Children's behaviors change when they are aware that they are being observed. The techniques that follow can strengthen observation skills and, over time, increase the teacher's knowledge base about child development and learning. Let's examine the features and uses of some of the more practical methods for recording and assembling observation data.

Recording Observation Data

Anecdotal Records

An *anecdote* is a short account of some significant event or incident in a child's day. The record of this event can be quite detailed or very brief. Usually written after the event, these short reports (or vignettes) describe, in a factual way, the incident, its

When children engage in shared learning and problem-solving activities, they learn to recognize and define a problem and plan or negotiate a solution.

Todd Yarrington/Merrill

context, and what was said or done by the participant(s). Skilled observation and accurate recording provide an opportunity to capture the essence of an event. The less time that elapses between the incident and the recording of it, the more detailed and accurate the anecdotal record can be.

Ideally, the anecdotal record should be recorded as it unfolds or immediately thereafter. However, this is not always possible in a busy classroom with few adult helping hands. Anecdotal records usually have to be written later, perhaps during a planning period or at the end of the school day. Because it is sometimes difficult to remember all aspects of an event for later recording, keeping brief notes on sticky pads or index cards carried in a pocket or placed about the room for ready accessibility can be helpful. Jotting one-word reminders or short phrases on the cards as the event unfolds (or immediately following it) can provide a set of handy reminders for the expanded version recorded later in the day. One can record information such as the child's initials; time; place (playground, writing center, music activity, and so on); other participants; any words, phrases, or quotations that will help one remember what was said; antecedents to the episode; and the outcomes or other items germane to the event. The index card might look like the example in Figure 4.5.

Figure 4.5
Anecdotal Record Note Card

CEP	11/16/07
	9:15 AM
block center	
w/ MH, DP, JB	
crowded	dispute over truck
"…we are friends…"	
prosocial solution	

Figure 4.6
Anecdotal Record

Child's Name: _Catherine E. P._

Date and Time: _11 / 16 / 07   9:15 am_

Observer: _J. Nowell_

Place or Learning Center: _block center_

Observed Event and Behaviors:

  While working together in the block center, Maria, Darrell, Jamie, and Catherine began to argue over who would be the driver of the dump truck. Maria allowed that none of the others could be her friend if she was not the driver. Catherine suggested that there were two other trucks and an airplane—she could be the pilot and everyone else could drive a truck. They were each satisfied and soon settled back into their roadbuilding play theme. Catherine soothed feelings by saying "I like it when we are friends."

Comments / Summary

  Catherine, while meeting her own needs to "be the pilot," nevertheless revealed unusual facility in negotiation and compromise. Her prosocial skills were evident in this incident. Observe for further evidence of this skill with other classmates.
  Reminder: Reduce number of children allowed in the block center at one time to alleviate crowding.

These short notes can be extended into full descriptions later, using a form designed for anecdotal records. The completed form should be placed in the student's portfolio. The anecdotal record might look like the form in Figure 4.6.

These and more-detailed records take some time to do well. However, their ability to capture the richness and complexity of the moment as children interact with one another and with materials provides a valuable source of information. Meisels (1992) suggests that at least one anecdotal record per child per week be completed, but more are certainly enlightening when feasible. These records of child behavior and learning accumulated over time enhance the teacher's understanding of the individual child as patterns or profiles begin to emerge. Behavior change can be tracked and documented, and suggestions for future observations, curriculum adjustments, and student or parent conferences can be included in teacher planning.

Checklists

More expeditious than anecdotal records, a checklist helps focus the observer's attention on the presence or absence of selected behaviors or learning. Checklists may focus on growth and development indicators or on learning objectives. They may contain lists of traits, skills, behaviors, interests, concepts, or developmental or curricular benchmarks. Checklists can be used to assess student performance, student products, and student processes. Checklists may be teacher designed or developed by experts in particular developmental or skill areas. Some published learning systems and textbooks include checklists of objectives.

Regardless of origin, checklists should be designed to portray well-defined criteria. Criterion-referenced checklists may be based on local or state-mandated learning objectives or perhaps on school site-based goals and objectives for specific curriculum areas or grade levels. Further, checklists must reflect current knowledge in child growth, development, and learning and be sensitive to cultural and linguistic diversity and special needs and talents.

A developmental checklist assists the teacher in monitoring the growth and development of each child. A good developmental checklist provides a sequential overview of expected patterns of development, from which an emerging profile of the student becomes evident and from which decisions can be made about the types of classroom experiences that will be most beneficial. Figure 4.7 is an example of a sequential checklist for observing emerging fine motor development. Checklists may also alert the teacher to the need for additional, more in-depth assessment for a particular child. A practical way to use checklists is to focus on a small group of four to five

Figure 4.7
Fine Motor Development Checklist

	Date	Date	Date	Comments
Picks up objects easily with pincer movement				
Releases grasp with ease				
Builds stable vertical structures with unit blocks				
Handles feeding utensils efficiently				
Manages clothing (buttons, zippers, ties, snaps, belt buckles, etc.)				
Demonstrates hand preference				
Pours from small pitcher				
Turns knobs and handles				
Manipulates bead stringing, peg board activities, puzzles, and other small manipulatives				
Turns pages of book, one at a time				
Holds crayon in fist				
Holds crayon with fingers				
Manipulates clay and sculpting material				
Molds discernable shapes or objects with clay				
Draws using wide circular marks				
Draws discernable shapes or pictures				
Folds paper				
Traces shapes and figures with finger				
Traces shapes and figures with crayon or pencil				
Copies shapes and figures				
Cuts with scissors—straight lines				
Cuts with scissors—curved lines				
Cuts with scissors—outlined shapes				
Grasp pencil correctly				
Uses pencil to make letters, numerals				
Copies letters, shapes, designs				
Writes in a horizontal line				
Writes within guidelines				

Figure 4.8
Class Summary Report

Target Behaviors

Student's name

children per day. Attempting to complete whole group checklists in one day increases the risk of mistakes, oversights, and overgeneralizations and simply is not practical.

Using developmental checklists to date the emergence of each developmental indicator provides a criterion against which to compare other data—performance, processes, and products. Other checklists may address curriculum-related areas and the developmental progression toward expected learning or skill outcomes.

For summative reports used for grade or school progress reporting, for assessing class progress in selected curriculum areas, and for planning for curriculum modification or enrichment, whole group checklists may be useful. Such lists can be assembled into a class summative portfolio for periodic assessment and summary data. Such a report includes identical information collected on each student in the class and depicted on a matrix such as the one in Figure 4.8.

A major disadvantage of the checklist is that it provides no context cues surrounding the observed behavior or learning. A checklist tells little or nothing about the frequency with which the behavior or event occurs or the duration of the behavior or episode being observed. The checklist does not describe or elaborate. It is necessary to complement checklists with other, more detailed observations of student performance and with actual samples or representations (e.g., photographs, audio or video recordings, or electronic storage) of student products.

Inventories

The checklist's "cousin," the inventory, can also be useful. The inventory has more meaning in terms of the overall picture. Inventories are generally more comprehensive and detailed than checklists and provide a way to keep track of what is currently happening or, in developmental terms, what observed development is emerging. This differs from checklists in that no single item on the inventory represents a necessary achievement. Checklists generally suggest the direction that growth, development, and learning should be following. Inventories, on the other hand, highlight growth, development, and learning as they occur. As Engel (1990) points out, the difference between the two is the difference between *prescription* and *description*. For example, Figure 4.9 illustrates a descriptive inventory of

Check (✓) observed behaviors	Comments

____ Observes actions of objects and people

____ Intentionally repeats behaviors or pleasurable actions

____ Employs imitative behaviors

____ Demonstrates the concept of object permanence

____ Motorically explores physical surroundings

____ Listens intently and curiously

____ Visually focuses on speaker or source of sound

____ Auditorily focuses on speaker or source of sound without visually searching

____ Engages in tactile exploration of objects

____ Engages in taste exploration of edibles

____ Uses sense of smell to identify objects, places, or events

____ Uses objects to represent ideas, events, play themes, or experiences

____ Connects sounds and rhythms with bodily movement

____ Expresses thought, ideas, and mood through movement, music, and/or art production

____ Verbally labels objects and events

____ Uses trial and error strategies to solve problems

____ Verbalizes previously learned concepts

____ Repeats previously learned behaviors

____ Applies previously learned concepts or behaviors in new situations and different contexts

____ Uses prior experiences and knowledge to verbally explain current event or dilemma

____ Demonstrates concept of cause and effect

____ Applies concept of cause and effect in play with objects

____ Applies concept of cause and effect in problem solving

____ Applies concept of cause and effect in social interactions

____ Experiments with new or novel uses for familiar objects

____ Solves concrete problems using physical objects

____ Manipulates and explores objects and classroom materials

____ Uses classroom materials in traditional ways

____ Uses classroom materials in creative, imaginative ways as a means to convey meaning or to further understanding

____ Contrasts and compares objects, events, and ideas

____ Formulates hypotheses

____ Tests predictions

____ Seeks verification through dialogue

____ Seeks verification through experimentation with objects

____ Attempts to explain or interpret new information

____ Generates and verbally suggests procedures for problem solving

Figure 4.9
"Observed" Cognitive Processes Inventory

Check (✓) observed behaviors	Comments

____ Works independently to solve problems

____ Interacts with classmates to solve problems

____ Enlists adult interaction to solve problems

____ Asks meaningful questions

____ Responds thoughtfully to answers

____ Challenges answers when necessary

____ Applies answers in subsequent situations

____ Engages in meaningful dialogue using questions to expand understanding

____ Uses a variety of speech forms to sustain conversation/dialogue

____ Demonstrates observant behaviors by calling attention to less obvious objects, events or situations

____ Relates objects and/or events to one another

____ Demonstrates functional relationships (objects, events, or ideas that are mutually dependent)

____ Classifies by one attribute

____ Classifies by more than one attribute

____ Classifies by complex or novel attributes

____ Uses concepts of conservation to understand or explain change phenomena

____ Uses pictures and other classroom visuals to obtain information

____ Uses books and other print sources to obtain information

____ "Reads" pictures in books

____ Finds meaning in print

____ Reads for meaning as well as enjoyment

____ Uses context clues to read

____ Uses sound/symbol associations to read

____ Creates drawings to express ideas and knowledge

____ Remembers and recites fingerplays, songs, chants, simple proverbs, classroom procedures, predictable stories, and so on, and uses them to guide own behaviors and facilitate understanding

____ Uses associative strategies to remember and recall

____ Uses a variety of written symbols to convey meaning

____ Uses ordering and sequencing strategies

____ Looks for patterns and relationships

____ Uses number and number concepts

____ Identifies incongruences (as with riddles and jokes)

____ Employs abstract concepts

____ Verbalizes cognitive dissonance ("that can't be so, because . . . ")

____ Reflects on own learning

____ Verbally describes own thinking

____ Verbally contrasts own point of view with that of another

____ Verbally contrasts own current point of view with a past perspective

Figure 4.9   (continued)

"observable" cognitive processes. Note that in this particular inventory, although the items are arranged from less to more complex and sophisticated levels of cognitive abilities, they do not necessarily represent an invariant step-by-step stage sequence. The descriptor, "observed," is surrounded by quotation marks to convey the obvious, that the classroom observer cannot actually get into the mind of the learner and know with certainty the cognitive processes that are taking place, but the observer can attend to the outward manifestations (i.e., language, behaviors, and activities) emanating from the learner's thinking processes. This OCP inventory is by no means a complete list of cognitive processes. The observer can use this inventory to profile the types of processes a learner uses in different contexts and with different tasks.

Figure 4.10
Problem-Solving
Rating Scale

Level	Problem Solving	Rating			Comments / Notes
		Frequently	Sometimes	Never	
EXPLORATION	1. Exhibits curiosity/ interest in the problem				
	2. Asks questions about the problem				
	3. Draws on past experience to understand the problem				
DISCOVERY	4. Verbally or graphically represents the problem				
	5. Draws on past experience to plan a solution				
INQUIRY	6. Engages others in the solution				
	7. Accepts assistance				
UTILIZATION	8. Initiates a plan				
	9. Evaluates the solution				
	10. Applies solution in other contexts				

Rating Scales

Another device for recording observations is the rating scale. The rating scale requires that the observer make judgments about knowledge, skills, feelings, and dispositions in the domains being observed by assigning them a numerical or descriptive rating. Rating scales can be difficult to construct because it is necessary to keep descriptors and numerical ratings within the common understanding of each person who will use the scale. There is also a heightened possibility for bias to creep into rating scales. Although such scales help teachers to record observations quickly and efficiently, they must be used prudently and must fairly (without bias) represent the observed behavior. Figure 4.10 illustrates rating scales in which descriptive categories are assigned frequency ratings.

Time Sampling

Using the time-sampling techniques, an observer or teacher attempts to record the occurrence or nonoccurrence of selected behavior(s) within certain time frames. For instance, a teacher may want to ascertain how many times a child moves from one learning center to another during periods when students are encouraged to self-select and initiate their own learning activities. A time-sampling chart might look like the example in Figure 4.11. Time sampling is helpful in determining the frequency with which certain behaviors occur and can be designed to include context clues such as time of day, place of event, other individuals involved in the event, and so on.

Event Sampling

Using the event-sampling technique, observers can record events or categories of events as they occur. For example, teachers may wish to observe creative effort with art media. They must first identify the behaviors to be observed and then record each

Figure 4.11
Frequency of Activity
Changes

Activity Changes	Time Unit										Comments
	9:00		9:15		10:00		10:15		10:30		
(child's name)	U	F	U	F	U	F	U	F	U	F	

U = unfocused/undecided about what to do next
F = focused/next activity pursued with obvious intent

Figure 4.12
Event Sampling:
Creative Activity

Creative Endeavor							
(child's name)	Draw	Paint	Clay	Paste	Multi-media	Other	Comments
10-12-07	I I		I	I			
10-15-07	I I I	I					

event when it is observed. This record can be designed several ways; Figure 4.12 illustrates one such method. Event sampling can be as brief or as detailed as time and need dictate. Always, the more information provided by an observation record, the more useful it can be later when interpretation or summarization is required.

Interviews

Student interviews are particularly helpful in deepening understanding of each child. Through interviews, teachers can gain insight into students' prior knowledge and experience, current understandings, learning styles, interests, motivations, anxieties, and so on. Teachers can observe students' responses and reactions to questions and dialogue without looking for the "correct" answer or "good" or "right" behaviors. The interview establishes a collaborative relationship between child and teacher and leads to mutual goal setting. The interview provides a special opportunity to help students reflect upon their own products, processes, performance, and portfolio contents. It also sets the stage for determining each student's **zone of proximal development (ZPD)**, described by Vygotsky (1930–1935/ 1978) as that distance between what a child is capable of doing independently and what he or she can accomplish with assistance and encouragement.

zone of proximal development (ZPD) The level of development in learning a particular concept or skill in which assistance from an adult or more skilled child is needed but may soon be unnecessary.

JUDGING STUDENT PERFORMANCE, PROCESSES, AND PRODUCTS

Fair, valid, and reliable assessment depends on having clearly defined the developmental domains and the specific behaviors, skills, or knowledge expected to emerge within each. Having done so, assessment instruments can be designed to reflect the degree to which the student exhibits the identified behaviors or is progressing toward specific learning outcomes. The term *rubrics* is commonly used to refer to the descriptions of the criteria in each level or gradation of a performance, product, or process. Rubrics are useful because they establish what is important; they define target outcomes and clarify expectations. The development of rubrics helps to focus observations and assessments on essentials and assists both learners and teachers in defining progress and quality. Well-framed rubrics, although time consuming to develop, ultimately reduce assessing and grading time and render more consistent, complete, context-specific information.

Rubrics provide immediate feedback to learners, thus giving them positive support and encouragement while helping them to identify and correct their mistakes or practice an emerging skill. Further, rubrics provide a clear frame of reference for articulating student progress and performance to various stakeholders: learners, their parents or guardians, appropriate school personnel, and policy-makers. Well-framed rubrics have the following characteristics:

◆ They are tied to clearly stated learning objectives, benchmarks, or developmental outcomes.

◆ They articulate a sequence that moves logically from emergent to proficient.

◆ They are stated in positive ("can-do") terms.

◆ They are free of bias relating to age, gender, socioeconomic status, ethnicity, and ableness.

◆ The terminology is understandable and meaningful to the learner.

◆ The terminology is universally understood by all professionals who are involved in the use of the particular assessment instrument.

◆ Rating scales or codes are fair and easily interpreted.

◆ The rubrics as stated and the scores thus derived facilitate decision making.

Scoring rubrics can be described several ways. Stiggins (1997a) classifies scoring rubrics into two categories: analytic and holistic. An *analytic* scale sets forth a series of statements describing characteristics associated with each score in a range of scores. The statements describe the progression the learner should go through to get more proficient. The scale provides a precise picture and is more "diagnostic" than other scoring systems, though it takes considerably more time to develop. Analytic scales are frequently used to describe levels of acceptable performance in academic achievements and are keyed to content area standards. The learner's performance or products are judged according to how close they come to the standard at the time of the assessment. Figure 4.13 illustrates rubrics for an early childhood mathematics assessment.

In line with this paradigm, we could construct a rubric that indicated where in the recursive learning cycle (Bredekamp & Rosegrant, 1992; Rosegrant, 1989) a student might be with regard to particular concepts or content. The four-part rubric would denote how a learner is relating to various aspects of the current curriculum and progressing toward new awarenesses. Such a rubric would help focus observation on learner processes while providing guidance to the teacher seeking to facilitate the learner's pursuit of understanding. The descriptors would be those described by Bredekamp and Rosegrant (1992): *awareness, exploration, inquiry*, and *utilization*. The rubrics for such an instrument might look like those in Figure 4.14.

A *holistic* approach entails assigning a single score based on the overall quality of the student performance or product. Quick and simple, this approach yields little specific information to guide instruction, although it may be used to flag individual students who may need more focused assessment. An example of holistic scoring might be to assign a score of 1, 2, 3, or 4 (1 representing the lowest score and 4 representing the highest) to a student's participation in a cooperative group

Not observed yet	Emerging	Gaining competence	Proficient
Counts by rote 1 to 10	Counts by rote beyond 10	Counts by rote to 30	Counts by rote to 100
Uses one-to-one correspondence to count up to 5 objects	Uses one-to-one correspondence to count 10 objects	Uses one-to-one correspondence to count 10 to 30 objects	Uses one-to-one correspondence to count more than 30 objects
Attempts to count objects for a purpose, e.g., a napkin for each of 6 members of the group	Counts objects for a purpose with no more than one or two miscalculations	Counts objects for a purpose with no miscalculations	Helps others count objects for a purpose with no miscalculations
Identifies objects as being a member of a set	Identifies objects as being a member of a set that is verbally described	Creates sets of objects	Creates sets of objects and describes the sets' attributes
Attempts to group objects by one attribute	Groups objects by one attribute	Attempts to group objects by more than one attribute	Groups objects by two or more attributes
Responds appropriately to most positional language, e.g., up, down, over, under, behind, in front, etc.	Responds appropriately to all positional language	Uses positional language to describe own behaviors	Uses positional language to describe and explain own and others' behaviors and to direct problem-solving activities

Figure 4.13
Mathematics Rubrics

Awareness	Exploration	Inquiry	Utilization
Experiences new concept or phenomenon	Observes materials, events, interactions	Extended exploration of the materials or information associated with the concept or event	Applies new learning to new situations or in other contexts
Shows interest	Explores the materials, attends to components or attributes	Engages in focused information gathering activities	Demonstrates new learning through a variety of representations, drawing, writing, construction, interactions with others
Attends to its characteristics or elements	Engages in play associated with new concept or phenomenon	Proposes own explanations	Uses language associated with new learning
	Attempts to apply labels, descriptions, attributes to new concept or event	Compares own perceptions with that of others	New awarenesses are created, new hypotheses formulated
	Attempts to represent new concept through drawing, writing, constructions, and sociodramatic play	Relates new information to prior experiences or learning	
		Generalizes to other concepts, events or phenomena	

Figure 4.14
Recursive Learning Cycle Observation

Meaningful assessments are collaborative, partnering with students to guide and celebrate their accomplishments.

Hope Madden/Merrill

endeavor. A set of general guidelines would describe the meaning of each numerical score. For instance, in the cooperative group endeavor, the following might describe the types of behaviors typically exhibited:

1. reticent, timid, reluctant, or interfering behaviors
2. minimal participation with some constructive suggestions and some counter-productive or interfering behaviors
3. participation with constructive contributions
4. focused participation with goal-oriented suggestions and meaningful contributions

Gredler (1996) refers to a "key features" approach that determines to what degree certain characteristics or features occur—for example, the extent to which a child's retelling of a story contains the following features: title, author, beginning, middle, and end; or perhaps the child might include more detail such as setting, characters, story problem (plot, climax), and story solution/conclusion. The evaluative code might include a three-part scale, such as:

Not yet   Sometimes   Most of the time

Emerging   Developing   Proficient

An assessment of a child's emergent drawing ability is an example of a key features approach and might look like the one in Figure 4.15.

As you can see, this paradigm is detailed and follows an expected developmental sequence. It can be used to assess many drawings over time. Information derived from this approach can be used to assess levels of development from very specific indicators and inform and complement other assessments. For example, the drawing assessment in Figure 4.15 can provide information about emerging symbol awareness, use, and meaning; writing and reading; concept

Emergent	Beginning	Developing	Proficient
Controlled fine motor strokes	Hand-eye coordination	Controlled eye-hand movements	Drawings represent familiar objects or experiences
Controlled use of implements, e.g., paint brush, crayons, markers, etc.	Curved line drawings	Drawings, sculptures, and so on are goal oriented	Demonstrates own unique ways of drawing certain pictures or symbols
Random line or shape drawings	Creates recognizable forms	Drawings include symbols	Uses some stereotypes observed in other art
Focus is primarily on sensory enjoyment and exploration of the media	Draws specific shapes, e.g., squares, rectangles, circles	Names symbols in drawings	Person drawing is elaborate with numerous details
	Curious about art media, e.g., clay, glue, finger paint, etc.	Stick figure person showing greater detail (eyes, hair, finger, toes, clothing, etc.)	Size of individual objects in drawings represent their importance to the child
	Repetition in drawings of same or similar pictures	Dictates labels or a one or two sentence story for art	Pictures contain a base line
	Draws stick figure person	Requests name be printed on art work	Dictates or writes labels or extended story on art work
		Distinguishes own art work from that of others	Most objects in drawings are recognizable to others
		Enjoys and takes pride in art work	Interested in the end product
			Saves art to share with others

Figure 4.15
Drawing: Key Developmental Features

development associated with the content of drawings; spatial awareness reflected in drawings (e.g., left/right, top/bottom); story-construction capabilities; and so on. The drawing assessments then can be triangulated (or merged) with assessments in other developmental or content areas to cross-reference and verify initial inferences. Thus, the key features approach provides a very useful and meaningful set of data that can integrate across developmental and curriculum areas.

Each scale value or dimension must be chosen for the message to be conveyed and to whom it is to be conveyed. For instance, some scales are designed to assist nonreaders and beginning readers in evaluating their own performance and, therefore, use pictures or symbols (e.g., a series of smiley faces or geometric shapes); others are intended to provide general developmental information to adults and to use descriptive terminology. Whether intended for the adult or student, the scales must be tied to and relate meaningfully to the criteria, standard, or developmental sequence being assessed. In addition to simply documenting the presence or absence of an attribute, scale values can be labeled in numerous ways. When using a range of values, each level must be clearly described and defined, so that all raters use the same criteria. The following are some examples of scale values:

Cannot do   Can do with assistance   Can do independently

Not yet   Developing   Achieving   Extending

Not yet   In process   Proficient

Never   Sometimes   Always (or consistently)

Not very much   A little bit   Much of the time   Always

Working on   Demonstrated some of the time   Effectively demonstrated

Not assessed   Not yet demonstrated   In progress   Consistently demonstrated mastery

Novice   Apprentice   Proficient   Distinguished

Emerging   Beginning   Developing proficient (or for reading: fluent)

Initiated   In progress   Completed

Early   Advanced   Early   Advanced   Early   Advanced
Emergent   Emergent   Beginning   Beginning   Independent   Independent

A scale that is clearly tied to a particular standard or benchmark might read as follows:

1. Performance is below standard expectation.
2. Performance shows minimal progress toward standard expectations.
3. Performance is progressing toward standard expectations.
4. Performance meets standard expectations.
5. Objective has not been introduced.

Scales can range from two points (yes/no) up to six or even nine points. Although we would not suggest limiting yourself to one particular type of point value, we like a four-point scale for several reasons. Using four levels, or dimensions, prevents the tendency to pull the score to the middle when undecided; it forces the assessor to be explicit about whether a ranking represents upper- or lower-level expectations or performance. Recognizing that systems for reporting student progress still include report cards, many of which continue to use grades of A, B, C, and D, an additional reason for favoring a four-point paradigm is that it facilitates translation into letter or numerical grades when such is required. As discussed earlier, many student attributes measured through authentic assessment processes cannot and should not be translated into letter grades or numerical scores. Nevertheless, school policy may dictate letter grades for certain attainments in behavioral or content areas, and meaningful instruments can be developed that provide descriptive information that can be scored in such a way that the scores can be translated. When numbers are attached to the grades in a four-point scale, 4 = A, 3 = b, 2 = C, and 1 = D, averaging is quick and easy.

WHEN AND WHERE ASSESSMENT TAKES PLACE

A skilled observer is alert to behaviors and performances in all contexts: the classroom, playground, with individuals, in groups, with parents and other adults, on a field trip, in the cafeteria, and all other places where children and teachers are together. For most teachers, observing children is a natural part of their work; they do so without conscious effort. However, becoming skilled at drawing valid inferences, selecting and using a variety of assessment instruments, assessing student products from an emergent development perspective rather than a deficit identification approach, and, finally, recording and showcasing student progress takes conscientious planning, focused observation, and practice.

A frequent concern associated with authentic assessment is the time involved in doing a good job. This is a legitimate concern, but it does not need to discourage the effort. The rewards in terms of professional development as teachers become more knowledgeable about their individual students and about child growth, development, and learning, the opportunities to effectively enrich curricula to meet needs, and the possibilities of better performance and sustained learning on the part of students are all valid reasons to make the time for a better system.

It helps to begin slowly with areas in which one has the greatest confidence and gradually increase the domains and the methods used to assess. It is best not to try to assess the whole class at once; work with small groups, week by week, rotating, observing, assessing different small groups until all children are involved in the assessment process. As with any new skill, the more one practices, modifies and refines the process, the easier it becomes. Indeed, integrating meaningful informal assessments into one's instructional repertoire can lead to more efficient and purposeful use of time—both the teacher's and the students'—as priorities change and former less essential practices are discarded.

WHOM TO INVOLVE IN THE ASSESSMENT PROCESS

Studies have shown that children perform best on assessments with which they are familiar and in which they have a warm and trusting relationship with the assessor (Atkins-Burnett, Rowan, & Correnti, 2001; Kami, 1990; Meisels & Atkins-Burnett, 2005). Additionally, when children are assessed in their "natural environments," the information obtained is more likely to reflect a child's typical behaviors and abilities (McLean, Wolery, & Bailey, 2004).

Meaningful assessments are collaborative. The teacher/assessor becomes a partner with each learner, helping to set realistic and obtainable goals, showcase accomplishments, and celebrate progress. Collaborating with parents to meet each child's unique needs and interests brings the home and school into shared responsibility for student outcomes. Working collaboratively with students, parents, and other professionals within the school, assessments become more authentic and, therefore, more useful. Students and parents can play an active and very significant role in the assessment process. In the next chapter we discuss the design, development, evaluation, maintenance, and uses of the portfolio, a process that depends on collaboration for its success.

REQUIREMENTS FOR A MEANINGFUL ASSESSMENT SYSTEM

In summary, a framework or blueprint for planning a meaningful system for assessing young children lays out the following required elements:

1. a statement of purpose and goals
2. identification of developmental and learning domains that will be assessed and the benchmarks by which progress will be measured
3. determining the behaviors that reflect knowledge, skills, feelings, and dispositions
4. selecting appropriate tests and instruments and refining informal strategies for meaningful assessments
5. determining who shall be involved in the assessment process
6. determining time and place(s) for formal and informal assessments
7. determining how assessment information will be communicated and to whom and how student records and products will be stored, retrieved, and referenced for further planning
8. establishing criteria by which developmental and learning outcomes will be measured and the types of rubrics that can best reflect student progress or mastery

The final step in the process should, as in Figure 3.1, return the planner to the stated goal and objectives and the defined development and learning benchmarks.

REVIEW STRATEGIES AND ACTIVITIES

Vexing Questions

1. What types of systemic changes in traditional education practices are needed to facilitate meaningful assessments?
2. Informal assessments take time. How might classroom priorities and schedules be configured to support comprehensive and well-executed informal assessments?

Activities

1. With a partner, observe the same child for thirty minutes. Decide in advance what recording form or forms you will use. Write separate summary reports from your observations, but do not reveal your observations to one another. Draw inferences where possible and make some suggestions regarding the

education of the child you both observed. Later, in class, compare your observations.

    a. What did one of you notice that the other did not?

    b. What did you notice but not record?

    c. Why did you choose not to record that incident?

    d. How objective were your observations?

    e. Do you think your inferences were valid, based on what you were able to observe?

2. Conduct your own survey of the literature for developmental and curricular checklists. Compare the items and sequences with principles of development and learning described in your child-development textbook.

3. Compare the essential characteristics of the type of test you have reviewed and the essential characteristics of performance-based assessment. Discuss the purpose(s) each strategy serves in the education process.

SUGGESTED LITERATURE AND RESOURCES

Allen, K. E., & Marotz, L. R. (2003). *Developmental profiles: Prebirth through twelve* (4th ed.). Clifton Park, NY: Thomson/Delmar Learning.

Beaty, J. J. (2006). *Observing development of the young child* (6th ed.) Upper Saddle River, NJ: Merrill/Prentice Hall.

Curtis, D., & Carter, M. (2006). *The art of awareness: How observation can transform teaching*. Upper Saddle River, NJ: Merrill/Prentice Hall.

Fraser, J. (2002). *Listen to the children: From focused observation to strategic instruction*. Portsmouth, NY: Heinemann.

Jensen, R. (2005). *Enriching the brain: How to maximize every learner's potential*. Indianapolis, IN: Jossey-Bass.

Kohn, A. (2004). *What does it mean to be well educated? and more essays on standards, grading, and other follies*. Boston: Beacon Press.

National Conference of State Legislatures. (2005). *Delivering the promise: State recommendations for improving No Child Left Behind*. Denver, CO: Author.

National Research Council. (2000). *How people learn: Brain, mind, experience, and school*. Washington, DC: National Academy Press.

Schecter, S. R., & Cummins, J. (2003). *Multilingual education: Using diversity as a resource*. Portsmouth, NH: Heinemann.

Smith, A. F. (2000, Summer). Reflective portfolios: Preschool possibilities. *Childhood Education, 76* (4), 204–208.

5

Portfolio Development and Assessment

To function adequately across the life span, children and youth need formative experiences that aid their growth and development along the physical, social-interactive, social-emotional, moral-ethical, linguistic, and cognitive pathways. Indeed, academic learning is not an isolated capacity, but an aspect of development. The two are inextricably linked and mutually facilitative.

Students who are developing well overall are more likely to perform well academically.

James P. Comer, *Education Week,* January 5, 2006

Just as high-quality assessments give meaning to report card grades, so too do they permit portfolios to tell rich and compelling stories about student academic growth and development. But, they can help us to communicate more effectively and thus improve schools only if they tell an accurate story.

Stiggins (1997a, p. 453)

After reading and studying this chapter, you will demonstrate comprehension by being able to:

❑ define and describe the portfolio process for student assessment and curriculum planning.

❑ identify student products and processes that provide meaningful assessment information.

❑ describe the different types of portfolios according to their purposes.

❑ articulate guidelines for the appropriate uses of the assessment portfolio.

ASSEMBLING AND USING ASSESSMENT INFORMATION

In Chapter 4, we began our development of a "grand plan," or blueprint, for implementing a meaningful assessment system in early childhood education. Such a plan entails making decisions about how to align assessment measures with curriculum goals and content, what developmental and content domains to assess, what strategies or techniques to use, what measures are needed to ensure reliability and validity, and where and when assessment can (or should) occur. In this chapter, we extend the discussion of the overall plan to include how assessment information is assembled and accessed and how assessment information can be amalgamated into a dynamic and meaningful portfolio system.

PERFORMANCE, PROCESSES, AND PRODUCTS

Recall from Chapter 3 the ways in which students reveal to us their feelings and knowledge, their capabilities and interests. Authentic assessment derives its information and inferences from astute attention to students' performance on both required and self-selected tasks, on the products of their work and play, and on the processes they employ when they are engaged in meaningful, purposeful activities.

The preceding chapters focused on the distinctions between formal and informal assessments and the need for wise selections and cautious use of standardized tests with young children. The subject of skilled observation as integral to assessment was also introduced. Portfolios provide a systematic way to assemble observation data and to sample student work. Portfolio assessments are well received by students and parents and have been found to provide reliable information about children's progress and achievements (Meisels, Xue, Bickel, Nicholson, & Atkins-Burnett, 2001; Meisels, Liaw, Dorfman, & Nelson, 1995). Portfolio development relies on information from both formal and informal assessments. In this chapter we focus on the processes and products of student learning while exploring how prior formal assessment information (e.g., standardized test scores) can be used to corroborate and complete the assessment picture.

Appreciative parents and grandparents over the years have saved the products of their children's learning, collecting them in drawers and boxes and proudly displaying them on refrigerator doors. Photographs record special events that showcase their children. In school, student performance and products are not only shown at special events, but they are also an integral part of each child's day-to-day schooling and contribute to an ongoing assessment process. Student products provide a medium through which teachers gain insight into a student's learning processes, uncovering important information about characteristics such as how individuals explore, discover, invent, and solve problems. Figure 5.1 lists examples of products available across curriculum areas, through which children demonstrate their knowledge, skills, feelings, and dispositions.

When we broaden assessment beyond the limited knowledge or skill universe of a single formal test to include this eclectic array of student products, we expand and deepen our knowledge about children. The term *authentic* is fitting when

author lists	silly sayings	signs
activity choices	songs	tales and stories
audiotapes	collages	dialogues
block constructions	conversations	dictations
book titles	computer productions	dictionaries
book illustrations	counting objects	dioramas
charts and graphs	creative movement	drawings and paintings
child-authored books	coordinated gross motor movement	dreams and secrets
clay and dough manipulations	demonstrations	exhibits
fact files	diaries	experiments
finger plays	instructive discourse	lists
flannel board depictions	innovations	love notes, greetings, thank-you notes and other written messages
game and game rules	jokes and riddles	
group projects	jump rope rhymes	news
manipulative constructions	humor	opinions
maps	labels	pantomime
math journals	math games and manipulatives	picture journals
plans and journals	monologues	props
plans and projects	models and replicas	photographs
posters	murals	theater arts projects
puppets	sortings and classifications	tunes and melodies
puzzles	special interest collections	verse manipulations
questionnaires	sticker designs	vocabulary cards
raps	sociodramatic themes	videotapes
rebus stories	surveys	word banks
recipes and menus	story illustrations	writing journals
rhythms	sculptures	word play
rhymes	skits	wood-working projects
role play		

Figure 5.1
Student Products

assessments are attached to concrete productions and to observed behaviors and skills as they are occuring. Howard Gardner's (1983; 1999) multiple intelligences (Figure 5.2), for example, are dramatically made real for us through student writings, art productions, musical activities, social interactions, and unique interests. Jean Piaget's cognitive theory (1952) comes to life when we observe the ways in which children use real objects to explain a phenomenon or new understanding. Eric Erikson's psychosocial theory (1963) is played out in the satisfying interactions in which children become engaged and that culminate in rich sociodramatic play with cleverly improvised props and coherent themes. Learning styles and cultural and linguistic strengths come into clearer focus and are valued for the individuality they represent. Looking at the products of student learning heightens our empathy and sharpens our insights. Instruction and curricula benefit from broader,

Adding to our understanding of cognitive development is Gardner's multiple intelligence theory (1983, 1991a, 1993a, 1993b, 1998; 1999) in which intelligence is defined as the ability to solve problems or to create products that are valued in one or more cultural settings. Gardner proposes that there are multiple forms of intelligence. In *Frames of Mind* (1983), he outlined seven separate intelligences: linguistic, musical logical-mathematical, spatial, bodily-kinesthetic, interpersonal, and intrapersonal; later, he added an eighth intelligence: naturalistic (1997). He continues to explore two additional possibilities: spiritual and existential (1999). Multiple intelligence theory suggests that individuals possess various combinations of different types of intelligence to greater or lesser degrees. Thus, individuals have unique intelligence profiles. Unlike the traditional perspective of defining and measuring intelligence in terms of an intelligence quotient (IQ), multiple intelligence theory asks not How smart are you? but How are you smart?

Gardner's proposed intelligences and the manner in which they might be expressed are as follows:

1. *Linguistic intelligence* includes sensitivity to meaning, order, sounds, rhythms, and inflections of words. Children who exhibit this type of intelligence listen intently to the words of others and enjoy engaged conversation; playing games with words; creating stories; rhymes; songs, nonsense phrases; and sentences; and puns and riddles. These children may spin tall tales, ask many questions, seek adult conversation, and play out unusually rich and elaborate sociodramatic themes. They are creative and expressive writers and usually have exceptional ability to remember names and places and to colorfully and cleverly describe events and personal experiences. This intelligence is characteristic of authors, poets, orators, politicians, commentators, and drama and literary critics.

2. *Musical intelligence* is described as an exceptional awareness of pitch, rhythm, and timbre. According to Gardner, this intelligence can often be observed in infancy when, as well as babbling, the infant/toddler formulates musiclike sounds and prosodic patterns and tones and imitates patterns and tones sung by others with some degree of accuracy. Children with musical intelligence enjoy singing and being sung to; remember and repeat songs and rhythms; often hum, chant, or sing to themselves; are curious about and enjoy experimenting with musical instruments; are often eager to master one or more musical instruments; and are sensitive to sounds in their environment. This intelligence is characteristic of composers and song writers, professional singers, instrumentalists, orchestra and band leaders, orchestrators, and sound-track specialists.

3. *Logical-mathematical intelligence* consists of the abilities to attend to patterns, categories, and relationships. Children with logical-mathematical intelligence have the ability to sort, classify, reason, form logical patterns and relationships, discover analogies, develop hypotheses, infer, calculate, and use numbers effectively. They enjoy activities that involve using numbers, counting, grouping, classifying, ordering, measuring, and estimating. These children ask many questions and enjoy what-if and if-then problems and analyses of wholes and parts. This type of intelligence is characteristic of scientists, mathematicians, and logicians.

4. *Spatial intelligence* includes exceptional visual perception, the ability to transform one's perception of visual stimuli, and the ability to reconstruct components of these perceptions with the removal of the visual stimuli. Children with this intelligence are keenly aware of color, shape, line, and form and can visualize spatial configurations and ideas. They have a good sense of direction and distance, pay close attention to pattern, and are often as intrigued by the pictures or types and spaces of print in a book as they are with the story itself. This intelligence is characteristic of interior designers, track and field athletes, golfers, choreographers, stage-set designers, architects, and anthropologists.

5. *Bodily kinesthetic* intelligence relates to the capacities of directing one's bodily motions and manipulating objects in a skillful fashion. It is characterized by refined large and fine motor coordinations; balance; agility; strength; speed; dexterity; and expressive, interpretive body language. Children exhibit this intelligence through their interest and skill in rhythm and movement activities, interpretive dance, finger plays, puppetry, mime, use of the balance beam and other sports equipment that requires precise movement or coordinations, obstacle courses, swimming, and follow-the-leader activities. These children tend to be more "fidgety" than others, tapping their fingers, clapping their hands, and rocking about in their chairs. Dancers, tennis players, gymnasts, mimes, surgeons, and mechanics are examples of individuals who possess this intelligence.

Figure 5.2
Gardner's Multiple Intelligences Theory

6. *Interpersonal intelligence* pertains to the capacity to recognize distinctions among others' feelings, moods, temperaments, motivations, and intentions. Individuals with this intelligence are sensitive to and respond appropriately to facial expressions, tone of voice, and body language. Children with this intelligence are sociable, enjoy the company of others, make friends easily, and are loyal friends themselves. They are skilled in negotiating and conflict resolution and are usually popular among their peers. These children easily accept guidance when it is just and reasonable and are keenly aware of injustices to self and others. They enjoy being helpful. Skilled parents, counselors, ministers, and teachers have this intelligence.

7. *Intrapersonal intelligence* involves the ability to access and understand one's own feelings and range of emotions. It is the capacity to discriminate among and label a variety of complex sets of feelings and to use this discrimination to understand and guide one's own behaviors. Intrapersonal intelligence is demonstrated by the ability to adapt thinking and behavior on the basis of one's own strengths, limitations, moods, temperaments, desires, motivations, and intentions. Children with this intelligence have high self-esteem and a good sense of autonomy, are reasonably self-disciplined, and show aspirations commensurate with their current capabilities. They verbalize their feelings well. These children are introspective and happy with their own company, although they are pleasant companions for others. They know when and how to remove themselves from situations that evoke unpleasant emotions. They enjoy hobbies and often prefer to study independently, but they also enjoy interacting with and helping others. The "community sage" comes to mind as an individual who possesses this intelligence, but counselors, child psychologists, religious leaders, psychotherapists, and, perhaps, novelists who can skillfully describe the inner feelings of their characters also possess this intelligence.

8. *Naturalistic intelligence* concerns the ability to classify nature by recognizing critical distinctions in the natural world among plants, minerals, and animals. This includes the ability to differentiate between ecological, geographic, topological, and anthropological characteristics and phenomena and changes that affect the life and growth of plants and animals and, hence, enhance or impede the capacities of the human organism. Children with this intelligence show an early interest in natural phenomena, bugs and "crawly things," identification, care, and nurture of animals of all sorts, weather phenomena, seeds and plants, and trees and their leaves, bark, berries, and so on. Depending on the types of exposures and experiences they have had, they may show an interest in activities associated with astronomy, oceanography, forestry, farming, health, or physiology. They enjoy describing and classifying natural phenomena and making distinctions between the natural and the unnatural. Individuals who have this type of intelligence include botanists, anthropologists, geologists, astronomers, oceanographers, space scientists, physical therapists, culinary artists and chefs, and members of farming and hunting cultures.

Yet to be further elaborated by Gardner are:

9. *Spiritual intelligence,* which is the ability to relate to the mysteries of life and death and the "why" questions of human existence.

10. *Existential intelligence,* which is related to spiritual intelligence and includes the ability to locate oneself within the cosmos—the infinite—while dealing with issues associated with the meaning of life and death and attempting to explain such life experiences as profound love, awe, or absorption in a work of art or music.

Figure 5.2   (*continued*)

more learner-centered perspectives and content that is driven by diverse student interests and capabilities.

Because a variety of methods are employed to assess all these aspects of learning, finding meaningful and functional ways to assemble and use information about student performance, products, and processes is a complex but important task. Combining all the assessment instruments, observation notes, and student products into some kind of meaningful whole is one of the challenges of a meaningful assessment system. Hence, a portfolio system provides a useful way to organize and access student work and assessments. The portfolio encourages continual assessment across developmental domains and content areas and provides for more flexibility in curriculum planning (Grace & Shores, 1998). According to the Northwest Evaluation Association (Meyer, Schumann, & Angello, 1990):

> [A portfolio is] a purposeful collection of student work that exhibits to the student (and/or others) the student's efforts, progress or achievement in given areas. The collection must include:
>
> ◆ student participation in selection of portfolio content.
> ◆ the criteria for selection.
> ◆ the criteria for judging merit.
> ◆ evidence of student self-reflection.

A portfolio can portray student accomplishments at selected time intervals and provide data for permanent or long-term records of student progress, but it differs from the traditional cumulative folder in the following ways. A portfolio:

◆ is created primarily by the student.
◆ provides an opportunity for the student to select and examine work in progress, reflect upon efforts and accomplishments, and revisit, review, and revise past performance and products.
◆ includes information that is meaningful to the learner and useful in planning for current and future instructional needs.
◆ is assembled to convey student strengths and progress toward developmental and content standards and goals.

It is important to be clear about what types of student products and assessment information will be included in the portfolio. All information and contents in the student's portfolio should be designed to assist, in positive and supportive ways, the student's efforts to learn and acquire skills. Remember, authentic assessment of student learning focuses on what the learner *can do,* not on deficits or comparisons of performance and products with other students. The materials for the portfolio meet the following criteria:

◆ The student products are primarily selected by and are personally meaningful to the learner.
◆ The products and assessment instruments reflect development and/or learning in all domains, in varying contexts, and on an ongoing basis throughout the school year.
◆ The contents of the portfolio are representative of learning in the content areas and can be tied to school or district content standards and benchmarks.
◆ The contents provide a medium for shared meaning between the student and teachers, parents, and, when appropriate, peers.

Reliability of data and inferences drawn from portfolio information depend on the consistency with which the same or similar results are found with similar tasks and show coherent trends when observations or products are compared with previous ones. To establish reliable information and to be able to accurately prescribe subsequent learning experiences for individual learners, portfolio contents must contain examples of similar work in the same domain or content area that can be contrasted and compared with previous items or observational data on an ongoing basis. For reporting purposes or for parent conferences, these comparative data tell a more complete story about the learner's developmental and educational journey. To do this, materials in the portfolio must always be dated and sequenced to reflect the most recent work. Categorizing student products according to specific developmental and content area domains and benchmark subcategories will help to organize the materials and focus analysis and interpretation. Color-coded portfolio files can be created for the assembly of items in specific content areas: mathematics, science, language arts, music, art, social studies, and physical education.

At the early childhood level (prekindergarten through grade three), contents should be representative of emerging development, keeping in mind that there is a developmental continuum associated with the content areas, as illustrated in the appendices to Chapter 3 and in Figure 5.3. It is this continuum of emerging development that early childhood assessment must address. The use of well-framed rubrics—that is, rubrics that lay out a logical evidence-based continuum that moves from some point of origin to an expected mature or mastery level—gives clarity to both expectation and student progress. There is, then, less confusion and vagueness to the "score,"—which is a major fallacy in traditional grading schemes. Traditional grades for the most part score a final product—or whether a student grasps certain information or performs a certain skill at a predetermined level that ostensibly represents mastery. (On a scale of A to F, A equals mastery). When development and learning are viewed as *emergent*, placing a letter grade or numerical score on them is of little use. Most portfolio entries provide evidence of emerging development, as opposed to academic achievements per se. One can neither excel nor flunk "*emerging* development." Therefore, the portfolio and its contents become a "picture story" of continuous child growth and development and the child's concurrent aquisition of content knowledge and skills. As such, portfolios in early childhood education are evaluated on the basis of whether the design and contents satisfy the following conditions:

- exemplify *progress toward* target behaviors and benchmarks and toward preestablished state, district, and school standards
- reflect the various contexts in which learning occurs: culture, home, school, peer group, and individual endeavors
- reflect individual intelligences and learning styles
- reflect individual capabilities and interests
- invite student self-reflection and dialogue
- provide a basis for meaningful mind-engaging communication between teacher and student
- provide a basis for meaningful and helpful collaboration among teacher, student, and parents or guardians
- inform instruction and curricular decisions

Using these criteria, the portfolio can be a rich source of data on student performance and learning processes and a meaningful guide for the development of learner-focused curriculums.

In early childhood education the portfolio is ongoing; it is never a completed product intended to culminate in a final "portfolio grade" or ranking, as associated with some upper-grade portfolios, such as portfolios that indicate fulfillment of requirements for high school graduation, special placement, or college entrance applications or visual or performing arts auditions. The contents of the early childhood education portfolio are forever changing, reflecting dynamic human growth and development as it is occurring in individual children.

What Goes into Portfolios?

Portfolios are as unique as the children they represent. They consist of materials that reflect and describe the child's development. Here are some typical contents:

Infant Portfolios

Anecdotal records - objective observations written by a caregiver that describe something the baby did or how the baby reacted in a situation—how Maria laughed out loud when the sparrow jumped on the windowsill, for example.

Science process skills - a caregiver's assessment of the child's thinking process, such as how Michael uses his eyes, hands, and mouth to observe a new rattle.

Learning cycle - a caregiver's assessment of the child's learning process, such as how LaKeesha finds an object hidden under a blanket.

Language sample - an audiotape of a baby cooing and babbling, with dated sections showing the child's progress.

Daily schedule - description of a day's events written by the caregiver, noting the baby's activities by hour such as sleeping, eating, and playing.

Target skills - listing of physical, cognitive, social-emotional, and self-help skills that an infant is practicing or has achieved.

Toddler Portfolios

Anecdotal records - objective observations written by a caregiver. Example: After Joseph puts on his shorts, he discovers that both legs are in one pant leg. He refuses help, saying, "Me do it."

Scribbling or drawing - sample of the child's drawing with the teachers' assessment of the child's verbal comments, attention span, and level of scribbling.

Social play record - teachers' observation and written assessment of the child's stage of social play such as onlooker, parallel, or associative.

Attention span mapping - a floor plan of the classroom with the teacher's notes about how and where the child spent 30 minutes, such as stacked blocks for 5 minutes, climbed steps for 4 minutes, pushed the wagon for 7 minutes, and scribbled at the art table for 14 minutes.

Language development checklist - a checklist of typical language skills that the teacher has used to assess the child's development at a given date.

Preschool Portfolios

Anecdotal Records - objective observations written by a teacher. Example: When a light rain begins to fall in drought-ridden South Texas, Charlene jumps up and says, "Look, it's spitting."

Logic interview - the results of a series of five Piagetian tests to determine whether a child has reached the pre-operational level of thinking.

Use of scissors - samples of materials the child has cut with scissors and the teacher's written assessment of the child's skills.

Physical checklist - a checklist used by the teacher to assess the child's small-motor and large-motor skills.

Draw-a-person picture - a sample of a child's drawing in response to the teacher's request to "draw a person" and the teacher's written assessment.

Dictated story - a story told by a child to a teacher who writes as the child dictates. The teacher may ask the child to describe something that has happened, to re-tell a storybook tale "in your own words," or to make up a story.

Math assessment - the teacher's written assessment of a child's performance during a series of math activities such as counting objects, following a pattern with beads, or identifying coins by name.

School-Age Portfolios

Work samples - a collection of homework or group assignments, often chosen by the child.

Handwriting - dated samples of the child's handwriting skills.

Journal entries - photocopied samples of journal entries written and selected by a child.

Taped reading - an audiotape of a child reading a section from a book. A tape may contain several reading segments over time that document the child's progress.

Block construction - drawings or photographs of the structures the child has built with blocks.

Jokes - photocopies of the child's favorite jokes with a written assessment by the teacher. Jokes often reflect a child's level of thinking and language development such as knowing that similar sounding words do not have the same meaning.

Figure 5.3
What Goes into Portfolios?
Note: From Texas Association for the Education of Young Children (1997). Appropriate Early Childhood Assessment: A Position Statement (D. Diffily, Ed.), Austin, TX: TAEYC. By permission.

TYPES OF PORTFOLIOS

How can a portfolio enhance student understanding and performance, communicate student and class progress, inform curriculum, and assure accountability? That is a lot to ask of one pedagogical process. To get at how this is possible, we need to return to our discussion of formative and summative data. Recall that formative data are collected on an ongoing basis and can reflect the student's day-to-day efforts or accomplishments. Summative data, on the other hand, are collected from information and products gathered over time and periodically evaluated and compared with earlier data to reveal developmental and learning trends (including indications of progress, plateaus, or regressions) in student performance, products, or processes. Each set of data is essential for both short- and long-term planning for individual and group student needs.

In addition to formative and summative data on individual students, summative data can be derived from the class as a whole by collecting random samples of products and assessment information to be assembled to form a class profile. These collected data are then used to determine group needs and interests, curricular content and direction, and any need for pedagogical modification. Class summative information also helps to establish progress toward preestablished class, grade, school, or district goals. In time, program effectiveness, when measured against grade or content area standards, can be documented to meet accountability requirements.

Thus, we have a three-tier system in which portfolios are assembled according to how they are to be used and what information they are designed to convey. Each tier represents a work in progress that fulfills different purposes at different times:

process portfolio A method of collecting products of and documenting the emerging processes of children's learning.

archival portfolio A portfolio in which representative selections from and information about the student is maintained over time.

aggregated portfolio An assemblage of samples of student or class products and assessments to provide a holistic report of progress toward goals and benchmarks

- ◆ the individual formative assessment process, or the **process portfolio**
- ◆ the individual summative assessment process, or the **archival portfolio**
- ◆ the whole class summative assessment process, or the **aggregated portfolio**

Let's elaborate on each of these types of portfolios.

The Process Portfolio

To follow a student's growth, development, and day-to-day learning, to address short-term goals, and to evaluate current performance, processes, and products, a *process portfolio* is established. This portfolio assembles work *in progress* and is organized so that the student's most recently completed pieces are a place mark.

Included in this portfolio are teacher comments and observation notes, student contracts and self-evaluations, jointly prepared progress notes, planning notes for continued work, and dialogue journals, in which certain types of work are entered and the students and teacher communicate in writing about the work. The process portfolio may include photographs of three-dimensional work, such as block or clay constructions; large items such as a mural or panoramic display; or sorting or classifying activities in which manipulatives are used. A tape recording of the student reading a passage, retelling a familiar story, or explaining a mathematical or scientific phenomenon might also be included. The student places work in progress in the portfolio as needed or required to meet short-term goals and revisits work as needed to revise, refine, complete, or review it.

Sometimes the process portfolio contains a daily or weekly "contract" between the teacher and the learner that gives focus and direction for daily activities and

Figure 5.4
Individual Student Contract (for Nonreaders)

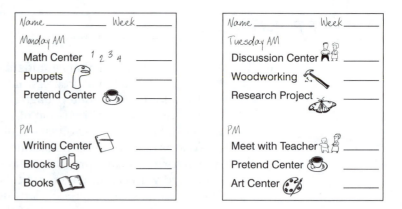

anticipated accomplishments. Contracts can be designed with picture or graphics to be "read" by nonreaders or with rebus or word-only formats for emergent readers (see Figures 5.4 and 5.5). Contracts suggest the learning centers that should be visited during the day (or week), a particular storybook to be shared with a reading buddy, a concept game to be played with a classmate, a special writing project, or an art activity to pursue. During a specific time each day, the teacher can review the day's activities with the learner, checking off the contract items completed and activities that remain to be done on another day or can be eliminated for lack of need or interest. Where classes are large, the teacher may review the contracts with, for example, one-third of the total number of students in the class each day, making certain that each learner is given an opportunity to share his or her work and receive important feedback and support at anticipated regular times.

Although contracts are not essential, simple ones help children organize themselves and focus on selected activities during the school day. At the beginning of the school day, students can take a look at their contracts and proceed to the activities suggested. The contract should not preclude self-selected and self-initiated activity, because these choices are important aspects of development, learning, and assessment as well. For example, as children become more accustomed to the classroom and its resources and routines, they may create individual daily plans and goals. Figure 5.6 illustrates a child's plan for "Rainy Wednesday."

Figure 5.5
Individual Student Contract (for Beginning Readers)

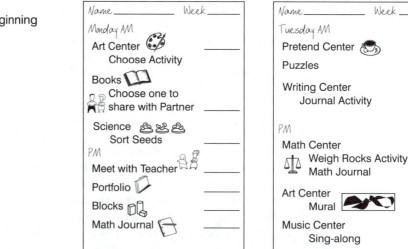

Figure 5.6
A Child's Plan for the Day

Three important points about the use of contracts are:

1. The suggested activities on the contract are developmentally appropriate, taking full advantage of the classroom learning centers, through which strategically selected materials and activities provide meaningful, hands-on, interactive learning opportunities.

2. Contracts are designed to include opportunities for learners to make choices and initiate much of their own learning.

3. Classroom design and learning center content is rich, meaningful, challenging, and connected in relevant and developmentally sensitive ways to the goals and learner outcomes established for content areas and grade.

The accumulation of dated contracts helps the teacher assess, over time, student interests, learning modalities, and capabilities. From these assessments, planning for subsequent learning is timely and ongoing. The contract system also serves as a powerful communicator with parents, who often mistakenly measure what happens at school by the types of worksheets, arts, or crafts that the student brings home. The contract portrays all the other types of tasks and learning that can take place at school and helps adults in the home understand school curricula and expectations. With this knowledge parents and guardians are better prepared to support school learning through developmentally appropriate support and activities at home.

The Archival Portfolio

Students regularly review the contents of the daily process portfolio to make selections for their individual *archival* portfolios or the portfolios from which summative data might be derived. The teacher works with students on their process portfolios, reviewing and revising the work, planning for work to follow, and deciding on products from the process portfolio to be transferred to archival portfolios. When skillfully handled, this process provides a developmental view of accomplishments, informing the learner, teacher, and parent about areas of accomplishment or need and building a sense of shared schooling experiences among child, parent, and teacher.

The student's archival portfolio might include both "novice" and "accomplished" products, notes about how and why each piece was selected, what meaning the products or process had for the learner, student-dictated notes about the choices, and a table of contents. At regular intervals (three or four times during the year), the archival portfolio contents can be assessed for progress toward content area standards and benchmarks and state, district, and school outcome goals; then the portfolios can be shared with parents or guardians in a portfolio conference. At the end of the school year, the archival portfolio can be either taken home by the student for continued visitations or forwarded to the student's next-grade teacher as a portrait of the student's emerging capabilities. (Selected products from the process portfolio can also be divided between an archival portfolio that goes home at the end of the year and another that remains at school to be forwarded to the next teacher.) The end-of-the-year archival portfolio provides a summative report of the year's accomplishments for each student.

The Aggregated Portfolio

There are two levels of summative data. In one, individual student effort, progress, and performance are aggregated and analyzed, as suggested in the preceding paragraph. The other, which brings us to the third type of portfolio in our assessment system, contains a sampling of exemplary student products representative of the whole class. Representative samples of student assessment items collected over time throughout the school year are assembled in an *aggregated portfolio* for use by teachers and school administrators in evaluating program effectiveness.

The class aggregated portfolio includes representative work samples (spanning the school year) from each student's portfolio, along with class summaries, analyses, and interpretations of beginning-, middle-, and end-of-year individual or group checklists, rating scales, anecdotal records, and summary notes from time or event studies. Also included are reports of special or formal evaluations, home visits, case studies as appropriate, and student and parent conference reports. This information can be analyzed and contrasted with expected developmental trends, grade-level goals, content area standards, and expected learner outcomes to determine how the class as a whole is doing. Periodic summary analysis of the aggregated portfolio can guide plans for follow-up, plans for meeting individual or group needs, and goals for ongoing curriculum development.

These reports, then, should serve the need for administrative accountability data and, when combined with required group-administered standardized tests, can place such test scores in a more holistic and meaningful context. At the end of

Figure 5.7
A Three-Tiered System of Portfolio
Development

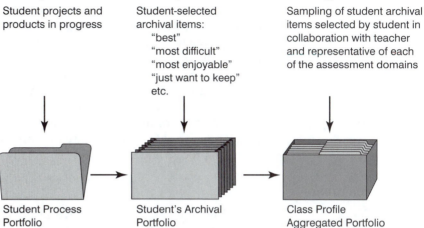

I	II	III
Student projects and products in progress	Student-selected archival items: "best" "most difficult" "most enjoyable" "just want to keep" etc.	Sampling of student archival items selected by student in collaboration with teacher and representative of each of the assessment domains

Student Process
Portfolio

Student's Archival
Portfolio

Class Profile
Aggregated Portfolio

the school year, the aggregated portfolio can be measured against national, state, or district standards, providing additional verification of student outcomes. Figure 5.7 illustrates this three-tier system of portfolio development.

PORTFOLIO STORAGE AND RETRIEVAL SYSTEMS

There is no one way to assemble, store, and retrieve portfolio contents. Methods will depend on the types of portfolio products chosen. Deciding what type of container or containers to use and how to store them to be readily accessible to the student for

Observations of the socio-dramatic play of young children reveals important information about their knowledge and skills.

University Christian Church Weekday School, Fort Worth, TX

use and review is a first step. File folders, expandable folders, hanging files, pocket folders, oversize sheets of construction paper folded in half and stapled, stacking baskets, corrugated cubbyhole units, wall filing units, and uniform-size boxes are some possibilities. If permanent or stationery units are used, students will still need a folder or container to transport their portfolio and contents to their workstation, home, or other places where it is to be used.

Although there will always be a desire and a need for children to create, manipulate, and interact with the concrete tools of learning and to have hard-copy representations of the products of their learning, the use of technology in portfolio development holds some promise for simplifying and organizing the many-faceted portfolio process and can serve to complement other assessment strategies.

Electronic Portfolios

As technology has expanded beyond the computer literacy level and the use of computers for skill-and-drill practices, sophisticated hardware and software are providing innovative electronic tools for children and teachers to pursue an ever-expanding knowledge universe and to store, retrieve, and assess all sorts of student products and performance indicators. Sophisticated electronic linkages have expanded the curriculum borders well beyond the school or classroom walls through distance learning networks and well beyond the curriculum "tool subjects" of reading, writing, and arithmetic into subject and content areas heretofore inaccessible. Telecommunications networks have made it possible for students to:

◆ send and receive electronic mail from people around the world.

◆ access thousands of databases containing information on almost every topic imaginable.

◆ access libraries around the world.

◆ participate in discussions with other students in faraway places.

◆ obtain current, up-to-the-minute information by accessing weather reports, news events, and late-breaking scientific discoveries.

◆ "visit" their family members' worksites or perhaps their siblings' classrooms in other parts of the building or in other schools.

◆ engage in multimedia projects of all sorts.

◆ store pictures, photographs, and video and audio recordings of students and their work.

◆ create presentations of their work.

Multimedia systems are providing new possibilities for assembling, recording, and storing individual student and group assessment data. These new systems allow for permanent storage of written, drawn, and photographed images as well as audio data. Most information that is stored in hard-copy portfolios can now be stored digitally on computer disks. Technological capabilities are such that sound (a sample of a child reading a passage or singing) can be stored and retrieved; images of students and their works can be scanned (photos of students engaged in an activity, the student's block construction, artwork, written work, tests and review exercises) and video presentations can now be stored in individual student electronic portfolios.

Electronic portfolios typically have the following components:

Name and information card with the student's name, grade, and teacher's name. The card could include a photo or video of the student

Table of contents card, which links the reader to all other cards in the portfolio. The contents can be divided into content areas and developmental domains, each including representative samples of the student's work.

Work sample cards, which hold the actual examples of the student's work (the scanned and audio items) as well as information detailing the content or developmental objectives fulfilled by the activity. The rubrics used to evaluate the activity can also be described or illustrated.

Dialogue cards, in which the student, teacher, and parent can write comments to one another.

Electronic portfolio assessment and reporting systems are commercially available and are widely used. Report cards are frequently being replaced by software programs designed to collect and organize detailed histories of student progress—information that can be made readily available to the student, parents, and teachers. Data banks of school or districtwide assessment data provide storage and retrieval systems for selected information on individual students, and modem linkages connect home and schools through electronic mail and creative Web sites. Through these linkages, schools now have the capabilities to conference with parents, share the contents of electronic portfolios, and access needed resources for individual learners.

As teachers are expected to manage increasingly more information, both for curriculum enrichment and student assessment, the ability to use such technology is becoming more vital. However, the use of technology for portfolio development and assessment with young children is in its infancy, and much is yet to be learned about its practicality. The need continues to find ways to economically and effectively incorporate new and emerging technologies into classrooms and to maintain upgraded systems. Teacher training and in-school technicians are necessary to keep pace with expanding technological capabilities. Additionally, research is needed to guide the wise use of assessment-related technology in early childhood classrooms. We, of course, keep in mind that the use of technology with all its promise should never overshadow the human dimension in education—a warm, friendly, mutually supportive relationship that builds between teacher, student, and family when communications are less mechanical.

ASSESSMENT PRACTICES AND RIGHTS TO PRIVACY

individual education program (IEP) A written plan for the education of a student with disabilities that follows procedures for development and implementation that have been set forth by federal legislation.

individual family service plan (IFSP) A written plan of child and family needs, outcomes to be achieved, and the specific services that will be provided. Its development involves the family and must meet criteria established by federal law.

Individual state laws require schools to maintain various cumulative records on each student. In addition to basic demographic information, such as name, address, birthdate, parent or guardian's name, ethnicity, current grade, schools attended, and so on, which is often restricted, cumulative files include a range of information to which access must also be restricted. Student cumulative files may contain any of the following: previous and current report cards; results of standardized tests and other assessments; attendance records; reports from other professionals, such as the school psychologists and speech, hearing, and language professionals; and physician's health care reports; records of parent conferences. Where special needs are concerned, student files may also contain **individual education program (IEP)** and **individual family service plans (IFSP)** and other state- or district-required reports associated with eligibility for certain federal or state funds, such as the free lunch program. These records are accessed legally by school personnel (such as school nurse, psychologist, counselor, or teacher) who have a *legitimate* need for the information and those individual professionals outside of the school whom the parents have authorized to receive or provide information about their child, such as their family physician.

Obviously, a considerable amount of personal and private information can be contained in these records. Therefore, both the law and professional ethics dictate that information about students and their families be held in strict confidentiality. This same level of professionalism applies to files and portfolios maintained by individual teachers within their classrooms. Pupil performance, processes, and products are a matter of individual learner concern and, therefore, are protected from perusal by anyone other than the learner, the learner's parents or guardians, the classroom teacher, and individuals who have a legitimate reason or have been authorized by the parent or guardian.

Therefore, teachers must use sound judgment in determining the contents of portfolios and how, when, and under what circumstances they are to be displayed and shared with others. Given that teachers have always displayed student work on bulletin boards and in hallways, a good rule of thumb is to allow the student to decide which items to publicly discuss or display and to expose no student work that would embarrass or demean the students or preclude his or her chances for fair and unbiased relationships with others, particularly other teachers and school personnel or classmates. A young child's "cute" rendition of a song, story, or drawing may make charming conversation with a colleague or other adult but might be embarrassing to the child and would be considered inappropriate, unprofessional, and potentially litigious.

Special interests and talents are revealed through children's choices and uses of classroom materials.

Nancy P. Alexander

By the same token, portfolios themselves, when not in use, should be stored in a private place, inaccessible to others. If they include sensitive information, such as family issues that have been shared with the assessor, the manner in which this information is recorded (if at all) must be kept confidential to protect the privacy of the child and the family. Information about individual students and their families is never appropriate for conversation outside the context of professional assessment for current instructional decisions. A first-grade teacher, curious about how kindergartner Jamie is going to perform in first grade next year, might wish to ask the kindergarten teacher, "How's Jamie doing in your class?" But such a conversation would be a violation of Jamie's privacy and, therefore, inappropriate and unethical. The first-grade teacher will have to wait until the appropriate records are forwarded to her.

With regard to video, audio, and photographic representations of children and their work, teachers must obtain parent permission to record and use these images for assessment and instructional purposes and must assure parents that these images will be used only for assessment and instructional decisions. The use of electronics, for all its fascinating possibilities, must never infringe on the individual privacy rights of the students and families and should be designed to prevent access by unauthorized individuals.

INITIATING A PORTFOLIO SYSTEM

In recent years the use of portfolios in classrooms has become quite popular. The portfolio process can begin with simple introductions, as illustrated in Figure 5.8.

This initial exercise provides some helpful information about Jason that will guide the manner in which Ms. Mercer interacts with him. She might infer from this limited information that Jason is reluctant, timid, or insecure about being in this particular context. Maybe he has some separation issues associated with an absent

Figure 5.8
Do You Know Me?

Ms. Mercer invited her second-grade students to write her a letter of introduction, telling her anything they wanted her to know about them. During the same week, Ms. Mercer jotted down notes about her first impressions to share and compare with the students. She also wrote a letter to each student introducing herself. These items were the first items entered into students' individual process portfolios and served as a starting point for interacting with students on an individual basis and as the precursor to dialogue journals between teacher and students that would continue and become more focused throughout the school year. Here is what one student wrote:

"My name is Jason. I dont want to be hir. But I think I mite lik it. I go to socer practis today. My dad is gon. My mom works at the bakry. I hop you lik kids. Jason

Here is what Ms. Mercer had already observed and recorded in her observation journal about Jason:

Jason (first day of school):

Reluctant to say good-bye to mother.

Uncomfortable with new friends.

Notices the visuals on the wall and bulletin boards.

Not very comfortable in seeking teacher's help.

parent. Maybe he needs help in learning to approach and make friends with class-mates. Maybe he needs assurances that Ms. Mercer is a kind and gentle teacher who wants to be helpful. Maybe Ms. Mercer can take a cue from his soccer interest to plan learning activities. She now has a hunch that he takes in visual cues to learn, and she has a beginning measure of his reading and writing skills. All the hunches await verification, but they provide a starting point for interactions, observation, and planning. Ms. Mercer will want to avoid allowing first hunches to become her reality; instead, she will want to keep a question mark at the end of each hunch.

Many tend to view the portfolio as an assessment process in and of itself. This is inappropriate. The portfolio is a way of assembling relevant information about a learner, much of which has been assessed prior to entry into the portfolio. In the case of the process portfolio, we are talking about a work in progress, with in-progress assessment feedback to guide the student's immediate and continuing performance. Hence, the portfolio should be viewed as a process, not an end prod-uct, until it can be used to inform summary reports and be released to the student, the parents, or the student's next teacher. However, even then, the process can continue. The portfolio's contents—varied and representing multiple forms of assessment—do not lend themselves to a final portfolio grade. In the context of early childhood education, the portfolio contents are used on an ongoing basis to collaborate with individual students, to collaborate with a student's parents, and to inform instruction. The portfolio then can be thought of as more a "communication system" than an assessment system (Stiggins, 1997a). The following are some guide-lines for initiating and developing a dynamic and worthwhile portfolio system:

1. Analyze district, school, or grade standards, benchmarks, and outcomes require-ments. Establish preliminary short- and long-range goals for the class.

2. Collaborate with other teachers to explore what to assess and how. Think through the developmental domains, the school or district goals and expecta-tions, and content area standards and grade-level benchmarks. Then refine and align short- and long-range goals with them.

3. Some schools have developed their own systems or adopted commercial systems for portfolio development. Become thoroughly acquainted with your system and analyze its elements to determine how well it aligns with your developmental and curriculum goals, mandated and professional standards, and expected out-comes. Determine if this program needs to be supplemented with additional in-formation. If your school does not have an assessment system in place, explore a variety of assessment forms and instruments and put them through the same scrutiny. Explore available electronic systems.

4. Make preliminary decisions about how and when to use individual assessment items, aligning each with your curriculum plans. The assessment instruments may change over time as you become more acquainted with individual students, as curricula emerge, and as you become more comfortable with the process.

5. Get organized. Assemble all the necessary materials needed to begin a portfolio system: Storage units, folders, spiral notebooks, carpenter's apron, sticky pads of assorted colors, index cards of assorted colors, clip boards, assessment forms and instruments, curriculum and assessment planning book with calendar, camera, audio and visual equipment, blank computer disks, and other computer-related software and materials.

6. Collect baseline information on each student as a starting point. Parents or guardians should be engaged to provide initial information about the child's early growth and development, child-care and preschool experiences, current interests, capabilities, and needs.

Infant/toddler portfolios contain anecdotal information along with photos depicting emerging development. For example, note posture, balance, pincer skill, and of course, apparent curiosity.

Lisa H. Witkowski

7. Begin informal and holistic observations of students in the class. Observe behaviors in a selected developmental domain (e.g., large motor characteristics, social interactions, literacy behaviors), observing small groups of five or six children at a time. Then move to other domains one at a time until you have additional baseline information sufficient to determine your starting place(s) for more individualized, focused observation. Use developmental checklists and take notes.

8. List and analyze your findings from these holistic observations.

9. Indentify the target behaviors in your short- and long-range goals and begin integrating informal assessments and student interviews into your daily plans.

10. Develop initial assessment plans for each student. Explain the portfolio process to each student during individual interviews. Begin with a general process portfolio or, for very young children who are new to the idea, begin with a quasi-archival portfolio of "favorite" products that can be taken home and shared. Because very young children do not always part with their products willingly, learning to maintain an in-school collection will be a gradual process. You may need to make photocopies of items deemed particularly significant and worth noting. Eventually, the young child will learn to maintain the portfolio at school. Begin with one portfolio folder (or other storage unit), adding color-coded, content-specific portfolios as the need arises. Keep it simple.

11. Continue to peruse, critique, select, or develop observation and assessment instruments that align with curriculum and efficiently and accurately portray student processes, products, and performance.

12. Analyze your scoring systems (Herman, Aschbacher, & Winters, 1992):

   ◆ Are all important goals, standards, or outcomes being addressed?
   ◆ Are your rating strategies appropriate for their intended purposes (key features, holistic, analytic)?
   ◆ Do rating scales provide adequate, accurate, and objective information that is easily interpreted?
   ◆ Are the scoring rubrics stated in clear and understandable language so that students, parents, and other professionals can understand?
   ◆ Do your expectations and assessment processes reflect current best practice in early childhood education?
   ◆ Are your expectation and assessment practices free of bias and fair to all students regardless of their age and development, socioeconomic status, gender, ethnicity, or ableness?
   ◆ Is your overall assessment plan manageable with appropriate domains and a limited, yet sufficient, number of items or dimensions in each domain to provide meaningful information?
   ◆ Can the information obtained from your assessment instruments and their scoring rubrics inform assessment in other domains (as with the drawing assessment in Figure 4.15) or, perhaps, suggest additional areas for assessment?

13. Determine how assessment scores and evaluations will be used to inform curriculum planning.

14. Make necessary adjustments in curriculum content and pedagogy, as indicated by assessment data.

15. Collaborate and celebrate with students and parents in both scheduled and informal interviews and dialogue. We elaborate on these student and parent collaborations in Chapters 6 and 7.

Archival portfolios may contain photographs of a students' completed projects.

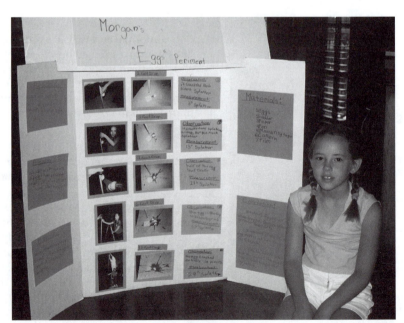

Paige Killian

The development of a portfolio system is not easy; it takes time and commitment. However, the rewards are immeasurable, as we come to value more fully all the processes of learning, focus more clearly on emergent development, and share the joy of each student's accomplishments. Valencia (1990, p. 340) says it well:

> The real value of a portfolio does not lie in its physical appearance, location, or organization; rather, it is in the mind-set that it instills in students and teachers. Portfolios represent a philosophy that demands that we view assessment as an integral part of our instruction, providing a process for teacher and students to use to guide learning. It is an expanded definition of assessment in which a wide variety of indicators of learning are gathered across many situations before, during, and after instruction. It is a philosophy that honors both the process and the products of learning as well as the active participation of the teacher and the students in their own evaluation and growth."

In Chapter 6 we explore how portfolios can be used to focus teacher student collaborations and lead to informed assessments. In Chapter 7, we explore how the portfolio can be used to engage students with their parents in collaborative assessments.

REVIEW STRATEGIES AND ACTIVITIES

Vexing Question

1. Portfolio development and use as an instructional strategy can be time consuming. Its value is without question. An analysis of daily schedules and activities often reveals a variety of superflous and unnecessary time-consuming activities that, if eliminated, would release more time for meaningful assessment procedures. What activities might be reduced in time or eliminated?

Activities

1. Work with a classroom teacher who is implementing authentic assessment strategies. Use the planning format illustrated in Figures 3.1 and 3.2 to plan a portfolio system for one of the students in the class. This should be a collaborative exercise among you, the teacher, and the student. Consider the developmental domains to be assessed and also the following questions:

   a. What kinds of performance, products, and processes will you assess?

   b. Against what criteria will you measure these elements?

   c. What types of rubrics and scoring devices will you use?

   d. How will you use the assessment information?

2. What do you consider to be the strengths and the limitations of a portfolio process? Brainstorm ways to address the limitations you have identified with your classmates and the instructor.

3. Visit a classroom in which portfolios are prominent. How does the teacher schedule assessment activities? What uses do the students make of their portfolios? Can you identify connections between the contents of the portfolios and the goals of the grade or content area?

SUGGESTED LITERATURE AND RESOURCES

Carey, S. (2000). *Working with second language learners: Answers to teachers' top ten questions.* Portsmouth, NY: Neinemann.

Gardner, H. (1999). *The disciplined mind: What all students should understand.* New York: Simon & Schuster.

Gardner, H. (1999). *Intelligence reframed: Multiple intelligences for the 21st century.* New York: Basic Books.

Gould, P., & Sullivan, J. (2005). *The Inclusive early childhood classroom: Easy ways to adapt learning centers for all.* Upper Saddle River NJ: Prentice Hall.

Helm, J. H., & Beneke, S. (Eds.). (2003). *The power of projects: Meeting contemporary challenges in early childhood classrooms: Strategies and solutions.* New York: Teachers College Press.

National Institute for Early Education Research. (2006). State standards database. (Retrieved from http://nieer.org/standards/summary.php.)

Means, B., & Haertel, G. D. (2004). *Using technology evaluation to enhance student learning.* New York: Teachers College Press.

Moss, W. L. (2004). *Children don't come with an instruction manual: A teacher's guide to problems that affect learners.* New York: Teachers College Press.

Stefanakis, E. H. (2002). *Multiple intelligences and portfolios: A window into the learner's mind.* Portsmouth, NH: Heinemann.

Wein, C. A. (2004). *Negotiating standards in the primary classroom: The teachers' dilemma.* New York: Teachers College Press.

Zigler, E. F., Singer, D. G., & Bishop-Josef, S. J. (Eds.). (2004). *Children's play: The roots of reading.* Washington, DC: Zero to Three Press.

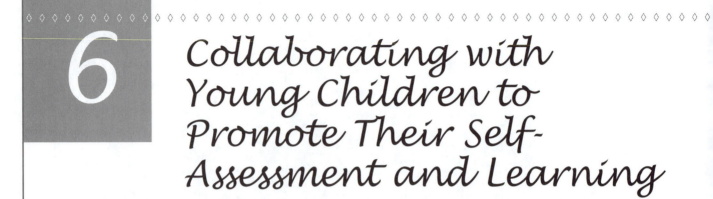

6

Collaborating with Young Children to Promote Their Self-Assessment and Learning

Observations and interviews have revealed that most kindergarten and first grade students rank themselves at the top of the class regardless of actual teacher-ranking. Young children consider themselves "smart" because for them, intelligence occurs any time something is learned.

Thomas (1989, p. 235)

A child's success is not accurately measured by how quickly she learns, or whether her method resembles that of others, but by how well she learns when taught in a manner suited to her needs.

Greenspan (1997, p. 213)

The very process of helping kids prepare to be intelligent reflectors upon their own performance may be one of the most powerful instructional interventions that it's possible to conceive.

Stiggins (1997b, p. 6)

After reading and studying this chapter, you will demonstrate comprehension by being able to:

❑ discuss the value and critical elements of effective collaborations with children.

❑ describe the various processes and strategies that can be used to help children reflect on their own products, processes, performance, and accomplishments.

❑ identify practices that facilitate meaningful teacher–child dialogue.

❑ describe how collaborating with learners informs curriculum and instruction.

SETTING THE STAGE FOR COLLABORATION WITH YOUNG CHILDREN

As the first epigraph in this chapter suggests, young children generally view themselves as smart. They arrive at school eager to learn and to interact with one another. Learner-centered classrooms based on the principles of developmentally appropriate practices provide numerous opportunities for interactions that sustain and support this early sense of self as a competent learner. In classrooms in which children are engaged in meaningful curricula and mind-engaging hands-on activities, working in small groups or independently and using the spaces and contents of learning centers to focus their learning, this view of themselves as smart is allowed to flourish. Opportunities to self-select and self-direct make way for the emergence of Erikson's important early stages of psychosocial development, autonomy, initiative, and industry, further enhancing this sense of self as capable (Erikson, 1963). In such classrooms, both guided and self-initiated learning opportunities expand the student's awareness and insights, and interactions with classmates encourage social development and perspective-taking abilities. Well-executed, developmentally appropriate classroom practices nourish each child's enthusiasm for learning and an unembarrassed personal "sense of smart." Settings where young children are personally and actively involved in varied and challenging pursuits provide the context for an insightful multidimensional assessment system—a system that can broadly and effectively focus on development and learning in all developmental and content area domains.

A key ingredient in the developmentally appropriate classroom and its assessment system is the interaction between the adult and the child (teacher and student) (Hamre & Pianta, 2001; Kluger, & DeNisi, 1996; Kontos & Wilcox-Herzog, 1997; Saft & Pianta, 2001). Carefully building a genuine relationship of trust and rapport entails a certain amount of quality time, in which student and teacher can interact in meaningful ways around relevant topics and issues of mutual import. This chapter explores building time for these important interactions and structuring them in such a way as to benefit both the learner and the assessment process.

WHAT IT MEANS TO COLLABORATE WITH STUDENTS

Collaboration with students is a positive and supportive way to engage individual children in meaningful and developmentally appropriate ways in thinking about and planning for their own learning. Within the context of grade and content area goals and standards, a student and teacher can explore together individualized goals and expectations. The student's reflections on his or her efforts, interests, challenges, and successes can be derived from exploring together the student's products, performance, and processes. A collaborative conference provides dialogue and feedback to focus and give direction to the student's efforts and insights for the teacher's assessments. Collaborations need not be lengthy, but they do need to occur fairly often. Student–teacher collaborations often occur spontaneously but are also regularly and predictably scheduled for focused dialogue and feedback.

ROLE OF COLLABORATION IN ENCOURAGING STUDENTS' LOVE OF LEARNING

There is no question that focused, empathic interactions between adult and child play a profound role in supporting and sustaining a child's typical eagerness to learn and to "prove" how smart he or she can be (Kontos & Wilcox-Herzog, 1997; Thomas, 1989). Collaboration in assessment and planning can shift the emphasis in instructional practices from the teacher as authority and primary source of ideas and information to the student as idea-generator, choice-maker, coplanner, initiator, and contributor to the learning process (Earl, 2003). Student-teacher collaborations provide important and in-context feedback (Pellegrino, Chudowsky, & Glaser, 2001). At the same time, personalized dialogue between student and teacher provides the teacher insights unobtainable in a large-group context. When young students and teachers collaborate, students:

◆ get to know their teacher and their teacher's expectations.

◆ develop a sense of trust in their teachers.

◆ talk about topics or concerns of importance to them.

◆ showcase their work.

◆ receive timely, specific, and helpful feedback.

◆ receive clarifications and scaffolding that supports their learning.

◆ learn to think about and reflect on their products and performance.

◆ learn to make choices and organize their efforts.

◆ begin to learn about learning and to talk about their learning.

◆ learn about the sequences of daily activities and gain a sense of time needed for task completion.

◆ receive guidance for directing their behaviors.

When young students and teachers collaborate, teachers:

◆ get to know and appreciate the individuality of each child.

◆ have an opportunity to dialogue with students about topics and issues of mutual interest and importance.

◆ observe and assess development in many domains, and determine special needs, interests, talents, dispositions, and learning styles.

◆ observe, analyze, and discuss student processes, products, and performance.

◆ answer questions and correct misperceptions.

◆ give specific directions and clarify expectations.

◆ provide instructional support and scaffolding for new concepts, content, and skill development.

◆ help children make connections between prior learning and new information.

◆ discuss and provide guidance to help individuals self-direct their behaviors.

◆ set challenging, yet attainable, goals with individual learners.

◆ help children compensate for skills they cannot master.

◆ plan together ways to work toward benchmarks and goals.

◆ obtain relevant information to guide ongoing assessment.

◆ obtain important information to guide curriculum development toward individual interests and capabilities.

◆ obtain relevant and meaningful assessment information to share with parents or guardians.

◆ collaborate with parents in planning educational opportunities for children.

◆ sustain children's views of themselves as competent learners.

ROLE OF TEACHERS IN COLLABORATING WITH STUDENTS

In authentic assessment classrooms, the teacher does not separate curriculum and assessment but intertwines them into a meaningful, ongoing process. (Revisit Figure 1.2.) Through this process, assessment entails continuous observation and reflection on child behaviors and learning. These observations and assessments depend on close and individualized interactions with students. The goals of collaboration are:

1. to promote student satisfaction in work and learning in a manner that builds self-confidence, self-esteem, and self-respect.
2. to guide students toward autonomous and divergent thinking.
3. to help students focus on target goals for skill development and content-related learning.
4. to obtain information to guide the development of appropriately challenging curriculum content and activities.

Moreover, in classrooms where informal assessments are ongoing, curricula become more customized, meeting both whole group goals and the needs of individuals. Collaboration with students is a key element in this process. For collaboration to be successful, the teacher:

◆ assumes an apprenticeship role in which the child is the novice and the teacher is the mentor.

◆ is committed to shared experiences and shared responsibility for learning.

◆ views the students as members of a community of learners in which shared goals and mutual respect are promoted while each learner is allowed to explore, discover, inquire, and use new knowledge and skills in unique ways.

◆ appreciates and incorporates children's ideas and interests into the curriculum.

◆ is willing to follow the student's lead.

◆ trusts children to learn from self-initiated as well as teacher-directed activities.

◆ serves as a resource and facilitator.

◆ recognizes and respects the fact that learning is not simply a matter of intellectual pursuit but has deeply personal emotional and social elements as well.

◆ recognizes that many ways exist for children to demonstrate what they know and can do and that different intelligences are manifested through different cognitive processes, products, and performance (revisit Figure 5.2).

◆ recognizes that students come from different cultural orientations and linguistic backgrounds and engages in culturally responsive interactions.

◆ provides specific types of assistance and accommodations as needed for children with special needs.

PEDAGOGICAL FEATURES THAT SUPPORT COLLABORATION

The following are important aspects of early childhood education that support the collaborative process.

Communicating Goals and Expectations

Children need to know what is expected of them and how they are to proceed. Recall that in the master plan for meaningful assessments, state and district goals and benchmarks are identified and sequenced to align with curriculum and assessment practices. The collaborative process begins with making certain that assessment goals and strategies are directly and intimately related to developmental goals and content standards and benchmarks. Students and teachers need to be equally clear about expectations. As Stiggins (1997a, p. 458) writes, " . . . students can hit any target that they can see and that holds still for them."

Classroom Design

Another pedagogical feature that supports collaboration is classroom design. The typical early childhood classroom arrangement of learning center spaces that focus on specific content and skills provides the most feasible setting for individualized child-teacher interactions. This setting and its inherent encouragement of student choice and self-initiated activities exposes a wide range of student behaviors and abilities. This setting allows the teacher to move about and among learners, observing, listening to, and interacting in timely ways with students as they work and play. The teacher can join a group or partner with one or two individuals to instruct, coach, model, and facilitate learning. In this context, scaffolding naturally occurs as students seek help and teachers observe and assess.

Daily Schedules

Because authentic assessment is an ongoing process in which students are observed and assessed in many contexts, teachers must first determine how to integrate assessment activities into the daily schedule. Again, practices typical of early childhood education work quite well. Daily schedules are divided into reasonable blocks of time determined by the activities that need to occur. At least two large blocks of time are scheduled each day for learning center instruction and activities. Smaller blocks are used for whole group instruction and guided or structured activities and for the routines of rest, snack, lunch, and recess.

Collaborations with individuals or small groups can occur during these large blocks of time. While students are engaged in small-group or independent activities, the daily plan might include a "meet with the teacher" period, in which a few students each day are invited to independently go over their work in progress, products, or portfolios and contracts or engage in other assessment procedures. Regardless of how the day is scheduled, it is important that students be able to predict and anticipate these collaborative moments. Setting them out in the student contract, creating a portfolio conference calendar that includes both student-teacher conferences and student-parent-teacher conferences, or including the "time with the teacher" on the posted daily schedule helps both students and teachers to anticipate and plan. As appropriate, students can be asked to organize their portfolios in prescribed ways (for example, organize the contents with most recent work first, prepare a table of contents, or write or draw a message about the portfolio to the teacher or their parents) in preparation for their interview with the teacher or an upcoming portfolio conference with their parents.

Scaffolding Student Learning

scaffolding A process by which an adult or a more skilled child facilitates the acquisition of knowledge or skills in the learner through coaching or providing needed information.

The concept of **scaffolding** children's learning is integral to authentic assessment practices. According to Vygotskian theory, learning and development are interdependent. This theory suggests that although maturation influences whether a child can perform certain tasks or engage certain cognitive processes at given points in time, it is the interdependence in which development influences learning and learning influences development that is important. One causes the other to occur. So it is in authentic assessments that we employ aspects of Vygotsky's theory when we engage in collaboration with children to support and enhance both learning and development. Helping children to become self-directing learners means understanding and using the important concept of *scaffolding*—a metaphoric term that attempts to describe adult participation in joint activities with students. Scaffolding occurs when teachers (or, in some instances, classmates) initially provide and execute the major parts of a task or learning event and then gradually decrease their help, allowing the student to assume more and more of the task, until the student begins to feel competent to pursue the task independently, so the "scaffold" can be withdrawn. Collaborating with students helps the teacher to determine if the student has sufficient background ability or knowledge to proceed to each new level of learning. This means becoming sensitive to the child's zone of proximal development (ZPD) (Vygotsky, 1930–1935/1978). The ZPD is the point at which a skill is "on the edge of emergence" (Bodrova & Leong, 1996, p. 38). This concept is important to the assessment process because it expands assessment beyond simply what a child knows and can do independently at a given point in time to what a child can do with different levels of assistance. Bodrova and Leong encourage assessors to note how children use the teacher's help and what types of hints are the most useful to them. By using the ZPD in assessment, these authors believe that estimates of children's abilities are more accurate and less likely to be viewed as dichotomous—that is, viewing the ability or attribute as either present or not present or mastered or not mastered.

Campione (1983, cited in Cazden, 1988) describes three components of scaffolding:

1. The teacher instructs, models, demonstrates, and explains.
2. The teacher and student engage in guided practice in which the teacher gradually relinquishes responsibility for the task, transferring it to the student.
3. The student engages in practice and application.

Through scaffolding interactions, the teacher becomes intimately aware of the processes by which children come to know and do. Through collaboration with in-

Assessments of young children should always support the development of positive self-regard and a sense of competence.

Anne Vega/Merrill

dividual students, teachers converse with them to determine the extent of their understanding and the amount of help they need. Teachers become engaged in scaffolding spontaneously during the day's activities as children interact with materials and with one another. Scaffolding also occurs when the student and the teacher are engaged in planning and evaluating portfolio contents and assessment data.

Classmates provide scaffolding for one another as they work in pairs or small groups. In small interactive groups, children quite naturally scaffold one another as one who has grasped a concept or mastered a skill assists others who need help. Sometimes, the teacher may purposely place students together who can assist one another, thus setting the stage for scaffolding to spontaneously occur among students. Observing these events reveals information about the levels of understanding of both students—the one who provides the scaffold and the one who is being assisted.

Interactive Group Work and Problem Solving

Much has been written about the benefits of interactive and cooperative group activities, group problem solving, and shared projects in early education (Katz, 2003; Katz & Chard, 2000; Slavin, 1991). Even opportunities to argue in safe contexts have been found to enhance cognitive development (Goldman, 1994; Kuhn, 1991; Salmon & Zeitz, 1995). Studies indicate that work in cooperative groups leads to positive student achievement outcomes when (1) group goals are established and (2) each member of the group is held accountable for the success of the whole group. Positive outcomes have been found in the areas of self-esteem, intergroup relations, acceptance among students of diverse backgrounds and abilities, attitudes toward school, and the ability to work cooperatively (Slavin, 1991).

When children engage in shared endeavors that require group problem solving, they learn to recognize and define a problem and negotiate and plan a solution. Problem-solving opportunities occur in both instructional and social interactions and are a naturally occurring part of a student's day-to-day experiences (Diffily & Sassman, 2002). As children gain experience in interactive group endeavors, they learn to negotiate and collaborate with others, to consider other points of view, and to assert their own point of view appropriately. They learn to compromise, achieve consensus, and enjoy the outcomes of shared decision making.

Consider, for instance, students planning, organizing, and collaborating on a project to develop a mural depicting their recent field trip to the planetarium. As these students pursue their work, they are practicing cooperation, negotiation, problem solving, and perspective taking—all essential skills—while gaining concepts and knowledge related to several content areas. As this project proceeds, the students:

◆ recall and reflect on important impressions and concepts from the field trip.

◆ share mutual and individual experiences both verbally and in writing.

◆ establish what the mural project will entail, which involves a number of cognitive tasks relating to artistic components, space, size, color, texture, appeal, message, labels and other print components, and expected final product and social skills relating to planning, cooperating, and fulfilling individual responsibilities.

◆ determine what elements of the project each student might pursue and in what sequence to pursue them.

◆ assemble necessary materials and supplies.

◆ become physically and cognitively engaged in mural construction.

◆ engage in both formative and summative evaluations of their individual and collective contributions.

◆ compare and analyze the relationship of the ongoing and final product to the original experience and their individual understandings of it.

◆ describe the field trip experience and the mural both verbally and in writing.

Certainly not lost in this project are the academic opportunities to read, write, and solve mathematical problems, acquire scientific information, explore the visual arts, and acquire and use new vocabulary.

Observing and recording the strategies children use and the outcomes of those strategies helps teachers to assess individual performance and processes in both content area and developmental domains, particularly in the social-development domain in which social cognition and social competence can be observed. During teacher-student collaborations, children can be skillfully guided to reflect on their participation and contributions to a group effort.

Related content area concepts and skills development can be assessed through both structured observations and interview questions. Progress toward content or developmental benchmarks can be noted. A class meeting can be held to reflect and discuss the experience and its outcomes, providing a valuable culminating opportunity for the students and additional insights for the teacher into students' perceptions of the project and its importance to them.

Psychologically Safe Classroom Dynamics

Meaningful assessments occur in learner-centered classrooms—that is, classrooms in which the focus is on helping individuals succeed (Bransford, Brown, & Cocking, 2000). To this end, every effort is made to assure a psychologically safe learning environment. Such a classroom environment is as sensitive to the emotional and social dimensions of learning as it is to the cognitive or academic aspects. Psychological safety in the classroom is best described as the comfort level children feel in the classroom context—with expectations and tasks, in their relationship with the teacher or other adults, and as a member of a social group (Charney, 2002; Eggen & Kauchak, 1992; Kohn, 1999). Psychologically safe classrooms are characterized by:

◆ **Challenging, yet reasonable and achievable, expectations.** Developmentally appropriate classrooms set achievement expectations within the developmental reach of individual learners while encouraging best efforts and high standards. Teachers are sensitive to cultural and linguistic differences among children and learn about each child's perceptions of school and its expectations. Teachers are alert to the challenges faced by children with special needs and set appropriate developmental and academic goals for them.

◆ **Empowerment.** By allowing students to make choices and participate in group decision making, teachers transfer some of their "power" to the students. Thus, ownership of what goes on in the class and among its members is shared by each participant. The growth of the psychosocial dimensions of trust, autonomy, initiative, and industry are encouraged in such a context. In a community of learners where there is group sharing of responsibility for what happens in the classroom, where class meetings provide opportunities to solve problems as a group, and where solutions are derived from group consensus, students experience the tenets of a democratic society (Developmental Studies Center, 1996).

◆ **Mutual respect.** In psychologically safe classrooms, the teacher strives to create a group dynamic that is characterized by mutual respect between teacher and students and among all students. In such a classroom, every contribution is valued, group problem solving and consensus building are practiced, and learning to accept individual differences and take the perspectives of others is an integral part of the interpersonal dynamics modeled by the teacher and expected of members of the class.

◆ **Freedom from embarrassment, guilt, ridicule, and negative or hurtful interactions.** A major aspect of mutual respect is setting a climate of intolerance of mistreatment of others. Neither teacher nor classmates may embarrass, humiliate, or demean another classmate in any way. All students are treated equitably, and when behavior limits are set, they are fair, reasonable, clearly stated, and consistently applied in a manner that protects the dignity of each student.

◆ **Encouragement of risk taking and freedom to make mistakes.** In a psychologically safe classroom environment, mistakes are valued on several fronts. They provide insight into the learner's thinking processes and their willingness to put forth effort, to take a risk, and to try. Mistakes also provide an opportunity to define a student's zone of proximal development and to coach or scaffold emerging understanding or skills. When a spirit of risk taking exists, student mistakes can serve as intrinsic motivation to continue efforts toward finding solutions. Students need not be embarrassed by their mistakes; indeed, fear of mistakes leads to the manifestation of any of a variety of counterproductive defense mechanisms (denial, rationalization, projection, withdrawal, or others)

In Chapter 3, we met a young gifted reader named Dorsey. Dorsey's test scores were quite high on a standardized reading test at the end of her kindergarten year. However, her scores on subsequent reading tests in first, second, and third grades revealed a declining trend. Although she was proud of her designation as a "gifted and talented" student, this sociable, gregarious, and fun-loving child found the requirements of the GT classes were more than she had bargained for. Her classroom behaviors began to be described by her teacher as off-task behaviors: declining ability to focus during instructions, chatting with classmates at inappropriate times on topics other than the lesson, giggling and teasing others, and taking frequent restroom breaks. She was, however, seemingly obsessive about getting her homework done (although she tended to hurry and was careless), keeping an orderly portfolio, and maintaining a clear and uncluttered work space. Can these behaviors be explained?

During the 1990s, a burst of literature from the biological and neurosciences brought educators' attention to the importance of brain growth and neurological development in infants and young children. Scholars began to translate this research into child-rearing and education practices that respond most effectively to the brain's need for certain inputs or experiences in order for successful neurological "wiring" to take place. Educators became challenged to reconsider traditional pedagogies in favor of more "brain-based" approaches. The research of scholars Renate and Geoffrey Caine (1994, 1997) relating to brain-based learning and pedagogy has been particularly helpful. One of the concepts described by Caine and Caine is that of *downshifting.* According to these scholars, downshifting is a psychophysiological response to threat, which can be associated with the learner's perceived sense of helplessness. It may result from mental or physical fatigue and is stress related. Downshifted learners are less able to use their capacities for creative thinking and problem solving, exploring options, and thinking about outcomes. Caine and Caine suggest that, absent appropriate interventions, the brain can become hardwired to less competent ways of thinking and learning—a process that leads to diminishing interest and success in school.

In Dorsey's case, the implications are fairly clear if we believe that downshifting is what is occurring. Restoration of her interest in reading and learning can begin by removing the high expectations that have been placed on her as a result of her accelerated performance as a young reader. Her teachers and parents need to redirect their ambitions for her in a way that facilitates her ability to tap her own resources in an appropriately timed manner. Dorsey can benefit from collaborations that redirect her energy toward reachable goals and learning to take small steps in accomplishing each task. She will need honest, though comparable, affirmation for her efforts and achievements, because she has come to judge herself on the basis of the GT label. Educators must never lose sight of the fact that young children are not just little academicians. Their needs for physical, playful, and emotionally and socially satisfying interactions persist even when they demonstrate accelerated academic abilities. There must always be room in their schooling for all these aspects of childhood development to flourish.

Figure 6.1
Downshifting

downshifting A psychophysiological response to perceived threat, which is accompanied by a sense of helplessness or lack of self-efficacy.

metacognition The ability to think about and regulate one's own thinking.

and may also result in a phenomenon referred to as **downshifting,** described in Figure 6.1.

These responses impede learning and distort the assessment process. It is far better to help learners value their mistakes and to use them to think about their own thinking. Frequently, we find that the thinking process was correct, even though the answer was not. Mistakes then, can bring about **metacognition,** a very important intellectual process, as described in Figure 6.2.

◆ **Reasonably stress-free.** Research has effectively demonstrated that children in programs in which they are confronted with developmentally *in*appropriate practices exhibit nearly twice the levels of stress behaviors as children in more developmentally appropriate situations (Burts et al., 1992), and have been found to do less well in academic achievement (Bryant, Burchinal, Lau, & Sparling, 1994; Stipek, Feiler, Daniels, & Milburn, 1995). See Figure 6.3. When expectations are developmentally appropriate, communicated in a friendly and sensitive manner, understood by the learner, and supported with appropriate and challenging materials and activities, the issue of stress need not arise.

Dorsey, now in second grade, just took a short test about a science unit on animal habitats. She was certain that she answered all the questions correctly. But when the unit test was returned later in the day, she discovered that she had missed one of the questions. Confidently, she made her way to the teacher and asked in a whisper, "Do you have a teacher's manual?" To which the teacher responded respectfully, "Sure, would you like to look at it?" After turning the pages to the unit section of the manual, she told Dorsey she could take it to her own desk and look at it. After studying the pages for several minutes, looking first at her test page, then at the manual, and then back at her own work, Dorsey closed the manual and returned it to the teacher, saying, "Well, you were correct."

Dorsey was demonstrating an ability known as *metacognition,* or the ability to think about one's own thinking. Although older children and adults apply metacognitive strategies to understand their own cognitive processes and outcomes, young children also do so, though at a less sophisticated level (DeLoach, Miller, & Pierroutsakos, 1998). Metacognition entails the ability to think about what one already knows and purposefully apply that knowledge or skill to a new situation or problem. It is the ability to reflect on one's mistakes, detect the origin of the mistake, and generate possible corrections or preventions. It can entail proposing alternative ways of thinking about a problem and projecting the outcomes of another course of action. In Dorsey's situation, a comparison of her original thinking with that of the Instructor's Manual provided an opportunity for Dorsey to think about what made her thinking (unit test answer) incorrect and then to find agreement in her own mind with the information provided by the manual.

Figure 6.2
Metacognition

Figure 6.3
Signs of Stress in Young Children

Regressions from more to less mature forms of behaving, such as toileting accidents, thumbsucking, clinging to adults, temper tantrums, and impatience

Daydreaming

Difficulty concentrating and staying with a task to completion

Little tolerance for change or frustration, easily overwhelmed

Moods may be depressed or inauthentically happy with silly, acting-out behaviors

Psychosomatic symptoms: eating and sleep disorders, aches and pains, upset stomach, diarrhea, headaches

Restlessness

"Nervous habits," e.g., nailbiting, hair twitching or pulling, scratching or picking at sores or scabs, overeating or loss of appetite

Irritability

Crying frequently

Difficulty making friends and enjoying social interactions

Increased need for reassurance

Increase in fears and preoccupation with frightening things

Speech and language difficulties, e.g., stuttering, speaking too softly or too loudly, too fast, or whining

Withdrawing behaviors

Muscular tensions revealed in taut facial muscles, poor motor controls, trembling hands, facial twitches, frequent accidents, and less coordinated use of pencils, crayons, scissors, computer keyboard, and other manipulatives

Aggressive behaviors toward others

In psychologically safe classrooms, teachers create a climate in which students can demonstrate affirmation and mutual respect for one another's efforts.

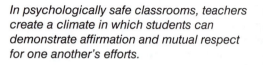

Todd Yarrington/Merrill

INITIATING ASSESSMENT COLLABORATIONS

Most teachers collaborate with children in many contexts every day and frequently go over assignments and expectations with individual students and with the class. In a meaningful assessment system, the teacher tries to structure these important instructional practices to fit specific goals and outcomes outlined in a class (or grade) assessment plan. Assessment in this context systematically focuses on particular domains as identified in the overall assessment plan and utilizes criteria-based scoring and rating systems to develop profile data on individual students. To begin this process, it is helpful to know something about each child's early development and background experiences.

Obtaining Baseline Information

Obtaining baseline biographical and developmental information about each child is one of the first steps in authentic assessment and individualized planning. Baseline information helps teachers to acquaint themselves with children and their families and to plan more appropriately for the experiences they will have at school. Baseline information is derived from parent conferences, home visits, previous records, and initial observations and interactions with the student. From this information a preliminary plan for each student can be developed—a plan that uses information about developmental characteristics and special interests to provide appropriate initial learning and assessment activities. Rapport with the student and family is more easily established when teachers can begin planning for individuals based on knowledge of their prior experiences and their current abilities and interests. Baseline information may include the following:

Important Developmental Information Associated with Physical Growth and Health History

◆ general health
◆ eating habits

- sleeping habits
- allergies, accidents, traumas, disease

Information Derived from Early Screening Tests

- special needs and talents
- current treatment, instructional and service plans, recommended instructional adaptations

Special or Unique Early Experiences

- favorite toys and activities
- special interests or proclivities
- important relationships (family and friends)
- memorable events

Child Care and Preschool Experiences

- age enrolled
- type(s) of nonparental child care
- types of early learning experiences
- relationships with caregivers
- relationships with other children

Family Life Experiences

- family members/siblings/extended family
- home language(s); preferred language
- traditions, family hobbies and interests
- family play, recreation, vacations
- types of discipline or guidance
- educationally enriching experiences
- chores and responsibilities

Feelings About Child Care, School, Classmates, and Learning

- prior knowledge about school
- prior experiences with books, writing, reading, numbers
- stress, fears, or anxieties relating to child care or school
- familiarity with classmates and preestablished friendships
- enjoyment of learning, eagerness to learn, curiosity
- unique capabilities and interests

Parents' Goals, Expectations, and Concerns

- parents' prior experience with their child's child-care setting or school
- expressed hopes, concerns, or anxieties
- congruency between parent goals and expectations and the schools' goals and standards

Using the Portfolio as a Tool for Effective Collaboration

Perhaps the most important aspect of portfolio development is the opportunity it provides for student-teacher collaboration. These focused interactions have enormous potential for enhancing learning through the opportunities they provide for students to discuss and reflect on their work in positive and self-affirming ways. The portfolio process begins with encouraging children to collect samples of their work and helping them devise ways to organize their collections. Once students have been introduced to the concept of collecting and storing their work (both in-progress and completed items), the teacher begins to think about helpful ways to communicate progress and expectations to students and engage them in thoughtful reflection and purposeful planning.

As presented in Chapter 5, introducing students to the concept of the portfolio should begin simply and on a small scale. For example, a strategy used by a kindergarten teacher to collect children's writing activities (both regularly scheduled and child initiated) is illustrated in Figure 6.4. Each child was given a legal-size folder with his or her name printed in large letters on the outside. Stapled to the inside was a sheet of paper blocked into six sections. As the teacher reviewed the writing with each child, he wrote a brief comment in one of the squares, dated it, and shared the comments with the student. When all the squares were filled, the teacher and student revisited the portfolio, reread together the teacher's notes, and talked about each item in the folder. The student was asked to choose one or two writing samples to be placed in the student's archival portfolio and perhaps an item for the class aggregated portfolio for later summative reports. The student also selected items to take home, along with a copy of the teacher's dated comment sheet for the child's parents to read. The teacher's comment sheet (or a photocopy of it) was placed in the student's archival folder for later summary review and a soon-to-be-scheduled collaborative conference with the parents. Writing projects in progress were left in the folder to be completed later. This plan can be adapted for other content areas.

The contents of a portfolio are, for the most part, controlled by the student, but guidance is needed to assure that the contents of the portfolio eventually accomplish the following:

◆ provide evidence of growth and development across all domains
◆ are related to instructional goals and indicative of progress toward benchmarks
◆ reflect events or learnings that are personally meaningful to the student
◆ reveal performance and processes as well as products
◆ assist the student in clarifying performance expectations

Figure 6.4
Beginner's Writing Portfolio

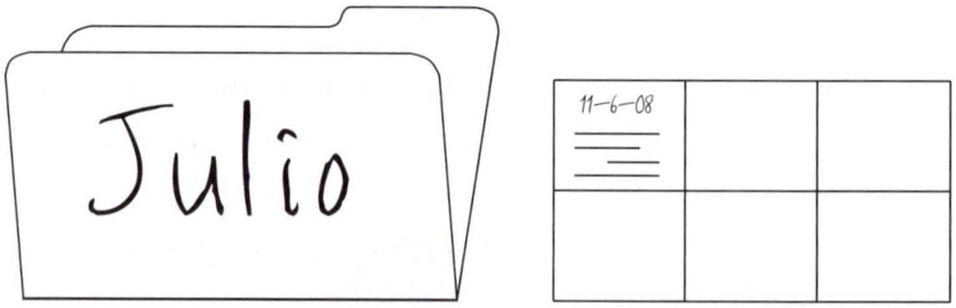

◆ provide a medium for shared meaning between the student and teacher, between the student and parents, and, when appropriate, among the student and classmates

When students take the lead in selecting the contents for their portfolios, their interests become vested and their motivation to learn becomes more intrinsic. Students may choose items on the following bases:

most meaningful
best work
favorite piece
most difficult to do
sentimentality or serendipity—reminiscent of home, family, or significant
    personal events
just to save

During the ongoing collaborative assessment process, the contents may grow to include additional items:

process samples and final products
student reflections and self-evaluations (see Figure 6.5)
teacher's observation notes
dialogue notes through which the teacher and student communicate
dialogue journals
progress notes jointly prepared by the student and teacher
copies of text students are now able to read
content-related structured assessments
audio and video devices (tapes, computer disks)
a variety of student work examples
summary reports (that are compiled and shared at selected intervals during
    the school year)

Student Reflection

When collaborating with students at both scheduled and nonscheduled times, the teacher engages them in thoughtful reflection about their work. The goal of collaborative assessment is to help students become cognitively engaged in their own work and to be able to talk about and reflect on their choices, procedures for doing things or figuring things out, and the products of their efforts. During collaborative interactions the teacher focuses on student strengths and interests, feelings and dispositions, demonstrated knowledge and skills, and the cognitive processes that appear to characterize their learning. Seeking "right" or "correct" answers to the teacher's questions is not the focus of these collaborations. What is important is determining how students think and perceive their assignments and what strategies they use to pursue them. For example, through properly posed questions, the teacher may discover that the student's wrong answers reflect right thinking. This question was posed to a kindergarten student: Which is taller, a grown-up or a child? The student answered, "a child," and then explained, "My big brother is taller than my dad." Questions are often used to open dialogue and foster discussion between the student and the teacher. Questions should be open-ended for the most part and should lead to supportive and

Figure 6.5
Student Self-Evaluation
Form

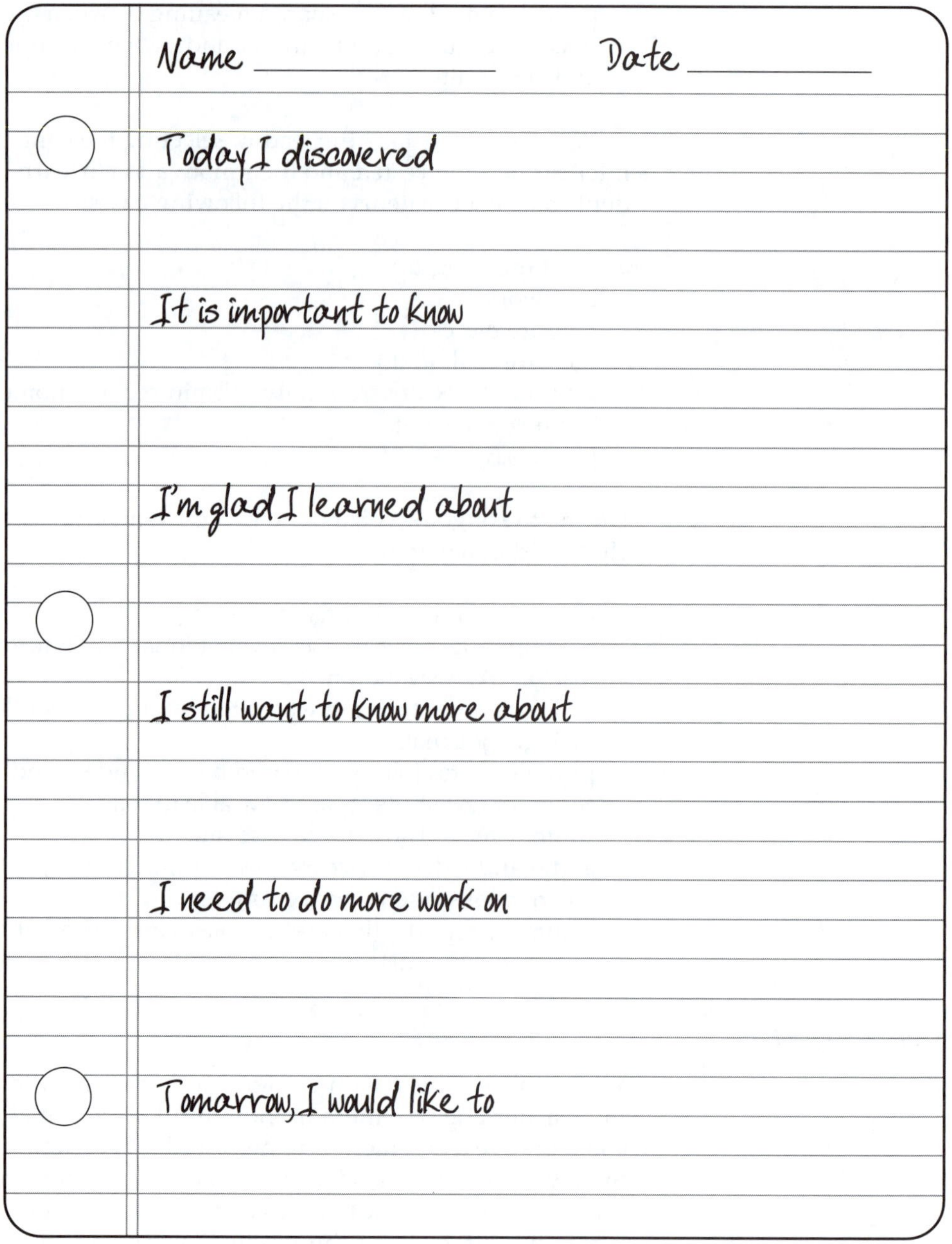

Name _____   Date _____

○ Today I discovered

It is important to know

I'm glad I learned about

○ I still want to know more about

I need to do more work on

○ Tomorrow, I would like to

informing dialogue between the student and the teacher. Questions should be genuinely posed, well timed, challenging, relevant, and focused on the student's work.

If students are to be able to think clearly and talk frankly about their work and their efforts, dialogue with them must put them at ease and convey that the teacher is interested in how and what they think and what they have to say. As well, collaborations with students must be nonthreatening and nonjudgmental.

According to Sigel and Saunders (1979), questions that promote cognitive development and inquiry should solicit the following types of responses:

- labeling (What is this called?)
- reconstructing previous experience (Tell me about your visit with your cousin.)
- proposing alternatives (Is there another way to do that?)
- resolving conflict (There are only two trucks; how will the three of you share them?)
- classifying (How did you decide what to put in each group?)
- estimating (How many pieces of wood will you need to build that airplane?)
- enumerating (How can we tell how many beads you have on your string?)
- synthesizing (What kinds of ideas have we shared, and how can we decide which to try?)
- evaluating (What is it about this writing example that you feel makes it your best?)
- generalizing (We watched ice melt on the windowsill in the sun; what will happen to the snow when the sun shines?)
- transforming (If we mix these ingredients together, what will we have?)

Dialogue should flow naturally from the student's answers and be allowed to evoke additional comments and questions. As part of ongoing assessment, the teacher may later record the types of questions posed during such dialogue and the types of answers they elicited. Inferences are more carefully drawn when questions and dialogue are framed to allow students to fully reveal their knowing. Anecdotal records (Figure 6.5) or simple self-reflecting questionnaires—what I knew; what I know now (Figure 6.6)—are helpful ways to record the richness of these interactions and should be included in the student's portfolio to be revisited in subsequent collaborative sessions.

Just as questions must be relevant and meaningful, so must the dialogue that accompanies them. Students need authentic dialogue with adults that responds specifically and helpfully to their responses, inquiries, and comments. Authentic dialogue involves focused and active listening to what the student is saying and providing useful feedback and suggestions. Although positive and supportive, this

Figure 6.6
Reflecting On What Has Been Learned

What I Knew Before the Field Trip About How Candy Is Made	What I Know Now About How Candy Is Made
1.	1.
2.	2.
3.	3.
4.	4.
5.	5.
6.	6.

approach uses praise judiciously. Inauthentic praise does little to instill intrinsic motivation and undermines the student's trust and respect for the adult's point of view (Kohn, 2004). The following types of responses go beyond the perfunctory and encourage mutually engaged participation in the collaborative process.

This idea interests me. How will you . . . ?
Another way to look at this is . . . .
Another way to think about this is . . . .
Perhaps this item tells a better story.
Perhaps this item shows what you do best.
Perhaps this item answers that question about . . . .
My feelings about this are . . . .
You seem very pleased with what you just did; tell me about it.
I would like to hear more about that.
You seem to be very interested in . . . (curious about . . . , puzzled about . . .).
These are the strong points that I see.
The reason I think so is . . . .
If you change this part, then you may need to think about . . . .
Another way to do this would be . . . .
Let me show you another example.
That is a really good question. How can we find the answer?
This is a difficult task and hard to figure out. You might try _____ to help you get started. If that doesn't work, we could explore other possibilities.
Have you tried . . .?
Did you think about . . .?
Yes, that makes good sense to me because . . . .

Collaborating with students supports their natural desire to learn.

University Christian Church Weekday School, Fort Worth, TX

Dialogue Journals and Notes

As the student becomes more involved with portfolio development, a diary or journal can be initiated that may or may not relate to the contents of the portfolio. A simple diary or log of meaningful activities might start this process and can begin with headings such as What I Do at School or What I Am Learning Today. Depending on the developmental level of the students, the journal entries may be drawings, cut-and-glued pictures, copied letters or other representations, dictations, or beginning writing.

These dialogue journals invite students to record their thinking, planning, and learning and to exchange ideas and information with others. Through dialogue that supports, reacts, questions, and challenges, students can be guided into deeper understandings and broadened perspectives. Journals can be used to enhance just about any activity. Journal writing is particularly helpful in the areas of language development, writing, spelling, and reading. Writing in journals emphasizes writing as a way of communicating and develops in the writer a sense of audience. In non-English-speaking children, journals can reveal their progress toward acquiring English, and the teacher's written responses can provide models for conventional forms of English. Math journals (Figure 6.7) provide an opportunity to illustrate the many uses of mathematics in everyday life, an awareness found to be limited in early childhood and primary grades (Perlmutter, Bloom, Rose, Rogers, 1997). Dialogue journals may be created for science, social studies, and other content areas as well, and for special curriculum activities. For example:

A *research journal* through which students are taught the concept of "research" and its components, including strategies for framing questions, looking for answers, summarizing findings, and telling where to get information on the topic. Figure 6.8 illustrates a set of questions one second-grade student posed relative to his chosen research topic.

A *current events journal,* in which students may draw, dictate, write about (or cut and glue from newspaper, magazine, fliers, event programs, and so on) significant happenings at school, in the community, or elsewhere.

A *thematic project journal,* in which each student keeps a diary of the class project, its progress, and his or her individual contributions to it.

A *learner's book of lists,* in which students collect all sorts of informational, or "hobby," lists: books I have read; places I have visited; people I know; names I can spell; flowers I can name; towns/cities/states I can name; friends and what I like about them, and things I want to know more about; I wish I had . . . , I wish I could . . . , and so on.

Over time, journal activities develop into more sophisticated processes and complex topics and activities. Throughout, dialogues need to be meaningful and focused on extensions such as those suggested in the questions and comments listed here.

Dialogue notes placed in the student portfolio can include such things as:

◆ comments on personal experiences similar to the student's.

◆ questions designed to stretch the student's thinking.

◆ comments about parts, sections, and characteristics of the product that the teacher found interesting, enlightening, helpful, and so on.

◆ an invitation to talk about the project or share it with classmates.

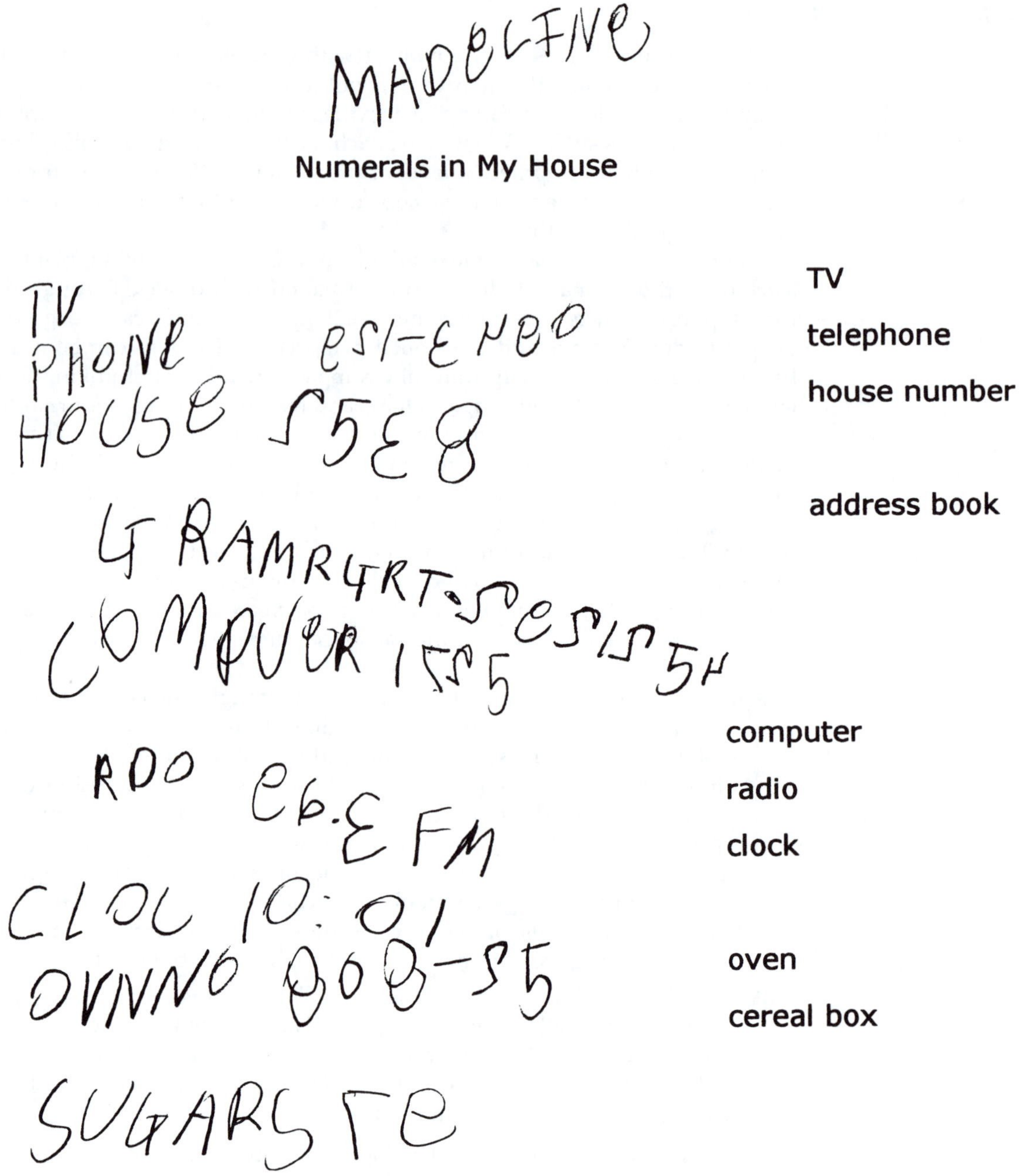

MADELINE

Numerals in My House

TV
PHONE   eSI—E NOO
HOUSE S5E8

4 RAMRYRT-SeSIS 5H
COMPUR 1SS5

RDO   e6.E FM
CLOL 10:01
OVNNO 808-S5

SUGARS re

TV

telephone

house number

address book

computer

radio

clock

oven

cereal box

Figure 6.7
A Kindergarten Math Journal (Teacher's translation is noted to the right of the student's list entries.)

◆ encouraging notes about student progress.
◆ offers to help with revising, expanding, or completing the project.
◆ reassurance of the value of trying, of taking risks, and of making mistakes.

Students may respond to dialogue notes with their own drawings, dictations, or writings. They may wish to respond to the teacher's notes or place short reminders

KATie

My Own Numbers

age   7

birthday   January the 12

number of people in my family   four

telephone   924-fo2ɔ

address   2ɔ1ɔ Boydɔ Ave

mother at work
        address/phone number

daddy at work   3 3 f - 9 4f3
        address/phone number

grandmother's phone number   292-1254

grandfather's phone number   292-1254

emergency phone number   911

time I go to bed   8'00

time I get up in the morning   7:30

minutes to travel from my house to school   5

blocks or miles to school from my house   2 miles

how many cups of water I drink each day   2

how many cups of milk I drink each day   1

how many ounces of juice I drink each day   24

number of trees in my yard   5

number of windows in my house   18   windowɔ

number of stuffed toys in my room   4

Figure 6.8
Second-Grade Student's Research Questions

to themselves of things to do or say. Dialogue such as this leads to additional discussion and, often, further inquiry and should expand the student's range of experience and expose other interests and challenges.

Students' responses to questions and dialogue reflect their level of understanding of (1) the requirements, expectations, or reasons for the work being assessed and (2) the reflective, self-evaluation process itself. It is important to ascertain if students are clear about a required task and what their responsibilities are. Teachers will want to be sensitive to the students' ability to work within this collaborative structure and ensure that the structure provides a psychological context in which it is safe to express themselves, perhaps challenge the teacher, pose questions, take risks, and make mistakes. Evidence of student self-reflection is found in answers to questions such as these:

◆ How does the student go about choosing portfolio or journal contents, and on what basis is the final decision/choice made?
◆ What meaning does the student attach to the choice?
◆ How does the student communicate this meaning?
◆ What observations, connections, and generalizations does the student make?
◆ Does the collaboration generate expanded or new goals for learning?

A summary of student portfolio entries and their evaluations should be completed at least three times a year. Figure 6.9 shows a form for this process. From a summary report the teacher can identify strengths, analyze attempts and processes, decide what next step(s) to encourage, determine instructional and scaffolding needs, and plan curriculum modifications and logical progressions.

Portfolio Collaboration

Providing predictable times for student-teacher collaboration helps children to organize themselves and their work. As students learn to anticipate these special interactions with their teacher, they can begin to collect and select portfolio items and think about what they want to say or do during the conference. Recall the comments earlier in this chapter on the importance of predictable scheduling for individual assessments. Children might be assigned to a day-of-the-week conference group (four or five children on Monday, three or four on Tuesday, etc.). If this procedure is followed predictably each week, both teacher and children can organize and plan for it. It is during these revisits that timely and meaningful dialogues take place; it is also when students have opportunities to complete unfinished work or reconstitute or reorganize their portfolio products. Some items may be withdrawn to take home, others assigned to the archival or aggregated (class) portfolio, and still others brought out for display, demonstration, or group work. Predictable scheduling of conferences with students should not, however, preclude what Graves (1983) refers to as the *roving conference,* in which the teacher captures special teachable moments to collaborate with individuals or with small work groups on their progress and plans.

Setting Goals and Plotting New Directions

Young children can learn to "think ahead" and to plan for things to come; they can set realistic goals for learning (White, Hohn, & Tollefson, 1997). When teachers engage in collaborative dialogue such as has been described in this chapter, they begin to develop skills in organizing and planning their work and anticipating what comes next. These processes help young children learn to set goals and anticipate the next steps. Young children should be involved in this type of planning. Children engaged in setting goals and planning next steps are assuming more and more responsibility for their own learning. A beginning step for this process is to have children dictate or write lists with headings such as the following:

When I finish this (task, assignment, job, activity), I am going to do . . . .
When I come to school tomorrow, I want to . . . .
I want to learn about (read about, write about, draw about, talk about) . . . .
I plan to build (construct, make) . . . .
Today, I will start a project in the science center (art center) . . . .
Next week I would like to . . . .
I don't know how to _____. I will ask _____ to help me.

Figure 6.9
Portfolio Summary

Name _____	**Teacher** _____
Grade _____	

Date _____   *Exemplary items (list)*

Fall Report

*Developmental domains
or learning objectives:*

Comments:

Date _____   *Exemplary items (list)*

Mid-Year Report

*Developmental domains
or learning objectives:*

Comments:

Date _____   *Exemplary items (list)*

End-of-Year Report

*Developmental domains
or learning objectives:*

Comments:

Through student-teacher collaborations, students can share and reflect upon what they know and can do.

Todd Yarrington/Merrill

These discussions and lists help children to think ahead, plan, organize, collect materials, seek advance information, and initiate personally relevant activities. As the year progresses, these projections can evolve into lists of complex plans involving two or more levels (First I will do A; then I will need to do B.), and goals can become more complex and multifaceted. (Caitlin and I are going to draw a spaceship and then make one out of wood.) With guidance, the time frames for goals can become more extended as children engage in increasingly more complex tasks and long-term projects. Their goal statements might look something like the following:

> By the end of this week, I want to have finished . . . .
> When I complete A, then I will start on B. To get started, I need . . . .
> This next step is going to take a long time. I think I will need three days to do it.
> By the next holiday, our group project will be ready to share with the class.
> I want to finish _____ before my next portfolio conference.

This type of planning and goal setting guides and motivates learners. The clarity of purpose and sense of accomplishment when goals are completed contributes to the child's sense of self as a competent learner. Guided goal setting and choice making help children to become wise choice-makers. As these goals inspire both teaching and learning, the collaborative process becomes even more dynamic and generative, and we learn that children's ideas and interests can extend and enrich the curriculum.

Taking cues from student's portfolios, journals, dialogue, and goal statements, the teacher can match curriculums to children's interests and emerging capabilities. For example, Chad, a second grader, initiated a research journal and selected his own topic. His interesting research was shared with the class and subsequently extended into a thematic unit. Chad's research journal included both his own and dictated writings. Yes, students' own ideas can enrich the curriculum for everyone, and collaborative assessments open the windows for that to happen.

Reflecting on Collaborations and Student Reflections

Teachers themselves benefit from setting aside time for reflection. Several tools assist this process.

The Teacher's Reflective Journal

The teacher can prepare a loose-leaf notebook with tabbed sections for each student in the class. Its contents provide a running log of on-the-run notes—a place to put stickies on which ideas have been jotted, a place to write notes that can jog memory prior to a student or parent collaborative interview, a place to record notes that would be inappropriate for dialogue journals or portfolios but can assist in framing the questions for interviews and conferences, and a reminder of behaviors to observe further. In this log, the teacher can record the dates and topics of each dialogue session or assessment event, both planned and impromptu. It is important to remember that this, like other information regarding children, is private information and should be kept in a secure place available only to those who have a legitimate reason to access it. As with all records, the contents of this document must be professionally worded, accurate, and unbiased. Beware: Anything written can be read by others, including students who can read.

A section of the journal can be created in which the teacher records his or her thoughts about assessment processes and how they might be improved to better serve the learning process. After each interview or conference, reflective questions such as the following can stimulate thinking about particular assessment processes and how the behaviors and learning of children are affected:

> What child behaviors did you observe?
> What do these behaviors tell you about child development? Learning? A child's immediate physical or psychosocial needs?
> Are you detecting any signs of stress? What do you think might be causing stress behaviors?
> What can you do to minimize stress at school?
> How does context (time, place, people, physiological or emotional needs) influence a child's behavior?
> What is the social and emotional climate within this group or classroom?
> Are the tasks that children pursue sufficiently challenging, meaningful, relevant, mind engaging, and developmentally and culturally sensitive?
> Are the children in this class developing a sense of community?
> Are individuals growing into a sense of self-efficacy, autonomy, initiative, industry, and social and moral competence?

Reflect on the assessment process itself:

> What glitches or stumbling blocks have you encountered?
> Have any of your colleagues run into these or similar problems?
> What resources do you need to enhance or streamline the process?
> What ideas have been generated for working with and meeting parents' or guardians' needs for assessment information?
> What curriculum ideas have emerged from the collaborations and assessments with children?
> In what ways have assessments enhanced learning? Curricula? Tracking progress toward goals and benchmarks?
> What resources are needed to improve the assessment processes?
> How are parents responding to portfolios, journals, conferences, and test scores?

REVIEW STRATEGIES AND ACTIVITIES

Vexing Question

Revisit the first quotation at the beginning of this chapter. If it is true that young children perceive themselves as "smart," what are the experiences that can (and often do) undermine this self-perception? What can or should be done to perpetuate a continuing "sense of smart" in young learners?

Activities

1. Visit an early childhood classroom in which children are engaged in portfolio development. With the permission of a child and the teacher, invite the child to select and share several items from his or her portfolio. Use some of the questioning and dialogue strategies mentioned in this chapter and those that flow naturally from the interaction to practice a collaborative dialogue. What observations were you able to make?

2. Make a list of your observations of the child's development or capabilities in any of the developmental domains (personal and social development, language and literacy, mathematical thinking, scientific thinking, social and cultural understanding, art and music, physical development).

   a. Without identifying the student, discuss your observations and notes in class. What have you learned about child development in general? What have you learned about learning styles, diversity and special needs, and the connection between child development and curriculum development?

   b. From this brief encounter, can you draw any initial inferences about the child's knowledge, skills, feelings, or dispositions?

   c. How would you plan to collaborate with the child on projects, processes, and performance?

SUGGESTED LITERATURE AND RESOURCES

Charney, S. C. (2002). *Teaching children to care: Classroom management for ethical and academic growth, K–8*. Greenfield, MA: Northeast Foundation for Children.

Diffily, D., & Sassman, C. (2000). *Project-based learning with young children*. Portsmouth, NH: Heinemann.

Donovan, M. S., & Cross, C. T. (Eds.). *Minority students in special and gifted education*. Washington, DC: National Academy Press.

Gentry, J. R. (2006). *Breaking the code: The new science of beginning reading and writing*. Portsmouth, NH: Heinemann.

Hamre, B., & Pianta, R. (2001). Early teacher-child relationships and the trajectory of children's school outcomes through eighth grade. *Child Development, 71*(2), 625–638.

Nelson, B., & Fritschi, J. (2004). Tour, inventory, and retool—Assistive technology for all students. *ACEI Focus on Inclusive Education 2*(3), 1–7.

Parson, S. (2005). *First grade writers: Units of study to help children plan, organize, and structure their ideas.* Portsmouth, NH: Heinemann.

Rose, D. H., Meyer, A. & Hitchcock, C. (2005). *The universally designed classroom: Accessible curriculum and digital technologies.* Cambridge, MA: Harvard Education Press.

Sadowski, M.(2004). *Teaching immigrant and second-language students: Strategies for success.* Cambridge, MA: Harvard Education Press.

Selverstone, H. (2003). Tech for kids with disabilities. *School Library Journal 49*(6), 36–37.

7

Collaborating with Families to Promote Meaningful Assessments

We begin, where we must, with parents. When all is said and done, mothers and fathers are the first and most essential teachers. It's in the home that children must be clothed, fed, and loved. This is the place where life's most basic lessons will be learned. And no outside program—no surrogate or substitute arrangement— however well planned or well intended, can replace a supportive family that gives the child emotional security and a rich environment for learning.

Boyer (1991)

Adherents of the whole child approach do not devalue the importance of cognitive skills, including literacy. The current initiative to ensure that every American child will be a proficient reader is admirable. However, reading is only one aspect of cognitive development, and cognitive development is only one aspect of human development. Cognitive skills are very important, but they are so closely inter- twined with physical, social, and emotional development that it is narrow-minded, if not pointless, to dwell on the intellect and exclude its partners.

Zigler & Bishop-Josef (2004)

After reading and studying this chapter, you will demonstrate compre- hension by being able to:

- ❏ describe the benefits of collaborating with families to promote and assess their children's growth, development, and learning.
- ❏ discuss factors that influence the abilities and inclinations of families to work with schools.
- ❏ describe the important features of a school-family collaborative as- sessment process.
- ❏ discuss the importance of sharing with families the school and dis- trict goals and expected learning outcomes, with emphasis on mutu- ally established roles for supporting children's learning and accomplishments.
- ❏ discuss the importance of sharing with families the various elements of a meaningful assessment system, including classroom based and mandated assessments.
- ❏ identify types of school and community resources that might be tapped to augment the assessment processes.

The full spectrum of developmental progress in early childhood is influenced by the types of relationships children experience between and among themselves and those who care for and about them—their families, caregivers, teachers, and health-care professionals (National Scientific Council on the Developing Child, 2004). To the extent that the many circles of influence (Bronfenbrenner, 1986, 1989, 2004; Bronfenbrenner & Morris, 1998) in a child's life are reciprocally supportive and collaborative, the child's development and learning benefits.

Early childhood educators have historically valued and promoted family involvement as an important contributor to children's success in school. Most federally funded programs for young children require parent-involvement components as a requisite for funding. School and early childhood program accrediting agencies, as well, expect quality programs to have strong family-school partnerhsips. The belief that parent involvement has positive influences on academic achievement and school adjustment is widely held and continues to be confirmed by research (Fan & Chen, 2001; Henderson & Mapp, 2002; Kraft-Sayre & Pianta, 2001; Marcon, 1999; Meisel & Reynolds, 1999; Pena, 2000).

However, the positive outcomes of quality relationships that surround and include the child influence growth, development, and learning in all domains (Lansdown, 2005). The National Scientific Council on the Developing Child (2004, p. 1) states it quite indisputably:

> Young children experience their world as an environment of relationships, and these relationships affect virtually all aspects of their development—intellectual, social, emotional, physical, behavioral, and moral. The quality and stability of a child's human relationships in the early years lay the foundation for a wide range of later developmental outcomes that really matter—self-confidence and sound mental health, motivation to learn, achievement in school and later in life, the ability to control aggressive impulses and resolve conflicts in nonviolent ways, knowing the difference between right and wrong, having the capacity to develop and sustain casual friendships and intimate relationships, and ultimately to be a successful parent oneself.

Past parent-involvement models focused on home-school relationships that provided more vicarious than direct experiences for children while promoting and supporting the larger school needs. Parent-involvement efforts were characterized by parents' (mainly mothers') attendance at several scheduled, school-based meetings during the school year, at special programs in which their children participated, and at fund-raising events such as school carnivals, spaghetti suppers, and sports or other types of booster club activities. The success of these models depended on the extent to which members of families volunteered in the classroom, assisted on field trips, planned school parties and special events, and assisted children at home with school assignments. This model of parent involvement is still helpful to schools and teachers and may strengthen (at least for some) the home-school relationship. However, the changing economic and family life contexts in which children are being raised today and the changing view of schooling that emphasizes not only educating, but promoting, the general well-being of children presupposes another parent-involvement model. This model emphasizes family participation through home-school *collaboration*.

FORMULATING A COLLABORATIVE MODEL

A collaborative model links home and school in nontraditional and unique ways. The goal of the collaborative model of home-school relationships is to engage families, students, teachers, and appropriate school personnel in meaningful and relevant interactions and shared responsibilities. In a collaborative model, parents and educators exchange information through a reciprocal process. The relationship is characterized by mutual respect, in which educators are open to the expertise and insights that parents provide about their children, and parents are engaged in meaningful and relevant dialogue and shared responsibilities for their children's learning outcomes. The underpinnings of this model were outlined a number of years ago by a Task Force on Early Childhood Education of the National Association of State Boards of Education (1988, p. 19), in which it was proposed that parents are purposefully invited into a partnership of shared visions characterized by programs that:

- ◆ promote an environment in which parents are valued as primary influences in their children's lives and are essential partners in the education of their children.
- ◆ recognize that the self-esteem of parents is integral to the development of the child and should be enhanced through positive interactions with the school.
- ◆ include parents in decision making about their own child and the overall education program.
- ◆ facilitate opportunities for parents to observe and volunteer in classrooms.
- ◆ promote exchange of information and ideas between parents and teachers which will benefit the learning process.
- ◆ provide a gradual and supportive transition process from home to school for those young children entering school for the first time.

These broad goals continue to provide a framework for thinking about meaningful and relevant ways to link homes and schools. At the classroom level, we propose that a collaborative model can be based on six principles:

1. shared goals
2. trust and mutual respect
3. shared knowledge of child growth, development, and learning
4. respect for diversity
5. ongoing communication
6. identification and utilization of resources

Shared Goals

A collaborative relationship model begins with establishing rapport with children and their families through interactions that convey mutual respect and shared goals and responsibilites. Early in this relationship it is important to share basic information with families about the early childhood and primary grades program and how each group or class and teacher functions. Parents want to know how their children will be treated, how and what they will be taught, how teachers respond to certain types of behavior, and what is expected of them as parents. Families need additional assurances that their children will be physically and psychologically safe in the school or center environment and that their concerns, questions, and interactions are encouraged. Further, families need assurances that they are welcome in their child's school and classroom and are encouraged to participate in helpful ways.

Initial interactions, whether in a formal group setting with other families or in impromptu interactions with individuals, need to provide information that describes school and program goals, grade-level expectations, and testing and assessment practices. For public school settings, this discussion can include conversations about school accountability requirements as established in federal and state laws and school district policies and what that means for children, families, and the teachers in the classroom. Figure 7.1 lists the elements of a successful collaborative model.

The primary goal of initial conversations is to open communication with parents to begin the process of forming a relationship that can identify mutually shared goals and expectations for individual children. Subsequently, parents and teachers throughout the year will explore together their mutual desire for the child's success—revisiting, revising, and projecting specific developmental and learning goals and collaboratively planning strategies that help the child reach these goals.

Importantly, in a collaborative model, the student is a contributing member of the collaboration. As described in the preceding chapter, young children can take some responsibility for their own learning and can reflect on and describe their learning when given appropriate opportunities. For assessment to be meaningful and to achieve its goals of celebrating learner accomplishments and setting new achievement goals, the learner is the key player (Lansdown, 2005). As we shall see,

---

Collaboration can be defined simply as working together in a joint effort.

Collaboration is successful when it:

- is initiated by either parent *or* teacher.
- emphasizes and celebrates student progress and accomplishments.
- enlists the student's participation and input.
- includes both parents and/or guardians, as appropriate.
- defines what the collaborators hope to accomplish.
- stays focused on clearly stated goals or achievable outcomes.
- emphasizes the shared interest in the student's success.
- is characterized by open and flexible minds.
- models respect, cooperation, empathy, encouragement, support, good humor, and optimism.
- culminates in a plan for the student's continued learning and success.

Collaboration is not successful when it:

- focuses on defining or describing student deficits.
- fails to include the students and to listen sensitively to what they have to say or demonstrate.
- allows either teacher or parent to dominate the discussion.
- ascribes criticism, fault, or blame.
- lacks a clear purpose or identified goals.
- has goals that are not truly shared.
- allows interactive dynamics that are uncomfortable for any of the participants.

Figure 7.1
What Is Collaboration?

three-way conferences (student, teacher, parent) and collaboration can be quite effective in helping children learn. As goals are identified, *all* participants identify and commit to their individual and collective roles and responsibilities.

Trust and Mutual Respect

In line with Erik Erikson's (1963) theory of psychosocial development, the basis for all healthy relationships is a sense of trust. So, it follows quite appropriately that the establishment of trusting relationships with children and families is basic to successful collaboration. Mutual trust is fostered when parental input is pursued on matters relating to their child's growth development and learning and when that input is treated with respect and thoughtful response. When parents are encouraged to share concerns or questions regarding their child's school experiences, school policies, programs, curricula, and assessments and when they are included in decision-making processes and feel that their suggestions have been heard, they come to view themselves as collaborators. Teachers who listen to parents with genuine intent to learn and understand the parent's perspective(s) are better prepared to be appropriately responsive and guide the collaborative process. Enhancing this development is the teacher's ability to listen and convey an open and flexible mind while communicating a consistent message regarding goals, standards, and expectations.

Building a relationship of mutual trust may be difficult with some families and may take more time for some than for others. Berger reminds us that there are parental levels of participation, to which teachers must learn to respond in positive and supportive ways. According to Berger (1995, p. 124) parent participation falls on a continuum as follows:

◆ parents who avoid schools like the plague
◆ parents who need encouragement to come to school
◆ parents who readily respond when invited to school
◆ parents who are comfortable and enjoy involvement in school
◆ parents who enjoy power and are overly active

family systems theory The theory purporting that each family includes members who are interconnected in individualistic ways, each influencing and also being influenced in individualistic ways by one another.

Additionally, and, at least in part, explaining these levels of participation is an understanding of **family systems theory** (Christian, 2006; Conchenour & Chrisman, 2004). It should be helpful for educators to explore this theory in more depth than is possible here. (See "Suggested Related Literature and Resources" at the end of the chapter.) This model helps us understand individual behaviors in the context of the family collective. A systems model describes families as made up of members who are interconnected in individualistic ways, each influencing and being influenced by the others, also in individualistic ways. Family systems theory explores whole family interaction and communication patterns, autonomy and dependency patterns, loyalty behaviors, the sense of being connected to one another, and family ways of handling issues, crises, or stress. As Christian (2006, p. 13) describes, there are a number of characteristics of the family as a system that are relevant to early childhood educators: boundaries, rules, roles, heirachy, climate, and equilibrium, each lying on a continuum. Each has some impact on the manner in which families and children respond to the requirements and expectations of early childhood programs and school expectations. For example, all families have rules, some more strict than others; all familes have boundaries that govern their activities and relationships with others outside of the family; and within every family, individual members have roles with certain behavior expectations. These roles often carry over into other settings such as school and playgroups. Hierarchy portrays the family "pecking order," which is often culturally derived. Ladies first, ask your father (or mother), and deference to family elders are examples of hierarchy within the family. Hierarchy is often portrayed by the one who, at a given time or situation, controls the decision making. Family climate is related to the views that members hold about one another and their interactional patterns. Just as a classroom can be described by its physical characteristics and emotional tone, so can the home and family climate be characterized. Equilibrium refers to the extent to which there is consistency in the life of the family. Equilibrium is present in the predictable routines of family life and enhanced through family rituals and traditions. However, all families experience disequilibrium from time to time due to change in any of the elements or routines of family life, such as extended work or extracurricular schedules; change of residence, school, or workplace; change in the parents' marital status; change in finances; illness; and a myriad of others. Each of these dimensions of the family system is seen in the internalized behaviors of a family's members. Thus, family systems theory helps us understand why members of a family behave the way they do in different contexts (Fingerman & Bermann, 2000, cited in Christian, 2006). Armed with such understanding, educators are better prepared to interact in helpful ways that respond to the uniqueness of individual families and their children.

A sense of trust can emerge when teachers are sensitive to this uniqueness of families. Insightful teachers structure their relationships with children and families in ways that acknowledge individualistic perspectives in order to promote a sense of trust and mutual respect. Thus, both the reluctant and the overly active parent, as described by Berger (1995), can be assured that their interests and concerns will be thoughtfully considered and appropriately addressed.

Finally, families need and are entitled to confidential and ethical treatment of any information shared with the teacher or other school personnel. As families come to trust the professionalism and integrity of their child's teacher and school, they are more willing to enter into candid conversation and engage in meaningful assessments of their child's school experiences. They become invested partners in assuring their child's success.

Shared Knowledge of Child Growth, Development, and Learning

Teachers are knowledgeable about child growth and development and share this knowledge with parents in appropriate and affirming ways. Parents, as well, have particular knowledge about their child that, when shared, provides insights not otherwise available to the teacher. Both teacher and parent share their knowledge about a child in order to set appropriate and achievable goals. In this sharing, teachers may find that interpretations of behaviors and accomplishments may differ, particularly when parents have not had the advantage of formal training in child development and early education.

A case in point is a national survey of American parents' knowledge about early childhood development, which revealed that although parents know quite a bit about child growth and development, there are some significant gaps in their knowledge (Lally, Lerner, & Lurie-Hurvitz, 2001). The study found that adults need more and better information on a variety of topics, such as the extent to which early experiences with a caregiver's moods and emotionality or witnessing violence affects infants' and toddlers' emotional development. The fact that infants and young children can experience sadness and depression is not well known. Many adults fail to recognize that very young children respond to many types of emotionally charged experiences and that these experiences can have lifelong impact on their development. The study found gaps in parents' knowledge about toilet learning, discipline, play, and age-appropriate expectations. The study also found that many parents have misguided notions of what very young children can reasonably be expected to know and do. For example, it was revealed that many parents believe that a three-year-old should be able to sit quietly for an hour—a truly unachievable expectation for very young children. Many parents indicated that they believed such play activities as educational flashcards, solitary play on the computer, and educational TV were "very effective" for helping two-year-olds develop intellectually. Some believed that children's language development could benefit as much from language heard on TV as from hearing a person in the same room talking with them. A large percentage of the parents studied believed that play was more important for five-year-olds than for children ten months old. Of course, play is essential to healthy growth and development in all domains throughout childhood (American Academy of Pediatrics, 2006; Stegelin, 2005; Zigler, & Bishop-Josef, 2004). These and other gaps were identified in the study, illustrating that parents and teachers may have disparate information and thus different views on how child development and learning issues should be addressed.

Meaningful assessments help parents learn and appreciate the unique development and capabilities of their own child while acquiring some very basic knowledge of child development and learning. When the parents' education performance expectations are age or developmentally *in*appropriate, the dialogue and demonstrations that occur during collaborative interactions help parents understand what is reasonable to expect of children within age groups and how to set achievable, yet challenging, goals for their children. Assessments that use developmentally sequenced rubrics (see Chapter 3) assist parents in conceptualizing a developmental continuum. For example, when parents have questions about or express concerns regarding particular behaviors, time-and-frequency sampling can help both parents and teachers assess the context in which the behaviors occur, revealing possible causes and frequency of the behaviors. Such research suggests the level of concern the behavior warrants.

Sharing program objectives and benchmark information also helps parents to focus on appropriate indicators of child learning (assuming that such benchmarks are, indeed, developmentally sound and age appropriate). Each grade level illustrates the level of expectation appropriate for the age of most children in that grade. This paradigm can be used with other developmental and curricular domains. For selected benchmarks, a storyboard or storybook can be created, with photos of children participating in activities that demonstrate the instructional strategies associated with the benchmarks.

Children with Special Needs and Talents

An important aspect of shared child development knowledge is that of observation, screening, and assessment for early detection of children who may have developmental anomalies. In 1975, Congress enacted PL 94-142, the Education for All Handicapped Children Act, requiring states to ensure that all school-age and some preschool-age children with disabilities receive a free, appropriate public education and to establish a Child Find program in each state for children from birth through age 21 to identify those who are eligible for education, health, or social service programs. In 1986, the enactment of PL 99-457 amended this act and extended services to preschool children ages three through five years and provided incentives for states to serve infants and toddlers as well. In 1990, the act was further amended and renamed through PL 101-476, the Individuals with Disabilities Education Act (IDEA). Part C of the IDEA provides services specifically for birth through age two and provides funds to states to develop, establish, and maintain a statewide system that offers early intervention services for this age group. The law basically provides for three groups:

1. children who have a measurable developmental delay in one or more of the following areas: cognitive, physical, language/communication, social, emotional, or adaptive or self-help behaviors

2. children who have a diagnosed physical or mental condition that could result in a developmental delay (e.g., Down syndrome, multiple sclerosis)

3. at-risk children who must experience early intervention to prevent a developmental delay

The latest version of the IDEA, PL 108-446 (2004), continues funding for special education and related services for children with special needs through the year 2011 and supports the individualized education program (IEP) as a basic right of children with disabilities (Figure 7.2). Parent involvement continues to be a fundamental principle, and the law stipulates that parents must be fully informed of their children's rights and their own right to participate in all decisions affecting their children. The IEP no longer must include benchmarks and short-term objectives unless the student will be taking alternative assessments as allowed under the No Child Left Behind Act. An IEP must include a description of annual goals, how goals will be measured, and when and how periodic progress reports will be provided to parents.

The law recognizes the importance of the family in the child's development and thus provides that families may receive services to help them promote the healthy development of their children. Such services may include family counseling or guidance for working with school- or behavior-related issues and involve families in collaborative efforts to design and implement early intervention programs. The law requires that services for young children be provided in *natural environments,* defined as settings that are natural or normal for the child's peers who have no disability. As such, the law encourages a family-centered approach to early identification and intervention and requires the development of individualized family service plans (IFSPs).

Part B of this law requires state education agencies to provide all eligible children ages three through five with early intervention programs. Evaluation of a child's eligibility for these services is based on:

◆ poor performance on hearing, vision, and speech or other screening activities that are routinely administered by school personnel as part of the Child Find activities.

◆ a need to determine whether a student exiting the early intervention program needs available preschool services.

◆ a parent or legal guardian making a referral for evaluation.

In these cases, a multidisciplinary team evaluates the student to determine if special education services are required. The committee, usually composed of an administrator, evaluator, classroom teacher, parent, and other professionals, when appropriate, meets to assess the student's eligibility for services. Eligibility falls under the broad classification of "preschool" or under specific disabling conditions: behavior disorder; aural, visual, mental, or speech/language impairment; or specific learning disability. These exceptionalities are described in Figure 7.3.

*INDIVIDUAL EDUCATIONAL PLAN (IEP)[1,2]   Page _____ of _____

☐ *INSTRUCTIONAL SERVICES   ☐ DRAFT_____
☐ *RELATED SERVICES   DATE
   SPECIFY _____   ☐ ACCEPTED BY ARD COMMITTEE

_____   _____   _____
NAME OF STUDENT   SCHOOL   GRADE
*Duration of services from: _____ to: _____
                        MONTH/DAY/YEAR   MONTH/YEAR

*Measurable Annual Goal[3] : _____   Language of delivery _____
                                              ESL Required   ☐ Yes   ☐ No

*BENCHMARKS OR SHORT-TERM OBJECTIVES[3] THE STUDENT WILL BE ABLE TO:	***INDICATE LEVEL OF MASTERY CRITERIA**	***EVALUATION PROCEDURE**	***SCHDULE FOR EVALUATION**	**EVALUATION CODES**				**DATE**
				DATE	DATE	DATE	DATE	REGRES-SION?
				C,M	C,M	C,M	C,M	
								Y/N
								Y/N
								Y/N
								Y/N
								Y/N
								Y/N
								Y/N
								Y/N
								Y/N
								Y/N
								Y/N
								Y/N
								Y/N

Evaluation Procedure Codes: **Evaluation Codes:**

1. Teacher-made tests   4. Unit Tests   7. Portfolios   C – Continue
2. Observations   5. Student Conferences 8. Other: _____   M – Mastered
3. Weekly Tests   6. Work Samples

[1]Goals and objectives for English as a second language and/or primary language development shall be included for limited English proficient students as appropriate.
[2]Criteria and schedule must allow for determining student's eligibility for participation in extracurricular activities.
[3]Must be related to meeting the child's needs resulting from the disability to enable the student to be involved in and progress in the general curriculum and related to meeting each of the student's other educational needs that result from his/her disability.
*Denotes required items

Figure 7.2
Sample Individualized Educational Plan

Figure 7.3
Exceptionalities That
Qualify Children for
Special Services

A number of different classification systems are used in schools today to specify the exceptionalities that entitle a child to special education services. Because it is tied to access to funds for special education services, the most commonly used classification system however, is that defined in the Individuals with Disabilities Education Act (IDEA, 2004). The following are the IDEA criteria with the definitions (in part), provided in federal guidelines:

Autism
. . . a developmental disability significantly affecting verbal and nonverbal communication and social interactions generally evident before age three that adversely affects a child's educational performance. Other characteristics often associated with autism are engagement in repetitive activities and stereotyped movements, resistance to environmental change or change in daily routines, and unusual responses to sensory experiences.

Mental Retardation
. . . significantly subaverage intellectual functioning existing with concurrent deficits in adaptive behavior, and manifested during the developmental period, that adversely affects a child's educational performance.

Learning Disability
. . . a disorder in one or more of the basic psychological processes involved in understanding or in using language, spoken or written, that may manifest itself in the imperfect ability to listen, think, read, write, spell, or do mathematical calculations. The term includes such conditions as perceptual handicaps, brain injury, minimal brain dysfunction, dyslexia, and developmental aphasia. The term does not apply to children who have learning problems that are primarily the result of visual, hearing, or motor disabilities, or mental retardation, emotional disturbance, or environmental, cultural, or economic disadvantage.

Serious Emotional Disturbance
. . . one or more of the following characteristics [exhibited] over a long period of time and to a marked degree that adversely affects educational performance: (a) an inability to learn which cannot be explained by intellectual, sensory, or health factors; (b) an inability to build or maintain satisfactory interpersonal relationships with peers and teachers; (c) inappropriate types of behavior or feelings under normal circumstances; (d) a general pervasive mood of unhappiness or depression; or (e) a tendency to develop physical symptoms or fears associated with personal or school problems.

Traumatic Brain Injury
. . . an acquired injury to the brain caused by an external physical force resulting in total or partial functional disability or psychological impairment or both that adversely affects a child's educational performance. The term applies to open or closed head injuries resulting in impairments in one or more areas, such as cognition, language, memory, attention, reasoning, abstract thinking, judgment, problem-solving, sensory, perceptual and motor abilities, psychosocial behavior, physical functions, information processing, and speech. The term does not apply to brain injuries that are congenital or degenerative, or brain injuries induced by birth trauma.

Speech and Language Impairment
. . . a communication disorder such as stuttering, impaired articulation, a language impairment, or a voice impairment that adversely affects a child's educational performance.

Visual Impairment
. . . impairment in vision that, even with correction adversely affects a child's educational development. [Visual impairment] includes both partial sight and blindness.

Figure 7.3
(*continued*)

Deafness and Hearing Impairment
. . . impairment in hearing that is so severe that the child is impaired in processing linguistic information through hearing with or without amplification, [and] that adversely affects the child's educational performance.

Orthopedic Impairment
An impairment that . . . adversely affects a child's educational performance. The term includes impairments caused by congenital anomaly (e.g., clubfoot, absence of some member, etc.), impairments caused by disease (e.g., poliomyelitis, bone tuberculosis, etc.), and impairments from other causes (e.g., cerebral palsy, amputations, and fractures or burns that cause contractures).

Other Health Impairments
. . . conditions that limit strength, vitality or alertness, [or] chronic or acute health problems, such as a heart condition, tuberculosis, rheumatic fever, nephritis, asthma, sickle cell anemia, hemophilia, epilepsy, lead poisoning, leukemia, or diabetes that adversely affect a child's educational performance.

---

least restrictive environment (LRE) A learning environment in which children with disabilities are allowed to participate to the extent possible while still having their special needs met.

Services for preschool children must be provided in the **least restrictive environment (LRE)** to the maximum extent possible; where a regular preschool program in not available in a particular public school, opportunities for participation in preschool programs operated by other public agencies, another elementary school, or a private program are provided.

The No Child Left Behind Act (2002) requires students with disabilities to take state-mandated tests, just as their peers do. The NCLB Act lists *protected classes* of students, which include students in special education programs, major racial and ethnic groups (African Americans, Hispanics, and Asians), and low-income students, who may receive alternative forms of accountability tests. This law requires that alternative assessments for special populations be aligned with the state's "challenging academic content standards and student academic achievement standards" (§ 300.160 of IDEA, 2004). Certain accommodations are allowed for these students. For example, accommodations for students with diabilities may include tests provided with Braille text, word processors, or any of a wide range of high- or low-tech **assistive technologies,** extra time, a low-distraction environment, or a scribe. These accommodations help students to more accurately reveal what they know and are able to do.

assistive technologies Defined by Federal Individuals with Disabilities Education Improvement Act of 2004 (P.L. 108-446) as "any item, piece of equipment, or product system, whether acquired commercially off the shelf, modified, or customized, that is used to increase, maintain, or improve the functional capabilities of a child with a disability."

The early childhood educator plays an important role in early identification and assessment of young children who may qualify for intervention programs and services. Their daily interactions and ongoing observations and assessments, coupled with information that parents provide, establishes evidence that is used to obtain services for children who need them. Data collected through classroom observations and assessments can be combined with mandated standardized group tests and diagnostic assessments administered by school-licensed diagnosticians or other professionals to comprise a comprehensive and meaningful set of data.

Through meaningful and collaborative assessment practices, teachers have a unique opportunity to enhance parents' education-related experiences with their children and further each child's chances for success. Studies have found that parents of children with special needs value and more readily become partners with professionals who have knowledge of child development, who can teach them how to meet their child's individual needs, and who can help them identify relevant community resources (Dinnebeil & Hale, 1999; Dinnebeil, Hale, & Rule, 1994). Conversations with

---

Teachers and families help children succeed when they:

- share observations and knowledge.
- learn from one another.
- focus on individuality and uniqueness.
- listen to what children have to say.
- connect with children's interests and capabilities.
- talk about ways to support learning through school and home activities, routines, play, and enrichment opportunities.
- explore together relevant resources needed to address specific needs or difficult issues.
- provide a model of mutual respect and working together for a "good cause."
- celebrate together children's achievements and successes.

Figure 7.4
Collaborating to Help Children Succeed

parents about their children naturally lead to shared understandings of how children grow, develop, and learn. But teachers have a profound responsibility to provide accurate and sound child-development information to parents. Whether identifying children for special services or tracking academic progress toward goals and benchmarks, information shared with parents (both verbal and written) must be based on current understandings, drawing on research-based knowledge and the educator's own practical experiences and objective observations.

Sometimes teachers provide published material to parents or newsletters with tips on helping children succeed in school. It is critical that this material be wisely chosen to truly represent the current science of child growth, development, and learning and be sensitive to differently abled children and diverse cultures. Well-designed developmental checklists and other strategies discussed in earlier chapters provide a medium for meaningful dialogue about child growth, development, and learning and how that information translates into developmentally appropriate expectations and goals for individual children. The goal of collaboration is to help children succeed (see Figure 7.4).

Respect for Diversity

Successful collaborations depend on the educator's knowledge of and ability to respond appropriately to diversity among children and families, including culture, language, capabilities, and circumstances. A genuine effort to learn about child and family diversity is requisite to the ability to communicate and collaborate in a meaningful way (Barrera & Corso, 2003; Kidd, Sanchez, & Thorp, 2004). Further, it is necessary for teachers to acknowledge their own preconceived notions or biases. Teachers themselves represent "culture, language, capability, and circumstance" and as such see children and families through their own "cultural lens" (Maude, Catlett, Moore, Sanchez, & Thorp, 2006). Both educators and families hold views of the purposes and goals of schooling. Recognizing that these views may differ is the first step in conceptualizing ways to collaborate with parents about the education and assessment of individual children.

Implicit in Berger's characterization of family/school participation levels (p. 173) is the realization that families differ in their knowledge of and ability or inclination to access resources through which to broker the schooling experience for their children. Although families generally share the common hope that their children will do well in school, they tend to pursue this hope in different ways. For example, Lareau's (1989) now well-known and provocative study of social class and school relationships uncovered a litany of differences between lower-income working-class and higher-income middle-class family relationships and attitudes toward schooling experiences. These different perspectives appear to hold true today.

Working-class families were found to separate family life from educational institutions. Although they helped to prepare their children for school by teaching manners and perhaps some rudimentary skills, they did not attempt to intervene in their children's schooling, expecting and assuming that the school would take charge of their children's education needs. In so doing, these families depended on teachers to ensure equitable and suitable educations for their children.

In contrast, upper-middle-class families were found to be "connected" to educational institutions and to devote more time and energy to preparing their children both academically and socially for school. Further, these families were more likely to supervise, supplement, and intervene in their children's schooling: hiring tutors, requesting certain teachers, challenging appropriateness of curriculums or grades, and sometimes even circumventing school policy. They formed and participated in friendship networks with other families and teachers, thus obtaining more detailed information about the schools (teachers, administrators, policies, and so on) and what schools wanted from them. As such, their roles more closely matched teachers' expectations and wishes than did those of the working-class families. There was some evidence, however, of increased stress for children whose parents became heavily involved.

Lareau's research found that middle-class parents were more likely to hold college degrees and, therefore, felt competent to communicate about education issues, even when they didn't completely understand the educator's professional jargon. On the other hand, working-class parents—most of whom were, at most, high school graduates—tended to leave parent-teacher conferences confused and felt incapable of engaging in routine interactions with the teacher. In terms of social interactions, middle-class parents viewed teachers as social equals, often thinking that they, too, could have been a teacher had they so chosen. Working-class parents, on the other hand, looked up to teachers and felt the social difference between themselves and "educated" people, often holding teachers in awe.

Income influenced the quantity and quality of clothing, toys, and books children had, and constraints of child care and transportation influenced the parents' ability or willingness to provide at-home school preparation or enrichment and to attend school events. Occupations also placed different demands on workers. Lareau refers to the work-family connections of middle-class families as paralleling the family-school connection.

Work-family connections of many upper-middle-class jobs give employees a vision of work as a diffuse, round-the-clock experience taking place at home *and* at the workplace—which is similar to the vision held by teachers. Parents provide role models for children as they labor at home in the evening and on weekends. Parents also embrace a notion of children's schoolwork as legitimately taking place in the home on a regular basis.

Working-class jobs give the employees a different vision of work—as discrete, time-limited, and taking place only at the worksite. Workers holding these positions have less experience and less enthusiasm for work taking place at home on a sustained and regular basis. This conflicts with the teachers' vision of children's schoolwork as well as teachers' own diffuse work experience. Conceivably, this perspective influences the support and help that children receive on homework assignments and, hence, the teachers' misperception of the parents' level of concern for their children's education.

As for student progress in school, Lareau found that working-class parents take grades very seriously, superordinating them to other indicators of school success, such as comprehension or understanding certain content. They often fail to understand what grades mean in terms of what their children have learned or their rate of progress and can be confused by or disinterested in psychometric measures that are communicated in percentile rankings or grade equivalents. In many of the families studied, there was often little understanding of broad curricular goals. Moreover, their awareness and understandings of changing methodologies lag behind their middle-class counterparts; therefore, they are not as equipped to communicate about or to help their children with schoolwork or career choices.

A later study found that different racial and ethnic groups have different beliefs about child rearing and what they expect from their children in school (Okagaki & Frensch, 1998). In a study of the relationships between parenting and school performance of fourth- and fifth-grade children in three groups—Latino, Asian American and European American—it was found that Asian American parents held the highest educational aspirations of the groups studied, expecting their children to have more years of education than did other parents in the study; they were least satisfied with grades of B or C. This suggests that they place at least as much, if not more, emphasis on effort as they do on their child's possible innate ability. Latino parents placed considerable importance on the development of children's autonomy and on monitoring their children's behaviors and tended to perceive grades as more related to innate ability. Although parent reports of the frequency with which they made efforts to help children with schoolwork were similar among the groups, the study found that European American parents felt more confidence about their ability to help their children succeed in school.

In order for teachers and parents to become engaged in a collaborative relationship in which meaningful assessments can occur, an awareness of the challenges faced by many families is necessary. These challenges include:

> economic hardships.
> language barriers.
> immigration issues such as:
> > immigration status.
> > disruption in the homeland.
> > contrasting views of education practices.

Economic Hardships

Poverty has become quite pervasive in the United States in recent years.* In fact, poverty rates among children in the United States are higher than in any other advanced industrial country. One in six children in the United States is reported to be

---

*To access the most current statistical data on child well-being in America, go to the Children's Defense Fund, *www.childrensdefensefund.org*, and the Annie E. Casey Foundation, *www.kidscount.org*.

living in poverty. Three of five of these children are living in extreme poverty. Many of these families have incomes that are less than $8,000 a year. Poverty exists disproportionately among African American and Hispanic families, who are three times as likely to be poor as non-Hispanic white children (Children's Defense Fund, 2006). At least a fourth of all young children of immigrant parents live in households with incomes below the federal poverty level (Matthews & Ewen, 2006).

It is projected that a majority of Americans will experience poverty at some point during their adult lives (Children's Defense Fund, 2006). Poverty may last for only a short time for some, but for others, poverty can persist throughout childhood and into adult life. A review of research on the association between the timing and duration of poverty on children and children's health, achievement, and behavior found that children who live in extreme poverty or who remain poor over an extended period of time appear to suffer the most deleterious outcomes (Brooks-Gunn & Duncan, 1997). This research suggests that poverty during early childhood can have a greater effect on children than poverty experienced only during later childhood years.

Children living in poverty are at risk for poor health associated with inadequate nutrition, limited health care, and crowded and often substandard living conditions. Children living in families with incomes that are less than $15,000 are twenty-two times more likely to be abused or neglected than children whose family income is greater than $30,000 (Children's Defense Fund, 2006). Compared with nonpoor children, children living in poverty are more likely to suffer a variety of health issues, such as anemias and stunted growth, vision and hearing problems, and physical and mental disabilities, and are more susceptible to diseases such as asthma and pneumonia. Poverty places children at greater risk of falling behind in school (Lennon, 2002).

These children have lower achievement scores on standardized tests, exhibit more learning disabilities and below-grade-level achievements, are more often placed in special education classes, and are more likely to drop out of school during adolescence (Children's Defense Fund, 2006; Sherman, 1997). One study found that children from very low-income families knew only one-fourth the number of words as children the same age from other families (Hart & Risley 1995). Another study found large differences by race and ethnicity in children's test scores when they began kindergarten, finding that before kindergarten, the average cognitive score of children in highest socioeconomic status (SES) groups was 60 percent above the lowest SES group. Additionally the study found that the average math achievement was 21 percent lower for African American children than for white children and 19 percent lower for Hispanic children (Lee & Burkam, 2002).

Not all children living in poverty are so predisposed; indeed, many manage to do quite well socially and academically. Nevertheless, educators who are aware of and sensitive to the life realities of children of meager means are better equipped to relate in appropriate ways to children and their families and plan for their needs for an enriched and remedial education. They understand that some families may not be able to participate in the life of the school to the extent that other families do and avoid further disadvantaging these families through their own expectations and actions. These parents may not know how to seek the best advantages for their children in terms of placement, tutoring, special enrichment programs, and free or reduced-cost school nutrition programs. Families with limited education and resources may not be able to assist their children with homework or provide appropriate print and creativity materials, computer access, or other educationally enriching experiences typically available to more-advantaged families and typically valued by middle-class teachers. Some may be financially unable to provide needed school supplies, appropriate clothing or fees for special events or activities, or transportation to off-campus events. In such situations, teachers can become child advocates, who work with parents to identify and access school- and community-based resources.

Language Barriers

Chapter 2 described the increasing number of different languages spoken by children enrolled in Head Start and other early childhood education programs (see the box on p. 33). It has been reported that more than 460 languages are spoken by English-language learners in the United States (Hepburn, 2004), and in the United States, the largest population of non-English-speaking students is Hispanic (Abedi, Hofstetter, & Lord, 2004). Ideally, children who do not speak English would be taught by a teacher who is fluent in the child's native language. Given the many different languages of today's school population, however, many children will not have a teacher who speaks their language. Revisit NAEYC Recommendations on Screening and Assessment of Young English-Language Learners (Figure 2.3.).

Depending on several factors—the dominant language spoken in the home, family language preferences, length of time in the United States, and amount and quality of English-language coaching or tutoring—children enter school with varying levels of and motivations to acquire English-language proficiency. Thus, the length of time it takes for children to acquire proficiency in English will also vary. Assessment of language development and English-language acquisition must take these factors into consideration.

Regardless of nativity, language development during early childhood plays a critical and dynamic role in learning. Language is intimately and interactively related to cognitive development (Piaget, 1926; 1952; 1963; Vygotsky, 1934/1962; 1930–1935/1978). Language allows us to express and share feelings, emotions, and ideas; to record history; and to project and plan for the future. Language has both verbal and nonverbal properties that are expressed differently in various cultural groups (Otto, 2006). In short, culture and language are mutually and simultaneously derived, and linguistic expression is unique and often idiosyncratic between and among members of diverse cultures.

Vygotskian theory proposes that language is a "tool of the mind" (Vygotsky, 1934/1962; 1930–1935/1978). As such, language plays a major role in cognitive development because it provides a mechanism for thinking. During infancy, before language has begun to emerge, concrete objects and firsthand experiences provide the impetus for the formation of mental concepts and schemes (Piaget, 1963). As language emerges, children can use these concepts and schemes to think, to frame ideas, to imagine, and to enhance their understanding of their experiences and of life around them. Language makes it possible for children to convey their needs; share ideas; ask and answer questions; and generally participate in social, emotional, and academic discourse. Language helps children think about and modulate their emotions and self-regulate their behaviors. Through language, learners create strategies for mastery of a variety of mental functions, including learning to mentally focus, sustain attention, remember, recall, process new information, problem solve, and develop reasoning ability and a sense of logic.

The intimate linkage between culture, language, and cognitive development and the mutual dependence of cognition and language on one another make it imperative that young children have ample opportunity to become proficient in

simultaneous bilingualism
The process of learning two languages at the same time, beginning at birth.

multilinguilism Proficiency in three or more languages.

successive (or sequential) bilingualism The process of learning a second language after acquiring proficiency in a first language.

metalinguistic awareness The ability to think about the forms and meanings of language.

receptive language Language that is comprehended but not necessarily produced.

preproductive language Earliest attempts to communicate (vocalizations and imitations of speech sounds, pointing, gesturing, facial expressions and other body language).

expressive language Oral communication; spoken language.

their native language. However, some children are exposed from infancy to two or more languages; thus, **simultaneous bilingualism** or **multilingualism** occurs. Reviews of research in first- and second-language acquisition have concluded that the level of proficiency in a child's native language (where only one language is spoken in the home) directly influences the ability to become proficient in a second language (Lewelling, 1992). This is referred to as **successive bilingualism,** where a second language is learned after the age of three (Otto, 2006). Because of the complexity of learning more than one lexicon at a time, children growing up learning more than one language may be somewhat delayed in their vocabulary development in each of the languages. However, these children often have more advanced **metalinguistic awareness** than monolingual children; that is, they can think about the linguistic nuances of different languages (Gleason, 1997).

In assessing second-language learning and acquisition, teachers need to observe children's natural language behavior in a variety of contexts, such as communication with family members, nonverbal behaviors and interaction with other children and with teachers, peer talk in lunchrooms and playgrounds, and the nature and themes of pretend play, as well as observing children's dictations and written work and other approaches to learning. This ongoing observation of natural language behavior in a variety of contexts throughout the school day reveals capabilities not typically identified by formal language proficiency tests. Through these naturalistic observations, teachers are able to document indicators of both first- and second-language acquisition as it progresses along a developmental trajectory from **receptive** and **preproductive language** to **expressive language** that evolves from early productions to fluency.

Clearly, language development and its relationship to learning is a crucial assessment domain and an area for which early childhood education makes an important contribution (Haskins & Rouse, 2005; Otto, 2006; Takanishi, 2004). Indeed, it is a place where early education *must* make an important contribution (Hart & Risley, 1995; Shonkoff & Phillips, 2000). Assessing the language development of children whose native language is not English involves learning about and appreciating the cultural contexts in which language is learned in the home, community, school, and classroom and the challenges associated with learning a second language.

Often, a language—for example, the language of Cambodians, Thai, and Laotians—has little relationship to the English-language system or to the Roman alphabet. Some languages, such as that of Creole-speaking Haitians and the Hmong, have been codified only within the past fifty years or less (Kellogg, 1988). Some immigrant families may not have had the opportunity to acquire their own native written language before entering a new country, having relied primarily on an oral tradition.

Assessment practices must consider the difficulty of acquiring a language that is significantly different from one's first language in semantic, syntactic, phonetic, morphemic, or pragmatic features. Children attempting to learn a language that is quite dissimilar from their own will have more difficulty than they would if they were attempting to learn a new language that has similarities. For example, the romance languages of French and Spanish have similar features, whereas Japanese and Spanish are very dissimilar.

Adding to the challenges faced by children with limited English proficiency is the fact that some families may not access available support systems, such as interpreters, tutoring, English-language classes, or school-based bilingual or English as a Second Language (ESL) classes for their children; thus, the children may have difficulty acquiring essential communication skills. Many children and families experience prejudice due to their inability to speak English.

Again, classroom teachers play an important role in assessing early language development and helping non-English-speaking children and families identify and access available resources. Children and families benefit from resources that help them both encourage and facilitate their children's native-language development and acquire proficiency in standard American English (SAE).

The No Child Left Behind Act of 2002 sets forth provisions about administration of mandated state or district accountability tests to children with limited English proficiency. Key provisions of the NCLB law are stated in Titles I and III, which require schools to improve the performance of limited English proficient (LEP) students in reading and mathematics beginning in third grade. As with children enrolled in special education classes, children with limited English proficiency are included in the protected classes of children defined by the U.S. Department of Education for testing required by the NCLB Act.

The law requires that states be held accountable for improving English proficiency on an annual basis, with the goal of LEP students being able to meet the same standards expected of all students. Though LEP students are required to learn the same content and are to be held to the same accountability levels as other students, the law allows for some flexibility. States and school districts may develop specific assessments of English proficiency and alternative assessments in children's native languages and may provide certain accommodations on English-language tests to facilitate accurate measures of LEP student performance. The law requires that to the extent practicable, communications with parents regarding student assessments be in the languages that the parents speak.

Immigration Issues

High rates of immigration into the United States in recent years places greater responsibility on educators to understand the challenges many families encounter as they integrate themselves into a new cultural milieu. Conditions associated with immigration groups can help explain the complex social and educational realities that newcomers experience in the United States. Their unique perspectives on schooling often challenge our assumptions about families, about how educators and families should relate, and about what we can or should expect of their children.

Undocumented Immigrant Status   Families and children of undocumented immigrant status deal with long-term stress associated with unsuccessful attempts to enter the country as legal immigrants, separation from their families, and, sometimes, dangerous circumstances.* Although the Supreme Court ruled in 1982 in *Plyer v. Doe* that states must educate the children of undocumented families, sometimes these families delay or avoid interactions with school personnel. In

---

*As this book goes to press, Congress is considering changes to current immigration laws. Several bills before Congress offer different points of view regarding the rights of undocumented persons living and working in the United States. Educators will need to assess the impact of new immigration laws on children and families.

school, these children are often fearful of revealing information that could jeopardize their families and possibly lead to deportation. These fears, combined with economic pressures, the necessity to move frequently, and the hesitancy of parents to become involved with teachers or the school, create an often overwhelming state of existence for the children of immigrant families. Again, educators who use mainstream populations as their frame of reference may mistakenly view these parents as disinterested or irresponsible and their children as withdrawn or, perhaps, defiant.

Contrasting Education Practices   In addition to language barriers, immigrant families have had prior experiences with educational systems that differ from those in the United States. Many immigrant children have experienced schooling that is more didactic than what is common in American schools; that is, they may have been judged on their rote memory and recitations. They may have been in school settings where teachers' authority is strict and unquestioned. They may have experienced schools in which books, paper, and pencil were not classroom staples, as they are in American schools. For some children, political indoctrination may have been the main course of study. They may find their new schools disorienting and unsettling as they encounter more democratic approaches; informal interactions among teachers and children; and unfamiliar teaching strategies, such as self-initiated learning, interactive groups and cooperative group projects, play, creative expression, physical education, and field trips.

Oppression by the Dominant Society   Children and families who have lived with a sense of disenfranchisement and powerlessness in their homelands may relate to education institutions in fearful, negative, or even futilistic ways. Their behaviors often militate against positive social adjustment and school success. Educators, in turn, sometimes respond on the basis of false assumptions about the interests and abilities of immigrant children and families to assimilate, to participate effectively in the education process, or to value learning. There is ample evidence to the contrary, however (Behrman, 2004).

Disruption in the Homeland   Some immigrants may have experienced years of war, political oppression, or social and political instability in their homelands. Or, after becoming residents of the United States, they may be burdened by uprisings, wars, or natural disasters in their homeland, where family members and friends remain. These conditions create anxieties and psychological trauma that compound the adjustment process for all members of the family, both children and adults.

Clearly, members of families who have immigrated to the United States face complex and diverse challenges. Some families navigate these challenges quite well, with few or no school-related issues. Others may experience greater difficulty. Teachers should anticipate various types of behaviors indicative of issues associated with learning to live in a new country. Children's behaviors often reflect the existence of family challenges. Timidity, acting-out behaviors, anxieties, fears, inattention, frustrations, and anger may be related to the child's and family's efforts to adapt. Misperceptions and miscommunications can arise due to language differences and nuances of nonverbal behaviors. Awareness of these possibilities should motivate teachers to expand their knowledge of the cultures immigrant families represent and to plan for culturally sensitive and responsive classroom practices and interactions with families (Gay, 2000; Obegi & Ritblatt, 2005). See Kem's Story in Figure 7.5.

Teachers and families help children succeed when they connect with children's interests.

Nancy P. Alexander

Figure 7.5
Kem's Story

The authors are reminded of a first-day-of-school encounter with a young and frightened mother of a five-year-old just entering kindergarten. The family had been in the United States only five weeks, having just arrived from their homeland, Korea. Neither mother nor child spoke English, except for a few sentences and phrases they recently had been taught. As the kindergarten teacher circulated among her new enrollees and their parents, greeting and welcoming each one before the school day would formally commence, she noticed the young, frightened mother at a distance from others and hovering in a classroom corner, positioned so that she seemed to be shielding her child. Compassionately and as unobtrusively as possible, the teacher made her way toward the mother and child. She smiled, but before she could say "Welcome," the mother's tearful eyes looked up, her arms wrapped protectively around her little girl, and recited; "This my child; be good to her."

The Korean child, whom we shall call Kem, became so fluent in English by the end of the kindergarten year that her score on the standardized achievement test administered to her grade was the highest in her class. To her teachers, Kem's rapid and what might be described as deliberate acquisition of the English language was quite impressive. It was, however, a family project. Her parents enrolled in an intensive English course at the local community college, and although they did not make the same rapid progress in acquiring English, they provided every opportunity for Kem to be exposed to English-speaking models and they, themselves, modeled their own commitment to becoming proficient in English. At school, in addition to formal English-language coaching, Kem enlisted her own keen observation skills, noticing change when it was occurring. She seemed to employ several sensory modes—the sounds of change, inflections in voices, sensitivity to motion and movement around her, awareness of movements and positioning of her teacher or classmates, behaviors in context, school-bell signals or other extra-classroom happenings (e.g., children transitioning from other classrooms passing in the hallway; the sounds of another class at recess on the playground), and her own "body clock." She learned to "read" the classroom visuals, particularly the daily routine rebus chart that helped her to

Figure 7.5
(*continued*)

learn "what comes next." She was friendly and receptive with classmates; interestingly, her quizzical facial expressions quickly elicited help and direction from them. Her teacher conscientiously used many strategic, yet subtle, techniques to help her learn another language, such as predictable and consistent scheduling of daily activities so Kem could anticipate changes, observe other children, and listen for instructions and verbal instructions that were always brief and consistently stated in the same manner or sentence format. For example, the teacher always said, "It is about time to put the blocks away." This sentence did not change on other days to "Please put the blocks away now," or "In five minutes it will be clean-up time," or some other sentence carrying the same intended message but different words. Verbal messages were supported with visuals and demonstrations (rebus charts, word/picture cards and games, photographs and posters with multicultural themes, and many labels, using pictures or drawings). The teacher used body language to convey meaning by, for example, positioning herself in locations where children were to convene. Instead of instructing, "When you have put the blocks away, go to the reading circle," the teacher stood or seated herself in the reading center and held a small poster used to identify the space and its activity and said, "When you have put the blocks away, come to the reading circle." She included in her daily planning many opportunities for small-group interactive experiences with concrete, hands-on materials. She also included high-interest class projects in her curriculum to engage children but also to stimulate verbal interaction among them. Importantly, she enlisted, from time to time, Kem's mother or father to sing or read a familiar story with the children in Kem's native language, to share Korean artifacts and family photos, and to teach some simple Korean words and phrases to assist their communication. On many occasions Kem translated or interpreted the teacher's words to her parents. As the year progressed, teacher, parents, and Kem grew more and more capable of communicating with one another.

These are only some of the techniques that were used in this classroom. There are, of course, many such techniques (Akhavan, 2006; Cary, 2000; Dragan, 2005; Gonzalez-Mena, 2007; Santos, 2004; Santos, Fowler, Corso, & Bruns, 2000). Thus, even without the ability to speak the child's native language, teachers can use many techniques to augment formal English-language-learning instructions and to communicate with non-English-speaking children and their families. Active pursuit of competence in communicating with children and families whose language is unfamiliar conveys respect and encourages interaction. Assessments that follow every effort to help children acquire Standard American English are then focused on emerging capabilities rather than on language deficiencies or inabilities to communicate.

ONGOING COMMUNICATION

The collaborative model includes timely communications about child progress, performance, and products, with both scheduled times for summary reports and conferences (usually three or four times a year in kindergarten and above, more often in prekindergarten and infant/toddler programs) and opportunistic and impromptu interactions. By establishing predictable times for summary reports and conferences with parents and their children, parents are given an opportunity to anticipate conversations about their child's progress and achievement and begin to gain a sense of inclusion in the assessment process. Meaningful impromptu interactions convey a spirit of shared interest and builds rapport.

Successful communications with parents occur when teachers are skilled in listening to what we like to refer to as the "deep structure" of parents' communications. For example, a parent who asks the teacher, "Why doesn't my child read, yet?" may actually be conveying other concerns or feelings, such as (1) the curriculum may not be challenging enough, (2) maybe we (the parents) are not doing things quite right at home, (3) my child may not be normal, (4) when do you begin reading instruction, or (5) some other question having little to do with the apparent subject of the question—in this example, learning to read. The teacher who listens for deep-structure messages gains valuable insights into what individual parents need and want to know. The more interactions a teacher can have with a parent, the more accurate he or she can become in understanding the concern behind the question or comment. Teachers who listen for deep-structure messages are in a better position to provide the most helpful feedback and to engage parents in meaningful dialogue about a child's progress and what assessment data reveal. Parents gain a sense of having been understood and thus are more inclined to participate comfortably in the conversation about their child's development and learning.

Some of the techniques for listening for deep-structure messages include:

1. *Taking time to pause and reflect* on what each participant has just said and how each comment or question has related to the other. (Ask: Did I fully understand the parent's comment or question? Did I respond too quickly? Did the parent "connect" with my response? Or, did the parent appear confused, defensive, or frustrated by my response?)

2. *Parroting or paraphrasing* what one believes to have heard; for example, "Let's see if I understood what you are asking: You want to know (if, when, how) your child will be learning to read. Is that what you are asking?"

3. *Taking the question to the next level.* Invite the parent to elaborate on the question or concern. "Tell me more about this concern."

4. *Attending to new information* or clues in the parent's extended discussion of the topic. For example, in this scenario, the parent reveals, "My child's older sibling has had difficulty on portions of the state-mandated reading test. I am worried that my other children will have similar problems."

5. *Responding with meaningful and helpful feedback* to the new and more particular information.

6. *Asking how the school or teacher can be helpful.*

These techniques are invitational without probing beyond levels of information parents wish to provide. With deep-structure insights, teachers can more effectively communicate with sensitivity and tact, share essential information and clarification, propose ideas or solutions to any perceived or real problems, and then guide the discussion toward the best next steps. Listening for deep-structure messages helps teachers avoid jumping to conclusions and beginning the conversation on topics or at a level beyond the parent's intent or readiness.

Communication and interactions with parents are also more successful when school policies and procedures have been developed with sensitivity to the demands on parents' time and resources. Schools or individual classroom or grade-

The early childhood educator plays an important role in identification and assessment of children who may qualify for specialized programs and services.

Krista Greco/Merrill

level teachers may wish to include conference schedules in a master calendar so parents can begin to plan in advance to schedule for them. When the school has established three or more scheduled summary conferences with parents (usually, fall, midyear, and spring), parents know what to expect during the year and can attempt to plan their work, babysitting, and transportation needs around these dates. For some parents, advance planning may not be that easy, so it is important that schedules be flexible in date, day of week, and time of day. There may be a need to plan before-school or Saturday conferences. There may be a need for the school to assist with transportation, perhaps by arranging carpools. Babysitting arrangements may need to be coordinated through the school Parent-Teacher Association (PTA) or other group to assist parents in keeping their conference appointments. Invitations (or reminder notes) to a collaborative conference should be warm and friendly, upbeat, and inviting. They should be written in language the parents understand. Sometimes, other school personnel can be enlisted to translate the invitation into the language of the home. By the same token, where low literacy skills exist in the home, written communications must incorporate familiar words, such as "Do you need a ride?" instead of "Please request transportation" (Bohler, Eichenlaub, Litteken, & Wallis, 1996). Formal letters can be off-putting and, for some, confusing or intimidating. The invitation should tell parents what the conference will entail and specifically how they might prepare for it. Facilitating parental participation is a major factor in the success of collaborative child-centered assessments. It may be necessary to convey to parents the importance of their role in collaborative assessment and the opportunities they will have to influence the types of experiences and learnings that their child will have and to participate in them throughout the school year.

When parents are informed participants in curriculum and assessment decisions involving their children, their investment in the education process can become more engaged and sustained. Their efforts to work with their own children can thus be guided by mutually established goals and mutually understood expectations. In this context, teachers can help parents understand school, district, and state standards, benchmarks, and testing requirements while reinforcing the importance of developmentally appropriate practices.

As parents begin to learn more about developmentally appropriate educational practices and alternative systems for "grading" children's school performance, they may find their long-held beliefs challenged. Many parents experienced traditional forms of assessment during their own schooling experience. Educators may need to help parents get beyond their concepts of traditional grading systems—report cards with letter and/or numerical grades and weekly unit test grades—in order for them to value new ways of viewing what children know and are able to do.

Although these traditional methods continue to be a part of many assessment practices today, they can be viewed as only part of a much more comprehensive, revealing, and meaningful assessment system. By experiencing meaningful dialogue and collaboration using authentic assessments that describe individual learning processes and example children's performance and products, parents are provided a more informing set of data about their child's learning. With this information, parents have a frame of reference for supporting their child's learning during out-of-school time and can benefit from suggestions teachers provide on how to facilitate individual acquisition of knowledge and skills. Figure 7.6 illustrates the important ways in which families can support learning at home. There are many professionally developed print and online sources giving tips for parents on how to help children succeed in school. (See "Identification and Utilization of Resources".) Frequently teachers or schools choose to customize their own "Tips for Parents," addressing topics of particular importance or timeliness to them.

It may take time for parents to acclimate to a new way of getting information about their child's school progress and achievements. Engaging parents in ongoing communication from the beginning of the school year, providing them with

---

Parents, other adults, and older siblings can support learning at home by:

talking, inquiring, conversing, and reading with children.

providing a variety of engaging, enlightening, and enriching educational experiences.

introducing children to individuals who share their special interests or talents.

providing space and resources for study.

helping (as needed) with and reviewing homework.

helping children prepare for tests.

establishing routines that allow time for homework.

collecting and organizing an at-home portfolio or a school memory box.

keeping test scores, grades, and performance expectations in perspective and balanced with other important aspects of healthy growth and development.

reflecting together and celebrating accomplishments.

seeking assistance when needed.

Figure 7.6
Helping Families Help Their Children at Home

opportunities to observe, and inviting and facilitating their participation in many home-school partnership efforts (see "Creating Opportunities for Enhanced Home-School Relationships"), displaying student products, and discussing processes and performances are some of the ways to help parents gain confidence in methods of assessment that may differ from the types of reporting and testing practices that characterized their own schooling experiences. As partners in planning, reviewing, and assessing student progress, both teachers and parents develop a healthy and positive regard for the individual learner's emerging development and capabilities.

Obtaining Initial Information from Families About Their Children

An initial parent conference should be scheduled with each parent as early in the school year as possible. During this conference, goals, curricula, and expectations can be clarified, and plans can be developed for obtaining and sharing assessment information. Initial conferences with parents should help teachers obtain baseline information about the parents' goals and aspirations and specific information about the child, including:

◆ special needs or accommodations.

◆ language proficiencies.

◆ personality and temperament characteristics.

◆ special interests and talents.

◆ response to guidance and discipline.

◆ prior learning experiences in preschool or other education settings.

◆ special and important family events or traditions.

◆ typical play and interaction behaviors.

◆ important attachments or relationships.

Each of these topics turns the adults' attention to the individuality of the learner, evoking greater empathy and understanding that will guide performance and achievement expectations and setting the individual learner's goals. The teacher then can develop or adjust curricula to meet the needs of individuals, thus assuring the greater likelihood of success (Bredekamp & Copple, 1997).

Subsequent conferences can address student achievements and progress toward expected benchmarks. Participants can be engaged in conversations that address such questions as (Katz and Chard, 2000):

1. What *knowledge* is the child acquiring? Knowledge includes ideas, facts, and concepts.

2. What *skills* is the child developing? Skills include such areas as physical, social, communicative, and cognitive—including reading, math, science, social studies, and so on.

3. What *dispositions* is the child developing? Dispositions include attitudes, personality traits, curiosity, creativity, resourcefulness, responsibility, initiative, interests, effort, mastery, and challenge seeking.

4. What *feelings* is the child developing? Feelings of success, positive self-esteem, empowerment, and autonomy as a learner are essential contributors to learning success and are included in a meaningful assessment paradigm.

If a child does not feel successful, changes or adjustments must be made. Otherwise, feelings of self-esteem and efficacy fail to develop, resulting in a disengaged learner. Disengaged learners, of course, are not as successful in school and subsequently develop negative feelings toward themselves and school. Disengaged learners often engage in disturbing and off-task classroom behaviors and can become potential school dropouts.

Teachers may wish to devise checklists, a brief questionnaire, or other forms to be completed by the parent and used during collaborative conferences. Figure 7.7 illustrates a goal statement that can be completed by the child, the child's parent(s), or the child and parent(s) together.

Figure 7.7
Goal Statement Form

Child's name: _____ **Parent's name(s):** _____

School: _____

Our/my goals for the school year are as follows:

I will get started by:

1.

2.

3.

I will need help from:

I will need these materials, supplies, books, etc.:

I will know I have accomplished my/our goals when:

Date: _____   _____
                               Child's signature

                               _____
                               Parent's signature

The Child-Parent-Teacher Collaborative Conference

The three-way child-parent-teacher conference is an invaluable contribution to meaningful assessment. This approach to assessment focuses everyone's attention on the student rather than on topics that are peripheral to the student's actual progress and performance. The collaborative conference is one in which student, parent(s), and teacher together examine and reflect on test results, summary reports, and portfolio contents. Figures 7.8a, 7.8b, 7.9, 7.10, and 7.11 contrast old and new methods for reporting student performance and progress to families.

Conference Foci

Where there are three assessment conferences during the school year, the first conference focuses on getting acquainted with one another and obtaining baseline information to guide goal setting. This conference also addresses what to anticipate during this grade and school year; what the child and parent hope will be learned during this grade; setting first or initial goals for the first third of the school year (or shorter period with very young children); and discussing how and when tests and assessments occur. The second collaborative conference takes a comparative look at the child's early products and accomplishments and current ones, revealing progress toward the goals and benchmarks named during the first conference. Figure 7.8 illustrates a summary report used in a three-way conference. The third conference reviews accomplishments toward goals and benchmarks identified in the second conference, but also takes a long, reflective and celebrative look at the achievements over the course of the school year. Each conference examines the prior established goals, looks at criteria in each of the developmental domains for determining progress, and explores areas of strength and areas needing more time, practice, or enrichment; it also suggests directions for review, remediation, and new learnings.

The first- and third-grade report cards in Figure 7.8a and b are dated 1909 and 1911–12. They are shown here to demonstrate and contrast both old (and, in some instances, continuing) and new practices. A number of contrasts can be drawn between current practices illustrated in Figures 7.9, 7.10, and 7.11 and yesteryear's emphases. Notice the size and simplicity of these historical school monthly reports, the "rubrics" at the bottom of the report card that explain the numerical grades, and, perhaps, the priority placement of "deportment" in the earlier grade. Parents are instructed to sign the report each month and are invited to ". . . confer with the teacher about anything which is not satisfactory." A quotation on the front of the card reads: "Write it on your heart that every day is the best day in the year.— Emerson" Instructions are also provided that read:

To The Pupil

1. Be clean in person, dress, habits, thought, and speech.
2. Be dutiful, polite, and respectful to parents, teachers, and all whom you may meet.
3. Strive to build up a good character, and your reputation will take care of itself.
4. Be earnest in play in the time for play and equally earnest in work in the time for work.

Figure 7.8
Contrasting Reports to Families

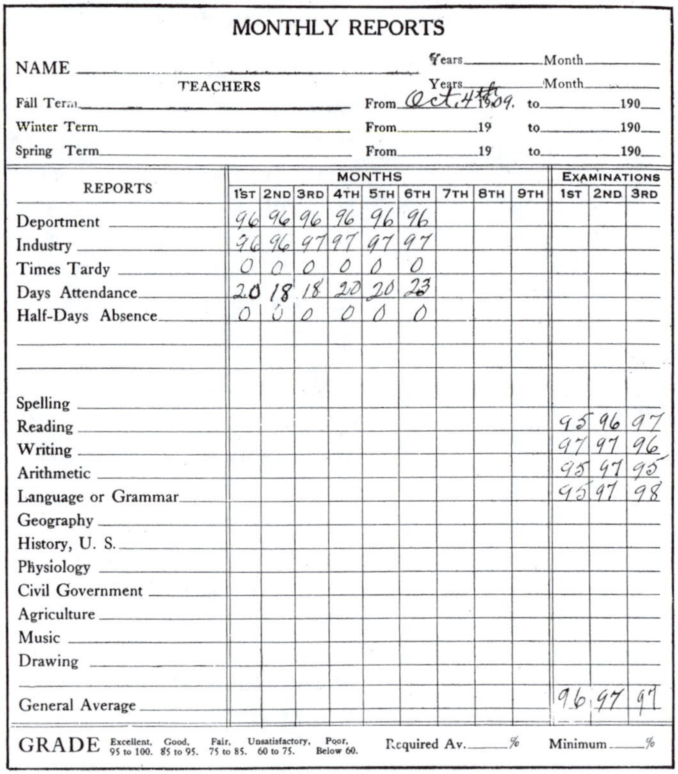

MONTHLY REPORTS

NAME ____________ Years ______ Month ______

TEACHERS Years ______ Month ______

Fall Term ____________ From Oct. 4th 1909. to ______ 190__

Winter Term ____________ From ______ 19 to ______ 190__

Spring Term ____________ From ______ 19 to ______ 190__

REPORTS	MONTHS 1ST	2ND	3RD	4TH	5TH	6TH	7TH	8TH	9TH	EXAMINATIONS 1ST	2ND	3RD
Deportment	96	96	96	96	96	96						
Industry	96	96	97	97	97	97						
Times Tardy	0	0	0	0	0	0						
Days Attendance	20	18	18	20	20	23						
Half-Days Absence	0	0	0	0	0	0						
Spelling												
Reading										95	96	97
Writing										97	97	96
Arithmetic										95	97	95
Language or Grammar										95	97	98
Geography												
History, U. S.												
Physiology												
Civil Government												
Agriculture												
Music												
Drawing												
General Average										96	97	97

GRADE Excellent, 95 to 100. Good, 85 to 95. Fair, 75 to 85. Unsatisfactory, 60 to 75. Poor, Below 60. Required Av. ____% Minimum ____%

a

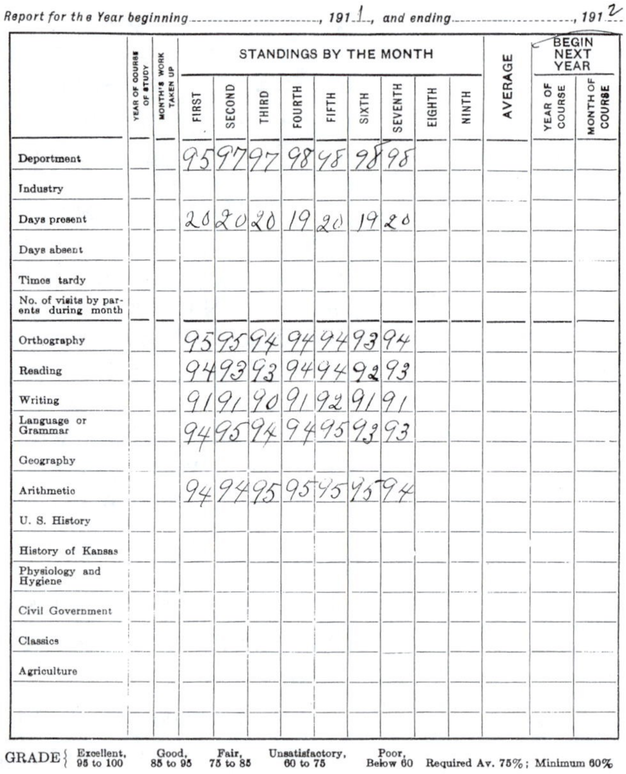

Report for the Year beginning ____________, 1911, and ending ____________, 1912

	YEAR OF COURSE OF STUDY	MONTH'S WORK TAKEN UP	STANDINGS BY THE MONTH FIRST	SECOND	THIRD	FOURTH	FIFTH	SIXTH	SEVENTH	EIGHTH	NINTH	AVERAGE	BEGIN NEXT YEAR YEAR OF COURSE	MONTH OF COURSE
Deportment			95	97	97	98	98	98	98					
Industry														
Days present			20	20	20	19	20	19	20					
Days absent														
Times tardy														
No. of visits by parents during month														
Orthography			95	95	94	94	94	93	94					
Reading			94	93	93	94	94	92	93					
Writing			91	91	90	91	92	91	91					
Language or Grammar			94	95	94	94	95	93	93					
Geography														
Arithmetic			94	94	95	95	95	95	94					
U. S. History														
History of Kansas														
Physiology and Hygiene														
Civil Government														
Classics														
Agriculture														

b GRADE { Excellent, 95 to 100 Good, 85 to 95 Fair, 75 to 85 Unsatisfactory, 60 to 75 Poor, Below 60 Required Av. 75%; Minimum 60%

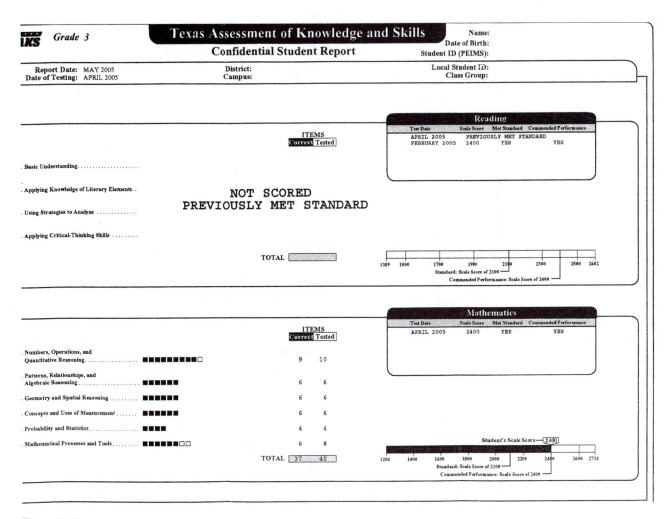

Figure 7.9

5. Cultivate promptness, energy, and patient industry. They are worth more to you than money or influence in securing success in life.

6. Finally, be courteous, obedient, thoughtful, earnest, atentive, studious, and industrious. If you would win the highest esteem of your teachers, school-mates, parents, and the general public."

A final note reads: "Please keep this report neat and clean. When you enter school next term, please present it to the teacher for inspection."

In Figure 7.9, a report of a state accountabiity test is quite specific about what was tested and whether the student's performance on the test met the state standard. It is straightforward. The report is accompanied by a school district form letter explaining how to intepret the scale score. Its usefulness to parents and learners is dubious; but, then, its intent is to track school accountability yearly progress. The information it reveals must be combined with other data if it is to be used to determine individual student progress or needs.

Figure 7.10 examples a recent narrative report that was used during a three-way conference. Notice that the first paragraph describes what the class has been

Figure 7.10

Alice Carlson Applied Learning Center

Narrative Report

2000-01 School Year • Second Nine-Week Cycle

		Attendance to date
Student **Macy**	Grade **Kindergarten**	_43_ days present
		_0_ days absent
Teacher _____	Date **Jan 25, 2000**	_____ days tardy

During this nine weeks, the students continued to develop language and literacy skills, mathematical thinking, and personal/social skills. The children read a variety of books for the purpose of enjoyment, raising his or her interest level, and attending to the print to discover reading strategies. They learned to use a variety of strategies to gain meaning from print which include exploring sound-letter relationships, looking at pictures for information, retelling stories so they are aware of the format, and learning some words that appear frequently in print. The children acquired the ability to identify the title, the author, and the illustrator of a book. In writing, the children drew pictures with more detail and began adding print to their stories. The children's print may be random letters, using their sound-letter knowledge to write words, using environmental print, and sight word vocabulary. They used the skills developed in writing workshop in writing letters to Santa. In mathematics, the children applied various strategies to solve a variety of problems. They participated in activities that focused on counting, developing one-to-one correspondence, and matching and comparing quantities. They recognized, described, and created a variety of patterns. Also, the children learned to see a variety of possibilities when sorting objects and recording their data. Concerning personal and social data, the children are encouraged to make responsible choices, take responsibility for their own behavior, and take risks as learners.

Macy enjoys reading books and she responds to literature in a variety of ways (reading logs, book talks, art, drama etc.). Macy is developing good reading strategies. She identifies the letters and sounds and can give words for the initial consonants. Her sight word vocabulary has increased. She is looking at the initial consonant for cues to the word and uses the picture effectively. Macy is beginning to transfer these skills into her writing. She is incorporating some sight words and environmental print in her stories and is using some inventive spelling to convey meaning. Macy needs to continue to develop a fluency in writing. Macy's ability to solve mathematical word problems is developing nicely. She is able to identify the problem and draw what she hears. Although she does not always calculate the correct response, her answer is usually reasonable. She is logical, sees patterns, and is able to apply what she knows to new situations. Macy sees a variety of possibilities when sorting, and realizes that counting is more than a rote activity. She understands that each counting number corresponds to a specific set of objects. Macy continues to work on her ability to utilize self-control and make responsible choices. She gets along well with other children and has made many friends at school.

Goals:
- continue to use inventive spelling in her stories
- develop a more fluent written story
- expand her sight word vocabulary
- continue to develop problem solving strategies
- use self-control

Macy

Teacher's signature	Student's signature	Parent's signature

---

studying and how the students are being taught. The second paragraph addresses specifically the student's learning and accomplishments and then identifies shared goals. The three participants sign the narrative report suggesting the shared agreement and shared responsibilites.

Figure 7.11 illustrates a school district form letter to parents describing a norm-referenced test that was given to all children in kindergarten and explaining how to interpret percentile scores. As with the state-mandated tests, it is straightforward and, absent dialogue with the teacher, provides little helpful or meaningful

Figure 7.11

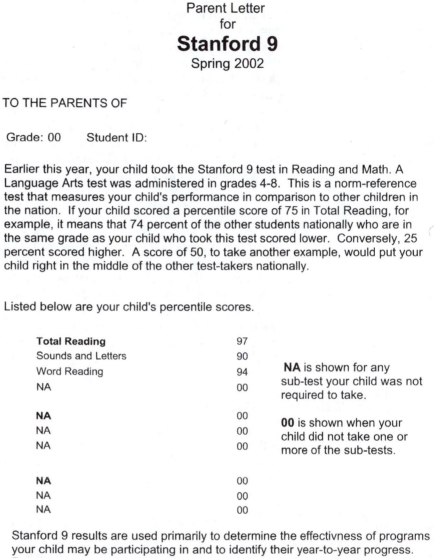

Parent Letter
for
Stanford 9
Spring 2002

TO THE PARENTS OF

Grade: 00   Student ID:

Earlier this year, your child took the Stanford 9 test in Reading and Math. A Language Arts test was administered in grades 4-8. This is a norm-reference test that measures your child's performance in comparison to other children in the nation. If your child scored a percentile score of 75 in Total Reading, for example, it means that 74 percent of the other students nationally who are in the same grade as your child who took this test scored lower. Conversely, 25 percent scored higher. A score of 50, to take another example, would put your child right in the middle of the other test-takers nationally.

Listed below are your child's percentile scores.

Total Reading	97	
Sounds and Letters	90	**NA** is shown for any
Word Reading	94	sub-test your child was not
NA	00	required to take.
NA	00	
NA	00	**00** is shown when your
NA	00	child did not take one or
		more of the sub-tests.
NA	00	
NA	00	
NA	00	

Stanford 9 results are used primarily to determine the effectivness of programs your child may be participating in and to identify their year-to-year progress. Results are not used to determine your child's course grade.

information for parents to use in supporting their child's learning. As with the state accountability test, the information it provides must also be combined with other more elaborative information if families and individual students are to make use of it. Notice that the report includes this information: "... results are used primarily to determine the effectiveness of programs .... Results are not used to determine your child's course grade."

Before a formal assessment conference, the teacher should send a copy of the summary report home so that parents will have a few days to read over it, think about its contents, discuss it with their child, anticipate questions, and be prepared before the conference occurs. It is unfair to surprise parents with information about their child's schooling and then expect them to respond in helpful and cooperative ways. (It may be necessary to have these report translated into the parent's language or verbally translated by an interpreter.) Again, planning and communication are the keys to the success of collaboration with parents.

The collaborative conference should not be rushed, nor should it drag on and detain a parent unnecessarily. Thirty to forty-five minutes should suffice; however, some conferences may take a little longer. If the teacher has prepared an agenda that lists the topics to cover and in what order to discuss them; includes time for the child to showcase, describe, and respond to comments or questions about the portfolio contents; and allows time for the parents to express their observations, pleasure, and concerns and to pose questions that will arise, the meeting can flow with some sense of focus and purpose. The agenda, however, should serve to focus the conference and should not be so binding as to interfere with meaningful and in-depth dialogue among teacher, parents, and student that naturally occurs following the examination of the summary report, the portfolio contents, and the child's comments and contributions.

Student's Role in the Three-Way Conference

The student's role in the collaborative conference is that of a team member or, perhaps, a conference leader, who is learning how to reflect on his or her own learning and accomplishments. During the three-way conference, the student showcases the contents of his or her portfolio, identifying and describing items according to selected assessment rubrics. (See Chapter 4.) Prior to the conference, the student and teacher collaborate on the selection of contents for the portfolio; if necessary, the student can role play or rehearse how he or she would like to talk about the portfolio items.

Strategies for Collaborative Assessment

Teachers can employ a variety of strategies for collaboratively assessing the child's performance, products, processes, and portfolio. The components of the collaborative conference portfolio are illustrated in Figure 7.12. Teachers may wish to include graphic material, such as that illustrated in Figure 7.13, to help

Figure 7.12
Portfolio Conference Components

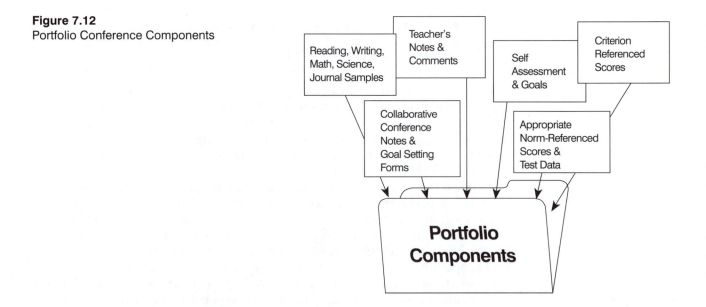

Figure 7.13
Graphic Representation of
Progress

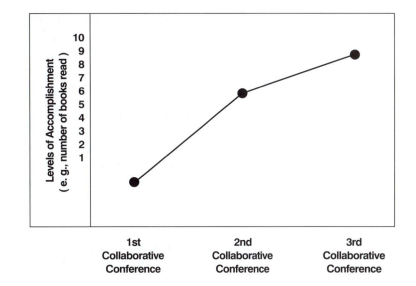

parents visualize the progress their child is making. If standardized tests have been used, these instruments and how they relate to other assessments must be explained.

When reviewing the products and contents of the portfolio, the teacher may pose questions to help the child and parent focus and reflect on the material. For instance, the following questions might be helpful:

Which item in the portfolio tells you the most about your child's ability in art? Math? Writing? Reading?
What strengths do you see in your child's schoolwork?
Have you observed similar performance (similar process, similar products) at home? Tell me about them.
What growth and progress do you see in these materials?
How is your child feeling about her or his work at school?
What areas do you think we should explore further?
Do you have concerns about any of the materials we have examined?
What suggestions do you have for helping your child to continue to improve?
Are additional resources needed?
How can I help?
How would you like to be involved in the next project (field trip, planning our open house, setting up the parent center, and so on)?

The teacher might address questions such as the following to the child:

Did you enjoy having your parent(s) share your portfolio with you?
What do you think your parent(s) learned today about your work in school?
What did you learn about your own knowledge or skills?
Where (when, how) do you think you do your best work?
How do you feel about your work in math? Reading? Art? Physical Education?
Is there anything else you want to share with us about your portfolio or how you feel about school?
Do you have any questions about what we have discussed today?

What else do you want to learn or learn to do?
How can your parent(s) help?
How can the teacher help?

To each of the collaborators, these questions may be helpful:

What did we all learn from this assessment conference?
Where do we want to go from here?
Are there subjects, skills, feelings, dispositions, and so on, that we should revisit and plan for their improvement?
Are additional assessments necessary?
Can we now set some additional goals for learning?
What curricular or pedagogical modifications need to take place now?

A summary report of the collaborative conference should be completed together and placed in the student's archival portfolio; a copy should be provided for the parent(s). This report can include the Goals Statement Form illustrated in Figure 7.7, along with other forms that were used and a narrative account. This summary will serve as a starting point for the next collaborative conference to assess what progress was made and if goals are being achieved.

Keep in mind that the collaborative conference is designed to identify student strengths, to celebrate learning. The assessment experience should leave children feeling competent and eager to go forward while identifying those areas of learning that everyone in a collaborative and helpful manner (child, parent, and teacher) will be working toward. Throughout the conference, the emphasis must be on evidence of progress, not on deficits and/or mistakes. Weaknesses or mistakes that show up should be used to illustrate how learning emerges—through trial and error; through making mistakes and discovering ways to correct them; through taking risks; and through exploration, inquiry, and use of new skills and knowledge. From this context, students can come to value mistakes as a natural part of the learning process and to view themselves as learners, capable of finding out. (See "Ask Marilyn.") They can also begin to trust adults to be supportive resources and advocates and view school as a psychologically safe place to learn.

When setting goals and assessing individual accomplishments, it seems appropriate to return to Gardner's theory of multiple intelligences. Quite clearly, not all children are mathematicians or linguistically skilled, the two intelligences most frequently emphasized in today's standards and mandated tests. In a new era of increasing tests and accountability standards, it is imperative that we maintain our goals for whole child development and for curricula that respond to children's strengths and learning styles. Meaningful, comprehensive, and holistic assessments help us to do that. Summarizing the benefits of collaborative goal setting around varied intelligences, Ellison (1992, p. 72) advises:

> Individual goal setting helps us honor student differences and plan for the wide range of diverse needs. And by using Gardner's multiple intelligences, all areas of growth become the domain for school learning and all kinds of excellence are celebrated.

Ask Marilyn

Life is so short, and the world of learning so vast, that I feel safe in stating that if you do not make mistakes, you don't know much.

Mariyn vos Savant
Parade Magazine
July 24, 2005, p. 6

*Meaningful assessment requires an under-
standing of the unique ways children use
language to communicate with others.*

Nancy P. Alexander

The outcomes of a collaborative conference should arrive at answers to these types of questions that can explain and guide the continuing assessment process:

1. Are the classroom expectations and curriculum topics a good fit for the age and individuality of this child?

   suffiently challenging
   engaging and interesting
   too difficult and stressful
   meaningless and not currently useful

2. In what types of contexts is the child most successful?

   independent activity
   small group or paired activity
   self-selected activity
   adult-selected and guided activity

3. What types of activities or information must be provided in order for the child to acquire necessary or additional skills or to benefit from new information?

4. Where can these activities occur to achieve their best outcomes—home, school, or other resource?

5. Does the child's behavior indicate a tendency for expressing intelligence from a particular frame of mind: linguistic, musical, logical-mathematical, spatial, bodily kinesthetic, intrapersonal, interpersonal, or naturalistic? (Gardner, 1983, 1997, 1998, 1999)

6. Does the child have any health- or disability-related challenges for which accommodations must be made?

   sensory impairment(s)
   motor coordinations or mobility needs
   nutritional issues
   chronic health issues
   attention disorder

7. Is there a need to adjust the learning environment in some manner: accessibility to materials, adaptations for visual, hearing, or mobility difficulties, alterations to light and/or sound ambiance, provision for more or less movement and interaction, seating arrangments, or others?

8. Are the child and family finding the school and classroom culturally sensitive and responsive? Are linguistic barriers being addressed and opportunities provided to learn Standard American English?

9. Would additional or alternative means for measuring and assessing progress be beneficial?

10. Do children and parents each find the assessment process encouraging and helpful?

Postconference Reflections

Specific child-outcome information should include the teacher's reflections on what was learned about the student.

> What strengths or challenges are (or became) apparent during the three-way conference?
> > academic strengths, interests, and talents (What appears to engage, excite, motivate, or cause stress, frustration, and defeat?)
> > social and emotional well-being and competences
> > language and communicating attributes
> > physical well-being and physical/motor attributes
> > communication and interactive style and abilities
> > understanding and use of classroom materials and resources
> > ways of pursuing concepts, knowledge, and skills and of seeking adult assistance
> > response to and benefits of formal test results
> > benchmark indicators
> What enrichments, accommodations, interventions, and further assessments are now indicated?

Documenting Child Development and Learning at Home

There are a number of ways that families can begin documenting their child's development and learning in out-of-school contexts. They can learn to keep dated samples of their child's at-home products, constructions, writings, and drawings. They can keep photo collections and albums depicting their child's growth and development, activities, and friends. Families can be provided with anecdotal record forms or observation guides and checklists and can keep logs or diaries themselves in spiral notebooks to be brought to collaborative conferences and shared. They can make lists of shared reading, writing, and math activities: favorite books read at bedtime; books recently checked out from the library; books read or stories shared; notes, letters, and lists shared with one another; mathematics-related experiences, such as counting out spoons and forks for the family picnic, measuring the distance from the back of the house or apartment to the front door, calculating the time it takes to drive to school at twenty miles an hour, or planning a savings account to buy Mom or Dad a birthday present; and an infinite number of other activities occurring in the regular course of the day and created for shared learning experiences. The richness of these activities and the enthusiasm they generate in parents and children enhances and informs both assessment and the parent-child relationship.

Contemporary studies of parent-child communications have focused attention on the conditions and contexts in which children and parents communicate and on developing strategies for enhancing this communication. Bradbard, Endsley, and Mize (1992) developed a checklist to examine and describe if, when, where, and to what extent parent-child conversations about preschool or day-care experiences occur and the topics and triggers of these conversations. Their findings suggest the role of the teacher in enhancing these communications as we learn more about them. For instance, from their study of well-educated parents whose children attended high-quality preschools, they found that parents communicated with their children about preschool nearly every weekday but significantly less often on weekends. Their topics centered more often on people at school or their particular child. They talked about schoolmates and teachers nearly every day; similarly, they talked daily about programmatic themes such as outside play, learning activities, and special events. They talked very little about health-related topics such as toileting and napping. Children communicated most frequently by describing what they did at school, asking questions, or performing (singing, dancing, and role playing, as opposed to emotional expressions, imitating, imaginary talking, or complaining).

Daily routines triggered parent-child conversations, as did parental classroom observations. Often conversations were motivated by conversations with the teacher, information in school newsletters, and subtle signals such as dirty hands or wet clothing. Mothers started conversations most frequently, although fathers and other children were also frequent initiators. Siblings and grandparents initiated conversations less frequently (i.e., once a week or less).

Studies such as these can help teachers and researchers begin to think about intervention strategies for low-communicating parents and children, helping them to learn to communicate more effectively. For instance, it is helpful to know that parent observations in the classroom enhance communications between the child and parent; it stands to reason that these observations provide topics about which parents and child can become engaged. Intervention strategies can be developed to help parents use the most likely times when they and their children can communicate and enjoy quality interactions with one another (i.e., en route to and from school, at mealtimes, just before bedtime, and those parent-child moments that simply occur spontaneously from time to time throughout the day). Bradbard et al. (1992) suggest that teachers can help parents use topics of interest with their children and help them understand that young children communicate through describing, asking questions, and performing. Parents can be guided toward framing conversations that elicit these ways of communicating. The parent may begin the conversation with, "Tell me about the science project you and Jeremy started today," and then talk with the child in a positive, nonjudgmental conversation. There is much to be learned in this area, but we do know that if parent-child communications can be improved, they can enhance the parents' understanding of their children's experiences and how they are responding to the activities and expectations of school. In turn, parent-teacher communications can be richly enhanced as the parent's interest, knowledge, and insights become more focused and revealing. Collaborations among families, children, and teachers are also enhanced.

Identification and Utilization of Resources

Authentic assessment practices reveal not only how children are progressing and what curricular adjustments need to occur, but also the extent to which the teacher(s) and families are familiar with and utilize available resources—both school-based and community resources. As student and family needs become apparent (Figure 7.14), teachers and other school personnel can identify and inform parents of additional resources, materials for learning, enrichment opportunities, tutoring, language courses and interpretors, support groups and neighborhood parent networks, social services, early screening and intervention services, health-care resources, transportation help, and others. Some parents may need help accessing suggested resources for their children. By helping families learn about available resources and how to access them, teachers and other school personnel help families meet the needs of their children and, in so doing, remove some of the obstacles to student success.

Figure 7.14
Family-Related Barriers to
Successful Home-School
Collaborations

Logistics
Work and family schedules
Overriding family issues
Transportation
Child care for siblings
Financial issues (e.g., inability to pay for fee-related school activities or to purchase school supplies)
In-home resources (e.g., computer access, resource and reference books, homework or project supplies)
Familiarity with school campus, building, and classroom
Disability accessibility

Perceptions and Attitudes
Limited information
Misunderstood or incomplete information
Disagreement or dissatisfaction with school policy
Feelings of intimidation or disconnect
Fear of being judged
Anxiety about child's behaviors or performance
Prior unsuccessful parent/teacher relationship

Participation dynamics
Language differences
Low literacy skills
Limited communication skills
Real or imagined bias toward class, race, gender, disability, marital status, education level, religion, or occupation
Immigration status

Within the school community, the expertise of available professionals should be readily tapped as needs arise. The psychological services counselor, the school nurse or health-care consultant, nutritionists, the director of special education and/or early screening and intervention services or licensed diagnostician, librarians, and technology experts are some of the more common supportive school-based resources.

Further, because teachers come into the profession with special content area interests and training, it is important to tap each other's expertise. In order to meet the needs of children with interests and talents in particular content ares, it could be quite enriching for both students and teachers to share consultations regarding developmentally appropriate curriculum enhancements in particular content areas: art, music, physical education, drama, science, social studies, reading, language arts, and others. By doing so, the needs of individual students who have been identified with talents, interests, or challenges in selected content areas can be met. In this process, it is important that the collaboration among teachers focus on curriculum content and pedagogy, not on individual student–assessment information.

Many communities provide local, regional, or state health and human resources offices, through which many services and resources can be made available to families. Printed fliers or other documents can be obtained for distribution to those families who might qualify for the services. For families who have access to electronic communication (computers or other technologies), much of this information is available online.

Additionally, philanthropic and faith-based organizations might also be accessed to assist with school supplies, clothing needs, special interest needs (e.g., musical instruments, art supplies, or sports equipment).

Local merchants and businesses are often quite eager to participate in efforts to improve educational opportunities within their communities. Some donate directly to the school or classroom; others provide special discounts to families for school supplies, school uniforms, or other needs.

Area colleges and universities can often make tutors and classroom assistants available to work with individuals or small groups of children. These students with appropriate instructions and/or training may also assist with assessments requiring certain types of observations or recording strategies.

Chapter 1 described the purposes of assessment in early childhood education. These purposes of assessment are best fulfilled when families are engaged and invested participants. Helping families identify and utilize available resources can, in many cases, remove barriers to their willing and collaborative participation. Children who lack the essential resources and background experiences to succeed in school can be helped through these types of supports and advocacy.

CREATING OPPORTUNITIES FOR ENHANCED HOME-SCHOOL RELATIONSHIPS

It is not the purpose of this chapter to explore the multiplicity of ways to connect families and schools. Early childhood literature is replete with traditional and innovative programs and strategies. A few are listed in the "Suggested Literature and Resources" section of this chapter. The following represent only selected suggestions, included here in the context of assessment practices to emphasize the importance of finding ways to support all the elements of the collaborative model: shared goals, trust and mutual respect, respect for diversity, ongoing communication, and identification and utilization of resources.

Home Visits

When school policies permit home visits, visits to students' homes before the beginning of the school year prove to be quite rewarding for teachers who can arrange for them. Through the home visit, the child and the parent have an opportunity to become acquainted with the teacher in the comfort of their own surroundings. For some, this reduces the stress of meeting for the first time at the school, with its seemingly impersonal atmosphere and frequent interruptions. The home visit provides an opportunity for the teacher to experience the child's home context firsthand. It also demonstrates for parents the teacher's genuine interest in the child. The child, of course, has a unique opportunity to become acquainted with the teacher in a personal way and in the secure surroundings of home, belongings, and parents. There may be some parents however, who are quite uncomfortable with a teacher's visit, fearing the teacher will judge their family, lifestyle, or home. In such a case, the teacher may wish to postpone the visit until the parents feel more at ease in the relationship and view the teacher as their child's advocate and friend, not as a professional who has come to judge the family and its surroundings. Teachers should follow certain procedures in planning for and carrying through with home visits:

◆ Ascertain the parents' desire or willingness to have the teacher visit in their home.

◆ Prearrange the date and time of the visit by telephone, e-mail, or a written note.

◆ Assure the parent(s) of the purpose of the visit.

◆ Encourage the parents to include their child in the visit.

◆ Plan the agenda—think through what to discuss or accomplish.

◆ Take every precaution to avoid causing the parents to feel uneasy.

◆ Bring along a photograph of the child's new school and/or classroom.

◆ Provide succinct materials (written in the family's home language) for the parents to read about the school and things they can do to prepare their child for the first days of school.

◆ As a guest in the home, follow the lead of the host or hostess.

◆ Dress in a conservative manner, neither "threateningly professional" nor too casual.

◆ Arrive on time and end the home visit within a reasonable length of time—no longer than forty-five minutes to one hour.

◆ Be friendly, relaxed, and assuring.

◆ If the parents are willing, take a photograph of them and the child together for a school bulletin board.

◆ Invite the parents, if they wish, to share family photos, memorabilia, or other significant items or events that have been special in their lives.

◆ Write a thank-you note as a follow-up and include some positive statements about some aspect of the visit, such as meeting the family pet, holding baby sister, accepting vegetables from their garden, and so on.

◆ Continue follow-up communications about specific goals, issues, or concerns discussed during the home visit through notes, conferences, e-mail communications, and in-school visits.

◆ Evaluate the conference and record pertinent information needed to plan curricula and assessment for the child.

◆ When feasible and appropriate, schedule another home visit later in the year to strengthen and continue the collaborative relationship.

Telephone and Electronic Communications

When home visits are not feasible, electronic or telephone communications can be employed. Communicating by phone or electronically can take place throughout the year as needed and should not occur only when there is a concern or problem to be discussed. It is helpful to parents to know the best times to contact the teacher and how soon they can expect a return call or electronic response. By the same token, teachers will want to ascertain and respect the most convenient times to contact parents. Teachers may also schedule regular times during the day or week to read and answer electronic communications between home and school.

E-mail provides an excellent and quick way to communicate with individual parents. Reminders of conference dates, field trips, special events, or simply what special curriculum topics, concepts, and skills are being addressed during selected time periods keep parents posted and connected to their child's school. Personal e-notes that include anecdotes with good news about challenges and successes go a long way toward establishing bonds between families and teachers. Classroom Web sites can share daily, weekly, and/or monthly school events and use photos to showcase the work and play activities of the classroom.

Electronic assessments and progress-reporting systems are becoming increasingly available and user-friendly (Lacina, 2006; Millon, 2000). Some are designed for individual teacher or classroom use; others are used by individual schools and/or school districts. Such systems, although efficient and time conserving, run the risk of distancing the home-school relationship, decreasing the opportunities for face-to-face relationships building. On the other hand, such systems could increase the number of opportunities to be in contact with families. Online gradebooks and assessment-reporting systems then should be chosen on the basis of how they might be used to share assessment information while maintaining the collaborative model that includes students, parents, and teachers in a sharing and caring relationship.

Open-Door Policy

Families need to feel that the doors to their child's school and classrooms are open to them. Some teachers may feel uncomfortable teaching with visitors in the room. However, it is the teacher who can set the stage for these visitations. Set purpose and goals for the visit in advance with the participating family members so that they arrive with a sense of what to do and what their focus will be. Provide a place for parents to hang their coats or store their personal belongings and a comfortable, yet unobtrusive, place for them to sit to observe; or provide some materials for them to peruse while visiting. One teacher we know has a handout for the parent's visit that describes a scavenger hunt (Figure 7.15), which directs parents to scan the room or quietly move about the classroom identifying the items on the list.

Another teacher encourages parents to peruse the classroom parents' center, which provides displays of children's work, information of use to parents, and

Figure 7.15
A Parent's "Scavenger" Hunt

Instructions:

With your child or another member of our class, explore the classroom and locate as many items on this list as you can. Give yourself 5 points for each correct find. Perfect score is 60 points.

1. How many learning centers can you count in this classroom?
2. Can you name them?
3. How many examples of student's creative works can you find?
4. Can you locate and read a "predictable" book?
5. Can you locate the parent information corner? Find something you would like to read.
6. Find two examples of learning materials that help children learn concepts of time.
7. Identify two ways children are encouraged to develop self-help skills.
8. Locate four mathematics activities. Have your child tell you about them.
9. Locate two activities that help children develop awareness of letters and letter sounds.
10. Find two ways large motor development is encouraged.
11. Find two ways small motor development is encouraged.
12. Ask your child if he or she would like to read their dialogue journal with you.

Answers:

1. 12, not counting the Parents' Corner.
2. Centers: Science, Sociodramatic, Writing, Listening, Mathematics, Creativity, Music, Blocks, Woodworking, Current Events, Library, Retreat/Relax Area
3. If you counted at least five, give yourself 5 points
4. How do you know what you read is a "predictable book"? If you are certain, give yourself 5 points.
5. What did you find there?
6. Clock, calendar, seasons chart, hour glass, timer, clock game, daily schedule, daily planning form, student daily contracts, and so on.
7. Individual cubbies for personal belongings, water fountain, hand-washing sink, dress-up clothes, self-help board games, low shelves for easy access and return of classroom materials, daily individual work contracts, and so on.
8. You will find numerous items and activities for developing math concepts in the Math Center.
9. Both letters and written words and messages can be found in every learning center.
10. Balance beam, bean bag toss, large balls, ladder to reading loft, rhythm and dance activities, and, of course, outdoor climbing equipment and space to run.
11. Puppetry, beads/strings, peg boards, artwork, puzzles, manipulatives, counting objects, and so on.
12. Did your child enjoy sharing his or her dialogue journal with you? What did you learn about your child's developing knowledge and skills?

sign-up rosters to assist with various class or school activities. When parents volunteer in the classroom, they should be given something specific to do, with simple instructions as needed: Read to a particular child or group of children; supervise the woodworking center, sort school supplies for storage, assist in the mathematics center; assist children with milk cartons at lunchtime, and so on). Provide parents with guidelines about expected classroom behaviors and how to respond to off-task or inappropriate behaviors. Be certain parent volunteers know the schedule and help children complete their activities and make transitions in a timely fashion.

If a parent conference is to occur during these volunteer visits, be certain the parent knows when and where it will take place. The more opportunities parents can have to observe and participate in the classroom and to be helpful in other areas of the school, the greater is their understanding of curricula and assessment processes and their commitment to a collaborative model of home-school relationships.

Breakfasts

These morning events, planned for those who cannot come at other times, allow parents to visit with the teacher briefly on their way to work. It is probably better to hold several breakfasts for a few parents at a time than to try to accommodate all in one class at the same time. These breakfast meetings will be brief by necessity, so supplying parents with succinct written or pictorial materials and perhaps questionnaires, which they can take with them to complete and return through the mail or by their child the next day, can expedite the purposes of the meeting. A short video showing the children's classroom in action or illustrating the curriculum and assessment practices can be shown, followed perhaps by a few minutes for questions and answers. Parents should be invited to visit the classroom following the breakfast or at some other time convenient for them.

The disadvantages of this event as an initial contact with parents are its group nature and limited time allotment. Obviously, there is less opportunity for parents and teachers to get to know one another. These breakfasts, however, do provide parents a chance to meet other parents and school personnel and begin to find their place in the school community.

Open Houses, Saturday Family Days, and Supper Specials

Special events, scheduled early in the school year, can encourage parents to participate and provide them opportunities to become acquainted with the teacher, school personnel, other parents and children, school policies, and the curricula and assessment practices that will be employed. Again, because these events involve large groups of parents, their purpose will be to communicate general information. Small groups of parents can be formed to discuss topics relating to the school and its curricula and assessment practices with a teacher. These groups often evolve into school committees, parent support groups, and other networks. Later in the year as assessment strategies get underway, a portfolio open house, when students can showcase their archival portfolio with others, is an effective way to help advance understanding of alternative methods of assessment.

"Ask the Expert" Meetings

Through surveys, ascertain the types of topics or concerns that parents have. Select one or more topics that are shared by many parents and invite an appropiate professional (local pediatrician, nutritionist, school diagnostician, school nurse, child psychologist, etc.) to spend an evening of question-and-answer dialogue on the topic with parents.

Friday Clubs

Invite parents to sign up to lead a once-a-month Friday afternoon special-interest activity with a small group of children. Parents can choose from a list of possible "clubs" to lead, in which they share their own talents or interests with children. (Some clubs that may appeal to young children: a hiking club can focus on safety tips, proper hiking gear, and a hike around the school grounds to focus on natural phenomenon; a cooking club, where age-appropriate food preparation can be enjoyed, along with learning about safe and nutritious food-preparation procedures and creating recipes. Other possible clubs are kite-making, music or a musical instrument club, dance and movement, arts and crafts, gardening, manners for kids, bird-watching, beautify the schoolgrounds, and so on. Have children select the club of interest to them and at least one Friday a month, arrange for parents and children to attend their club meeting. The teacher is responsible for the wise and safe selection of clubs and their meeting space within the classroom or school building. Parents will need to be advised about school policies, use of building and grounds, and child safety.

Classroom Parent Center

To support and encourage parents to visit and become knowledgeable about the school and its programs, space within the classroom or the school building can be provided for parents to have the opportunity to peruse selected journal articles, curriculum materials, parenting books, class-authored books, science and art displays, and other items of particular interest to parents. Space in the classroom allows the parents to visit, observe, and become better acquainted with their children's teacher and his or her methods of teaching and assessment. They also have a chance to explore the various materials the teacher has made available to inform parents about the classroom and its activities. (Some of these materials might be information on how to help in the classroom and a schedule for classroom volunteers; information on the current thematic unit or class project and materials needed to carry out themes and projects; classroom discipline and guidance strategies; a photo album of recent classroom events; weekly assignment logs; suggested books to read to children; a small bulletin board of school or classroom announcements; testing and assessment schedules, and ways parents can help their children at home.)

Information-gathering items might also be included, such as parent questionnaires, opinion polls, and checklists for selected topics of interest or concern to which the teacher or school might respond. The parents can also observe their own child's activities, behaviors, and choices during the school day and assess the child's capabilities and relationships within the school context. Providing checklists, rating scales, observation guidelines, and so on, helps parents to become engaged in the ongoing assessment process and invites them to provide additional

Students engaged in setting goals and plan-ning next steps begin to assume more and more responsibility for their own learning.

Anne Vega/Merrill

helpful information. This information, combined with classroom observations and portfolios, is used to guide and inform the child-parent-teacher collaborative conferences. When parents can visit or volunteer in the classroom, teachers and parents have an opportunity to become better acquainted. Every child benefits from a parent visit because the presence of a parent in the classroom helping and interacting with the students affirms the importance of the school experience.

Parent Resource Room

Sometimes schools provide a parent resource room, in which a variety of activities can take place. Such a room can provide space for small-group meetings (support groups, committees, informal gatherings) and, if space can be so configured, for private collaborative conferences. The resource room can display and make available various types of information to parents: grade-level curriculum materials; school handbooks and policy manuals; audio and visual materials of school events and topics of importance to parents and equipment for listening to and viewing them; video access to individual classrooms for observation; computer linkages to the classrooms; bulletin boards with calendars, school announcements, volunteer schedules, and small-group meeting dates; book and toy lending library and ex-change programs; recyclables programs; and opportunities to donate materials for arts and crafts projects and for thematic units and other long-term projects.

The parent resource room can provide a place where materials to assist parents in locating and using community resources are displayed and fliers, brochures, and other materials about local community-health and human-services agencies are made available. Resource people from these various community programs can be scheduled for small-group discussions in the parent resource room from time to time. Information about before- and after-school programs and child care, summer programs, tutoring sources, transportation and car pools, and nannies and babysit-ters can also be exchanged. When scheduling the hours of availability of the parent resource room, consideration will need to be given to the many parents who have limited opportunities to visit the school during regular school hours. Again, inno-vative and creative thinking will assure that no parent is disadvantaged by their family circumstances or employment obligations. These types of activities and events bring families into the community of parents and teachers, help them grow in a sense of belonging and ownership within the school, and open communication and collaboration between and among families and school personnel.

This chapter has attempted to convey the profound importance of establishing partnerships with families. As educators become skilled in the art of collaborating with parents and with parents and children, assessment and curriculum planning become more focused on strengths of individuals and, ultimately, more sensitive and constructive. Meaningful communications and supportive relationships among students, parents, and teachers are the foundation upon which relevant curricula and assessments are built and antecede excellence and equity in education.

The following poem perhaps best summarizes the effect of parent-teacher collaboration:

Unity

I dreamed I stood in a studio
And watched two sculptors there.
The clay they used was a young child's mind,
And they fashioned it with care.
One was a teacher; the tools he used
Were books, and music, and art;
One, a parent with a guiding hand,
And a gentle, loving heart.
Day after day the teacher toiled,
With touch that deft and sure
While the parents labored by his side
And polished and smoothed it o'er.
And when at last their task was done,
They were proud of what they had wrought.
And each agreed he would have failed
If he had worked alone,
For behind the parent stood the school
And behind the teacher, the home.

Author Unknown

REVIEW STRATEGIES AND ACTIVITIES

Vexing Questions

1. If large-scale standardized tests are intended to evaluate schools or programs, how can or should parents respond to their child's test-score reports?

2. How can child caregivers and early educators avoid inaccurate assessments when assessor and child and family speak different languages, apply different meanings to words, deeds, or body language, or have different value systems and understandings about the purposes of education?

   a. How can educators assure non-English-speaking families that testing and assessment practices are fair and equitable?

b. Should all teachers be bi- or multilingual?

c. Because letter and numerical grades are so universally understood, should they always be a part of progress reporting to parents? What do these markings actually tell parents about their child?

Activities

1. Interview a number of parents (10 to 15 or more) whose young children are in school. Ask each the following questions; then share and compare your findings with your colleagues. From this information, develop a plan for establishing a collaborative model for home-school interactions.

   a. What elements or features of your child's school (or classroom) solicit, encourage, or motivate you as a parent to take an active role in your child's schooling experience?

   b. What elements or features, if any, tend to impede your participation?

   c. What would you recommend to make your child's school more user-friendly for parents?

2. In groups of four or five, plan a brief skit in which some groups role-play a collaborative assessment conference demonstrating its purpose, process, and expected outcomes. Discuss and compare skits describing the successes and challenges of the collaborative approach to assessment of learning.

3. List and analyze the various resources available to parents in your school and community. Do parents use these resources? How are these resources made known to parents? How might resources be tapped to enhance the education process for children? Are there other resources needed by parents that the school or classroom teacher might access?

4. Prepare a welcome booklet for parents that explains the collaborative assessment process, defines the roles of children, teachers, and parents, and creates a calendar for collaborative assessment opportunities.

SUGGESTED LITERATURE AND RESOURCES

Cary, S. (2000). *Working with second language learners: Answers to teachers' top ten questions*. Portsmouth, NH: Heinemann.

Christian, L. G. (2006). Understanding families: Applying family systems theory to early childhood practice. *Young Children, 61*(1), 12–20.

Copple, C. (Ed.). (2003). *A world of difference: Readings on teaching young children in a diverse society*. Washington, DC: National Association for the Education of Young Children.

Diffily, D. (2004). *Teachers and families working together*. Boston: Allyn & Bacon.

Diffily, D., & Morrison, K. (Eds.). (1997). *Family-friendly communication in early childhood programs*. Washington, DC: National Association for the Education of Young Children.

Division for Early Childhood of the Council for Exceptional Children (2002, April). *Position statement on responsiveness to family cultures, values, and languages*. Denver, CO: Author.

Gauvain, M. (2000). *The social context of cognitive development*. New York: Guilford Press.

Helm, J. H., Berg, S., & Scranton, P. (2004). *Teaching your child to love learning: A guide to doing projects at home*. New York: Teachers College Press.

Lundgren, D. & Morrison, J. W. (2003). Involving Spanish-speaking families in early education programs. *Young Children 58*(3), 88–95.

Perry, T. C., Steele, C., & Hillard, A. (2003). Young, gifted and black: *Promoting high achievement among African American students*. Boston: Beacon Press.

Small, M. F. (2001). *How biology and culture shape the way we raise our children*. New York: Doubleday.

Young, D., & Behounek, L. M. (2006). Kindergarteners use PowerPoint to lead their own parent-teacher conferences. *Young Children 61*(2), 24–26.

ONLINE RESOURCES

Charles and Helen Schwab Foundation, http://schwablearning.org

Harvard Family Research Project, http://www.gse.harvard.edu

National Association for Bilingual Education, www.nabe.org

National Association of Elementary School Principals (Online Grade Books), www.naesp.org/content_oad.do?contentid=230

National Clearinghouse for English Language Acquisition & Language Instuction Educational Programs, www.ncela.gwu.edu

National Coalition for Parent Involvement in Education, www.ncpie.org

National Parent Teacher Association, http://www.PTA.org

Parents' Action for Children, http://www.parentsaction.org

III

Completing the Picture: Shared Responsibilities for Child Outcomes

8

Making Readiness Assessment Meaningful

There is good reason for the claim that early childhood years are formative. Indeed, virtually every human capability first makes its appearance during childhood.

Restak (2001, p. 35)

Ideally, children would enter kindergarten engaged in school, with good health, and with age-appropriate social development and cognitive skills. And, ideally, children would maintain their engagement in school and physical well-being throughout their early school years, while developing their social skills and advancing their cognitive achievement.

Vandivere, Pitzer, Halle, & Hair (2004, p. 11).

After reading and studying this chapter, you will demonstrate comprehension by being able to:

❑ provide several perspectives on the term *readiness* and discuss how definitions of readiness influence expectations of infants, toddlers, and preschoolers.

❑ list key developmental areas in which readiness is most frequently assessed.

❑ discuss how knowledge of a child's well-being indicators can contribute to our understanding of readiness.

❑ describe the critical nature of early development, relationships, and experiences.

❑ list reasons for early screening and intervention.

❑ describe the types of screening instruments frequently used to assess infants, toddlers, and preschool-age children.

❑ describe how families promote readiness attributes in children.

❑ discuss the uses and potential abuses of readiness assessments administered to preschool-age children.

Greta is a university senior with an early childhood education major who is completing the last of several student-teaching practica. Today she is observing a kindergarten teacher-directed reading lesson. The teacher has expressed some concern about the ability of some of the children to sit still, listen, and participate appropriately in the reading lessons required by the state-adopted kindergarten reading curriculum. The teacher convenes small groups of six children each for brief reading instructional periods. Greta is asked to record the types of behaviors she observes during the lesson. As the lesson begins, Greta looks at her watch, records the date and beginning time, and begins to take notes.

The children are each given a small paperback copy of a beginning reader, a pencil, and a worksheet containing pictures associated with words in the book. The kindergarten teacher instructs children to hold their readers so they can see the cover and begins the lesson by pointing out the illustrations on the cover, inquiring about what children think the book's story might be and then pointing to the print that spells the title of the book. She invites children to sound out the letters of each word and to orally read along with her as she points to each word. She then solicits student participation in phonetically decoding the simple words on each page and asks the children to recite in unison larger segments of print that they decode.

The lesson is brief, lasting less than fifteen minutes. In that time span, however, Greta records the following behaviors:

watching other children working in nearby learning centers
pulling T-shirt over face
rocking back and forth
poking pencil in navel
rolling up the thin paperback book, making a "horn" of it, and then humming
    through it
picking the eraser off a pencil
licking the page of the book
holding hands and giggling with a classmate
drawing with pencil on the teacher's chair
twirling pencil between fingers
rubbing eyes, as though sleepy
hiding face behind opened book
resting head in hands, staring at the floor
poking a classmate with foot
staring off in space
shouting out wild guesses in response to teacher's questions
requesting to go to the restroom
second request to go to the restroom
rearranging blocks on nearby shelf
soon joined by a second person rearranging blocks
covering worksheet entries with arm as though embarrassed for others to see
classmate attempting to assist another
turning worksheet over and drawing a picture
soon joined by second and third classmates turning worksheets over and
    drawing pictures

With but one or two exceptions, Greta observes that the children were "remarkably disengaged" for the duration of this reading lesson.

Was the reading lesson too advanced for these children? Were these children simply derelicts needing to be disciplined? Were the artifacts of the lesson uninteresting? Was the pedagogy developmentally *in*appropriate? Was the presentation boring? Were the children simply not "ready" for this type of reading instruction? How should the benefits of this lesson be gauged?

This vignette illustrates how child behavior suggests capabilities, interests, and approaches to learning. We see in this situation an apparent mismatch between children's interests and capabilities and the curriculum, instructional strategies, and participation/performance expectations. The concept of readiness certainly comes into play here. But how should readiness be defined, and who is responsible for "being ready"? In this vignette, should readiness rest with the children? The teacher? The school's textbook-adoption committee? The authors and publishers of the reading program? Let us see if we can give the concept of readiness a meaningful place in an early childhood–assessment system.

WHAT IS READINESS?

Readiness is a term that holds different meanings for different situations. The most frequent use of the term is to address the knowledge, skills, and abilities that individual children are expected to demonstrate in order to proceed to new experiences. This is most often applied to children's transition from the preschool years to the school-age years, in which they will be introduced to formal instruction and academic-achievement expectations. It is also used to address the eligibility of students to advance to more challenging tasks or subject matter or to advancing grade levels.

Theoretical Perspectives on Readiness

The term *readiness* first came into use in the 1930s when Arnold Gesell, a physician and psychologist who established the Clinic of Child Development at Yale University, conducted research on how children grow and develop (Gesell, 1925; Gesell & Amatruda, 1941). Gesell's studies led to age-related *norms* for motor skills, adaptive behaviors, language development, and personal/social behaviors. Gesell's research established what came to be known as *ages and stages* data, in which he found that each child grows and develops at an individual pace determined primarily by his or her genetic makeup. He also established that although growth and development generally follow similar and predictable patterns for all children, rates of growth and development vary among children. As such, Gesell believed that school entry and grade placements should be based on a child's behavioral level or developmental age rather than on chronological age.

But this *maturationist* theory is not the only perspective on readiness. There are others (Hogue, 2005). The *behaviorist* point of view purports that there are certain sets of skills and abilities that can or should be taught and mastered in order for a child to demonstrate readiness. The *social constructivist* definition of readiness suggests that readiness is defined by the demands or expectations of families, teachers, schools, communities (Graue, Kroeger, & Brown, 2003; Meisels, 1999). The *ecological* point of view addresses the different circles of influence in the lives of children that contribute to or impede optimal growth, development, and learning (Bronfenbrenner & Ceci, 1994; Rimm-Kaufman & Pianta, 2001).

The current emphasis on *school accountability* directs attention to readiness as an essential concept to be promoted among families, preschools, and communities in order for children to have the types of prerequisite experiences that ostensibly assure their success with formal instruction. Scores on accountability tests that will be administered during the early grades are expected to reveal this early preparation (National Governor's Association, 2005a, b). This focus has origins in recognition of the importance of early growth and development (maturationism) and contemporary emphasis on an interactionist (the interplay between heredity and environmental influences) point of view, particularly with regard to early brain growth and neurological development (Shonkoff & Phillips, 2000). But the implementation of policies intended to boost child readiness is based on a comingling of behaviorism, social constructivism, and ecological perspectives. As we shall see as our discussion proceeds, how one defines readiness influences how one attempts to measure and facilitate it.

Readiness Domains

The readiness movement took wings at the turn of the century when the U.S. Congress enacted the Goals 2000: Educate America Act (P. L. 103-227, 1994). As described in Chapter 2, this act listed eight goals (Figure 2.4), the first of which focused on school readiness: ". . . all children in America will start school ready to learn"—a goal that, in actuality, was not met. Nonetheless, in social and political circles today, there is continuing (indeed, increasing) emphasis on early school readiness.

Theory aside, many parents and educators tend to think narrowly of readiness as a level of maturity prerequisite to learning to read, write, and benefit from formal academic instruction (Graue, 1993; Graue et al. 2003; Hatcher, 2005; NAEYC & NAECS/SDE, 2000). This pervasive concept of readiness is characterized by what Graue et al. (2003) have described as a **kindergarten prototype.** According to these scholars, adults (teachers and parents) hold prototypical images of the kindergarten-ready child. This image comprises what adults perceive in a child's attributes that ostensibly foretell the child's readiness or unreadiness for the kindergarten experience. In this kindergarten prototype, readiness is associated with:

kindergarten prototype A perceptual model of the characteristics typically thought to represent a child's readiness or unreadiness for the kindergarten experience.

1. **Age**—for example, a child may be chronologically five years old but may be perceived as not ready if his or her birthday is close to the school entry date. Distinction is made between "young" fives and "older" fives, with youngness being perceived as a disadvantage. Conversely, birthdates further away from the school entry date are supposed to ensure an older kindergartener ready to participate at an optimal level.

2. **Stamina**—the need for a nap during the kindergarten hours is associated with a concern that the child might not be able to withstand the rigors of kindergarten (particularly where full-day kindergarten is provided) and suggests a physical level of immaturity thought to disadvantage the child.

Early childhood experiences that encourage physical/motor development contribute to individual readiness characteristics.

Lisa H. Witkowski

3. **Maturity**—a vague term that tends to describe social interactions characteristics of confidence, choice of playmates (with choice of younger versus older playmates denoting immaturity), compliance, and related attributes. Idiosyncracies are viewed as problematic.

4. **Work Habits**—primarily address the extent to which children rely on the teacher as opposed to being able to make choices and work independently. The less involved with the teacher the child is, the more likely the child is to be perceived as a compliant and ready learner.

This study underscores the fact that the prototypical concept of child readiness is frought with misjudgment and error potential and can lead to inappropriate placement and retention decisions. Further, this concept leads to inappropriate expectations for children who enter kindergarten at the legal age for admission but are among either the youngest or oldest in their class. Notice that each of these criteria (age, stamina, maturity, and work-related behaviors) are characteristics over which the child or parent has limited or no control. When explored deeper for the types of behaviors suggested by "younger or older fives," "low or high stamina," "mature or immature" behaviors, and expected "work" behaviors, we might well find that individual differences rather than readiness deficits are evident.

Other studies reveal that in many instances expectations for readiness may be unrealistic for some populations of children (McLanahan, 2005). Differences among white, African American, and Hispanic children in prior participation in child care and preschool, coupled with ranges in the quality of their early edcuation experiences, lead to varying readiness characteristics between and among children of different races and ethnicities.

So, what model is available to guide our definition of readiness and associated policies on school-entry-level expectations? The National Association for the Education of Young Children in its position statement on school readiness (NAEYC, 1995, p. 1) states that, ". . . the commitment to promoting universal school readiness requires:

1. addressing the inequities in early life experience so that all children have access to the opportunities that promote school success;

2. recognizing and supporting individual differences among children including linguistic and cultural differences; and

3. establishing reasonable and appropriate expectations of children's capabilities
upon school entry."

The National Education Goals Panel (NEGP) concluded that readiness was much
more than simply being ready to learn to read and carry out academic tasks and
identified a range of factors associated with child readiness (National Education
Goals Panel, 1995, 1997). Subsequently, a NEGP subcommittee of child-development
experts and educators distilled a broad set of factors into the following developmental domains:

◆ *Physical well-being and motor development,* which include health factors such as issues associated with birth weight, nutrition, and gross and fine motor abilities.

◆ *Social and emotional development,* which include developmental histories of secure attachments and social/emotional support, self-confidence, self-esteem,
and positive social/emotional interactions.

◆ *Approaches toward learning,* which include dispositions and learning styles
rather than skills per se, and dispositions such as curiosity, iniative, cooperation, and task persistence.

◆ *Language usage,* which includes receptive and expressive language with emphasis on ability to communicate effectively with others—both children and
adults. This domain also includes emergent literacy skills such as book and
print awareness, book-handling skills, discernment of rhymes and articulated
speech sounds, word play, and enjoyment of stories.

◆ *Cognition and general knowledge,* which include social-conventional knowledge, problem-solving skills, representational thought, and emergent math
knowledge.

The federal Head Start Child Outcomes Framework (U.S. Department of Health
and Human Services, 2002–2006) for the assessment of child progress and accomplishments includes eight domains: Language Development, Literacy, Mathematics, Science, Creative Arts, Social and Emotional Development, Approaches to
Learning, and Physical Health and Development. Table 8.1 shows the Head Start
Child Outcomes expectations for children ages three to five years. (Note that there
are four specific domain elements and nine indicators that are legislatively mandated for children enrolled in Head Start.) Assessment data regarding these items
are used to evaluate the effectiveness of the federal Head Start program for accountability purposes but do not negate the importance of other indicators of development and learning.

Although the focus of readiness assessment in these domains is on children before school entry, these domains are quite similar to the domains identified by
Dichtelmiller, Jablon, Marsden, & Meisels (2001) and Meisels (1993) that lend themselves to meaningful assessments during the early grades—kindergarten through
third grade (described in Chapter 3). Recall that those developmental and academic domains were personal/social development, language/literacy, mathematical
thinking, scientific thinking, social studies, the arts, and physical development.
Each of these domain sets focuses attention on whole child growth, development,
and learning. However, the growing emphasis on testing for accountability in
the primary grades (K–3) has vectored many of the indicators in these domains

Table 8.1
The Head Start Child Outcomes Framework

RELEASED IN 2000, THE HEAD START CHILD OUTCOMES FRAMEWORK is intended to guide Head Start programs in their curriculum planning and ongoing assessment of the progress and accomplishments of children. The Framework also is helpful to programs in their efforts to analyze and use data on child outcomes in program self-assessment and continuous improvement. The Framework is composed of 8 general Domains, 27 Domain Elements, and numerous examples of specific Indicators of children's skills, abilities, knowledge, and behaviors. The Framework is based on the Head Start Program Performance Standards, Head Start Program Performance Measures, provisions of the Head Start Act as amended in 1998, advice of the Head Start Bureau Technical Work Group on Child Outcomes, and a review of documents on assessment of young children and early childhood program accountability from a variety of state agencies and professional organizations.

- The Domains, Elements, and Indicators are presented as a framework of building blocks that are important for school success. The Framework is not an exhaustive list of everything a child should know or be able to do by the end of Head Start or entry into Kindergarten. The Framework is intended to guide assessment of 3- to 5-year-old children—not infants or toddlers enrolled in Early Head Start and not infants or toddlers in Migrant Head Start programs.

- The Framework guides agencies in selecting, developing, or adapting an instrument or set of tools for ongoing assessment of children's progress. It is inappropriate to use the Framework as a checklist for assessing children. It also is inappropriate to use items in the Framework in place of thoughtful curriculum planning and individualization.

- Every Head Start program implements an appropriate child assessment system that aligns with their curriculum and gathers data on children's progress in each of the 8 Domains of learning and development. At a minimum, because they are legislatively mandated, programs analyze data on 4 specific Domain Elements and 9 Indicators in various language, literacy, and numeracy skills, as indicated with a star in the chart. Local program child assessment occurs at least three times a year. The National Reporting System (NRS) child assessment includes measures of the mandated child outcomes.

- Information on children's progress on the Domains, Domain Elements, and Indicators is obtained from multiple sources, such as teacher and home visitor observations, analysis of samples of children's work and performance, parent reports, or direct assessment of children. Head Start assessment practices should reflect the assumption that children demonstrate progress over time in development and learning on a developmental continuum, in forms such as increasing frequency of a behavior or ability, increasing breadth or depth of knowledge and understanding, or increasing proficiency or independence in exercising a skill or ability.

LANGUAGE DEVELOPMENT

Listening & Understanding

- Demonstrates increasing ability to attend to and understand conversations, stories, songs, and poems.
- Shows progress in understanding and following simple and multiple-step directions.
- **Understands an increasingly complex and varied vocabulary.***
- **For non-English-speaking children, progresses in listening to and understanding English.***

Speaking & Communicating

- **Develops increasing abilities to understand and use language to communicate information, experiences, ideas, feelings, opinions, needs, questions; and for other varied purposes.***
- Progresses in abilities to initiate and respond appropriately in conversation and discussions with peers and adults.
- **Uses an increasingly complex and varied spoken vocabulary.***
- Progresses in clarity of pronunciation and towards speaking in sentences of increasing length and grammatical complexity.
- **For non-English-speaking children, progresses in speaking English.***

(continued)

Table 8.1
The Head Start Child Outcomes Framework (*continued*)

LITERACY

Phonological Awareness*

- Shows increasing ability to discriminate and identify sounds in spoken language.
- Shows growing awareness of beginning and ending sounds of words.
- Progresses in recognizing matching sounds and rhymes in familiar words, games, songs, stories, and poems.
- Shows growing ability to hear and discriminate separate syllables in words.
- **Associates sounds with written words,** such as awareness that different words begin with the same sound.*

Book Knowledge & Appreciation*

- Shows growing interest and involvement in listening to and discussing a variety of fiction and non-fiction books and poetry.
- Shows growing interest in reading-related activities, such as asking to have a favorite book read; choosing to look at books; drawing pictures based on stories; asking to take books home; going to the library; and engaging in pretend-reading with other children.
- Demonstrates progress in abilities to retell and dictate stories from books and experiences; to act out stories in dramatic play; and to predict what will happen next in a story.
- Progresses in learning how to handle and care for books; knowing to view one page at a time in sequence from front to back; and understanding that a book has a title, author, and illustrator.

Print Awareness & Concepts*

- Shows increasing awareness of print in classroom, home, and community settings.
- Develops growing understanding of the different functions of forms of print such as signs, letters, newspapers, lists, messages, and menus.
- Demonstrates increasing awareness of concepts of print, such as that reading in English moves from top to bottom and from left to right, that speech can be written down, and that print conveys a message.
- Shows progress in recognizing the association between spoken and written words by following print as it is read aloud.
- **Recognizes a word as a unit of print,** or awareness that letters are grouped to form words, and that words are separated by spaces.*

Early Writing

- Develops understanding that writing is a way of communicating for a variety of purposes.
- Begins to represent stories and experiences through pictures, dictation, and in play.
- Experiments with a growing variety of writing tools and materials, such as pencils, crayons, and computers.
- Progresses from using scribbles, shapes, or pictures to represent ideas, to using letter-like symbols, to copying or writing familiar words such as their own name.

Alphabet Knowledge

- Shows progress in associating the names of letters with their shapes and sounds.
- Increases in ability to notice the beginning letters in familiar words.
- **Identifies at least 10 letters of the alphabet, especially those in their own name.***
- **Knows that letters of the alphabet are a special category of visual graphics that can be individually named.***

MATHEMATICS

Number & Operations*

- Demonstrates increasing interest and awareness of numbers and counting as a means for solving problems and determining quantity.
- Begins to associate number concepts, vocabulary, quantities, and written numerals in meaningful ways.
- Develops increasing ability to count in sequence to 10 and beyond.
- Begins to make use of one-to-one correspondence in counting objects and matching groups of objects.

Table 8.1 *(continued)*

- Begins to use language to compare numbers of objects with terms such as more, less, greater than, fewer, equal to.
- Develops increased abilities to combine, separate and name "how many" concrete objects.

Geometry & Spatial Sense

- Begins to recognize, describe, compare, and name common shapes, their parts and attributes.
- Progresses in ability to put together and take apart shapes.
- Begins to be able to determine whether or not two shapes are the same size and shape.
- Shows growth in matching, sorting, putting in a series, and regrouping objects according to one or two attributes such as color, shape, or size.
- Builds an increasing understanding of directionality, order, and positions of objects, and words such as up, down, over, under, top, bottom, inside, out-side, in front, and behind.

Patterns & Measurement

- Enhances abilities to recognize, duplicate, and extend simple patterns using a variety of materials.
- Shows increasing abilities to match, sort, put in a series, and regroup objects according to one or two attributes such as shape or size.
- Begins to make comparisons between several objects based on a single attribute.
- Shows progress in using standard and non-standard measures for length and area of objects.

SCIENCE

Scientific Skills & Methods

- Begins to use senses and a variety of tools and simple measuring devices to gather information, investigate materials, and observe processes and relationships.
- Develops increased ability to observe and discuss common properties, differences and comparisons among objects and materials.
- Begins to participate in simple investigations to test observations, discuss and draw conclusions, and form generalizations.
- Develops growing abilities to collect, describe, and record information through a variety of means, including discussion, drawings, maps, and charts.
- Begins to describe and discuss predictions, explanations, and generalizations based on past experiences.

Scientific Knowledge

- Expands knowledge of and abilities to observe, describe, and discuss the natural world, materials, living things, and natural processes.
- Expands knowledge of and respect for their bodies and the environment.
- Develops growing awareness of ideas and language related to attributes of time and temperature.
- Shows increased awareness and beginning understanding of changes in materials and cause-effect relationships.

CREATIVE ARTS

Music

- Participates with increasing interest and enjoyment in a variety of music activities, including listening, singing, finger plays, games, and performances.
- Experiments with a variety of musical instruments.

Art

- Gains ability in using different art media and materials in a variety of ways for creative expression and representation.
- Progresses in abilities to create drawings, paintings, models, and other art creations that are more detailed, creative, or realistic.

Table 8.1
The Head Start Child Outcomes Framework (*continued*)

- Develops growing abilities to plan, work independently, and demonstrate care and persistence in a variety of art projects.
- Begins to understand and share opinions about artistic products and experiences.

Movement

- Expresses through movement and dancing what is felt and heard in various musical tempos and styles.
- Shows growth in moving in time to different patterns of beat and rhythm in music.

Dramatic Play

- Participates in a variety of dramatic play activities that become more extended and complex.
- Shows growing creativity and imagination in using materials and in assuming different roles in dramatic play situations.

SOCIAL & EMOTIONAL DEVELOPMENT

Self-Concept

- Begins to develop and express awareness of self in terms of specific abilities, characteristics, and preferences.
- Develops growing capacity for independence in a range of activities, routines, and tasks.
- Demonstrates growing confidence in a range of abilities and expresses pride in accomplishments.

Self-Control

- Shows progress in expressing feelings, needs, and opinions in difficult situations and conflicts without harming themselves, others, or property.
- Develops growing understanding of how their actions affect others and begins to accept the consequences of their actions.
- Demonstrates increasing capacity to follow rules and routines and use materials purposefully, safely, and respectfully.

Cooperation

- Increases abilities to sustain interactions with peers by helping, sharing, and discussion.
- Shows increasing abilities to use compromise and discussion in working, playing, and resolving conflicts with peers.
- Develops increasing abilities to give and take in interactions; to take turns in games or using materials; and to interact without being overly submissive or directive.

Social Relationships

- Demonstrates increasing comfort in talking with and accepting guidance and directions from a range of familiar adults.
- Shows progress in developing friendships with peers.
- Progresses in responding sympathetically to peers who are in need, upset, hurt, or angry; and in expressing empathy or caring for others.

Knowledge of Families & Communities

- Develops ability to identify personal characteristics, including gender and family composition.
- Progresses in understanding similarities and respecting differences among people, such as genders, race, special needs, culture, language, and family structures.
- Develops growing awareness of jobs and what is required to perform them.
- Begins to express and understand concepts and language of geography in the contexts of the classroom, home, and community.

APPROACHES TO LEARNING

Initiative & Curiosity

- Chooses to participate in an increasing variety of tasks and activities.
- Develops increased ability to make independent choices.

Table 8.1 (*continued*)

- Approaches tasks and activities with increased flexibility, imagination, and inventiveness.
- Grows in eagerness to learn about and discuss a growing range of topics, ideas, and tasks.

Engagement & Persistence

- Grows in abilities to persist in and complete a variety of tasks, activities, projects, and experiences.
- Demonstrates increasing ability to set goals and develop and follow through on plans.
- Shows growing capacity to maintain concentration over time on a task, question, set of directions or interactions, despite distractions and interruptions.

Reasoning & Problem Solving

- Develops increasing ability to find more than one solution to a question, task, or problem.
- Grows in recognizing and solving problems through active exploration, including trial and error, and interactions and discussions with peers and adults.
- Develops increasing abilities to classify, compare and contrast objects, events, and experiences.

PHYSICAL HEALTH & DEVELOPMENT

Gross Motor Skills

- Shows increasing levels of proficiency, control, and balance in walking, climbing, running, jumping, hopping, skipping, marching, and galloping.
- Demonstrates increasing abilities to coordinate movements in throwing, catching, kicking, bouncing balls, and using the slide and swing.

Fine Motor Skills

- Develops growing strength, dexterity, and control needed to use tools such as scissors, paper punch, stapler, and hammer.
- Grows in hand-eye coordination in building with blocks, putting together puzzles, reproducing shapes and patterns, stringing beads, and using scissors.
- Progresses in abilities to use writing, drawing, and art tools, including pencils, markers, chalk, paint brushes, and various types of technology.

Health Status & Practices

- Progresses in physical growth, strength, stamina, and flexibility.
- Participates actively in games, outdoor play, and other forms of exercise that enhance physical fitness.
- Shows growing independence in hygiene, nutrition, and personal care when eating, dressing, washing hands, brushing teeth, and toileting.
- Builds awareness and ability to follow basic health and safety rules such as fire safety, traffic and pedestrian safety, and responding appropriately to potentially harmful objects, substances, and activities.

*Indicates the 4 specific Domain Elements and 9 Indicators that are legislatively mandated.

Source: United States Department of Health and Human Services, Administration for Children and Families, Office of Head Start (July, 2004). *The Head Start Child Outcomes Framework.* Washington, D.C.: Author.

toward academic subject matter. This runs the risk of an early childhood education that mimics upper-grade formats in content and pedagogy. There is no evidence that push-down curricula and developmentally inappropriate teaching strategies enhance the learning process for young children. Indeed, such practices are typically developmentally inappropriate and are thus more likely to impede rather than promote learning (Bredekamp & Copple, 1997; Burts, et al, 1993; Stipek, Feiler, Daniels, & Milburn, 1995).

Interpretation of the intent of specific readiness indicators for instructional practices can vary among educators and reflects both their philosophical/theoretical perspectives (conscious or unconscious), their knowledge of child growth, development, and learning, and their level of training for teaching young children. Many states and local school districts have developed and adopted lists of readiness indicators, and because these lists, although focused on similar domains, vary in their scope and specificity, it is important to be discerning in their use. Figure 8.1 suggests questions to ask when developing or using readiness indicators.

Today, although the NEGP is disbanded, most states have adopted the NEGP and similar readiness domains and have established readiness indicators for each (Saluja, Scott-Little, & Clifford, 2000). Each state sets its own expectations for school readiness and prekindergarten programs. In so doing, state policymakers can address regional and local population trends and unique regional and cultural characteristics.

Child Well-Being Indicators

Many of today's children face challenges and obstacles to smooth and optimal growth, development, and learning during their formative years. Many enter school less ready than others and, over time, may or may not catch up with their classmates. Are there identifiable limitations or risk factors that, if minimized or eliminated, could facilitate progress toward child readiness? Although **child well-being indicators** have been collected since the 1970s and national and international trends have been noted, this information has particular significance today.

child well-being indicators
Aspects of a child's life that represent potential risk to optimal development.

Figure 8.1
Assessing Readiness
Indicators

Do the readiness indicators reflect reasonable expectations for the age of children to whom they are applied?

Do the readiness indicators address growth, development, and learning in all domains?

Do the readiness indicators represent truly essential skills, knowledge, or dispositions for the age and the situation for which readiness is expected?

Are the readiness indicators applicable across many populations of children representing diverse cultures, linguistic abilities, special needs and talents, gender, and socioeconomic backgrounds?

Are the indicators worded or framed in such a way that interpretation is clear and unambiguous?

Are the readiness indicators listed in a logical developmental sequence representing an expected order of emergence?

Do the readiness indicators avoid teacher-centric expectations, that is, expectations that are more teacher pleasing than developmentally typical?

The child well-being data collected by contemporary demographers and social scientists help us to recognize challenges faced by children and families and to explore how best to facilitate optimal development for later school achievement among very diverse populations of young children.*

Several efforts are in place to identify and track indicators of child and family well-being (for example, Annie E. Casey Foundation, 2005; Federal Interagency Forum on Child and Family Statistics, 2005; Foundation for Child Development, Child and Youth Well-Being Index Project, 2006; National School Readiness Indicator Initiative, 2005).

These indicators can identify the types of challenges that impede progress toward child readiness in children from birth to school age. As with readiness domains, different agencies and organizations collect data on similar, but not identical, child and family characteristics. For the most part, child well-being is measured against data depicting family economic security, health, social environments, and education opportunities.

For example, Child Trends data (Annie E. Casey Foundation, 2005) track state-by-state well-being indicators such as rates of prematurity and low birth weight, infant mortality rates, teen birth rates, percent of teens who drop out of school, percent of children living in families where no parent has full-time, year-round employment, percent of children in poverty, and percent of children in single-parent households. Studies addressing these issues find that children faced with these types of challenges are less successful upon school entry, and through later grades, they tend to lag behind others whose lives are less challenged (Lee & Burkham, 2002; McLanahan, 2005; Vandivere et al., 2004; U.S. Department of Education 2000; Zill & West, 2001).

Researchers use these data to examine the relationship of well-being indicators to a variety of child outcomes. For example, one study related child well-being indicators to school success in specific developmental areas such as cognitive knowledge and skills, social skills, engagement in school, and physical well-being (Vandivere et al., 2004).

Additional research tracks the availability and participation in preschool among diverse populations (National Institute for Early Education Research, 2006). Many studies have demonstrated that the types and quality of early childhood child-care and preschool experiences influence later success upon entering kindergarten (Magnuson & Waldfogel, 2005; National Institute of Child Health and Development, 2002).

These studies reveal that child care and preschool participation matters, and enrollment varies among race, ethnicity, and socioeconomic levels. One study found that early care and education might widen readiness gaps among groups of children enrolled in low-quality child care but could, on the other hand, narrow readiness gaps for minority groups who attend high-quality programs (Magnuson & Waldfogel, 2005).

These tracking systems, the data they obtain, and the research studies that they spawn provide insights into the extent to which families are able to foster the types of early development and learning necessary for their children to be school ready. These data, although used primarily to guide an array of state and local policy decisions, can well be used to guide the development of curriculum and assessment systems in child care, preschools, and beyond. They certainly provide

*To learn about child well-being indicators in individual states, go to www.kidscount.org.

rationale for early screening and intervention. Additionally, these data should be used to guide the selection and use of readiness tests and assessments, and the decisions that are made regarding individual children based on readiness-assessment information.

WHO NEEDS TO BE READY?

The foregoing discussion suggests that readiness for school is a complex and complicated proposition. It begs the question: Who needs to be ready? Implicit in this question is the suggestion that in addition to the child, who is typically the primary focus of readiness efforts, there are others who are responsible for assuring that early schooling experiences are, indeed, beneficial to young children.

Typically, when educators speak of readiness, the general concept is that there is a certain time in a child's life, a certain level of "maturity," or a certain set of acquired skills that foretell a child's ability to benefit from formal instructional practices. Although it is true that there are characteristics of children that enhance school performance, the burden of success with the expectations of kindergarten and subsequent grades does not rest solely with the child. Families, child-care programs, schools, communities, and policy-making bodies each have responsibilities for readiness-related and education outcomes. So, it is important to examine how each contributes to school-ready child development. Let us begin this discussion with the primary focus of readiness, the child.

Child Readiness

The expectation that children should or can be ready for school or formal forms of instruction assumes that something comes into existence during early growth and development that can predispose children to success. If this is so, when does this something emerge? Asked another way, does readiness have origins? This is a good question because it directs our attention to the growth, development, and learning that has occurred since birth (and before). Readiness does not appear at some magical moment months or a year or so before kindergarten entry. The point can be made that the health and integrity of prenatal development begin the journey toward school readiness, and from birth onward, children are growing, experiencing, and learning in ways that enhance or impede their chances for success in school. Profound developments during the infant and toddler periods are worth noting.

Two major areas of contemporary research are enhancing our knowledge of what and how infants and young children learn. The complementary bodies of research in the biological and behavioral sciences emphasize:

1. the importance of early brain growth and neurological development.
2. the types of nurturing experiences available to infants and young children that promote optimal growth, development, and learning (Shonkoff & Phillips, 2000).

Additionally, studies of intervention practices stress the importance of early screening to identify infants and very young children who may be at risk for

Studies have demonstrated that the types and quality of early childhood play influence later school success.

University Christian Church Weekday School, Fort Worth, TX

developmental and learning difficulties (Guralnick, 2001; Karoly, Kilburn, & Cannon, 2006; Shonkoff & Meisels, 2000; Shonkoff & Phillips, 2000).

Early Brain Growth and Neurological Development

Stunning advances in recent years in the fields of neuroscience and technology are expanding our knowledge about the brain and how it develops. Modern technology has made it possible for scientists to witness how, where, and when neurological connections occur and to observe this process as it actually occurs within the brain. Technologically sophisticated tools such as high-resolution ultrasound recordings, magnetic resonance imaging (MRI), positron emission tomography (PET) scans, brain electrobiology chemistry and analysis capabilities, and others have facilitated precise study of the brain's development and functioning. This research has shed light on the biological origins of conscious and unconscious behaviors by examining how brain cells process information at the molecular level and how literally billions of neuron and glial support cells become organized into elaborate networks that process complex forms of information and govern behaviors.

During prenatal development, the brain emerges as a cluster of cells, out of which neurons will emerge. As the brain grows, neurons migrate to various regions to fulfill a multitude of specialized purposes. When any of these neuron migrations are diverted, normal neurological development can go awry. Neurological development can be adversely affected by poor prenatal nutrition and health, disease, genetic mutation, and exposure to drugs or toxins.

sensitive periods Periods in growth and development when aspects of the environment and relational experiences have their greatest potential for help or harm (also referred to as *prime times*).

prime times Periods in growth and development when aspects of the environment and relational experiences have their greatest potential for help or harm (also referred to as *sensitive periods*).

The human brain becomes "wired" at an astounding rate during the early months and years of development as migrations, connections (synapses), and pruning take place. During the early years the brain appears to be quite sensitive to specific types of experiences (negative or positive) during certain developmental time periods (Perry, 1999; Shonkoff & Phillips, 2000; Thompson, 2001). Scholars refer to these periods as **sensitive periods,** or **prime times** (Greenough, Gunnar,

The human brain becomes "wired" at an astounding rate during the early months and years of development.

Lisa H. Witkowski

Emde, Massinga, & Shonkoff, 2001; Restak, 2001; Shore, 1997). A sensitive period is defined as "... a point in development when development is optimal if an event occurs, but the constraints are less" (Greenough et al, 2001, p. 18).

Frequently, these periods are referred to as *windows of opportunity.* This characterization has been criticized as suggesting an "open" or "closed" state, in which—when closed—further migrations and synapses cease (Bailey, Bruer, Symons, & Lichtman, 2001; Bruer, 1999). Early experiences are certainly and profoundly influential in early brain growth and neurological development. However, the concepts of prime times or windows of opportunity should not be construed to imply that beyond these "opportunities," growth and development is foregone. Rather, it is important to understand that although sensitive or vulnerable during certain growth periods, the brain remains open to experience throughout the life span. Table 8.2 illustrates some of these prime times during infancy and early childhood and the types of learning and experiences generally associated with facilitating brain growth and neurological development.

Other research has identified core neurocognitive systems associated with the types of learning and behaviors necessary for school success (Noble, Tottenham, & Casey, 2005). These scholars explored the neurobiological basis for (1) *cognitive control,* which is the ability to self-regulate or override inappropriate thoughts and behaviors; (2) *memory and learning,* which involve the ability to store and retrieve information; and (3) *language and reading,* which—importantly—include language development as a precursor to reading and, concomitantly, phonemic awareness (the sounds of language) as crucial to learning to read. Each of these systems develops within specific regions of the brain. With this knowledge of anatomical loci of development, it is possible to design tests that assess each type of learning as a single cognitive system. Such tests enable scientists to evaluate precise cognitive processes and the brain region where development is taking place. Hence, variations in readiness among children can be more precisely attributed. Armed with such capabilities, future screening and interventions can be more targeted and precise than is now the case, and school readiness tests as currently in use can be rendered obsolete.

Table 8.2
Growth Promoting Experiences During Prime Times in Early Brain Growth and Neurological Development

Age	Developmental Domain	Essential Experiences
0–2	Social Attachment	Consistency of care that is warm, nurturing, and predictable. Gentle, loving, dependable relationship with primary caregivers. Immediate attention to physiological needs for nourishment, elimination, cleanliness, warmth, and exercise and attention to discomforts and symptoms of illness and to psychological needs for comforting and enjoyable interactions.
0–3	Control of Emotions/ Ability to Cope with Stress	Age- and individually appropriate expectations. Responsive, empathic, predictable adults who understand and relate in positive and accepting ways to the child's unique personality traits, including play preferences, styles of interacting, expressions of emotion and moods. Assistance and coaching in understanding and learning to modulate emotions. Instructive, constructive guidance that teaches alternatives rather than punishes. Psychologically safe (nonthreatening and free of stress) interactions with adults. Playful engagement with others, both adults and children.
0–2	Vision	Early and regular professional vision examinations. Varied and interesting visual fields accompanied by verbal interactions that label and describe. Toys and personal belongings that enlist interest in color, shape, texture, size, movement, and other qualities.
0–5	Motor Development	Opportunities to use emerging muscle coordinations in a safe and encouraging environment. Play equipment and toys that engage both large and small muscles. Encouragement and positive feedback for physical/motor effort.
0–3	Vocabulary	Enriched and engaging verbal interactions: singing, talking, chanting, sharing picture books, stories, tales, wordplay, rhymes, and poetry. Interactions that label and describe objects and experiences as they occur. Social interactions that encourage all efforts to communicate and provide responsive feedback. Opportunities to pretend play and to both watch and interact with other young children.
0–10	Language	Enriched and engaging conversations that explore a variety of topics and employ interesting vocabulary, expressions, inflections, and sentence structures. Many and varied firsthand experiences. Social interactions with other children. Positive encouragement and focused responses and feedback for all attempts to communicate: speaking, listening, writing. Varied and interesting experiences with good literature, music, poetry, and drama.
0–10	Second Language	Focused and responsive verbal interactions in both native and second languages. Verbal interactions that label, describe, and extend opportunities to use language. Encouragement and positive feedback for all efforts to communicate, verbally and in writing. Opportunities to interact and converse with others who speak the second language. Shared stories, songs, dance, and other cultural artifacts and traditions.
1–5	Mathematical and Logical Thinking	Daily/weekly schedules and routines that are predictable. Playthings and curriculum materials that encourage mathematical and logical thinking: i.e., manipulatives that can be arranged, rearranged, sorted, grouped, sequenced, counted, and used to create and construct in a variety of ways. Many and varied opportunities to solve "real-life" problems; formulate hypotheses; experiment with solutions; challenge answers. Adult-child interactions that employ inquiry, reason, logic, and analytic thinking.
3–10	Music	Enjoyable and engaging experiences with many types of music and in varied contexts: at rest, during work and play periods. Both shared and privately enjoyed musical experiences: listening to many forms of music, singing and being sung to; rhythm and dance; music and dance programs and special events. Opportunities to explore and learn to play a musical instrument.

Infinity?

The brain is made up of seemingly infinite numbers of cellular units, intricately interconnected and engaged in an infinite array of electrochemical activity. It has been reported that during the first week of prenatal development, neurological cells form at a startling rate of 250,000 a minute. At birth, the brain's 100 billion or more neurons and glial cells have formed more than 50 trillion connections or synapses (Sylwester, 1995).

By age three the number of synapses is reported to be twice that of an adult, an enormous number that holds steady throughout the child's first ten years (Shore, 1997). After age ten, synapse density gradually declines, and by adolescence, the brain has discarded about half of the synapses that were present in the early years. Thereafter, and throughout life, the brain continually and actively produces and eliminates synapses (Caine & Caine, 1994, 1997; Shore, 1997; Sylwester, 1995).

First Experiences

Over the years, child-development literature has repeatedly documented the importance of warm, nurturing, supportive, and cognitively stimulating early experiences (Puckett & Black, 2005). Scholars now assert that the types of experiences that children encounter in their human and physical surroundings determine the extent to which their inborn potential can and will be expressed (Nelson, Thomas, & deHaan, 2006; Thompson, 2001). It is generally believed that positive early life experiences are essential to healthy growth and development in all developmental domains. This is affirmed by the fact that neuroscientists are able to demonstrate how early experiences influence the very architecture of the brain. Numerous studies have documented the influence of early life experiences on the way the human brain grows and forms neurological connections (Nelson, Thomas, & deHaan, 2006; Perry, 1999; Perry, Pollard, Blakley, Baker, & Vigilante, 1995; Shonkoff & Phillips 2000; Shore, 1997). Certain early life experiences have been shown to be of critical importance:

◆ early relationships
◆ opportunities for meaningful and pleasurable play
◆ engaging learning experiences
◆ health care and safety oversight

Early Relationships   The types and quality of the relationships that infants and young children experience have a decisive and long-lasting effect on how they will develop. Scientists believe that the infant's and young child's early attachment relationships directly affect the formation of certain neural pathways (Shonkoff & Phillips, 2000; Siegel, 1999). Affectionate, nurturing, dependable, engaging, healthy relationships with caregivers (mothers, fathers, family members, child-care persons, and early educators) are associated with later forms of social competence, stronger language and cognitive skills, and more effective work skills in school (Hart & Risley, 1995; National Scientific Council on the Developing Child, 2004).

Early relationships influence the extent to which children develop emotional competence, an important precursor to success in school (Peth-Pierce, 2001; Raver,

2002). Emotional competence includes the ability to modulate, express, and understand a wide range of feelings and emotions. Contemporary research is placing increasing emphasis on the need for environments and interactions that support the development of emotional competence in young children (Hyson, 2002).

Play   Play is what infants and children of all ages do. Play contributes to growth, development, and learning in all developmental domains. A childhood without play is unimaginable. However, trends in family life and early childhood care and education continually curtail the amount of time and opportunity that children have to play—spontaneously, freely, with toys, themes, playmates, and games of their own choosing. A century or more of scholarly research argues for more, not less, playtime in the lives of children (American Academy of Pediatrics, 2006; Isenberg & Quisenberry, 2002; Zigler, Singer, & Bishop-Josef, 2004; Zigler & Bishop-Josef, 2004). The relationship of play to early brain growth and neurological development is well established, as is the relationship to the types of knowledge and skills associated with readiness for and success in school that accrue when children have opportunities to engage in safe and pleasurable play (Nelson et al., 2006; Shonkoff & Phillips, 2000; Zigler et al., 2004; Stegelin, 2005). Indeed, the tenets of developmentally appropriate practices in early childhood education are based on a long history of research on how children learn through play and how pedagogies can capitalize on children's naturally evolving play mode by structuring classrooms, curricula, and materials in such a way as to invite young learners to become personally and actively engaged (Bredekamp & Copple, 1997; Copple & Bredekamp, 2006; Puckett & Diffily, 2004).

Need for Engaging Learning Experiences   From infancy onward, children thrive on sensory-rich, engaging environments that support their innate and compelling drive to grow, develop, and learn. Like play, learning is what children do. Play environments are learning environments, and learning environments can effectively and beneficially be play environments. Growth, development, and learning in all

The types and quality of experiences that infants and toddlers encounter determine the extent to which their inborn potential can and will be expressed.

Lisa H. Witkowski

domains are supported and facilitated by the structuring and provisioning of play and learning environments. This is true whether we are discussing infants or older children (Bredekamp & Copple, 1997; Copple & Bredekamp, 2006; Puckett & Diffily, 2004).

Need for Early and Continuous Health Care and Safety Oversight　Healthy growth and development depend on the type of caring that oversees and protects the health and safety of children. Timely and appropriate immunizations, protections from illnesses, avoidance of exposure to toxins, and monitoring children's environments for hazards that lead to injuries are essential. Additionally, nutrition, routine preventive physical (including vision and hearing) and dental checkups, and protection of children from undue stress and harmful relationships contribute to a child's health and well-being. All these health-related protections contribute to healthy brain growth and neurological development and increase the child's potential for benefiting from educational experiences, both in the present and as they make their way through the school years (Nelson et al., 2006; Shonkoff & Phillips, 2000). Poor health histories are often found among children of families living in poverty and families with low levels of education. Studies of children among low-income families and minority races find wide variations in readiness characteristics among children at school entry that are often associated with child mental-health problems, chronic physical conditions, environmental hazards, and poor nutrition. The health and well-being of parents is also a factor (Currie, 2005).

Not unrelated to the need for early and continuous health care and safety oversight and all the first experiences just described is the important need for screening and intervention. Timely screening by child development experts and diagnosticians can identify developmental issues and prescribe appropriate interventions.

Early Screening and Intervention

The following stories illustrate the importance of early screening and intervention.

Trevor

It was the first day of kindergarten. It was a very busy morning and dismissal time was approaching. Trevor appeared to be getting increasingly agitated. Seated on the floor with the group listening to his teacher instruct about dimissal and anticipate tomorrow's activities, he began to rock back and forth—his rocking becoming faster as he became less patient. He stopped rocking momentarily, brought his hands into his visual field, and began to flutter them in front of his face, trying hard to train his eyes on his fluttering fingers. He paused; then he looked at the clock, and in an impatient voice strained the words: "I i i . . . t's . . . twww . . . ellve . . . O' . . . clo . . . ck . . . ."

In the days that followed Trevor's teacher noticed that his fluttering-hand behaviors were often accompanied by jumping up and down in front of a particular bulletin board that had caught his attention or, sometimes, the classroom calendar. This behavior was repeated on the playground while standing facing a tree or post. He made little or no effort to interact with other children and monitored the teacher's movement about the clssroom, becoming disturbed if her routines varied.

Additionally, Trevor's teacher quickly observed that Trevor could read at an advanced level. He brought to school an advanced reader about Daniel Boone and retrieved it from is book bag at rest time. His mother advised his teacher that when he gets restless to "just give him a book to read." And indeed, a book to read did have a calming effect. It was soon determined by the school Reading Specialist that five-year-old Trevor was reading at a sixth-grade ("or beyond") level. Further, his math skills were equally advanced.

Angela

Angela suffered a head injury in an auto accident when she was three years old. At kindergarten-entry age, her difficulties were many. Both her speech and hearing were impaired, and her cognitive functioning was well below that of her age-mates. She was a pleasant and eager-to-please child who enjoyed play in the home-living area and giggling and interacting with both her classmates and the teacher. She loved music, and although her motor skills were seriously impaired, she enjoyed rhythm and movement activities.

Both Trevor and Angela reached kindergarten age without the benefit of comprehensive diagnostic and intervention services. Their health care had been adequately monitored through their respective health-care professionals. However, other aspects of their developmental histories did not receive adequate attention.

In Angela's case, her recovery from her initial injuries was closely supervised by her pediatrician; however, learning behaviors and opportunities and social and emotional behaviors did not appear to be as closely monitored. Angela's physician had made arrangements for her to participate in intensive physical therapy treatments, but her mother, a single mother with transportation issues, was not consistent in taking her for treatments. Angela's vision had been assessed, as indicated by the fact that she wore corrective lenses.

Trevor's parents, by contrast, were professionals whose lives were quite career oriented. Little was revealed to the teacher about Trevor's health history, and when the teacher began to describe his school behaviors and ascertain his parents' interest in further assessment for Trevor, they became quite anxious and avoided contact. Trevor's father expressed a vague kind of anger with the teacher for suggesting that Trevor might have problems that need to be identified. He viewed Trevor as simply a very smart child.

One of the first tasks of the early childhood educator is to observe and record these types of observations in order to determine if there are children in the class for whom additional information or specialized assessments may be needed. The teacher would want to ascertain the extent to which these children have had prior screening, diagnostic, and/or intervention services. This information may or may not have been provided by the parents and may require a parent conference to share observations and seek parental input.

Why is early screening important? The U.S. Department of Education's Office of Special Education and Rehabiliative Services has estimated that 759,000 children between the ages of birth and 21 received special education services in 2006 (US-DOE/OSER, 2006). This estimate does not include the number of infants, toddlers, and young children who had not been identified as eligible for services. A democratic society requires that all children be given their best opportunities to succeed. This is an inclusive goal that does not discriminate among children of different socioeconomic circumstances, race, religion, gender, or ableness. As indicated in Chapter 3, for this reason, there is a legal basis for early screening and intervention with children who may be at risk for health, psychological, or learning challenges.

There are many risk factors that presuppose a need for screening, diagnosis, and intervention. Such factors include genetic anomalies, premature birth and low birthweight, prenatal exposure to alcohol, drugs, or other toxins, maternal stress, maternal depression, under- and overnutrition, chronic and debilitating illnesses, disabling accidents, and living conditions characterized by low levels of education, poverty, abuse, neglect, negative or demeaning interactions, or violence. Early screening and identification increases the chance that interventions can take place as early as possible in a manner that serves the best interest of children and families and, importantly, when the effects of interventions can be most promising.

Through provisions of the Individual with Disabilities Act (Part C) (2004), screening is used to identify infants and very young children who may need additional assessments and/or diagnostic testing to determine their need and eligibility for intervention services. The IDEA defines infant or toddler disability as an individual under three years of age who needs intervention services because of developmental delays (as measured by appropriate diagnostic instruments) in one or more developmental areas: cognitive, physical, communication, social or emotional, or adaptive development. The law also defines disability as a physical or mental condition that has a high probability of resulting in developmental delay. Further, at risk is defined as one who would be at risk of experiencing a substantial developmental delay if early intervention is not provided.

The IDEA requires all states to have a Child Find system. Child Find is a program of public awareness, screening, and evaluation that is designed to locate, identify, and refer as early as possible all young children with disabilities and their families who are in need of early intervention services under Part C of IDEA or preschool special education under Part B of IDEA. Additionally, screening is required of pediatric health-care professionals who serve infants and children who are eligible for Medicaid. This screening includes comprehensive physical and mental health, vision, hearing, dental, and lead toxicity evaluations, followed by appropriate referral for treatment and intervention.

The law requires that all instruments used in screening and diagnosing children meet professional standards for reliability and validity. (Appendix F describes a number of commonly used assessment instruments.) Moreover, the screening process should always obtain information from several sources, including medical examinations, hearing and vision tests, necessary and appropriate standardized tests, and information provided by parents through interviews and questionnaires. Multiple sources of screening information are needed to provide sufficient information for professional diagnosticians to render an accurate diagnosis. Most effective intervention plans depend on an accurate assessment and diagnosis of the child's needs and risk factors (Meisels & Atkins-Burnett, 2005).

Equally as important as valid and reliable instruments and multiple sources of information is the need for screening and diagnostic techniques that provide, in a very practical way, meaningful and useful information. In an effort to meet this goal, some systems link early screening, intervention, and ongoing assessments in a contextualistic way (*Zero to Three,* Theme Issue, 2001). Referred to as **functional assessment,** these strategies are different from traditional screening tests. Functional assessments are, in effect, performance assessments in that they document physical, social, emotional, and cognitive behaviors in context. Rather than matching observed or tested behaviors to a set of developmental milestones, functional assessments focus on everyday, naturally occuring behaviors and accomplishments (Meisels, 2001). These behaviors and accomplishments are easily observed by parents and caregivers and describe the functional capabilities of an individual child. Hence, the focus is not just on whether or not an ability or behavior exists and/or at what age it occurs, but also on how the child uses his or her skills and abilities and how the child's environment nurtures and motivates—or impedes and frustrates—the child's attempts to function. For example, a caregiver taking care of children in her home discovered after a professional-development training seminar on infant

functional assessment An in-context performance assessment of how a child functions.

motor development that providing safe spaces for her infants and toddlers to move about rather than constraining them in their cribs and infant seats changed their behaviors in a variety of ways. The infants appeared less fretful and unhappy and made more frequent attempts to move and use their bodies to roll over, crawl, pull to a standing position, and attempt to stand alone and take steps. Their prior restrictive environment was impeding their abilities and desires to develop and utilize new skills—that is, to function. An example of a functional assessment system is the *Ounce Scale* (Meisels, Marsden, Dombro, Weston, and Jewkes, 2003), which is a performance-based assessment for use with infants and toddlers and engages families in the observation and assessment process. The Ounce Scale evaluates functionality in six developmental areas: personal connections, feelings about self, relationships with other children, understanding and communicating, exploration and problem solving, and movement and coordination. Another assessment system, the *DIR (Developmental, Individual-Differences, Relationship-Based)* focuses on infant core functional emotional and social capabilities (Wieder & Greenspan, 2001). [See *Zero to Three*, Theme Issue (2001) for additional examples.]

So what about Trevor and Angela? Trevor's teacher continued to monitor through a variety of techniques (observation notes, anecdotal records, time-and-event samplings, sociograms, and portfolio analysis) his behaviors and progress. She was particularly interested in keeping his mind challenged with meaningful and engaging curriculum content, but she set a major goal for him that focused on learning to play, independently and with others. Additionally, noticing that his locomotor movements and large-muscle coordinations in general were less controlled and fluid than typical for his age, she made certain that each day he had an opportunity to engage in movement and large motor activities. Because Trevor exhibited anxiety with change, his teacher maintained a very predictable schedule and followed sequenced instructional routines that seldom varied. When she knew she would be away from the class and another adult would be present, she always advised Trevor in advance of this change in his regular routine. Eventually, as he became more trusting, he acquired a small, but significant, measure of flexiblity. The time-and-event sampling charts in Trevor's portfolio over time revealed this ability to modulate his anxieties. These charts helped Trevor's teacher adjust her own timing and behaviors in ways that facilitated and supported this development.

Trevor's teacher skillfully led his parents to seek their pediatrician's assessment while offering the testing and diagnostic services of the school. Trevor was eventually diagnosed as having an autism-related syndrome, and adaptations for his advanced cognitive abilities were implemented in his kindergarten classroom. Although the suggestion was made that Trevor might benefit from placement in the third grade, his kindergarten teacher felt that his diminuitive size and his current emotional and social stage of development would place him at further risk in the upper grade. Further, his reading and math skills were well beyond the third-grade level, and, therefore, such grade placement would be superflous. His teacher reported that she thoroughly enjoyed working with and learning from Trevor, whose parents became quite active classroom volunteers. Trevor's social skills evolved slowly, but eventually he bonded with two of his classmates (one of whom was Angela) and began to show more and more pleasure in interacting with others. He continued to read advanced literature and particularly enjoyed algebraic math problems. An interesting class dynamic emerged; as children began to recognize Trevor's superior reading ability, they frequently sought his assistance with their own attempts to read. As the year progressed, they requested that Trevor be allowed to read to the whole class at storytime. Sometimes, Trevor would agree to do so; other times he declined. This peer admiration was a welcome contribution to Trevor's social development. Again, Trevor's portfolio effectively traced his social developmental progress through anecdotal records and time-and-event samples. His academic progress was revealed through logs depicting his reading selections and choices and use of materials. His teacher used this information to acquire the types of learning materials and literature best suited to Trevor's interests and abilities.

Angela's mother was encouraged to allow Angela to be tested for participation in a special education class at the school. Subsequently, as prescribed by her Individualized Education Program, Angela met with the special education teacher and speech therapist twice a week while remaining in her regular kindergarten classroom for all other instruction.

Assessments of Angela's progress were ongoing, and daily observation notes helped Angela's teacher monitor her play choices, her use of materials, her approaches to learning, and her interactions with other children. Angela's teacher met regularly, both formally and informally, with the special education teacher and the speech therapist so that the learning opportunities provided for Angela in these different settings were compatible and coordinated and so that her Individualized Education Program was followed and regularly revisited for needed revisions and adaptations.

Also, Angela's teacher provided many opportunities for her to develop large and small motor coordinations through music, rhythm, and other large motor activities and special equipment. Angela was provided many opportunities to gain literacy, numeracy, and other skills through her pretend play activities. A full portfolio documented Angela's progress with work samples, photographs, collaboration diaries, and anecdotal records. Her progress was promising, although her challenges were many.

As with Trevor, Angela's teacher worked diligently to establish rapport with Angela's mother and to keep communications open and frequent. Because Angela's mother was unable to visit the classroom due to employment and transportation constraints, communication took place through notes, scheduled conferences, and telephone and e-mail conversations.

Family Readiness

Families contribute to child readiness in many ways. Indeed, the family is the primary influence on child development and learning. Through family, children have their basic needs met, form first relationships, learn to communicate, experience the world in unique ways that are particular to their family's cultural, linguistic, and socioeconomic characteristics, and acquire value orientations. As the discussions of Trevor, Angela, and child well-being indicators suggest, there are many factors associated with individual child development and family life that contribute to or impede child readiness for school entry. Nonetheless, the following discussion assumes that there are contributions that families make that enhance their child's potential for early school success.

How Families Contribute to Readiness

Learning to Meet Whole Child Development Goals   It is important for families to recognize that child readiness does not mean that children must already have the skills that will be introduced in a particular grade or school setting. Nor should parents be left with the impression that cognitive and academic abilities are more important than other aspects of development and learning. Instead, they should recognize that children who are ready, enter with a background of varied and engaging educational experiences, a history of positive, affirming relationships, a repertoire of large and small motor skills and play behaviors, and the curiosity and enthusiasm for learning that undergird school success. To this end, families benefit from guidance that helps them to focus on all the developmental domains: physical/motor, emotional, social, language, cognitive, and moral.

A number of family-education initiatives address this important focus. One of the better-known parent-education systems is the *Parents as Teachers* program, which is an international early childhood parent-education and family-support program that serves families, starting with pregnancy and continuing through infancy and early childhood to age 5. The Parents as Teachers National Center (PATNC) develops curricula and trains and certifies early childhood professionals to work with families. The stated goals of the PAT program are to:

◆ increase parent knowledge of early childhood development and improve parenting practices.

◆ provide early detection of developmental delays and health issues.

◆ prevent child abuse and neglect.

◆ increase children's school readiness and school success (Parents as Teachers, 2006).

Many local communities across the country have established councils or task force groups to bridge home, child-care program, and schools in an effort to support child readiness. The Arlington (TX) Child Care Council of the Tarrant County Youth Collaboration (ACCC/TCYC) is one such initiative and is exemplary. We describe this and other community initiatives in Chapter 9. However, two examples of the ACCC/TCYC pamphlets reproduced in the appendix to this chapter suggest the types of interactions and activities that families (*and* teachers) can provide for infants, toddlers, and young children that support development and learning in all developmental domains (ACCC/TCYC, 2006). Intentionally brief, the practical information contained in these pamphlets is helpful without overwhelming parents.

Recognizing the Need for Health-Care and Safety Oversight   Infants and young children need ongoing professional health care that includes neonatal screening for birth anomalies, nutrition supervision, timely immunizations, timely attention to illness or accidents, and growth and development monitoring that includes dental, vision, and hearing examinations. Where health, disabilities, or developmental delay issues arise, early diagnosis, treatment, and referral for specialized services can occur. Where family challenges exist, referral to appropriate professionals and support systems can be made. Throughout early childhood, preventive physical, dental, and mental health care is essential. Good health at their school-entry age helps children meet the physical, mental, and social challenges of school.

In short, families contribute to health readiness by:

◆ making sure that children have regular health and dental checkups and timely immunizations and treatment for illness or injuries.

◆ providing nutritious meals and snacks.

◆ setting consistent routines for rest, sleep, play, and exercise.

◆ protecting children from avoidable accidents.

◆ assuring a safe and healthy living environment.

Wise Selection of Nonparental Care and Preschool Education Opportunities   Current contemporary family composition and employment patterns mean that more and more children are receiving nonparental child care during infancy and the preschool years. Additionally, the increasing awareness among families of the importance of growth and development during the early years has motivated many families to enroll their preschoolers in early education programs and to take advantage of assorted enrichment opportunities for their preschool-age children.

Years of research have demonstrated that quality early care and education foster growth, development, and learning in all developmental domains and contribute to later successes in school (Barnett, 1995; Barnett & Boocock 1998; Barnett et al., 1998; Behrman, 1995; Campbell et al., 2002; Lazar & Darlington, 1982; Peisner-Feinberg, et al., 2001; Ramey & Ramey, 2004; Schweinhart et al., 2005). Most of this research is related to children living in low-income families. However, contemporary research is finding that advantaged children benefit as well from well-designed, developmentally appropriate, high-quality early childhood education experiences (Barnett, Lamy, & Jung, 2005; Gormley, Gayer, Phillips, & Dawson, 2005).

Families are challenged to select appropriate child-care and early education programs that meet the unique needs of their individual infants and young children. They should look for care and education that:

◆ promotes and supports growth, development, and learning in all developmental domains.

◆ adheres to highest standards for the protection of health and safety of infants and children.

◆ provides positive, affirming, emotionally and socially healthy and satisfying relationships.

◆ holds developmentally appropriate expectations (age, individual, cultural) for infants and children.

◆ provides highly qualified adults and maintains small groups with low adult-child ratios.

◆ provides enriching play environments and language-rich interactions with children.

Importance of Family-Support Systems   All families benefit from available enrichment and support systems within their communities. Parent-education classes, literacy-development programs for children and adults, library story times for children, English-language tutoring, preschool and kindergarten tours and orientation, parks and recreation programs for children and families, and museums provide educational opportunities for children and families. Local service agencies and faith-based organizations provide other types of family support through adult education, counseling services, health-care resources, safety education, job training and employment services, and child-care resources and referral systems. The benefits to be gained from these types of supportive activities are many and contribute to *family readiness.* Educators who are familiar with local and state resources for families play a very important role in child and family readiness by helping families access needed support services.

Understanding the Purposes and Outcomes of Readiness Assessments   Readiness assessments are used to evaluate whether or not a child is "ready" for a particular experience, grade, or academic program. They are most often associated with school-entry decisions at the kindergarten and first-grade levels. There are wide variations in types of strategies used to determine child readiness: standardized tests and screening instruments, locally developed tests and screening instruments, checklists based on state- or locally developed lists of readiness indicators, and teacher observations before or during the first days or weeks of a particular grade or program.

Of the many types of assessments administered to children, readiness assessments are the most varied, controversial, and frequently difficult to justify. Hence, as a category of assessments, readiness assessments are the least clearly understood in terms of their purposes. Yet families have a need—indeed, a right—to know the purpose(s) for which readiness assessments are given, what type (s) of readiness assessment instruments will be administered, and how readiness scores are interpreted and used. Moreover, families, as primary decision-makers on behalf of their children, need clear and unambiguous guidance for the decisions they must make based on assessment results. Absent clear and viable options for children whose readiness scores (high or low) pose an exception or problem, assessment for readiness can be very frustrating for parents and, thus, can be deemed pointless.

Confounding this issue is the use of readiness tests that fail to meet professional standards for validity and reliability. In fact, scholars assert that there are few readiness tests that meet standards for validity and reliability (Meisels, 1987). This is particularly true of nonstandardized developmental checklists and screening instruments. Moreover, given the rapid and dynamic nature of early growth, development, and learning, such tests are poor predictors of later development. High or low scores on a readiness test at one point in time cannot adequately predict child performance in the upcoming weeks or months. Nor can such tests predict the rate or extent to which a child will respond to and learn from the new experience. Thus, readiness testing (particularly when only one form of assessment is used) has a high likelihood of leading to mistaken notions about what a child knows, can do, and will be able to do in an ensuing grade or new situation. Such tests pose ethical issues for educators and unnecessary angst-ridden dilemmas for parents (Hatcher, 2005).

Across the country, readiness test results are used variously to delay kindergarten or first-grade entry of "young" or "immature" children who are otherwise of the current (often legally prescribed) chronological entry age. A child who is delayed may be simply denied entry to kindergarten or first grade. The child may continue attendance in a child-care or preschool program or may not attend any type of educational program until the beginning of the next school year. Frequently, children who "fail" readiness tests for subsequent grades are retained in the same grade for an additional year.

transitional grade A grade placement, usually between two grades, designed to provide an additional year for growth and development prior to a particular grade entry (also referred to as a *bridge class*).

bridge class A grade placement, usually between two grades, designed to provide an additional year for growth and development prior to a child's entry into a particular grade.

In other instances children deemed "not ready," are assigned to **transitional grades** or **bridge classes,** which are intended to provide time for additional growth and development. For example, they may be assigned to a slightly more advanced prekindergarten or "junior kindergarten," pre–first grade (between kindergarten and first grade), pre–second grade (between first grade and second grade), and so on. This practice of delaying, retaining, or assigning to between-grade grade levels is often referred to as *the gift of time,* a concept and practice repeatedly challenged by scholars (National Association for the Education of Young Children, 1995; National Association of Early Childhood Specialists in State Departments of Education, 2002;

National Association for the Education of Young Children & National Association of Early Childhood Specialists in State Departments of Education, 2003). Some parents, fearing their child's inability to meet the demands of today's kindergarten, hold their age-eligible children back for an extra year with the hope that being older will advantage them, a decision referred to as **redshirting.**

redshirting Holding back a child who is eligible for school entry in the hope that an extra year of growth and development will be of benefit.

These types of decisions are generally referred to as high-stakes decisions, because they have important implications for families and children, both in the short and the long term, such as increased costs to families for an additional year of child care, for further corroborating assessments, and for enrollment in alternative programs. Schools, as well, incur additional costs for each added grade to the existing prekindergarten/kindergarten to grade twelve structure. The short- and long-term effects on children include, for example, issues associated with parental disappointment or anxiety, self-esteem, and sense of failure; missed opportunities to learn during the intervening year; elevated expectations upon entry as an "older" member of a class; increased potential for burning out and, later, dropping out of school. Placement and retention decisions associated with readiness test outcomes have been widely studied and, for most children, found to be unsatisfactory, if not deleterious (Atkins-Burnett et al., 2001; Ferguson, 1991; Meisels, 1986; 1987; 1989; 1992; 1999; Morrison, Griffith, & Alberts, 1997; Phillips, Crouse, & Ralph, 1998; Shepard & Smith, 1986; 1987; 1988; 1989).

In order to best guide parental decisions regarding school entry or grade placement, educators have an ethical responsibility to select valid and reliable readiness-assessment instruments and to consider carefully the pitfalls associated with their interpretation. Importantly, information obtained from assessments must be used in ways that are proven to benefit children.

The most effective use of readiness-assessment information is to provide families with information and ideas for helping their children gain specific types of knowledge and skills and to set school and program expectations that are responsive to individual differences and developmental variations among children. Readiness-assessment information should be used to benefit children, both within the home and family and in education settings, through strategic development of curricula and instructional strategies that meet established criteria for developmentally appropriate practices.

In spite of the pitfalls associated with readiness testing, its use is destined to increase as the nation moves rapidly toward providing universally available prekindergarten classes in public schools. The need for valid, reliable, and predictive instruments must be met if widespread readiness testing begins to take place. In the current context, given the pitfalls associated with these assessments, many scholars discourage their use in determining eligibility for school entry and, instead, recommend using entry age as the only truly ethically and legally defensible criteria for school admission (NAEYC, 1995; NAECS/SDE, 2002).

When chronological age becomes the criteria for school entry or grade placement, greater responsibility for readiness is transferred to schools and classroom teachers. Because no class of children at any age can be "homogenized" so that there will not be wide ranges in abilities, interests, background experiences, and development, the responsibility for children's success rests not with the readiness factor, but within a child-friendly school that supports teachers in their efforts to assess children in an ongoing manner as they work, play, grow, and learn over time. Thus, educators can continually adapt and refine curricula and instructional strategies to meet the unique needs of individuals and provide fair and equitable opportunities for all children.

A "ready child" welcomes new experiences that match her age and capabilities.

University Christian Church Weekday School, Fort Worth, TX

The need for schools and educators to use readiness-assessment information in ethical and useful ways and to anticipate the needs of young children in the planning and implementation of early childhood programs brings us to the topic of our next chapter, that of evaluating schools and programs for young children and assessing school and community readiness—the last and final part of a meaningful assessment system.

REVIEW STRATEGIES AND ACTIVITIES

Vexing Questions

1. What is the potential for an emphasis on readiness to trump the need for young children to enjoy a carefree childhood?

2. Is it reasonable to expect that all children could enter kindergarten prepared to meet the challenges kindergarten might pose?

3. Consider the options for the use of readiness assessments: denial of entry, retention, referral to a different program, or admission with or without preparation of classrooms, curricula, materials, and perhaps modified instruction procedures to meet individual needs and capabilities and/or screening for special needs and talents. How do we assure that decisions are made that "do no harm"?

4. How might more parents be given opportunities to learn about child growth, development, and learning?

Activities

1. Download, from your state's department of education, the definition of readiness and its accompanying readiness indicators. Compare your state with at least two other states in other U.S. regions. How does your state define readiness for school? How does this definition compare with other states' definitions? What accommodations are made in readiness assessments for children with special needs and children with limited English proficiency?

2. Take a survey of ten parents and ten kindergarten teachers regarding their beliefs about the following characteristics that are often associated with child readiness for kindergarten. Ask them to rank the following child characteristics on a scale from 1 to 4 (1 = important and 4 = essential):

   ◆ is physically healthy, well-nourished, rested
   ◆ manages personal needs (clothing, toileting, eating, and obtaining and using learning materials)
   ◆ speaks in complete sentences (in first language)
   ◆ is curious and enjoys new experiences
   ◆ enjoys pretend play
   ◆ follows directions and conforms to rules
   ◆ sits still and pays attention
   ◆ takes turns and shares
   ◆ shows a caring attitude toward classmates
   ◆ manages crayons, paints, pencil/paper
   ◆ knows letters of the alphabet
   ◆ phonetically sounds out some letters or words
   ◆ writes name
   ◆ knows full name, address, and phone number
   ◆ recognizes numerals
   ◆ counts to 20

   Compare parents' and teachers' responses. Compare your findings with those of your classmates. What trends do you find? On which characteristics do parents and teachers generally agree? Differ? How should professional educators address these differences in perceptions and expectations?

4. Look over this list again. Which of these characteristics are child-development oriented? Are any of these characteristics teacher-centric—that is, certain attributes are simply teacher-preferred behaviors and their presence or absence is more of a benefit or problem for the teacher than a representation of atypical child development?

SUGGESTED LITERATURE AND RESOURCES

Bergen, D., & Coscia, J. (2001). *Brain research and childhood education: Implications for educators*. Olney, MD: Association for Childhood Education International.

Blaustein, M. (2005). See, hear, touch: The basics of learning readiness. *Beyond the Journal.* Washington, DC: National Association for the Education of Young Children. Downloaded 7/1/05: www.journal.naeyc.org

Estok, V. (2005). One distict's study on the propriety of transition-grade classrooms. *Young Children, 60*(2), 28–31.

Finn-Stevenson, M., & Zigler, E. (1999). *Schools of the 21st century: Linkng child care and education.* New York: Perseus Books.

Fromberg, D. P. (2002). *Play and meaning in early childhood education.* Boston: Allyn & Bacon.

Gallagher, K. C. (2005). Brain research and early childhood development: A primer for developmentally appropriate practice. *Young Children 60*(4), 12–18, 20.

Jones, E., & Cooper, R. M. (2006). *Playing to get smart.* New York: Teachers College Press.

Lerner, C., & Dombro, A. L. (2004). *Bringing up baby: Three steps to making good decisions in your child's first years.* Washington, DC: Zero to Three Press.

Marshall, H. H. (2003). Research in review: Opportunity deferred or opportunity taken?: An updated look at delaying kindergarten entry. *Young Children, 58* (5), 84–93.

Meisels, S. J., & Atkins-Burnett, S. (2005). *Developmental screening in early childhood: A guide* (5th ed.). Washington, DC: National Association for the Education of Young Children.

Minogue, A., & Clothier, S. (2005). *Measuring progress toward school readiness.* Denver, CO: National Conference of State Legislatures.

Moyer, J. (2001). *The child-centered kindergarten: A position paper. Childhood Education, 77*(3), 161–166.

Parlakian, R. (2003). *Before the ABCs: Promoting school readiness in infants and toddlers.* Washington, DC: Zero to Three Press.

Scully, P. A., Seefeldt, C., & Barbour, N. H. (2003). *Developmental continuity across preschool and primary grades* (2nd ed.). Olney, MD: Association for Childhood Education International.

Walmsley, S. A., & Walmsley, B. B. (1996). *Kindergarten ready or not?: A parent's guide.* Portsmouth, NH: Heinemann.

Winton, P., Catlett, C., & James, A. C. (2005). Resources to help teachers and other adults to discover the evidence base for early childhood and early intervention practices. *Young Exceptional Children, 9*(1), 3032.

Wittmer, D. S., & Petersen, S. H. (2006). *Infant and toddler development and responsive program planning: A relationship-based approach.* Upper Saddle River, NJ: Merrill/ Prentice Hall.

ONLINE RESOURCES

Early Childhood Research & Practice (L. Katz & D. Rothenberg, Eds.) Internet journal from the ERIC Clearinghouse on Elementary and Early Childhood Education, http://ecrp.uiuc.edu/

Federal and state policy developments, www.naeyc.org/policy/federal

First Signs, www.firstsigns.org

Members of Congress, http://capwiz.com/naeyc/home

National Association for the Education of Young Children Accreditation Performance Criteria, http://www.naeyc.org/accreditation/performance_criteria/

NAEYC Public Policy Resources: Advocacy/public policy/critical issues, www. naeyc.org/policy; www.naeyc.org/ece/critical.asp

National Center for Fair and Open Testing, www.fairtest.org

National Center for Research on Evaluation, Standards, and Student Testing, www.cse.ucla.edu

National Child Care Information Center, http://www.nccic.org

National Education Goals Panel, www.negp.gov

National Institute for Early Education Research National Network for Child Care, www.nncc.org

National School Readiness Indicators Initiative, www.gettingready.org

National Scientific Council on the Developing Child, http://www.developingchild. net/about.shtml

Rethinking Schools: The Urban Education Journal, www.rethinkingschools.org

Appendix

| **Skill Set Building Activities** | **Now that you've identified the specific School Readiness Skills you would like to work on with your child, below are examples of some activities you can do to ensure that he or she is ready for school.** *For more skill set building activities check our web site:* www.tcyc4kids.org/accc. |

Large and Small Muscle Coordination

Skill Set builder:	**1 year old activities:**
Coordination, balance and flexibility	-Roll small ball back & forth -Bowl with child using a ball and plastic bottles
Holding and manipulating small play objects	-Finger Paint with pudding -Play with "Busy Boxes" with controls & buttons -Play dump and fill with small blocks and pail
Exhibiting age-related coordination	-Provide pull toys to use while walking -Make a game of carrying soft toys or objects while walking

Emotional and Social Resilience

Skill Set builder:	**1 year old activities:**
Positive self-regard	-Specifically & positively express your feelings for child and his/her accomplishments -Verbal & physical recognition
Pride in accomplishments	-Offer gestures and responses child can imitate when appropriate (clapping, "So Big!")
A "try-again" attitude with difficult or challenging tasks	-Offer activities child can master -Reinforce successes

Math, Social Studies and Art

Skill Set builder:	**1 year old activities:**
Reciting numbers in sequence	-Count child's toes and fingers -Count Cheerios or Goldfish -Explore counting books together
Counting (using one-to-one correspondence), sorting, ordering, making patterns	-Count blocks as the child puts them in a bucket to dump -Provide a shape sorter -Look at family photo and label family members for child -Explore board books about family
Exhibiting beginning awareness of the needs and rights of others	-Express your feelings and the feelings and rights of others while playing with child "Sue had that first, let's share." -Model expected behavior
Exhibiting beginning awareness of family and cultural membership and similarities and differences among people	-Look at family photo and label family members for child -Explore board books about family
Exhibiting beginning awareness of the importance of rules in family and school	-Set boundaries -Offer child an alternative when possible "Chairs are for sitting." -Follow through if necessary
Engaging all five sense to explore	-Offer toys & activities that stimulate all senses -During play encourage child to use all senses "Feel it, it's soft." -Put on music and dance with child -Encourage child to care for a doll

Self-Confidence

Skill Set builder:	1 year old activities:
Interacting with playmates	-Peek-a-Boo with caregiver -Play any game with gestures or actions to imitate -Set up play dates with other children
Self-selecting activities	-Provide child with appropriate choices in activities, toys and foods -Provide specific praise when child makes appropriate choices
Initiating an idea or activity	-Reinforce child positively with words and play when he/she brings a toy/activity to caregiver
Engaging in new or challenging activities	-Provide activities at which child can succeed -Talk to child, reassure and guide him/her through each step
Seeking adult assistance	-Positively respond to child when he/she seeks your assistance -Model words or gestures to use

Emotional Maturity

Skill Set builder:	1 year old activities:
Using language to express feelings and needs to resolve conflicts	-Label emotions child expresses -Model acceptable words or actions ("No", "Mine" "Juice" "Blanket" . . .) -Redirect unacceptable expressions
Demonstrating age-appropriate self-control	-Monitor to ensure child does not become over tired, hungry or frustrated -Calm child with speech & touch
Seeking and/or accepting comfort, assistance, and guidance	-Positively respond to child when he/she seeks your assistance -Model words or gestures to use
Employing age-appropriate self-comforting strategies	-Provide a "lovey" to soothe child (bear, blanket, doll) -Allow child ample time/place to soothe self -Stay calm & supportive

Uses Language Effectively

Skill Set builder:	1 year old activities:
Communicate needs and interests	-Provide words for gestures ("You want to go outside") -Encourage child to use one–two word requests ("juice, "bear")
Listen and engage in conversation	-Talk to child throughout the day -Provide child with labels for objects and actions
Communicate play and pretend intentions	-Provide words for gestures ("You want to go outside") and encourage child to use words
Share ideas and convey meaning	-Listen to child -Share ideas with child
Share stories and events	-Listen to child -Share ideas with child

Self-Care

Skill Set builder:	1 year old activities:
Self-dressing	-Label items of clothing and body parts as you dress child -Help child dress and undress; encourage him/her to finish
Toileting	-Talk to child using "potty terms" while diapering child -Use same terms when you notice child is having a BM
Hand-washing and personal cleanliness	-Give child a warm wash cloth to wash hands and face after diapering & eating -Let child "brush" teeth & hair
Self-feeding	-Provide finger foods -Encourage child to use cup
Responsibility for personal belongings	-Child shadows caregiver in putting away toys or clothes -Child "washes" eating space

Curiosity, Creativity and Inventiveness

Skill Set builder:	1 year old activities:
Asking questions; seeking information	-Be open and available -Answer specific question child asks (not too much information) and ask child questions
Exploring learning materials	-Create safe environment for exploration -Offer a variety of new learning materials
Using play equipment and learning materials for a variety of pretend and constructive purposes	-Provide a variety of ways to use materials -Reinforce creative uses
Participating in a variety of experiences	-Expose child to a variety of toys and experiences -Offer support and guidance as they explore
Engaging in creative and imaginative play	-Provide dolls, encourage child to "care" for baby (feed, clothe, diaper, cover with blanket)
Uses objects to represent ideas, or events	-Give child a play telephone to play with and imitate as you use the phone

Exhibits Increasing Awareness of Print

Skill Set builder:	1 year old activities:
Associating storys and books with pleasure and information	-Let your child see you reading -Read a variety of genre with child
Recognizing and beginning to print name	-Teach child to say his name
Showing interest in print and understanding that print conveys meaning	-Read to child
Demonstrating an awareness of sounds in spoken words (e.g., rhymes and alliterations)	-Read poems and rhymes to child -Sing rhyming songs with child (Open, Shut Them; Pat-a-Cake)
Demonstrating some book and story knowledge	-Lap read to the child

Skill Set Building Activities

Now that you've identified the specific School Readiness Skills you would like to work on with your child, below are examples of some activities you can do to ensure that he or she is ready for school. *For more skill set building activities check our web site:* www.tcyc4kids.org/accc.

Large and Small Muscle Coordination

Skill Set builder:

Coordination, balance and flexibility

Holding and manipulating small play objects

4 year old activities:

-Set up an obstacle course
-Play "Simon Says": stand on one foot, hop, run, jump, gallop, walk on tip toes
-Play "Duck, Duck, Goose"
-Play with peg boards, puzzles, or Legos
-Draw and paint shapes
-Work on writing name

Math, Social Studies and Art

Skill Set builder:

Shows an interest in real-life mathematical concepts by counting, sorting, ordering, making patterns with objects

Exhibiting beginning awareness of family and cultural membership and similarities and differences among people

Exhibiting beginning awareness of the importance of rules in family and school

Employing art, music, dance, drama, and pretend play as means of self-expression, creativity, and fantasy

4 year old activities:

-Talk about "subtraction" as child eats his/her goldfish snack using "the shark (child) takes one away, let's see how many are left"
-Make patterns with legos, beads using just two colors or shapes in pattern (AB pattern)
-Make cards with dots and coinciding number, child places one small toy on each dot, count and reinforce number
-Help child express his/her rights/feelings to others
-Help children to compromise "Caitlyn, Sue wants the doll too, how can we help her?"
-Positively reinforce compromise
-Set limits, follow through
-When enforcing set rules and boundaries ask child "David, can you tell me why we have that rule?" Then reiterate the purpose of the rule or clarify the purpose of the rule, offer alternatives
-Encourage child to paint or draw recent experiences or self
-Model drawing specific objects
-Draw with child, helping him/her to draw things by request

Emotional Maturity

Skill Set builder:

Using language to express feelings and needs to resolve conflicts

Demonstrating age-appropriate self-control

Seeking and/or accepting comfort, assistance, and guidance

Employing age-appropriate self-comforting strategies

4 year old activities:

-Provide assistance to child in expressing needs and emotions
-Encourage child to express feelings and offer compromises
-Show them alternatives through your actions
-Monitor child's needs and mood
-Label feelings and offer choices & independence
-Set limits and follow through
-Positively respond to child when he/she seeks your help
-Show words or gestures to use
-Monitor child's frustration level
-Allow enough time/space to soothe themselves
-Stay calm & supportive

Emotional and Social Resilience

Skill Set builder:

Positive self-regard

Pride in accomplishments

A "try-again" attitude with difficult or challenging tasks

4 year old activities:

-Help child identify their talents and successes
-Specifically and positively recognize their talents & traits
-Specifically & positively express your feelings for child and his/her accomplishments
-Break difficult task in small bites
-Reinforce each step of success

Exhibits Increasing Awareness of Print

Skill Set builder:

Associating storys and books with pleasure and information

Recognizing and beginning to print name

Showing interest in print and understanding that print conveys meaning

Demonstrating an awareness of sounds in spoken words (e.g., rhymes and alliterations)

Demonstrating some book and story knowledge

4 year old activities:

-Read a variety of types of stories to child
-Assist child in finding information in books
-Have child trace & erase name on a lamented strip with a washable marker
-Write on a dot-to-dot name plate
-Point out and trace title of book with child before you read it
-Help child write names of family
-Use clipboard for food "orders"
-Read poems and rhymes to child
-Play a fun game where you and the child make up silly rhymes
-Read to the child
-Point out the title & trace words
-After you read a book casually talk about the characters and story sequence

Self-Confidence

Skill Set builder:

Interacting with playmates

Self-selecting activities

Initiating an idea or activity

Engaging in new or challenging activities

Seeking adult assistance

4 year old activities:

-Play low level organized games: Candy Land and I Spy
-Plan play dates and encourage imaginary play
-Free choice in toys & activities
-Appropriate choices of day's activities, clothes, foods
-Variety of toys on child's level
-Praise appropriate choices
-Reinforce child positively with words and play
-Stretch child's thinking/ideas
-Build on successful activities so they require more thought & skill
-Talk to child, reassure and guide him/her through each step
-Positively respond to child when he/she asks for help
-Help child to ask other adults

Uses Language Effectively

Skill Set builder:	4 year old activities:
Communicate needs and interests	-Support child in expressing needs to other children or unfamiliar people
Listen and engage in conversation	-Listen to child and respond -Ask child questions about things of interest -Support child in conversation with others
Communicate play and pretend intentions	-Encourage child to use words -Support child when talking to others
Share ideas and convey meaning	-Clarify child's ideas -Support child as they share ideas with others
Share stories and events	-Share stories with child -Clarify events in child's story -Encourage child to share story with others -Help child put an event in sequence

Self-Care

Skill Set builder:	4 year old activities:
Self-dressing	-Allow child to pick outfits and let him/her dress him/herself -Use terms "right and left" with child as he/she dresses
Toileting	-Choose clothing that is easy to get in and out of -Encourage and reward his/her going by his/herself
Hand-washing and personal cleanliness	-Supervise & assist child in bathing, brushing teeth & hair -Talk through it as you do it
Self-feeding	-Let child make some food choices and help prepare food and clean-up
Responsibility for personal belongings	-Supervise & assist child in cleaning up his/her room -Help them break it into smaller tasks (putting away clothes, toys, etc)

Curiosity, Creativity and Inventiveness

Skill Set builder:	4 year old activities:
Asking questions; seeking information	-Be open and available -Answer specific questions -Show child how to seek out answers/problem solve
Exploring learning materials	-Offer a variety of new learning materials (routinely rotate toys) -Model and provide variety of ways to use materials
Using play equipment and learning materials for a variety of pretend purposes	-Model and provide a variety of ways to use materials -Allow children to use toys in a variety of learning centers -Reinforce creative uses
Participating in a variety of experiences	-Use child's interests and abilities to encourage play -Rotate children in small groups to different activities
Engaging in creative and imaginative play alone and/or with others	-Make & provide puppets to extend child's understanding of a book or experience -Act out child's favorite book or fairy tale

Source: Reproduced with permission by Arlington Child Care Council, a community initiative of the Tarrant County Youth Collaboration.

9

Program Evaluation

An Essential Component of a Meaningful Early Childhood Assessment System

Some day you are goin to make A+ on sometin.
   Seven-year-old's pretend-teacher's note to playmate-pupil

Expanding early childhood initiatives gives students a greater opportunity to learn and grow, giving them a brighter future in the classroom. If our children are well cared for, we know that our communities are strong and our future is bright.
   Pennsylvania Governor Edward G. Rendell (National Governors' Association, 2005a)

After reading this chapter, you will demonstrate comprehension by being able to:

❏ discuss the reasons for evaluating early childhood care and education programs.

❏ list important child, family, and societal outcomes of high-quality care and education programs for children.

❏ list the essential characteristics of high-quality early care and education programs for children.

❏ describe the various strategies employed to evaluate programs that serve young children.

❏ discuss how schools and communities fulfill readiness requirements for serving young children and families.

EARLY CARE AND EDUCATION READINESS

A meaningful assessment system includes not only the assessment of student progress and achievement, but—importantly—the environments in which such progress and achievements are expected to take place. In the previous chapter, we discussed the many facets of child readiness and the importance of the ready family in supporting and facilitating optimal development in children. In this final chapter we explore how child-care people and programs, schools, and communities also have responsibilities for child well-being, developmental progress, readiness, and learning and how their abilities to meet those responsibilities are assessed.

DEFINING EVALUATION

The recognition by scientists of the importance of the early months and years in human growth and development has brought unprecedented public and political attention to early childhood care and education (National Governors Association, 2005a, b). Additionally, there is now compelling evidence of the potential of early care and education programs to influence in positive or negative ways the course of development and learning in children. It is a legitimate societal concern that children's needs be met and their opportunities for optimal growth, development, and learning be supported. It is a professional responsibility to continue to explore and learn more about which types of programs, services, curricula, and assessments are most effective for which children and their families. To this end, we evaluate early care and education programs for quality and for child and family outcomes.

In 1993, the federal Performance and Results Act focused attention on accountability for publicly funded programs and mandated that such programs provide evidence of their effectiveness. As a result, there has been increased emphasis in recent years on evaluation of all early care and education programs.

Evaluation has been defined by Gilliam and Leiter (2003, p. 6) as: " . . . a systematic process of describing the components and outcomes of an organized intervention or service with the aim at improving the quality of the services received or documenting the program's beneficial impacts."

THE NEED FOR EVALUATING EARLY CHILDHOOD PROGRAMS

Evaluation of out-of-home settings and schools is as important as the assessment of child development and learning. It is the physical and interactional environments in which children grow, develop, and learn that either nourish and support or present risks and obstacles that frustrate or impede optimal outcomes. These environments are either physically and psychologically safe, wholesome, and enriching places for children, or they are potentially unsafe, boring, debilitating, and harmful places. The quality and developmental appropriateness of curricula and the training and expertise of teachers influence the extent to which outcomes are optimal. In these environments, the assessment systems used to assess child growth, development, and learning can contribute to or derail child progress, depending on the procedures employed, the level of training for assessment purposes of those who assess, and the accuracy with which assessment data are used for decision-making. Thus, the expectation that early childhood programs will meet certain standards for excellence is an important one.

Evaluation of early care and education programs serves many purposes. Chief among them is the goal of assuring that all children are cared for in safe and nurturing environments and that educational programs meet professional expectations for developmentally appropriate practices. Because society has an interest in the well-being of children in both home and out-of-home contexts, evaluations of early care and education programs are often a part of regulatory and monitoring systems. The age of accountability in education, which increasingly includes early childhood programs, the growing emphasis on child readiness for formal schooling, and the groundswell of public support for universally available prekindergarten, has generated additional emphasis on program evaluations. In this contemporary context, both internal and external evalauations of early care and education programs take place in order to:

◆ meet national and state licensing requirements.

◆ meet professional accreditation requirements.

◆ meet local, state, and federal mandates and accountability requirements.

◆ analyze curriculum content and teaching strategies and make needed adjustments to assure student success.

◆ support transitions from child-care and preschool programs into public and private early childhood and primary education programs.

The need for these types of early care and education evaluations is clear. As mentioned in Chapter 1, an enormous body of research has demonstrated that quality of child-care and early childhood programs (see Figure 9.1) is significantly associated with positive or negative outcomes for children. Studies that measure quality can be divided into three categories (Vandell & Wolfe, 2000):

◆ studies that assess health and safety characteristics

◆ process studies in which children's actual experiences and interactions with adults and peers, their participation in activities and use of materials, and the

Figure 9.1
What Is Quality Early Care and Education?

1. Well-trained, knowledgeable adults who care about and enjoy being with infants and children
2. Safe, sanitary, healthy, appealing, child- and family-friendly physical environments
3. Low teacher- and adult-to-child ratios
4. Health-promoting, appropriately configured daily routines that include both active and quiet periods, rest times, and nutritious meals, snacks, and beverages
5. Age, individually, and culturally appropriate expectations and interactions
6. Cognitively and linguistically enriching, socially stimulating, emotionally supportive interactions, curricula, and instructional practices
7. Sensitive, appropriate, antibias interactions, curricula, and teaching materials
8. Daily balance of teacher-directed and child-initiated activities
9. Parent-involvement and participation opportunities
10. Licensed and accredited

elements in the environment that support their interactions with people and materials are examined

◆ structural and caregiver studies that evaluate features such as group size, adult-child ratios, and caregiver education and specialized training

In addition, numerous longitudinal studies of the effects of exemplary early childhood programs have projected long-term outcomes and concomitant economic benefits associated with quality programs for young children (Barnett, 1995; Behrman, 1995; Campbell & Ramey, 1995; Campbell et al. 2002; Galinsky, 2006; Lynch, 2004; Schweinhart, 1997; Schweinhart et al, 2005).

A review of such studies is beyond the scope of this text. However, a few summary findings are worth noting (Behrman, 1995; Lee & Burkam, 2002; Peisner-Feinberg & Burchinal, 1997; Peisner-Feiner et al., 2001; Vandell & Wolfe, 2000):

◆ High-quality child care has positive effects on children's cognitive, language, and preacademic skills development and is associated with later academic success in reading and math (Burchinal, Roberts, Nabors, & Bryant, 1996; Clarke-Stewart, Vandell, Burchinal, O'Brien, & McCartney, 2000; Lamb, 1998; Peisner-Feinberg & Burchinal, 1997; Peisner-Feinberg et al., 2001).

◆ Higher levels of formal education and specialized training of child caregivers are associated with more positive adult-child interactions, less authoritarian approaches to guidance, higher levels of encouragement, and higher scores on standardized measures of process quality (e.g., ITERS, ECERS, and FDCRS) (Arnett, 1989: Berk, 1985, Howes, 1997; Howes & Smith, 1995; Clarke-Stewart et al., 2000; Howes, Phillips & Whitbrooke, 1992; Peisner-Feinberg et al., 2001; Phillipsen, Burchinal, Howes, & Cryer, 1997).

◆ High-quality child care is associated with positive emotional and social development outcomes, fewer behavior problems, and higher levels of sociability,

Of critical importance to the success of early childhood programs is the teacher who has had formal education and specialized training in child development and early education.

Nancy P. Alexander

cooperation, social problem solving, and engaged play behaviors (Clark-Stewart et al., 2000; Kontos, 1991; Peisner-Feinberg & Burchinal, 1997).

◆ Lower-quality child care has been associated with poor emotional and social development outcomes, including increased anger, defiance, and aggressive behaviors and delayed language development and reading and math skills (Hausfather, Toaharia, LaRoche, & Engelsmann, 1997; Phillips, 1995).

EVALUATING EARLY CHILDHOOD PROGRAMS

The safety and well-being of children has historically been the primary focus of evaluations of programs and institutions serving young children. This is the primary concern of federal, state, and local agencies that regulate and license programs that serve children and families.

Child-Care Licensing

Child-care programs in the United States have had a long history of regulatory and government oversight, dating back to the late 1700s, when volunteer and philanthropic groups took an interest in the care and protection of poor and, often, abandoned children. During the mid- to late 1800s, day nurseries began to be established in large cities, and in 1865, the first State Board of Charities and Corrections, which would later be named the State Board of Public Welfare, was established in Massachusetts. This board was charged with inspecting all state institutions caring for dependents, delinquents, mentally ill, and those in prison. They established standards for child care, presented reports to the state legislature, and solicited appropriations for continuing and maintaining facilities (Lundberg, 1935). Concurrently, charitable organizations made up of well-meaning, civic-minded, and wealthy citizens took an interest in helping the poor. Ironically, the first organized effort to protect children from neglect and cruelty had its origin in the New York Society for the Prevention of Cruelty to Animals. The New York Society for the Prevention of Cruelty to Children, established in 1875, was an outgrowth of that organization (Lundberg, 1935). The current professional field of social work had its origins in charity societies that followed and were formed primarily in large cities around the country during that time period (Lewis, 1966).

When the United States Children's Bureau was established in 1912, it was the first such agency in the world. It was charged " . . . to investigate and report upon all matters pertaining to the welfare of children and child life among all classes of people" (Lathrop, 1912). The Children's Bureau continues today as a federal agency within the U.S. Department of Health and Human Services. Its charge remains quite similar today:

> . . . to investigate and report . . . upon all matters pertaining to the welfare of children and child life among all classes of our people, and shall especially investigate the questions of immortality, birth rate, orphanage, juvenile courts, desertion, dangerous occupations, accidents, and diseases of children, legislation affecting children in the several states and territories. (U.S. Department of Health and Human Services, 2006).

licensing A system for assuring that certain programs that serve children and families meet standards set by the state.

In 1968, the federal government issued stringent **licensing** standards for programs receiving federal funds. These standards were known as the Federal Interagency Day Care Requirements (FIDCR). However, this effort received a lukewarm reception among the states, even after some revisions. In 1980, the government abandoned this effort to regulate child-care programs in the states.

Today, licensing laws are established by individual state legislatures and are promulgated for the express purpose of protecting the physical and psychological safety of children in nonparental and out-of-home care. In all states, certain individuals or programs that provide early care and education must obtain a state license or be registered with a designated child protective services agency. To obtain a state license and/or be registered, certain standards and requirements must be met.

Each state sets its own standards and spells out the requirements for meeting them. The stringency of the requirements that must be met in order to obtain a license varies from state to state. As a rule, the standards set a level of performance or compliance below which the early childhood setting or program would be deemed potentially harmful and thus would not be allowed to provide services to children and families. Thus, most of these state standards are *minimum* standards, and licensees are expected to exceed them. Some states have ranking systems or quality rating systems (QRS) to recognize programs that exceed the minimum standards. (For example, Kentucky uses a STARS scale of 1 through 4 to identify levels of quality. North Carolina has a five-star rating system in which centers can be licensed at the one-star level but can voluntarily elect to be licensed at higher-quality levels. Texas has a rising-star system. Each star indicates a level at which the program surpasses the state minimum standards. Some states include accreditation among the criteria in their quality-rating systems.

Licensing standards set rules governing such requirements as indoor and outdoor space, group size for age, adult-to-child ratios, appropriateness of equipment and teaching materials, nutrition and feeding procedures, sanitation, staff and child hygiene, safety requirements, security of medicines and chemicals, staff qualifications and training, schedules of routines and learning activities, discipline/guidance policies, protection of children from the spread of communicable diseases and accidents, record keeping, communications with families, transportation policies and procedures, emergency plans and procedures, and local health and fire department inspections.

Early Childhood Program Accreditation

accreditation Recognition of a program or school by a national or regional professional or governing organization whose quality standards and evaluation criteria have been met.

Another type of evaluation of early childhood programs and services is that of accreditation. **Accreditation** differs from licensing in the following ways:

Licensing	Accreditation
Required by state and local mandates	Voluntary
Baseline/minimum standards/requirements	Highest standards/exemplary requirements
Governmentally regulated at state or local levels	Promoted/sponsored by professional groups at regional or national levels
Consequences/sanctions for noncompliance	Reputation/recognition for high quality
Inspections, investigations, and technical assistance	Self-studies, validation, and verification visits

Unlike licensing, the accreditation of early care and education programs has a more recent history, although the promotion of program quality has been, since their inception, the primary goal or mission of the professional organizations or agencies that provide accreditation services. There are several organizations that accredit early childhood care and education programs. Some are developed for specific types of programs or services—for example, faith-based programs, foster care, adoption services, center-based proprietary programs, family childcare, and after-school programs. Other accrediting agencies provide services to a broad range of programs; for example, the Southern Association of Colleges and Schools extends accreditation services to programs from preschools through universities. The National Child Care Information Center provides an online list of early care and education accrediting organizations.

Possibly the most well-known early childhood accreditation program is provided by the National Association for the Education of Young Children (NAEYC). The NAEYC is the world's largest professional early childhood organization. This professional organization established its national, voluntary accreditation system in 1985. Its purpose was (and is) to improve the quality of group programs available to young children and their families and to recognize programs that substantially meet national standards for high quality (Bredekamp, 1990). In 2005, NAEYC launched revised criteria for accreditation that assume a profession and field of service better equipped to meet more particularized and stringent (and, for many programs, more costly) requirements than previously set forth. The "reinvented" program standards assess criteria in four broad categories, with very specific and lengthy lists of criteria for each (NAEYC, 2005e):

1. Children

    Relationships
    Curriculum
    Teaching
    Health
    Assessment of child progress

2. Teaching staff

3. Partnerships

    Families
    Community relationships

4. Administration

    Physical environment
    Leadership and management

According to the authors of this program, these standards and requirements are grounded in the following principles:

◆ Young children deserve careful attention to every aspect of their physical, social, and cognitive development. They are complex individuals worthy of respect and the recognition that they are each unique, valuable, and lovable.

◆ Each child comes to the early childhood environment with a unique set of defining characteristics, including family background, abilities, temperament, and learning styles.

◆ Positive relationships between children and adults are fundamental to a harmonious environment that promotes learning and growth.

◆ Teachers actively promote positive outcomes for all children through thoughtful assessment, well-implemented curriculum, and effective teaching practices.

◆ Children are active participants in the formation of relationships with adults and friends.

◆ Children bring their own thoughts and abilities to the learning process. They gain knowledge and skills from activities, materials, and interactions that are responsive to their interests and needs, are based in play, reflect their lives, are tailored to their developmental level, and encourage active participation and experimentation.

◆ Families matter, both in terms of their influence on their own child or children and as partners with the program's administration and teaching staff working to maximize the quality of children's experiences.

◆ High-quality early childhood programs address all aspects of children's development (social-emotional, language, cognitive, and physical) and provide a solid foundation for the development of skills and knowledge that contribute to children's future success in school. Programs are part of a community and have a responsibility to support their community and make the most of its resources. (NAEYC, 2005e, p. 8).

National accreditation systems are an essential part of a meaningful assessment paradigm proposed by this text and an essential part of the early childhood education profession. It is critical that accreditation systems be based on research that supports the requirements imposed and that truly reflects the standards of quality that are widely accepted within the profession. As with standardized tests, accreditation systems must be valid and reliable. Accreditation systems that fail to meet high standards for validity and reliability may actually do more harm than good if they promote standards that are at variance with the current child-development and education knowledge base.

Additionally, although accreditation systems need to be sufficiently comprehensive, their lists of requirements need not be tedious. Recognizing that child care and early education programs come in all forms and sizes—some with more financial and people resources than others—accreditation that is lengthy, complicated, and costly will discourage rather than invite participation.

High quality early childhood programs provide opportunities and materials for age-related play.

Anthony Magnacca/Merrill

Figure 9.2
Head Start National
Reporting System

> The NRS grew out of 1998 legislation that set standards for student outcomes in the federal Head Start program. These Child Outcomes Measures are used to assess the effectiveness of the Head Start program in achieving its goal of increasing the readiness of young children in low-income families. The Child Outcomes measures, administered to four- and five-year-old children are intended to provide comparative information about the performance of the nation's 1,300 Head Start programs. Additionally, combined with other locally selected assessment measures, these Child Outcomes data can yield important information that helps to identify the areas in which Head Start students and programs are most successful and/or need to improve.
>
> The purposes of the NRS are to help with educational planning and to identify programs needing technical assistance, which is designed to increase the capacity of a program to meet its goals.

Early Childhood Program Accountability

Current laws governing the allocation of public monies to child-care and education programs and services mandate annual reviews and outcomes assessments. These mandates apply to programs such as Head Start, Early Head Start, IDEA services, and other programs receiving federal funds for early care and education (Figure 9.2). The accountability requirements of the No Child Left Behind Act of 2002 are intended to assure the tax-paying public that monies spent on education are well spent. As well, other funding agencies, such as foundations and agencies that manage community funds (e.g., United Way), require evaluations that account for the manner in which funds are used and the extent to which programs fulfill the purposes for which funding was provided. Guidelines for early childhood programs are provided by the National Association for the Education of Young Children in Figure 9.3. The joint position statement (Appendix G) of the National Association for the Education of Young Children and the National Association of Early Childhood Specialists in State Departments of Education addresses the importance of shared responsibility for sound curriculums, assessments, and program evaluations.

cost-benefit analysis A process of calculating the costs of a program or intervention relative to the benefits. By dividing the total cost of a program by the number of children served, a cost-to-benefit ratio can be obtained that reveals how much it costs to achieve each specific outcome.

Accountability is usually assessed through measurements of outcomes and calculations of cost per unit of service. These data lead to additional information, resulting in a **cost/benefit analysis.** Thus, as in the many longitudinal studies of the long-term effects of specific types of preschool and intervention programs mentioned earlier, determinations can be made about the feasibility and advantages of certain types of programs. This information guides decision making regarding further funding and expansion or replication of successful programs. In some cases, where outcomes are not satisfactory, withdrawal of funds or other sanctions are imposed. For example, the No Child Left Behind Act mandates that failure to meet its average yearly progress (AYP) requirements, as measured by large-scale standardized testing, can result in sanctions that redirect monies to other programs.[*] In other cases, needs analyses, technical assistance, and revisions to program format

growth-based accountability model
An accountabiity model that grants schools credit for student improvement over time by tracking individual achievement year to year.

---

[*]The U.S. Office of Education is piloting an alternative approach to this mandate in several states that allows school districts to develop a **growth-based accountability model**, which allows schools to track student improvement over time, comparing year-by-year scores rather than basing achievement of AYP on the current year's scores.

PROGRAM EVALUATION and ACCOUNTABILITY
in programs for infants, toddlers, preschoolers, kindergartners, and primary grade children

Infants/Toddlers	Preschoolers	Kindergarten/Primary

Effective program evaluation and accountability: Programs serving children of all ages engage in ongoing evaluation in light of their identified goals and are accountable for producing beneficial results. Although many similarities are found across all high-quality early childhood programs, the specific standards of quality used to evaluate programs (e.g., program standards and early learning standards), issues about the kinds of evidence that are most appropriate, and specific risks inherent in accountability systems vary depending on the ages of the children served. Programs for older children are more likely to be mandated to participate in large-scale evaluations using norm-referenced assessments; in those cases, multiple safeguards should be in place, ensuring that the tests are developmentally appropriate, conducted in the language children are most comfortable with, and employ other accommodations as appropriate. Aggregated, not individual, data should be used as part of an accountability system, and gain scores should be emphasized rather than "snapshots" of scores upon exit from a program.

Infants/Toddlers	Preschoolers	Kindergarten/Primary
Program evaluation and accountability uses standards of quality (program and early learning standards) that are specific to infants and toddlers and address the developmental domains (physical well-being and motor development; social and emotional development; approaches to learning; language development; and cognition and general knowledge), as well as those that are relevant to all programs. In evaluating program effectiveness, great importance is placed on family-related goals and outcomes because of their critical developmental significance for infants and toddlers. Use of children's gain scores as part of an accountability system, while preferable over other types of comparisons, still warrant caution because of the wide variability and unevenness of early development.	Program evaluation and accountability attends to a comprehensive range of developmental and learning outcomes, both in identifying program goals and in evaluating effectiveness. As preschool programs increasingly become part of state accountability systems, outcomes should not be limited to academic disciplines but should include developmental domains—physical well-being and motor development; social and emotional development; approaches to learning; language development; and cognition and general knowledge—as well as address adherence with applicable program standards. Given the difficulty of using formal standardized assessments with preschool children, alternate methods and sampling procedures should be emphasized.	Program evaluation and accountability in programs serving kindergarten and primary-age children is typically conducted within a system of federal, state, and district expectations. Although more capable of participating in some kinds of formal assessments, children six to eight may still fail to show their level of competence under testing conditions, leading to erroneous conclusions about programs as well as individual children. Accountability systems for children this age run the risk of reinforcing a narrow range of program goals; special attention is needed to maintain a comprehensive, developmentally appropriate system that focuses on program standards as well as learning standards. Assessment of kindergarten and primary grade children using formal standardized assessments continues to be problematic. Alternate methods of sampling procedures should be emphasized.

The information in this chart is based on the recommendations of the NAEYC-NAECS/SDE Position Statement on Curriculum, Assessment, and Program Evaluation (www.naeyc.org/resources/position_statements/pscape.pdf). The chart provides examples of ways in which the recommendations of the NAEYC-NAECS/SDE Position Statement on Curriculum, Assessment, and Program Evaluation can be implemented in programs for infants/toddlers, preschoolers, and kindergarten/primary age children. The examples can best be understood within the context of the full position statement.

Figure 9.3
Guidelines for Early Childhood Programs from NAEYC

or policies are implemented to determine the extent to which continued funding might lead to better outcomes.

These systems, licensing, accreditation, and accountability entail formal and informal and internal and external evaluations. The evaluations used for these different purposes can range from observational, anecdotal, and carefully structured descriptive studies to very rigorous and detailed studies that involve specific and standardized measurement instruments or standardized procedures.

Depending on goals or purposes, evaluations are either conducted by teachers, directors, or others within the particular program or carried out by someone not associated with the program but specifically trained and/or employed by or representing licensing, accreditation, or accountability entities. Some, as with most accreditation systems, combine internal and external evaluations through program self-study procedures, followed by external validation. Whether the evaluations take place internally or are externally provided, the more rigorous the methods used, the more confidence we can have in their findings (Gilliam & Leiter, 2003).

MEASURING SPECIFIC INDICATORS OF QUALITY

There does not appear to be a wide range of valid and reliable instruments that measure health and safety, process, and/or structure characteristics in early care and education programs. Rather, studies of program quality tend to focus more specifically on child-outcome data relative to general and specific growth and development characteristics and learning or academic achievements in literacy and math. Few focus on characteristics that describe program qualities per se.

Perhaps the most well-known and widely used scales are the environmental rating scales researched and developed by scientists at the Frank Porter Graham Child Development Institute at the University of North Carolina at Chapel Hill. These process measures include:

> *Early Childhood Environment Rating Scale* (ECERS-R) (Harms, Clifford, & Cryer, 2005).
> *Infant/Toddler Environment Rating Scale* (ITERS-R) (Harms, Cryer, & Clifford, 2006).
> *Family Day Care Rating Scale* (FCCERS-R) (Harms & Clifford, 2006).
> *School-Age Care Environment Rating Scale* (SACERS) (Harms, Jacobs & White, 1996).

The scales are similar in format, and these most recent revisions include indicators that measure qualities associated with program accommodations and responses to disabilities and sensitivity to cultural diversity. The ECERS-R, for example, consists of a forty-three-item scale covering seven categories, or subscales:

> Space and Furnishings
> Personal Care Routines
> Language-Reasoning
> Activities
> Interaction
> Program Structure
> Parents and Staff

Within each of these subscales are specific items that are ranked on a scale of 1 to 7, indicating the level of quality for that item. A score of 1 indicates inadequate conditions, whereas a score of 7 indicates excellent conditions.

These scales have been used in establishing licensing quality-rating systems and accreditation standards. They have been used extensively in research studies of quality effects on child development and learning. They are suited to both internal and external evaluations.

Another well-known program-evaluation instrument is the High/Scope Program Quality Assessment (PQA) (High/Scope Research Foundation, 1998). The PQA is used in center-based early childhood settings and is consistent with the NAEYC accreditation criteria and the Head Start Performance Standards. The instrument has seventy-two items that are divided into seven sections, or categories:

> Physical Environment
> Daily Routines
> Adult-Child Interaction
> Curriculum Assessment and Planning

Program evaluations include both indoor and outdoor spaces.

Merrill Education

Parent Involvement and Family Services
Staff Qualifications and Staff Development
Program Management

A five-point rating scale is used, and the instrument includes space for recording supporting evidence and anecdotes. The measurement process includes classroom observations and interviews with teachers and administrators. Trained raters administer the evaluation.

ANALYSIS OF CURRICULUM CONTENT AND PEDAGOGY

Program evaluations are especially helpful in analyzing age-related expectations and curriculums. Recognizing that high-quality programs contribute to positive outcomes, which are expressed well into the adult years, setting quality goals and standards for curriculum and instructional practices, and continuously evaluating how a program is doing in meeting these goals is essential. From a contextualistic perspective, evaluations help us to focus on the different types of experiences children encounter in a particular program and the impact of these experiences on them. Further, the knowledge, skills, and dispositions of the adults (administrators, aides, teachers, and others in the program or school) determine the extent to which the curriculum is planned and delivered in a developmentally appropriate manner (Barnett, 2004). Analyzing curricula and instructional practices helps us to consider how children grow and change over time and have a need for learning experiences that match their changing interests and abilities. Program evaluations can provide useful data for determining what is working well with individual children or age groups and what types of modifications may be needed to meet the particular needs of children at particular points in their development and learning.

HELPING CHILDREN MAKE THE TRANSITION FROM PRESCHOOL TO FORMAL SCHOOLING

One of the most significant developmental events during the early childhood years is the transition from preschool or home settings into a formal schooling situation. This is an important event for children and families and for preschools and elementary schools because:

a. school entry marks the beginning of a child's formal education.

b. experiences and learning in the prekindergarten, kindergarten, and first grade establish social and learning competencies that are critical to children's later academic successes and achievements.

c. there is continuing emphasis on the importance of parent involvement, yet the opportunities for such involvement may differ from prior programs.

d. the learning environments that children have experienced in their preschool programs are most likely different from what they will encounter in their elementary school classrooms.

e. expectations and instructional practices may vary significantly from the child's prior experiences.

The ability to make a smooth transition does not depend solely on the child's readiness for school; it also depends on the shared responsibilities of schools and communities. Families, caregivers, preschool teachers, kindergarten teachers, elementary school principals, community leaders, and support agencies all participate in this shared responsibility.

DEFINING READY SCHOOLS AND COMMUNITIES

Ready Schools

Scholars have suggested that schools could take a more proactive role in connecting with children and families prior to school entry. A 1996 national survey of nearly 3,600 kindergarten teachers by the National Center for Early Development and Learning (Pianta, Cox, Early, & Taylor (1999) revealed that the majority of teachers reported using transition practices such as:

sending a letter to parents after the beginning of school.
holding an open house after school starts.
sending a brochure home after school.

Less commonly reported practices were:

calling the child before or after school starts.
visiting the child's home or preschool program.

Scholars lament that children and families are more likely to receive a form letter announcing first day of school and its schedule, a school supply list, and important dates such as open house, screening or testing dates, a calendar of special events, PTA dates and a membership invitation, and, perhaps, names of school contact persons. Although this information is important and useful to children and families, it would be considered low impact compared to a more personalized approach, such as a personal call or a letter from the child's teacher to the child or parent with specific and particularized information.

Pianta, Rimm-Kauffman, and Cox (1999) have suggested transition strategies that:

1. reach out by linking with families and preschools to establish relationships and two-way communication about the transition process.
2. reach backward in time, establishing links with families well before the first day of school.
3. reach with appropriate intensity, utilizing practices that are both low intensity (e.g., flyers or pamphlets) and high intensity (e.g., personal contacts or home visits).

Transition is but one of the important characteristics of ready schools. The National Education Goals Panel (1997) identified ten keys to school readiness:

1. smooth the transition between home and school
2. strive for continuity between early care and education programs and elementary schools
3. help children learn and make sense of their world
4. make a commitment to every child's success
5. show they are committed to every teacher's success
6. introduce and expand strategies that have been shown to improve achievement
7. function as learning organizations that change their practices if they do not help children
8. serve children in communities
9. take responsibility for results
10. maintain strong leadership

We would add some others:

1. Provide classroom teachers who have specialized knowledge and skills in early childhood education and have strong child-development academic backgrounds.
2. Prepare classroom environments that are child and family friendly.
3. Acknowledge the young child's unique ways of learning and employ age, individually, and culturally appropriate instructional materials and strategies.
4. Make parent involvement an inviting, engaging, and collaborative endeavor.
5. Learn about and prepare for children with special needs and diverse cultural and linguistic backgrounds.
6. Protect young children from expectations more suitable for older children and later grades.

In short, establish and maintain developmentally appropriate practices during the earliest grades of elementary school—prekindergarten through third grade.

High quality early childhood programs provide materials that engage the learning process.

Nancy P. Alexander

Ready Communities

Communities also have a role to play in supporting child and family readiness and do so in a variety of ways. The National Governors' Association (2005b) Task Force on School Readiness reports that a recent survey found that municipal leaders nationwide identified child care and early education as a pressing need for children and families in their communities. These officials overwhelmingly supported allocating resources to early childhood development, and more than half of the cities in the United States have increased spending on programs and services for children and families during the period from 1998 to 2003 (Katz, Hoene, & deKerver, 2003). The NGA (2005a) recommends that:

◆ Ready communities maintain a comprehensive infrastructure of resources and supports, which include such services as nutrition, health care, mental-health care, and high-quality early care and education programs. Communities are encouraged to conduct needs assessments and explore ways to leverage funding for local readiness initiatives.

◆ Ready communities set goals and track progress by establishing indicators of well-being to measure how children are faring and track child outcomes relating to health, safety, and learning. Local data on positive outcomes helps community leaders to obtain support for investments in early childhood programs within the community and in state legislatures.

Ready communities are engaged in partnerships with state decision-makers through the generation of innovative ideas and initiatives that meet child and family needs. An example of a local initiative to encourage and support child readiness is described in Figure 9.4. Successful local initiative can provide rationale for state-level policy decisions relating to children.

Figure 9.4
Arlington Child Care
Council Ready for
School Initiative

The Arlington Child Care Council of Texas is a freestanding, citizen-driven initiative composed of twenty-five members of the city's business, civic, and faith-based communities. This group formed in response to a comprehensive study that detailed the city's demographics associated with child-care needs, family choices, and the number and types of available child-care arrangements. The report *Caring for Our Kids* (Arlington Human Service Planners, 2003) identified several areas of concern, including the low number of centers with high-quality accreditation, caregiver-qualification requirements, high costs to families regardless of quality, and the need for some type of official community oversight. The report recommended the establishment of an oversight committee.

Thus, the ACCC convened to set a course that would enhance community awareness of child-care needs and begin to carry out a well-conceived strategic plan to ensure that ". . . all children in Arlington experience quality early childhood development opportunities and will be ready for school."

This diverse group of community leaders effectively engaged key stakeholders within the community, including school district leaders and the child-care providers themselves. Their stated mission is: "The Arlington Child Care Council will design and support a comprehensive Arlington early care and education system that will improve the quality, accessibility and utilization of informal and formal child care."

Working with area child development and early childhood education experts, child-readiness indicators were identified. Once the readiness indicators were defined, another group of professionals in early education developed *Skill Set Building Activities*. These professionally developed materials were then formatted and widely distributed throughout the community (see the Chapter 8 appendix).

The current strategic plan includes the following goals:

"*Support* parents as a child's first teacher and primary caregiver. Supporting parents means respecting their choices about how to rear their child, but expecting them to do all they can to help their child be prepared for school and for life.

Collaborate with the formal child care provider system to strengthen that system: Collaborating with the formal child care provider system means understanding the complex economic issues that face this vital industry and facilitating their efforts to work together in the best interests of the children whom they serve.

Enhance the relationship between the formal child care system and the Arlington Independent School District: Enhancing the relationships between the formal child care system and AISD means creating a fluid connection between the two while acknowledging that professionals within the formal child care system require as much respect as do public and private school educators.

Challenge the community-at-large through an ongoing public awareness effort to both understand and support the need for all young children to be ready for school: Challenging the community-at-large through an ongoing public awareness effort means changing some of our collective cultural values and investing time and money in honoring a commitment to ensure that all young Arlington children are ready for school."

Many projects and activities characterize this enthusiastic and collaborative group of community volunteers. Notable among them is the formation of the Arlington Alliance for Early Childhood Professionals, a group of dedicated child-care providers who have coalesced to work with and support the ACCC Readiness Initiative.

More specifically, communities can contribute to children's success in school through a number of support systems, such as the following:

1. Provide adequate nutrition, physical and mental health services to families, and publicize and encourage immunizations and regular health examinations.

2. Establish and/or support library programs that encourage family literacy, children's story hours, book fairs, and other literacy-enhancing activities. A librarian with special interest in children's literature can assure a wide and varied selection of books and other media.

3. Help families access available parent-education and parent-support systems, such as parent-education classes at the local library, community college, or parenting center.

4. Provide research-based family education and support programs, such as the nationally known Parents as Teachers, Home Instruction Program for Preschool Youngsters, and Touchpoints programs for families and early childhood personnel.

5. Promote and support high-quality child care and early education programs and provide child-care resource and referral services to help families make wise choices for the nonparental care of their children.

6. Insist on high-quality standards in child-care licensing and in center and school accreditation.

7. Publicize Child Find activities to encourage parents to obtain early screening, diagnosis, and intervention for children with disabilities.

8. Distribute information to families about child- and family-related resources that are available in the community.

9. Provide safe parks and recreation areas for children and families.

10. Support local schools through school-community collaborations and partnerships.

The National Governor's Association report concludes with these words that firmly assert the importance of multiple layers of support for children and families if readiness is to be achieved:

> Responsibility for school readiness lies not with children, but with the adults who care for them and the systems that support them. Starting at the top, states are responsible for making informed policy decisions, committing sufficient resources and connecting programs and services to all children who need them. (NGA, 2005a, p. 31)

Throughout this text we have attempted to describe the elements of a meaningful assessment system in early childhood education and to clarify the many "languages" of assessment. Beginning with learning to observe and record child behaviors, draw valid inferences from classroom assessment practices and large-scale standardized test results, collaborating with children to guide their own learning, collaborating with parents to support learning, and evaluating programs and holding them accountable for child outcomes is indeed a "system." Striving for a meaningful system means continually assessing all its parts with an eye on the reason for assessment in the first place, that of assuring best practices in educating young children. Assessment practices should never trump our responsibility to protect childhood, which is a precious period in the life span that can neither be repeated nor revised.

The concept of readiness neces-
sarily includes child, family,
schools, and the community.

Paige Killian

The field of early childhood assessment has greatly expanded since the first edition of this text. As with most textbooks, there is far more information available on the subject than is practical to include. Readings and online resources have been selected for your further research and study. Our goal is to promote a truly meaningful assessment system that respects and protects childhood. In the end, assessments are only as good as the ability they have to improve the types of experiences children have as they journey through our classes. We end this text with one story and a "mind game" for you to reflect upon.

A TEACHER'S STORY

The school building was getting new air-conditioning units that were being installed on the roof above the kindergarten classroom. It was late spring and was the week during which readiness testing for first-grade placement was taking place. As a safety precaution, the school principal arranged for the children to be given the test in the school cafeteria. It was 9:30 AM, and both cleanup from breakfast and preparations for lunch for the 500+ students in the school were underway. The kitchen was teeming with food-service personnel greeting delivery persons, visiting with one another, and talking loudly over the clang and bang of large pots and pans and the shrill of the giant bread dough mixer. Teachers on break wandered in and out to pour themselves cups of tea or sample warm cookies fresh from the oven and chatted loudly, if briefly, with cafeteria friends.

Twenty-two kindergartners seated precariously in chairs too large for them and at tables too tall for them were straining to maintain their physical balance, handle test booklets and pencils, and hear and follow the teacher's test directions. After several pages of the test, Keith, one of the brightest in my class, tensed, his body rigid to the point of shaking, his face buried in his fists that were attempting to rub away the tears he didn't want others to see. I drew near as unobtrusively as possible.

Without looking up, Keith sobbed, "I can't do this." I looked around at all the little intense faces, eager to please and show what they could do, but unsure and uneasy: signs of stress emerging throughout the class.

That marked the beginning of my distaste for mass standardized testing of young children. Inquiring of my colleagues and school leaders, I asked a number of questions:

Q: Given the construction work taking place on the roof of our building and outside our windows, did we have to administer the test on this particular day?

A: Yes. The district has so decreed and all kindergartens in the district will be testing on this day and for the next two days.

Q: Was there no other place in the building to give this test?

A: No. All other classrooms are in use; the library is in use by another grade (not for testing, by the way), and the auditorium would be less suitable than the cafeteria.

Q: Was it necessary to administer this test to Keith and others like him whose "readiness" for first grade was already apparent to me?

A: Yes. All kindergarten children must be so tested.

Q: Given the unbearable distractions—physical/motor, visual, auditory, and, yes, olfactory—how representative or valid can these test scores actually be?

A: It doesn't seem to matter, because children in this school usually do well on this particular test anyway.

Q: Who selected this test?

A: Not sure; it is the one we have used for years.

The answers to my questions left me perplexed and wanting. My concern for Keith and others who were brought to tears (and, sometimes, nausea) by an insensitive bureaucracy surrounding standardized testing in our schools was, and continues to be, profound. I ask myself often: Is this really necessary? If I must, how can I make the experience as benign as possible? On a perhaps defensive personal/professional level, of what value is professional training and a teacher's intimate knowledge of the capabilities of children in her classroom? Is there anything I, as a professional trained in early childhood education, can do about policies that, in my view, are potentially harmful to young children?

MIND GAME: "SOME DAY YOU ARE GOIN TO MAKE A+ ON SOMETIN"

The first quotation at the beginning of this chapter is loaded with possible meanings for educators. We cannot be certain what the author was thinking when she penned these significant words, nor do we know what inspired the school room play theme, nor do we know what the pretend pupil's "assignment" was or what the pretend teacher was intending for the pupil to learn from the "assessment" noted on the pretend-pupil's drawing. Nonetheless, this quotation arouses a search for its meaning. Reading into it maybe too much or maybe missing the mark, here are some of our curiosities. Does the note to the pretend pupil say something to us about children's perceptions and/or responses to assessment feedback? Does it suggest a child's sense of a teacher's control and how that control is conveyed through grades or assessments? Did the child have a pretend sense of control or power in withholding the A+ for another effort? Has the child experienced loss of control or feelings of helplessness in meeting school-related expectations or succeeding with self-imposed goals? And reaching even deeper, is there perhaps within this young pretend "assessor" some rudimentary sense of the meaning of "readiness"? And, finally, do we read optimism or pessimism into the statement? You may think of other questions about experiences and feelings possibly buried in the minds and hearts of these pretend players that, if known, could reveal a lot about what role assessment plays in child thinking and feeling and, hence, in child development and learning.

Moreover, though this pretend-play vignette is not described, the play theme that the quotation reveals and our fascination with its potential meanings serve as a metaphor for the culture of assessment that currently surrounds children, teachers, and administrators. Do we educators collectively agree on the purposes and goals of assessments and grades? Do we take time to reflect on children's perceptions of the testing process, assessments, and test scores—why they exist and how they are used? Do we take time to reflect on the promises and challenges of the current emphasis on testing and assessing, outcomes, and accountability? How do educators maintain a sense of autonomy and creativity in classroom practices when attempting to meet goals and benchmarks determined by a person or entities unknown to them? Are we optimistic or pessimistic about our ability to provide a well-rounded, enriched, engaging, challenging, and meaningful education for children in the face of accountability rewards and sanctions?

The child's pretend assessment summons us to reflect on the gestalt of a meaningful assessment system. When all the parts converge into a meaningful assessment system, will it be that "A+" we were supposed to make on "somethin someday"?

REVIEW STRATEGIES AND ACTIVITIES

Vexing Questions

1. What makes the "one size fits all" paradigm in teaching and testing so appealing to policy makers and some educators?

2. How might schools and communities be assessed for their readiness to meet the unique needs of young children and their families?

3. How might the message that school readiness does not rest solely with the child be effectively communicated?

Activities

1. Quality preschool and child care programs are generally described as having the following characteristics:
   a. developmentally appropriate curriculums
   b. age, individually, and culturally responsive expectations and interactions
   c. warm and supportive adult-child interactions
   d. child-friendly, safe, and healthy physical surroundings
   e. engaging materials and activities
   f. inclusive and bias-free interactions and curricula
   g. parent-friendly and engaging collaborations
   h. meaningful, valid, reliable assessment systems

With permission, observe one or more preschool programs and describe them using these aspects of quality as your frame of reference. To what extent does the program emphasize academic learning, employ teacher-directed lessons or upper-grade-level methods and materials, restrict movement and talk, or control behaviors with power-assertive strategies? To what extent are children allowed to make choices, move about, interact with one another, and suggest, plan, or initiate activities? How would you describe the level of engagement and interest of children, resistance or stress, and negative or aggressive interactions? How is child progress monitored and assessed?

2. Create a five-column chart with columns headed by Child, Family, School, Community, and State. In each column, list ten readiness indicators. Compare your chart with those of your classmates. What commonalities emerged? Did any indicators reflect high priority? Discuss how these indicators can best be encouraged, supported, and assessed.

3. Read and reflect upon the position statements in Appendix G. If you were to design an instrument to evaluate the readiness of a prekindergarten, kindergarten, or first-grade classroom, what features would you assess?

SUGGESTED LITERATURE AND RESOURCES

Bickart, T. S., Jablon, J. R., & Dodge, D. T. (1999). *Building the primary classroom: A complete guide to teaching and learning.* Washington, DC: Teaching Strategies, Inc.

Burk, C. J. F., & Burke, W. M. (2005). Student-ready schools. *Childhood Education, 81*(5), 281–285.

Egertson, H. A. (2004). Achieving high standards and implementing developmentally appropriate practice—both ARE possible. *Dimensions of Early Childhood, 32*(1), 3–9.

Eggers-Pierola, C. (2005). *Connections and commitments: Reflecting Latino values in early childhood programs.* Portsmouth, NH: Heinemann.

Halliburton, A. L., & Thornburg, K. R. (2004). School readiness: Children, families, schools, and communities. *Dimensions of Early Childhood 32*(1), 30–36.

Honig, A. S. (2002). *Secure relationships: Nurturing infant/toddler attachment in early care settings.* Washington, DC: National Association for the Education of Young Children.

Lally, J. R., Griffin, A., Fenichel, E., Segal, M., Szanton, E. S., & Weissbourd, B. (2003). *Caring for infants and toddlers in groups: Developmentally appropriate practice.* Washington, DC: Zero to Three Press.

Lombardi, J., & Bogle, M. M. (Eds.). (2004). *Beacon of hope: The promise of early Head Start for America's youngest children.* Washington, DC: Zero to Three Press.

Manning, J. P. (2006). Using the licensing visit to be all you can be. *Young Children, 61*(2), 84–87.

McDaniel, G. L., Isaac, M. Y., Brooks, H. M., & Hatch, A. (2005). Confronting K–3 teaching challenges in an era of accountability. *Young Children, 60*(2), 20–26.

National Institute of Child Health and Human Development Early Child Care Research Network (2005). *Child care and child development: Results from the NICHD study of early child care and youth development.* New York: Guilford.

Pack, J. A., & Knight, M. E. (2000). Developing a school portfolio: A tool for staff development. *Young Children, 55*(5), 42–46.

Sandall, S., McLean, M. E., & Smith, B. J. (2000). *DEC recommended practices in early intervention/early childhood special education*. Denver, CO: Division for Early Childhood of the Council for Exceptional Children.

Swick, K. J. (2004). *Empowering parents, families, schools and communities during the early childhood years*. Champaign, IL: Stipes Publishing.

U.S. Office of Elementary and Secondary Education & the Office of Special Education & Rehabilitative Services. (2006). *Tool kit on teaching and assessing students with disabilities*. (Free copy download at www.osepideasthatwork.org.)

ONLINE RESOURCES

Early Childhood Research & Practice (L. Katz & D. Rothenberg, Eds.). Internet journal from the ERIC Clearinghouse on Elementary and Early Childhood Education, http://ecrp.uiuc.edu/

Federal and state policy developments, www.naeyc.org/policy/federal

Members of Congress, http://capwiz.com/naeyc/home

NAEYC Public Policy Resources: Advocacy/public policy/critical issues, www.naeyc.org/policy; www.naeyc.org/ece/critical.asp

National Association for the Education of Young Children Accreditation Performance Criteria, http://www.naeyc.org/accreditation/performance_criteria/

National Center for Fair and Open Testing, www.fairtest.org

National Center for Research on Evaluation, Standards, and Student Testing, www.cse.ucla.edu

National Child Care Information Center, http://www.nccic.org

National Education Goals Panel, www.negp.gov

National Institute for Early Education Research; National Network for Child Care, www.nncc.org

National Scientific Council on the Developing Child, http://www.developingchild.net/about.shtml

Rethinking Schools: The Urban Education Journal, www.rethinkingschools.org

Naeyc Code of Ethical Conduct and Statement of Commitment*

Revised April 2005

A Position Statement of the National Association for the Education of Young Children

Endorsed by the Association for Childhood Education International

PREAMBLE

NAEYC recognizes that those who work with young children face many daily decisions that have moral and ethical implications. The **NAEYC Code of Ethical Conduct** offers guidelines for responsible behavior and sets forth a common basis for resolving the principal ethical dilemmas encountered in early childhood care and education. The **Statement of Commitment** is not part of the Code but is a personal acknowledgement of an individual's willingness to embrace the distinctive values and moral obligations of the field of early childhood care and education.

The primary focus of the Code is on daily practice with children and their families in programs for children from birth through 8 years of age, such as infant/toddler programs, preschool and prekindergarten programs, child care centers, hospital and child life settings, family child care homes, kindergartens, and primary classrooms. When the issues involve young children, then these provisions also apply to specialists who do not work directly with children, including program administrators, parent educators, early childhood adult educators, and officials with responsibility for program monitoring and licensing. (Note: See also the "Code of Ethical Conduct: Supplement for Early Childhood Adult Educators," online at www.naeyc.org/about/positions/pdf/ethics04.pdf.)

Core values

Standards of ethical behavior in early childhood care and education are based on commitment to the following core values that are deeply rooted in the history of the field of early childhood care and education. We have made a commitment to

◆ Appreciate childhood as a unique and valuable stage of the human life cycle

◆ Base our work on knowledge of how children develop and learn

◆ Appreciate and support the bond between the child and family

◆ Recognize that children are best understood and supported in the context of family, culture,[†] community, and society

◆ Respect the dignity, worth, and uniqueness of each individual (child, family member, and colleague)

[†]The term *culture* includes ethnicity, racial identity, economic level, family structure, language, and religious and political beliefs, which profoundly influence each child's development and relationship to the world.

◆ Respect diversity in children, families, and colleagues

◆ Recognize that children and adults achieve their full potential in the context of relationships that are based on trust and respect

Conceptual framework

The Code sets forth a framework of professional responsibilities in four sections. Each section addresses an area of professional relationships: (1) with children, (2) with families, (3) among colleagues, and (4) with the community and society. Each section includes an introduction to the primary responsibilities of the early childhood practitioner in that context. The introduction is followed by a set of ideals (I) that reflect exemplary professional practice and by a set of principles (P) describing practices that are required, prohibited, or permitted.

The **ideals** reflect the aspirations of practitioners. The **principles** guide conduct and assist practitioners in resolving ethical dilemmas.* Both ideals and principles are intended to direct practitioners to those questions which, when responsibly answered, can provide the basis for conscientious decision making. While the Code provides specific direction for addressing some ethical dilemmas, many others will require the practitioner to combine the guidance of the Code with professional judgment.

The ideals and principles in this Code present a shared framework of professional responsibility that affirms our commitment to the core values of our field. The Code publicly acknowledges the responsibilities that we in the field have assumed, and in so doing supports ethical behavior in our work. Practitioners who face situations with ethical dimensions are urged to seek guidance in the applicable parts of this Code and in the spirit that informs the whole.

Often "the right answer"—the best ethical course of action to take—is not obvious. There may be no readily apparent, positive way to handle a situation. When one important value contradicts another, we face an ethical dilemma. When we face a dilemma, it is our professional responsibility to consult the Code and all relevant parties to find the most ethical resolution.

*There is not necessarily a corresponding principle for each ideal.

Section I

Ethical Responsibilities to Children   Childhood is a unique and valuable stage in the human life cycle. Our paramount responsibility is to provide care and education in settings that are safe, healthy, nurturing, and responsive for each child. We are committed to supporting children's development and learning; respecting individual differences; and helping children learn to live, play, and work cooperatively. We are also committed to promoting children's self-awareness, competence, self-worth, resiliency, and physical well-being.

Ideals

I-1.1—To be familiar with the knowledge base of early childhood care and education and to stay informed through continuing education and training.

I-1.2—To base program practices upon current knowledge and research in the field of early childhood education, child development, and related disciplines, as well as on particular knowledge of each child.

I-1.3—To recognize and respect the unique qualities, abilities, and potential of each child.

I-1.4—To appreciate the vulnerability of children and their dependence on adults.

I-1.5—To create and maintain safe and healthy settings that foster children's social, emotional, cognitive, and physical development and that respect their dignity and their contributions.

I-1.6—To use assessment instruments and strategies that are appropriate for the children to be assessed, that are used only for the purposes for which they were designed, and that have the potential to benefit children.

I-1.7—To use assessment information to understand and support children's development and learning, to support instruction, and to identify children who may need additional services.

I-1.8—To support the right of each child to play and learn in an inclusive environment that meets the needs of children with and without disabilities.

I-1.9—To advocate for and ensure that all children, including those with special needs, have access to the support services needed to be successful.

I-1.10—To ensure that each child's culture, language, ethnicity, and family structure are recognized and valued in the program.

I-1.11—To provide all children with experiences in a language that they know, as well as support children in maintaining the use of their home language and in learning English.

I-1.12—To work with families to provide a safe and smooth transition as children and families move from one program to the next.

Principles

P-1.1—Above all, we shall not harm children. We shall not participate in practices that are emotionally damaging, physically harmful, disrespectful, degrading, dangerous, exploitative, or intimidating to children. *This principle has precedence over all others in this Code.*

P-1.2—We shall care for and educate children in positive emotional and social environments that are cognitively stimulating and that support each child's culture, language, ethnicity, and family structure.

P-1.3—We shall not participate in practices that discriminate against children by denying benefits, giving special advantages, or excluding them from programs or activities on the basis of their sex, race, national origin, religious beliefs, medical condition, disability, or the marital status/family structure, sexual orientation, or religious beliefs or other affiliations of their families. (Aspects of this principle do not apply in programs that have a lawful mandate to provide services to a particular population of children.)

P-1.4—We shall involve all those with relevant knowledge (including families and staff) in decisions concerning a child, as appropriate, ensuring confidentiality of sensitive information.

P-1.5—We shall use appropriate assessment systems, which include multiple sources of information, to provide information on children's learning and development.

P-1.6—We shall strive to ensure that decisions such as those related to enrollment, retention, or assignment to special education services, will be based on multiple sources of information and will never be based on a single assessment, such as a test score or a single observation.

P-1.7—We shall strive to build individual relationships with each child; make individualized adaptations in teaching strategies, learning environments, and curricula; and consult with the family so that each child benefits from the program. If after such efforts have been exhausted, the current placement does not meet a child's needs, or the child is seriously jeopardizing the ability of other children to benefit from the program, we shall collaborate with the child's family and appropriate specialists to determine the additional services needed and/or the placement option(s) most likely to ensure the child's success. (Aspects of this principle may not apply in programs that have a lawful mandate to provide services to a particular population of children.)

P-1.8—We shall be familiar with the risk factors for and symptoms of child abuse and neglect, including physical, sexual, verbal, and emotional abuse and physical, emotional, educational, and medical neglect. We shall know and follow state laws and community procedures that protect children against abuse and neglect.

P-1.9—When we have reasonable cause to suspect child abuse or neglect, we shall report it to the appropriate community agency and follow up to ensure that appropriate action has been taken. When appropriate, parents or guardians will be informed that the referral will be or has been made.

P-1.10—When another person tells us of his or her suspicion that a child is being abused or neglected, we shall assist that person in taking appropriate action in order to protect the child.

P-1.11—When we become aware of a practice or situation that endangers the health, safety, or well-being of children, we have an ethical responsibility to protect children or inform parents and/or others who can.

Section II

Ethical Responsibilities to Families   Families* are of primary importance in children's development. Because the family and the early childhood practitioner have a common interest in the child's well-being, we acknowledge a primary responsibility to bring about communication, cooperation, and collaboration between the home and early childhood program in ways that enhance the child's development.

*The term *family* may include those adults, besides parents, with the responsibility of being involved in educating, nurturing, and advocating for the child.

Ideals

I-2.1—To be familiar with the knowledge base related to working effectively with families and to stay informed through continuing education and training.

I-2.2—To develop relationships of mutual trust and create partnerships with the families we serve.

I-2.3—To welcome all family members and encourage them to participate in the program.

I-2.4—To listen to families, acknowledge and build upon their strengths and competencies, and learn from families as we support them in their task of nurturing children.

I-2.5—To respect the dignity and preferences of each family and to make an effort to learn about its structure, culture, language, customs, and beliefs.

I-2.6—To acknowledge families' childrearing values and their right to make decisions for their children.

I-2.7—To share information about each child's education and development with families and to help them understand and appreciate the current knowledge base of the early childhood profession.

I-2.8—To help family members enhance their understanding of their children and support the continuing development of their skills as parents.

I-2.9—To participate in building support networks for families by providing them with opportunities to interact with program staff, other families, community resources, and professional services.

Principles

P-2.1—We shall not deny family members access to their child's classroom or program setting unless access is denied by court order or other legal restriction.

P-2.2—We shall inform families of program philosophy, policies, curriculum, assessment system, and personnel qualifications, and explain why we teach as we do—which should be in accordance with our ethical responsibilities to children (see Section I).

P-2.3—We shall inform families of and, when appropriate, involve them in policy decisions.

P-2.4—We shall involve the family in significant decisions affecting their child.

P-2.5—We shall make every effort to communicate effectively with all families in a language that they understand. We shall use community resources for translation and interpretation when we do not have sufficient resources in our own programs.

P-2.6—As families share information with us about their children and families, we shall consider this information to plan and implement the program.

P-2.7—We shall inform families about the nature and purpose of the program's child assessments and how data about their child will be used.

P-2.8—We shall treat child assessment information confidentially and share this information only when there is a legitimate need for it.

P-2.9—We shall inform the family of injuries and incidents involving their child, of risks such as exposures to communicable diseases that might result in infection, and of occurrences that might result in emotional stress.

P-2.10—Families shall be fully informed of any proposed research projects involving their children and shall have the opportunity to give or withhold consent without penalty. We shall not permit or participate in research that could in any way hinder the education, development, or well-being of children.

P-2.11—We shall not engage in or support exploitation of families. We shall not use our relationship with a family for private advantage or personal gain, or enter into relationships with family members that might impair our effectiveness working with their children.

P-2.12—We shall develop written policies for the protection of confidentiality and the disclosure of children's records. These policy documents shall be made available to all program personnel and families. Disclosure of children's records beyond family members, program personnel, and consultants having an obligation of confidentiality shall require familial consent (except in cases of abuse or neglect).

P-2.13—We shall maintain confidentiality and shall respect the family's right to privacy, refraining from disclosure of confidential information and intrusion into family life. However, when we have reason to believe that a child's welfare is at risk, it is permissible to share confidential information with agencies, as well as with individuals who have legal responsibility for intervening in the child's interest.

P-2.14—In cases where family members are in conflict with one another, we shall work openly, sharing our observations of the child, to help all parties involved make informed decisions. We shall refrain from becoming an advocate for one party.

P-2.15—We shall be familiar with and appropriately refer families to community resources and professional support services. After a referral has been made, we shall follow up to ensure that services have been appropriately provided.

Section III

Ethical Responsibilities to Colleagues   In a caring, co-operative workplace, human dignity is respected, professional satisfaction is promoted, and positive relationships are developed and sustained. Based upon our core values, our primary responsibility to colleagues is to establish and maintain settings and relationships that support productive work and meet professional needs. The same ideals that apply to children also apply as we interact with adults in the workplace.

A—Responsibilities to co-workers

Ideals

I-3A.1—To establish and maintain relationships of respect, trust, confidentiality, collaboration, and cooperation with co-workers.

I-3A.2—To share resources with co-workers, collaborating to ensure that the best possible early childhood care and education program is provided.

I-3A.3—To support co-workers in meeting their professional needs and in their professional development.

I-3A.4—To accord co-workers due recognition of professional achievement.

Principles

P-3A.1—We shall recognize the contributions of colleagues to our program and not participate in practices that diminish their reputations or impair

their effectiveness in working with children and families.

P-3A.2—When we have concerns about the professional behavior of a co-worker, we shall first let that person know of our concern in a way that shows respect for personal dignity and for the diversity to be found among staff members, and then attempt to resolve the matter collegially and in a confidential manner.

P-3A.3—We shall exercise care in expressing views regarding the personal attributes or professional conduct of co-workers. Statements should be based on firsthand knowledge, not hearsay, and relevant to the interests of children and programs.

P-3A.4—We shall not participate in practices that discriminate against a co-worker because of sex, race, national origin, religious beliefs or other affiliations, age, marital status/family structure, disability, or sexual orientation.

B—Responsibilities to employers

Ideals

I-3B.1—To assist the program in providing the highest quality of service.

I-3B.2—To do nothing that diminishes the reputation of the program in which we work unless it is violating laws and regulations designed to protect children or is violating the provisions of this Code.

Principles

P-3B.1—We shall follow all program policies. When we do not agree with program policies, we shall attempt to effect change through constructive action within the organization.

P-3B.2—We shall speak or act on behalf of an organization only when authorized. We shall take care to acknowledge when we are speaking for the organization and when we are expressing a personal judgment.

P-3B.3—We shall not violate laws or regulations designed to protect children and shall take appropriate action consistent with this Code when aware of such violations.

P-3B.4—If we have concerns about a colleague's behavior, and children's well-being is not at risk, we may address the concern with that individual. If children are at risk or the situation does not improve after it has been brought to the colleague's attention, we shall report the colleague's unethical or incompetent behavior to an appropriate authority.

P-3B.5—When we have a concern about circumstances or conditions that impact the quality of care and education within the program, we shall inform the program's administration or, when necessary, other appropriate authorities.

C—Responsibilities to employees

Ideals

I-3C.1—To promote safe and healthy working conditions and policies that foster mutual respect, cooperation, collaboration, competence, well-being, confidentiality, and self-esteem in staff members.

I-3C.2—To create and maintain a climate of trust and candor that will enable staff to speak and act in the best interests of children, families, and the field of early childhood care and education.

I-3C.3—To strive to secure adequate and equitable compensation (salary and benefits) for those who work with or on behalf of young children.

I-3C.4—To encourage and support continual development of employees in becoming more skilled and knowledgeable practitioners.

Principles

P-3C.1—In decisions concerning children and programs, we shall draw upon the education, training, experience, and expertise of staff members.

P-3C.2—We shall provide staff members with safe and supportive working conditions that honor confidences and permit them to carry out their responsibilities through fair performance evaluation, written grievance procedures, constructive feedback, and opportunities for continuing professional development and advancement.

P-3C.3—We shall develop and maintain comprehensive written personnel policies that define program standards. These policies shall be given to new staff members and shall be available and easily accessible for review by all staff members.

P-3C.4—We shall inform employees whose performance does not meet program expectations of areas of concern and, when possible, assist in improving their performance.

P-3C.5—We shall conduct employee dismissals for just cause, in accordance with all applicable laws and regulations. We shall inform employees who are dismissed of the reasons for their termination. When a dismissal is for cause, justification must be based on evidence of inadequate or inappropriate behavior that is accurately documented, current, and available for the employee to review.

P-3C.6—In making evaluations and recommendations, we shall make judgments based on fact and relevant to the interests of children and programs.

P-3C.7—We shall make hiring, retention, termination, and promotion decisions based solely on a person's competence, record of accomplishment, ability to carry out the responsibilities of the position, and professional preparation specific to the developmental levels of children in his/her care.

P-3C.8—We shall not make hiring, retention, termination, and promotion decisions based on an individual's sex, race, national origin, religious beliefs or other affiliations, age, marital status/family structure, disability, or sexual orientation. We shall be familiar with and observe laws and regulations that pertain to employment discrimination. (Aspects of this principle do not apply to programs that have a lawful mandate to determine eligibility based on one or more of the criteria identified above.)

P-3C.9—We shall maintain confidentiality in dealing with issues related to an employee's job performance and shall respect an employee's right to privacy regarding personal issues.

Section IV

Ethical Responsibilities to Community and Society Early childhood programs operate within the context of their immediate community made up of families and other institutions concerned with children's welfare. Our responsibilities to the community are to provide programs that meet the diverse needs of families, to cooperate with agencies and professions that share the responsibility for children, to assist families in gaining access to those agencies and allied professionals, and to assist in the development of community programs that are needed but not currently available.

As individuals, we acknowledge our responsibility to provide the best possible programs of care and education for children and to conduct ourselves with honesty and integrity. Because of our specialized expertise in early childhood development and education and because the larger society shares responsibility for the welfare and protection of young children, we acknowledge a collective obligation to advocate for the best interests of children within early childhood programs and in the larger community and to serve as a voice for young children everywhere.

The ideals and principles in this section are presented to distinguish between those that pertain to the work of the individual early childhood educator and those that more typically are engaged in collectively on behalf of the best interests of children— with the understanding that individual early childhood educators have a shared responsibility for addressing the ideals and principles that are identified as "collective."

Ideal (Individual)

I-4.1—To provide the community with high-quality early childhood care and education programs and services.

Ideals (Collective)

I-4.2—To promote cooperation among professionals and agencies and interdisciplinary collaboration among professions concerned with addressing issues in the health, education, and well-being of young children, their families, and their early childhood educators.

I-4.3—To work through education, research, and advocacy toward an environmentally safe world in which all children receive health care, food, and shelter; are nurtured; and live free from violence in their home and their communities.

I-4.4—To work through education, research, and advocacy toward a society in which all young children have access to high-quality early care and education programs.

I-4.5—To work to ensure that appropriate assessment systems, which include multiple sources of information, are used for purposes that benefit children.

I-4.6—To promote knowledge and understanding of young children and their needs. To work toward greater societal acknowledgment of children's rights and greater social acceptance of responsibility for the well-being of all children.

I-4.7—To support policies and laws that promote the well-being of children and families, and to work to change those that impair their well-being. To participate in developing policies and laws that are needed, and to cooperate with other individuals and groups in these efforts.

I-4.8—To further the professional development of the field of early childhood care and education and to strengthen its commitment to realizing its core values as reflected in this Code.

Principles (Individual)

P-4.1—We shall communicate openly and truthfully about the nature and extent of services that we provide.

P-4.2—We shall apply for, accept, and work in positions for which we are personally well-suited and professionally qualified. We shall not offer services that we do not have the competence, qualifications, or resources to provide.

P-4.3—We shall carefully check references and shall not hire or recommend for employment any person whose competence, qualifications, or character makes him or her unsuited for the position.

P-4.4—We shall be objective and accurate in reporting the knowledge upon which we base our program practices.

P-4.5—We shall be knowledgeable about the appropriate use of assessment strategies and instruments and interpret results accurately to families.

P-4.6—We shall be familiar with laws and regulations that serve to protect the children in our programs and be vigilant in ensuring that these laws and regulations are followed.

P-4.7—When we become aware of a practice or situation that endangers the health, safety, or well-being of children, we have an ethical responsibility to protect children or inform parents and/or others who can.

P-4.8—We shall not participate in practices that are in violation of laws and regulations that protect the children in our programs.

P-4.9—When we have evidence that an early childhood program is violating laws or regulations protecting children, we shall report the violation to appropriate authorities who can be expected to remedy the situation.

P-4.10—When a program violates or requires its employees to violate this Code, it is permissible, after fair assessment of the evidence, to disclose the identity of that program.

Principles (Collective)

P-4.11—When policies are enacted for purposes that do not benefit children, we have a collective responsibility to work to change these practices.

P-4.12—When we have evidence that an agency that provides services intended to ensure children's well-being is failing to meet its obligations, we acknowledge a collective ethical responsibility to report the problem to appropriate authorities or to the public. We shall be vigilant in our follow-up until the situation is resolved.

P-4.13—When a child protection agency fails to provide adequate protection for abused or neglected children, we acknowledge a collective ethical responsibility to work toward the improvement of these services.

Glossary of Terms Related to Ethics

Code of Ethics. Defines the core values of the field and provides guidance for what professionals should do when they encounter conflicting obligations or responsibilities in their work.

Values. Qualities or principles that individuals believe to be desirable or worthwhile and that they prize for themselves, for others, and for the world in which they live.

Core Values. Commitments held by a profession that are consciously and knowingly embraced by its practitioners because they make a contribution to society. There is a difference between personal values and the core values of a profession.

Morality. Peoples' views of what is good, right, and proper; their beliefs about their obligations; and their ideas about how they should behave.

Ethics. The study of right and wrong, or duty and obligation, that involves critical reflection on morality and the ability to make choices between values and the examination of the moral dimensions of relationships.

Professional Ethics. The moral commitments of a profession that involve moral reflection that extends and enhances the personal morality practitioners bring to their work, that concern actions of right and wrong in the workplace, and that help individuals resolve moral dilemmas they encounter in their work.

Ethical Responsibilities. Behaviors that one must or must not engage in. Ethical responsibilities are clear-cut and are spelled out in the Code of Ethical Conduct (for example, early childhood educators should never share confidential information about a child or family with a person who has no legitimate need for knowing).

Ethical Dilemma. A moral conflict that involves determining appropriate conduct when an individual faces conflicting professional values and responsibilities.

Sources for glossary terms and definitions

Feeney, S., & N. Freeman. 1999. *Ethics and the early childhood educator: Using the NAEYC code.* Washington, DC: NAEYC.

Kidder, R.M. 1995. *How good people make tough choices: Resolving the dilemmas of ethical living.* New York: Fireside.

Kipnis, K. 1987. How to discuss professional ethics. *Young Children* 42 (4): 26–30.

The National Association for the Education of Young Children (NAEYC) is a nonprofit corporation, tax exempt under Section 501(c)(3) of the Internal Revenue Code, dedicated to acting on behalf of the needs and interests of young children. The NAEYC Code of Ethical Conduct (Code) has been developed in furtherance of NAEYC's nonprofit and tax exempt purposes. The information contained in the Code is intended to provide early childhood educators with guidelines for working with children from birth through age 8.

An individual's or program's use, reference to, or review of the Code does not guarantee compliance with NAEYC Early Childhood Program Standards and Accreditation Performance Criteria and program accreditation procedures. It is recommended that the Code be used as guidance in connection with implementation of the NAEYC Program Standards, but such use is not a substitute for diligent review and application of the NAEYC Program Standards.

NAEYC has taken reasonable measures to develop the Code in a fair, reasonable, open, unbiased, and objective manner, based on currently available data. However, further research or developments may change the current state of knowledge. Neither NAEYC nor its officers, directors, members, employees, or agents will be liable for any loss, damage, or claim with respect to any liabilities, including direct, special, indirect, or consequential damages incurred in connection with the Code or reliance on the information presented.

NAEYC Code of Ethical Conduct Revisions Workgroup

Mary Ambery, Ruth Ann Ball, James Clay, Julie Olsen Edwards, Harriet Egertson, Anthony Fair, Stephanie Feeney, Jana Fleming, Nancy Freeman, Marla Israel, Allison McKinnon, Evelyn Wright Moore, Eva Moravcik, Christina Lopez Morgan, Sarah Mulligan, Nila Rinehart, Betty Holston Smith, and Peter Pizzolongo, *NAEYC Staff*

Content-Area Standards Published by National Professional Organizations

The following content-area standards developed by professional organizations are not federal mandates but provide a framework for determining what students need to know and be able to do. Individual states have also established selected content-area standards that can be accessed through each state's education agency.

Civics

Center for Civics Education
National Standards for Civics and Government (K–4)
http://www.civiced.org/stds.html

Fine Arts

Consortium of National Arts Education Associations & National Committee for Standards in the Arts
National Standards for Art Education (K–12)
http://www.artsedge.kennedy-center.org/teach/standards/

Foreign Languages

American Council on the Teaching of Foreign Languages (K–12)
Standards for Foreign Language Learning: Preparing for the 21st Century (K–12)
http://www.actfl.org

Geography

National Geographic Society
United States National Geography Standards (K–12)
http://www.nationalgeographic.org

Health

American Association for Health Education & American Alliance for Health, Physical Education, Recreation, and Dance
National Health Education Standards (Pre-K–12)
http://www.aahperd.org/aahe/pdf_files/standards.pdf

Language Arts

National Council of Teachers of English and the International Reading Association
Standards for the English Language (K–12)
http://www.ncte.org
http://www.reading.org

Mathematics

National Council of Teachers of Mathematics
Principles and Standards for School Mathematics (Pre-K–12)
http://www.nctm.org

Music

National Association for Music Educators
National Standards for Music Education
http://www.menc.org/

Physical Education

National Association for Sport and Physical Education
Moving into the Future: National Physical Education Standards (K–12)

See also:
Active Start: A Statement of Physical Activity Guidelines for Children Birth to 5 years, and *Physical Activity: A Statement of Guidelines for Children 5–12*
http://www.aahperd.org/naspe/

Science

National Research Council of the National Academies of Science: Center for Science, Mathematics, and Engineering Education
National Science Education Standards (K–12)
http://www.nap.edu

See also: National Science Teachers Association
http://www.nsta.org/standards

Social Studies

National Council for Social Studies
Expectations of Excellence: Curriculum Standards for Social Studies (K–12)
http://www.ncess.org

Technology

International Society for Technology in Education
National Education Technology Standards
http://cnets.iste.org/

United States History

National Council for History Standards and the National Center for History in the Schools
National Standards for History (K–4)
http://nchsucla.edu/standards.html

Early Learning Standards*
Creating the Conditions for Success

Approved November 19, 2002

A Joint Position Statement of The National Association for the Education of Young Children (NAEYC) and The National Association of Early Childhood Specialists in State Departments of Education (NAECS/SDE)

EXECUTIVE SUMMARY

INTRODUCTION

Early childhood education has become part of a standards-based environment. More than 25 states have standards[1] describing desired results, outcomes, or learning expectations for children below kindergarten age; Head Start has developed a Child Outcomes Framework; and national organizations have developed content standards in areas such as early literacy and mathematics. This movement raises significant educational, ethical, developmental, programmatic, assessment, and policy issues. Rather than writing a new set of standards, in this position statement NAEYC and NAECS/SDE address those issues, describing four features that are essential if early learning standards are to be developmentally effective. The recommendations in this position statement are most relevant to young children of preschool or prekindergarten age, with and without disabilities, in group settings including state prekindergarten programs, community child care, family child care, and Head Start. However, the recommendations can guide the development and implementation of standards for younger and older children as well.

THE POSITION

The first years of life are critical for later outcomes. Young children have an innate desire to learn. That

[1]NCRESST defines *standards* as "the broadest of a family of terms referring to expectations for student learning." This position statement uses the term *early learning standards* to describe expectations for the learning and development of young children. Narrower terms included in standards and early learning standards are *content standards* ("summary descriptions of what it is that students should know and/or be able to do within a particular discipline" [McREL]); *benchmarks* ("specific description of knowledge or skill that students should acquire by a particular point in their schooling" [McREL]-usually tied to a grade or age level); *performance standards* ("describes levels of student performance in respect to the knowledge or skill described in a single benchmark or a set of closely related benchmarks" [McREL]). Important, related standards that are not included in this position statement's definition of early learning standards are *program standards*—expectations for the characteristics or quality of schools, child care centers, and other educational settings. It should be noted that Head Start uses the term *Performance Standards* in a way that is closer to the definition of program standards, describing expectations for the functioning of a Head Start program and not the accomplishments of children in the program. A working group of representatives from NAEYC, CCSSO, ERIC, and other groups is developing a more complete glossary of terms related to standards, assessment, and accountability.

desire can be supported or undermined by early experiences. High-quality early childhood education can promote intellectual, language, physical, social, and emotional development, creating school readiness and building a foundation for later academic and social competence. By defining the desired content and outcomes of young children's education, early learning standards can lead to greater opportunities for positive development and learning in these early years. The National Association for the Education of Young Children (NAEYC) and the National Association of Early Childhood Specialists in State Departments of Education (NAECS/SDE) take the position that early learning standards can be a valuable part of a comprehensive, high-quality system of services for young children, contributing to young children's educational experiences and to their future success. But these results can be achieved only if early learning standards (1) emphasize significant, developmentally appropriate content and outcomes; (2) are developed and reviewed through informed, inclusive processes; (3) use implementation and assessment strategies that are ethical and appropriate for young children; and (4) are accompanied by strong supports for early childhood programs, professionals, and families.

Because of the educational and developmental risks for vulnerable young children if standards are not well developed and implemented, the recommendations in this position statement are embedded in and refer to the principles set forth in NAEYC's code of ethical conduct. According to this code, early childhood professionals and others affecting young children's education must promote those practices that benefit young children, and they must refuse to participate in educational practices that harm young children. Thus, a test of the value of any standards effort is whether it promotes educationally and developmentally positive outcomes and whether it avoids penalizing or excluding children from needed services and supports.

ESSENTIAL FEATURES

A developmentally effective system of early learning standards must include four essential features:

1. **Effective Early Learning Standards Emphasize Significant, Developmentally Appropriate Content and Outcomes**

   ◆ Effective early learning standards give emphasis to **all domains** of early development and learning.

   ◆ The content and desired outcomes of effective early learning standards are **meaningful and important** to children's current well-being and later learning.

   ◆ Rather than relying on simplifications, of standards for older children, the content and desired outcomes of effective early learning standards are **based on research about** the processes, sequences, and long-term consequences of **early learning and development.**

   ◆ Effective early learning standards create **appropriate expectations** by linking content and desired outcomes to specific ages or developmental periods.

   ◆ The content of effective early learning standards, and expectations for children's mastery of the standards, must **accommodate variations**—community, cultural, linguistic, and individual—that best support positive outcomes. To do so, early learning standards must encompass the widest possible range of children's life situations and experiences, including disabilities.

2. **Effective Early Learning Standards Are Developed and Reviewed Through Informed, Inclusive Processes**

   ◆ The process of developing and reviewing early learning standards relies on relevant, valid **sources of expertise.**

   ◆ The process of developing and reviewing early learning standards involves **multiple stakeholders**. Stakeholders may include community members, families, early childhood educators and special educators, and other professional groups. In all cases, those with specific expertise in early development and learning must be involved.

   ◆ Once early learning standards have been developed, standards developers and relevant professional associations ensure that standards are shared with all stakeholders, creating multiple opportunities for **discussion and exchange.**

   ◆ Early learning standards remain relevant and research based by using a systematic, interactive process for regular **review and revision.**

3. **Early Learning Standards Gain Their Effectiveness Through Implementation and Assessment Practices That Support All Children's Development in Ethical, Appropriate Ways**

   ◆ Effective early learning standards require equally effective **curriculum, classroom practices, and teaching strategies** that connect with young children's interests and abilities, and that promote positive development and learning.

   ◆ **Tools to assess young children's progress** must be clearly connected to important learning represented in the standards; must be technically, developmentally, and culturally valid; and must yield comprehensive, useful information.

   ◆ Information gained from **assessments** of young children's progress with respect to standards must be **used to benefit children.** Assessment and accountability systems should be used to improve practices and services and should not be used to rank, sort, or penalize young children.

4. **Effective Early Learning Standards Require a Foundation of Support for Early Childhood Programs, Professionals, and Families**

   ◆ Research-based standards for early childhood **program quality, and adequate resources** for high-quality programs, build environments where standards can be implemented effectively.

   ◆ Significant expansion of **professional development** is essential if all early childhood teachers and administrators are to gain the knowledge, skills, and dispositions needed to implement early learning standards.

   ◆ Early learning standards have the most positive effects if **families**—key partners in young children's learning—are provided with respectful communication and support.

Child Outcomes Framework*

DOMAIN	DOMAIN ELEMENT	INDICATORS
LANGUAGE DEVELOPMENT	Listening & Understanding	◆ Demonstrates increasing ability to attend to and understand conversations, stories, songs, and poems. ◆ Shows progress in understanding and following simple and multiple-step directions. ☆ **Understands an increasingly complex and varied vocabulary.** ☆ **For non-English-speaking children, progresses in listening to and understanding English.**
	Speaking & Communicating	☆ **Develops increasing abilities to understand and use language to communicate information, experiences, ideas, feelings, opinions, needs, questions; and for other varied purposes.** ◆ Progresses in abilities to initiate and respond appropriately in conversation and discussions with peers and adults. ☆ **Uses an increasingly complex and varied spoken vocabulary.** ◆ Progresses in clarity of pronunciation and towards speaking in sentences of increasing length and grammatical complexity. ☆ **For non-English-speaking children, progresses in speaking English.**
LITERACY	☆ Phonological Awareness	◆ Shows increasing ability to discriminate and identify sounds in spoken language. ◆ Shows growing awareness of beginning and ending sounds of words. ◆ Progresses in recognizing matching sounds and rhymes in familiar words, games, songs, stories, and poems. ◆ Shows growing ability to hear and discriminate separate syllables in words. ☆ **Associates sounds with written words,** such as awareness that different words begin with the same sound.
	☆ Book Knowledge & Appreciation	◆ Shows growing interest and involvement in listening to and discussing a variety of fiction and non-fiction books and poetry. ◆ Shows growing interest in reading-related activities, such as asking to have a favorite book read; choosing to look at books; drawing pictures based on stories; asking to take books home; going to the library; and engaging in pretend-reading with other children.

(continued)

*U.S. Department of Health and Human Services, Administration for Children and Families Office of Head Start (July, 2003). *The Head Start Child Outcomes Framework.* Washington, DC: Author.

☆Indicates the 4 specific Domain Elements and 9 Indicators that are legislatively mandated.

DOMAIN	DOMAIN ELEMENT	INDICATORS
LITERACY (CONT.)		◆ Demonstrates progress in abilities to retell and dictate stories from books and experiences; to act out stories in dramatic play; and to predict what will happen next in a story. ◆ Progresses in learning how to handle and care for books; knowing to view one page at a time in sequence from front to back; and understanding that a book has a title, author, and illustrator.
	☆ Print Awareness & Concepts	◆ Shows increasing awareness of print in classroom, home, and community settings. ◆ Develops growing understanding of the different functions of forms of print such as signs, letters, newspapers, lists, messages, and menus. ◆ Demonstrates increasing awareness of concepts of print, such as that reading in English moves from top to bottom and from left to right, that speech can be written down, and that print conveys a message. ◆ Shows progress in recognizing the association between spoken and written words by following print as it is read aloud. ☆ **Recognizes a word as a unit of print,** or awareness that letters are grouped to form words, and that words are separated by spaces.
	Early Writing	◆ Develops understanding that writing is a way of communicating for a variety of purposes. ◆ Begins to represent stories and experiences through pictures, dictation, and in play. ◆ Experiments with a growing variety of writing tools and materials, such as pencils, crayons, and computers. ◆ Progresses from using scribbles, shapes, or pictures to represent ideas, to using letter-like symbols, to copying or writing familiar words such as their own name.
	Alphabet Knowledge	◆ Shows progress in associating the names of letters with their shapes and sounds. ◆ Increases in ability to notice the beginning letters in familiar words. ☆ **Identifies at least 10 letters of the alphabet, especially those in their own name.** ☆ **Knows that letters of the alphabet are a special category of visual graphics that can be individually named.**
MATHEMATICS	☆ Number & Operations	◆ Demonstrates increasing interest and awareness of numbers and counting as a means for solving problems and determining quantity. ◆ Begins to associate number concepts, vocabulary, quantities, and written numerals in meaningful ways. ◆ Develops increasing ability to count in sequence to 10 and beyond. ◆ Begins to make use of one-to-one correspondence in counting objects and matching groups of objects. ◆ Begins to use language to compare numbers of objects with terms such as more, less, greater than, fewer, equal to. ◆ Develops increased abilities to combine, separate and name "how many" concrete objects.

MATHEMATICS (CONT.)	Geometry & Spatial Sense	◆ Begins to recognize, describe, compare, and name common shapes, their parts and attributes. ◆ Progresses in ability to put together and take apart shapes. ◆ Begins to be able to determine whether or not two shapes are the same size and shape. ◆ Shows growth in matching, sorting, putting in a series, and regrouping objects according to one or two attributes such as color, shape, or size. ◆ Builds an increasing understanding of directionality, order, and positions of objects, and words such as up, down, over, under, top, bottom, inside, outside, in front, and behind.
	Patterns & Measurement	◆ Enhances abilities to recognize, duplicate, and extend simple patterns using a variety of materials. ◆ Shows increasing abilities to match, sort, put in a series, and regroup objects according to one or two attributes such as shape or size. ◆ Begins to make comparisons between several objects based on a single attribute. ◆ Shows progress in using standard and non-standard measures for length and area of objects.
SCIENCE	Scientific Skills & Methods	◆ Begins to use senses and a variety of tools and simple measuring devices to gather information, investigate materials, and observe processes and relationships. ◆ Develops increased ability to observe and discuss common properties, differences and comparisons among objects and materials. ◆ Begins to participate in simple investigations to test observations, discuss and draw conclusions, and form generalizations. ◆ Develops growing abilities to collect, describe, and record information through a variety of means, including discussion, drawings, maps, and charts. ◆ Begins to describe and discuss predictions, explanations, and generalizations based on past experiences.
	Scientific Knowledge	◆ Expands knowledge of and abilities to observe, describe, and discuss the natural world, materials, living things, and natural processes. ◆ Expands knowledge of and respect for their bodies and the environment. ◆ Develops growing awareness of ideas and language related to attributes of time and temperature. ◆ Shows increased awareness and beginning understanding of changes in materials and cause-effect relationships.
CREATIVE ARTS	Music	◆ Participates with increasing interest and enjoyment in a variety of music activities, including listening, singing, finger plays, games, and performances. ◆ Experiments with a variety of musical instruments.
	Art	◆ Gains ability in using different art media and materials in a variety of ways for creative expression and representation. ◆ Progresses in abilities to create drawings, paintings, models, and other art creations that are more detailed, creative, or realistic. ◆ Develops growing abilities to plan, work independently, and demonstrate care and persistence in a variety of art projects. ◆ Begins to understand and share opinions about artistic products and experiences.

(continued)

DOMAIN	DOMAIN ELEMENT	INDICATORS
CREATIVE ARTS (CONT.)	Movement	◆ Expresses through movement and dancing what is felt and heard in various musical tempos and styles. ◆ Shows growth in moving in time to different patterns of beat and rhythm in music.
	Dramatic Play	◆ Participates in a variety of dramatic play activities that become more extended and complex. ◆ Shows growing creativity and imagination in using materials and in assuming different roles in dramatic play situations.
SOCIAL & EMOTIONAL DEVELOPMENT	Self-Concept	◆ Begins to develop and express awareness of self in terms of specific abilities, characteristics, and preferences. ◆ Develops growing capacity for independence in a range of activities, routines, and tasks. ◆ Demonstrates growing confidence in a range of abilities and expresses pride in accomplishments.
	Self-Control	◆ Shows progress in expressing feelings, needs, and opinions in difficult situations and conflicts without harming themselves, others, or property. ◆ Develops growing understanding of how their actions affect others and begins to accept the consequences of their actions. ◆ Demonstrates increasing capacity to follow rules and routines and use materials purposefully, safely, and respectfully.
	Cooperation	◆ Increases abilities to sustain interactions with peers by helping, sharing, and discussion ◆ Shows increasing abilities to use compromise and discussion in working, playing, and resolving conflicts with peers. ◆ Develops increasing abilities to give and take in interactions; to take turns in games or using materials; and to interact without being overly submissive or directive.
	Social Relationships	◆ Demonstrates increasing comfort in talking with and accepting guidance and directions from a range of familiar adults. ◆ Shows progress in developing friendships with peers. ◆ Progresses in responding sympathetically to peers who are in need, upset, hurt, or angry; and in expressing empathy or caring for others.
	Knowledge of Families & Communities	◆ Develops ability to identify personal characteristics, including gender and family composition. ◆ Progresses in understanding similarities and respecting differences among people, such as genders, race, special needs, culture, language, and family structures. ◆ Develops growing awareness of jobs and what is required to perform them. ◆ Begins to express and understand concepts and language of geography in the contexts of the classroom, home, and community.

APPROACHES TO LEARNING	Initiative & Curiosity	◆ Chooses to participate in an increasing variety of tasks and activities. ◆ Develops increased ability to make independent choices. ◆ Approaches tasks and activities with increased flexibility, imagination, and inventiveness. ◆ Grows in eagerness to learn about and discuss a growing range of topics, ideas, and tasks.
	Engagement & Persistence	◆ Grows in abilities to persist in and complete a variety of tasks, activities, projects, and experiences. ◆ Demonstrates increasing ability to set goals and develop and follow through on plans. ◆ Shows growing capacity to maintain concentration over time on a task, question, set of directions or interactions, despite distractions and interruptions.
	Reasoning & Problem Solving	◆ Develops increasing ability to find more than one solution to a question, task, or problem. ◆ Grows in recognizing and solving problems through active exploration, including trial and error, and interactions and discussions with peers and adults. ◆ Develops increasing abilities to classify, compare and contrast objects, events, and experiences.
PHYSICAL HEALTH & DEVELOPMENT	Gross Motor Skills	◆ Shows increasing levels of proficiency, control, and balance in walking, climbing, running, jumping, hopping, skipping, marching, and galloping. ◆ Demonstrates increasing abilities to coordinate movements in throwing, catching, kicking, bouncing balls, and using the slide and swing.
	Fine Motor Skills	◆ Develops growing strength, dexterity, and control needed to use tools such as scissors, paper punch, stapler, and hammer. ◆ Grows in hand-eye coordination in building with blocks, putting together puzzles, reproducing shapes and patterns, stringing beads, and using scissors. ◆ Progresses in abilities to use writing, drawing, and art tools, including pencils, markers, chalk, paint brushes, and various types of technology.
	Health Status & Practices	◆ Progresses in physical growth, strength, stamina, and flexibility. ◆ Participates actively in games, outdoor play, and other forms of exercise that enhance physical fitness. ◆ Shows growing independence in hygiene, nutrition, and personal care when eating, dressing, washing hands, brushing teeth, and toileting. ◆ Builds awareness and ability to follow basic health and safety rules such as fire safety, traffic and pedestrian safety, and responding appropriately to potentially harmful objects, substances, and activities.

Continuum of Children's Development in Early Reading and Writing*

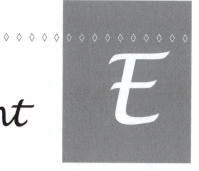

Note: This list is intended to be illustrative, not exhaustive. Children at any grade level will function at a variety of phases along the reading/writing continuum.

Phase 1: Awareness and exploration (goals for preschool)

Children explore their environment and build the foundations for learning to read and write.

Children can

- enjoy listening to and discussing storybooks
- understand that print carries a message
- engage in reading and writing attempts
- identify labels and signs in their environment
- participate in rhyming games
- identify some letters and make some letter-sound matches
- use known letters or approximations of letters to represent written language (especially meaningful words like their name and phrases such as "I love you")

What teachers do

- share books with children, including Big Books, and model reading behaviors
- talk about letters by name and sounds
- establish a literacy-rich environment
- reread favorite stories
- engage children in language games
- promote literacy-related play activities
- encourage children to experiment with writing

What parents and family members can do

- talk with children, engage them in conversation, give names of things, show interest in what a child says
- read and reread stories with predictable text to children
- encourage children to recount experiences and describe ideas and events that are important to them
- visit the library regularly
- provide opportunities for children to draw and print, using markers, crayons, and pencils

Phase 2: Experimental reading and writing (goals for kindergarten)

Children develop basic concepts of print and begin to engage in and experiment with reading and writing.

Kindergartners can

- enjoy being read to and themselves retell simple narrative stories or informational texts
- use descriptive language to explain and explore
- recognize letters and letter-sound matches
- show familiarity with rhyming and beginning sounds
- understand left-to-right and top-to-bottom orientation and familiar concepts of print

Note: Excerpt from "Learning to Read and Write: Developmentally Appropriate Practices for Young Children: A Joint Position Statement by the National Association for the Education of Young Children and the International Reading Association." In *Young Children*, 53(4), pp. 30–46.

- match spoken words with written ones
- begin to write letters of the alphabet and some high-frequency words

What teachers do

- encourage children to talk about reading and writing experiences
- provide many opportunities for children to explore and identify sound-symbol relation-ships in meaningful contexts
- help children to segment spoken words into individual sounds and blend the sounds into whole words (for example, by slowly writing a word and saying its sound)
- frequently read interesting and conceptually rich stories to children
- provide daily opportunities for children to write
- help children build a sight vocabulary
- create a literacy-rich environment for children to engage independently in reading and writing

What parents and family members can do

- daily read and reread narrative and informa-tional stories to children
- encourage children's attempts at reading and writing
- allow children to participate in activities that in-volve writing and reading (for example, cooking, making grocery lists)
- play games that involve specific directions (such as "Simon Says")
- have conversations with children during meal-times and throughout the day

Phase 3: Early reading and writing (goals for first grade)

Children begin to read simple stories and can write about a topic that is meaningful to them.

First-graders can

- read and retell familiar stories
- use strategies (rereading, predicting, question-ing, contextualizing) when comprehension breaks down

- use reading and writing for various purposes on their own initiative
- orally read with reasonable fluency
- use letter-sound associations, word parts, and context to identify new words
- identify an increasing number of words by sight
- sound out and represent all substantial sounds in spelling a word
- write about topics that are personally mean-ingful
- attempt to use some punctuation and capital-ization

What teachers do

- support the development of vocabulary by reading daily to the children, transcribing their language, and selecting materials that expand children's knowledge and language development
- model strategies and provide practice for identifying unknown words
- give children opportunities for independent reading and writing practice
- read, write, and discuss a range of different text types (poems, informational books)
- introduce new words and teach strategies for learning to spell new words
- demonstrate and model strategies to use when comprehension breaks down
- help children build lists of commonly used words from their writing and reading

What parents and family members can do

- talk about favorite storybooks
- read to children and encourage them to read to you
- suggest that children write to friends and relatives
- bring to a parent-teacher's conference evi-dence of what your child can do in writing and reading
- encourage children to share what they have learned about their writing and reading

Phase 4: Transitional reading and writing (goals for second grade)

Children begin to read more fluently and write various text forms using simple and more complex sentences.

Second-graders can

- read with greater fluency
- use strategies more efficiently (rereading, questioning, and so on) when comprehension breaks down
- use word identification strategies with greater facility to unlock unknown words
- identify an increasing number of words by sight
- write about a range of topics to suit different audiences
- use common letter patterns and critical features to spell words
- punctuate simple sentences correctly and proofread their own work
- spend time reading daily and use reading to research topics

What teachers do

- create a climate that fosters analytic, evaluative, and reflective thinking
- teach children to write in multiple forms (stories, information, poems)
- ensure that children read a range of texts for a variety of purposes
- teach revising, editing, and proofreading skills
- teach strategies for spelling new and difficult words
- model enjoyment of reading

What parents and family members can do

- continue to read to children and encourage them to read to you
- engage children in activities that require reading and writing
- become involved in school activities
- show children your interest in their learning by displaying their written work
- visit the library regularly
- support your child's specific hobby or interest with reading materials and references

Phase 5: Independent and productive reading and writing (goals for third grade)

Children continue to extend and refine their reading and writing to suit varying purposes and audiences.

Third-graders can

- read fluently and enjoy reading
- use a range of strategies when drawing meaning from the text
- use word identification strategies appropriately and automatically when encountering unknown words
- recognize and discuss elements of different text structures
- make critical connections between texts
- write expressively in many different forms (stories, poems, reports)
- use a rich variety of vocabulary and sentences appropriate to text forms
- revise and edit their own writing during and after composing
- spell words correctly in final writing drafts

What teachers do

- provide opportunities daily for children to read, examine, and critically evaluate narrative and expository texts
- continue to create a climate that fosters critical reading and personal response
- teach children to examine ideas in texts
- encourage children to use writing as a tool for thinking and learning
- extend children's knowledge of the correct use of writing conventions
- emphasize the importance of correct spelling in finished written products
- create a climate that engages all children as a community of literacy learners

What parents and family members can do

◆ continue to support children's learning and interest by visiting the library and bookstores with them

◆ find ways to highlight children's progress in reading and writing

◆ stay in regular contact with your child's teachers about activities and progress in reading and writing

◆ encourage children to use and enjoy print for many purposes (such as recipes, directions, games, and sports)

◆ build a love of language in all its forms and engage children in conversation

Examples of Frequently Used Assessment Instruments and Standardized Tests*

ASSESSMENT TOOLS FOR TEACHERS

The Creative Curriculum Developmental Continuum (Dodge, Colker, & Heroman, 2002)

The Devereux Early Childhood Assessment (DECA) (LeBuffe & Naglieri, 1998)

High/Scope Preschool Observational Record: Infants and Toddlers (COR) (High Scope Educational Research Foundation, 1992)

High/Scope Preschool Observation Record: 2½–6 (COR), 2nd Edition (High/Scope Educational Research Foundation, 2003).

Social Competence and Behavior Evaluation (SCBE) (LaFreniere & Dumas, 1995).

Teacher Rating of Oral Language and Literacy (TROLL) (Dickinson, McCabe, & Sprague, 2003).

The Ounce Scale (Birth to 3½ years) (Meisels, Marsden, Dombro, Weston, & Jewkes, 2002)

The Work Sampling System (Meisels, Jablon, Marsden, Dichtelmiller, Dorfman, & Steele, 1995)

STANDARDIZED TESTS

◆ *Achievement tests*
  ◆ *Brigance Comprehensive Inventory of Basic Skills—Revised*
  ◆ *Brigance Inventory of Essential Skills*
  ◆ *Iowa Test of Basic Skills*
  ◆ *Kaufman Test of Educational Achievement*
  ◆ *Peabody Individual Achievement Test, Revised*
  ◆ *Stanford Achievement Test*
  ◆ *Metropolitan Achievement Test*
  ◆ *Wide Range Achievement Test—3*
  ◆ *Woodcock-Johnson III Tests of Achievement*
◆ *Readiness tests*
  ◆ *Boehm Test of Basic Concepts*
  ◆ *Brigance Inventory of Early Development*
  ◆ *Dynamic Indicators of Basic Early Literacy Skills* (DIEBELS)
  ◆ *Metropolitan Readiness Test*
  ◆ *Naglieri Nonverbal Ability Test*
  ◆ *Peabody Picture Vocabulary Test*
  ◆ *Preschool Individual Growth and Development Indicators* (IGDIs)
  ◆ *Oral and Written Language Scales*
  ◆ *Social Competence and Behavior Evaluation—Preschool Edition*
  ◆ *Social Skills Rating System* (SSRS)
◆ *Developmental Screening Tests*
  ◆ *Ages and Stages Questionnaires: A Parent-Completed Child Monitoring System*

*This list of examples of assessment instruments and standardized tests is by no means exhaustive, nor does it represent endorsement of any of them by the authors or publishers of this textbook. For information about specific tests, the student should consult the most current publication of *Buros Mental Measurements Yearbook* and *Tests in Print*, *http://www.unl.edu/buros/*. Additionally, most informal assessments are described online by their individual publishers.

- *AGS Early Screening Profiles*
- *Developmental Indicators for the Assessment of Learning—Revised (DIAL-3)*
- *Early Screening Inventory, Revised; Denver II* revision of the *Denver Developmental Screening Inventory*
- *Preschool* Individual Growth and Development Indicators (IGDIs)
- *Transdisciplinary Play-Based Assessment*

- *Diagnostic Tests*
  - *Assessment, Evaluation, and Programming System for Infants and Children (AEPS)*
  - *Batelle Developmental Inventory*
  - *Bayley Scales of Infant and Toddler Development (3rd Ed.)*
  - *Infant Toddler Social Emotional Assessment*
  - *Kaufman Assessment Battery for Children*
  - *Peabody Developmental Motor Scales (2nd Ed.)*
  - *Pediatric Evaluation of Disability Inventory*
  - *Purdue Perceptual-Motor Survey*
  - *Southern California Sensory Integration Test*
  - Vineland Adaptive Behavior Scales (VBAS)

- *Intelligence* and Cognitive Development Tests
  - *Stanford-Binet Intelligence Scale (4th Ed.)*
  - *Wechsler Intelligence Scale for Children, Revised*
  - *Wechsler Preschool and Primary Scale of Intelligence*
- *Program Evaluation Instruments*
  - *Assessment of Practices in Early Elementary Classrooms (Hemmeter, Maxwell, Ault, & Schuster, 2001)*
  - Classroom Assessment Scoring System *(Pianta, La Paro, & Hamre, 2004)*
  - *Early Childhood Environment Rating Scale (ECERS-R) (Harms, Clifford, & Cryer, 2005)*
  - *Early Language and Literacy Classroom Observation Toolkit (Smith, Dickinson, Sangeorge, & Anastasopoulos, 2002)*
  - *Family Day Care Rating Scale (FCCERS-R) (Harms & Clifford, 2006)*
  - *Infant/Toddler Environment Rating Scale (ITERS-R) (Harms, Cryer, & Clifford, 2006)*
  - *Program Administration Scale (Talan & Bloom, 2005)*
  - *School-Age Care Environment Rating Scale (SACERS) (Harms, Jacobs, & White, 1996)*
  - *Student Teacher Relationship Scale (Pianta, 2001)*

Early Childhood Curriculum, Assessment, and Program Evaluation*

Building an Effective, Accountable System in Programs for Children Birth through Age 8

A Joint Position Statement of the National Association for the Education of Young Children (NAEYC) and the National Association of Early Childhood Specialists in State Departments of Education (NAECS/SDE)

INTRODUCTION

High-quality early education produces long-lasting benefits. With this evidence, federal, state, and local decision makers are asking critical questions about young children's education. What should children be taught in the years from birth through age eight? How would we know if they are developing well and learning what we want them to learn? And how could we decide whether programs for children from infancy through the primary grades are doing a good job?

Answers to these questions—questions about *early childhood curriculum, child assessment, and program evaluation*—are the foundation of this joint position statement from the National Association for the Education of Young Children (NAEYC) and the National Association of Early Childhood Specialists in State Departments of Education (NAECS/SDE).

THE POSITION

The National Association for the Education of Young Children and the National Association of Early Childhood Specialists in State Departments of Education take the position that policy makers, the early childhood profession, and other stakeholders in young children's lives have a shared responsibility to

◆ construct comprehensive systems of curriculum, assessment, and program evaluation guided by sound early childhood practices, effective early learning standards and program standards, and a set of core principles and values: belief in civic and democratic values; commitment to ethical behavior on behalf of children; use of important goals as guides to action; coordinated systems; support for children as individuals and members of families, cultures, and communities; partnerships with families; respect for evidence; and shared accountability.

- implement curriculum that is thoughtfully planned, challenging, engaging, developmentally appropriate, culturally and linguistically responsive, comprehensive, and likely to promote positive outcomes for all young children.

- make ethical, appropriate, valid, and reliable assessment a central part of all early childhood programs. To assess young children's strengths, progress, and needs, use assessment methods that are developmentally appropriate, culturally and linguistically responsive, tied to children's daily activities, supported by professional development, inclusive of families, and connected to specific, beneficial purposes: (1) making sound decisions about teaching and learning, (2) identifying significant concerns that may require focused intervention for individual children, and (3) helping programs improve their educational and developmental interventions.

- regularly engage in program evaluation guided by program goals and using varied, appropriate, conceptually and technically sound evidence to determine the extent to which programs meet the expected standards of quality and to examine intended as well as unintended results.

- provide the support, professional development, and other resources to allow staff in early childhood programs to implement high-quality curriculum, assessment, and program evaluation practices and to connect those practices with well-defined early learning standards and program standards.

RECOMMENDATIONS

Curriculum

Implement curriculum that is thoughtfully planned, challenging, engaging, developmentally appropriate, culturally and linguistically responsive, comprehensive, and likely to promote positive outcomes for all young children.

Indicators of Effectiveness

- *Children are active and engaged*—Children from babyhood through primary grades—and

beyond—need to be cognitively, physically, socially, and artistically active. In their own ways, children of all ages and abilities can become interested and engaged, develop positive attitudes toward learning, and have their feelings of security, emotional competence, and linkages to family and community supported.

- *Goals are clear and shared by all*—Curriculum goals are clearly defined, shared, and understood by all "stakeholders" (for example, program administrators, teachers, and families). The curriculum and related activities and teaching strategies are designed to help achieve these goals in a unified, coherent way.

- *Curriculum is evidence-based*—The curriculum is based on evidence that is developmentally, culturally, and linguistically relevant for the children who will experience the curriculum. It is organized around principles of child development and learning.

- *Valued content is learned through investigation, play, and focused, intentional teaching*—Children learn by exploring, thinking about, and inquiring about all sorts of phenomena. These experiences help children investigate "big ideas," those that are important at any age and are connected to later learning. Pedagogy or teaching strategies are tailored to children's ages, developmental capacities, language and culture, and abilities or disabilities.

- *Curriculum builds on prior learning and experiences*—The content and implementation of the curriculum builds on children's prior individual, age-related, and cultural learning, is inclusive of children with disabilities, and is supportive of background knowledge gained at home and in the community. The curriculum supports children whose home language is not English in building a solid base for later learning.

- *Curriculum is comprehensive*—The curriculum encompasses critical areas of development including children's physical well-being and motor development; social and emotional development; approaches to learning; language development; and cognition and general knowledge; and subject matter areas such as science, mathematics, language, literacy, social studies, and the arts (more fully and explicitly for older children).

- *Professional standards validate the curriculum's subject-matter content*—When subject-specific curricula are adopted, they meet the standards of relevant professional organizations (for example, the American Alliance for Health, Physical Education, Recreation and Dance [AAHPERD], the National Association for Music Education [MENC]; the National Council of Teachers of English [NCTE]; the National Council of Teachers of Mathematics [NCTM]; the National Dance Education Organization [NDEO]; the National Science Teachers Association [NSTA]) and are reviewed and implemented so that they fit together coherently.

◆ *The curriculum is likely to benefit children*— Research and other evidence indicates that the curriculum, if implemented as intended, will likely have beneficial effects. These benefits include a wide range of outcomes. When evidence is not yet available, plans are developed to obtain this evidence.

Assessment of Young Children

Make ethical, appropriate, valid, and reliable assessment a central part of all early childhood programs. To assess young children's strengths, progress, and needs, use assessment methods that are developmentally appropriate, culturally and linguistically responsive, tied to children's daily activities, supported by professional development, inclusive of families, and connected to specific, beneficial purposes: (1) making sound decisions about teaching and learning, (2) identifying significant concerns that may require focused intervention for individual children, and (3) helping programs improve their educational and developmental interventions.

Indicators of Effectiveness

◆ *Ethical principles guide assessment practices*— Ethical principles underlie all assessment practices. Young children are not denied opportunities or services, and decisions are not made about children on the basis of a single assessment.

◆ *Assessment instruments are used for their intended purposes*—Assessments are used in ways consistent with the purposes for which they were designed. If the assessments will be used for additional purposes, they are validated for those purposes.

◆ *Assessments are appropriate for ages and other characteristics of children being assessed*— Assessments are designed for and validated for use with children whose ages, cultures, home languages, socioeconomic status, abilities and disabilities, and other characteristics are similar to those of the children with whom the assessments will be used.

◆ *Assessment instruments are in compliance with professional criteria for quality*—Assessments are valid and reliable. Accepted professional standards of quality are the basis for selection, use, and interpretation of assessment instruments, including screening tools. NAEYC and NAECS/SDE support and adhere to the measurement standards set forth in 1999 by the American Educational Research Association, the American Psychological Association, and the National Center for Measurement in Education. When individual norm-referenced tests are used, they meet these guidelines.

◆ *What is assessed is developmentally and educationally significant*—The objects of assessment include a comprehensive, developmentally, and educationally important set of goals, rather than a narrow set of skills. Assessments are aligned with early learning standards, with program goals, and with specific emphases in the curriculum.

◆ *Assessment evidence is used to understand and improve learning*—Assessments lead to improved knowledge about children. This knowledge is translated into improved curriculum implementation and teaching practices. Assessment helps early childhood professionals understand the learning of a specific child or group of children; enhance overall knowledge of child development; improve educational programs for young children while supporting continuity across grades and settings; and access resources and supports for children with specific needs.

◆ *Assessment evidence is gathered from realistic settings and situations that reflect children's actual performance*—To influence teaching strategies or to identify children in need of further evaluation, the evidence used to assess young children's characteristics and progress is derived from real-world classroom or family contexts that are consistent with children's culture, language, and experiences.

◆ *Assessments use multiple sources of evidence gathered over time*—The assessment system emphasizes repeated, systematic observation, documentation, and other forms of criterion- or performance-oriented assessment using broad, varied, and complementary methods with accommodations for children with disabilities.

◆ *Screening is always linked to follow-up*—When a screening or other assessment identifies concerns, appropriate follow-up, referral, or other intervention is used. Diagnosis or labeling is never the result of a brief screening or one-time assessment.

◆ *Use of individually administered, norm-referenced tests is limited*—The use of formal standardized testing and norm-referenced assessments of young children is limited to situations in which such measures are appropriate and potentially beneficial, such as identifying potential disabilities. (See also the indicator concerning the use of individual norm-referenced tests as part of program evaluation and accountability.)

◆ *Staff and families are knowledgeable about assessment*—Staff are given resources that support their knowledge and skills about early childhood assessment and their ability to assess children in culturally and linguistically appropriate ways. Preservice and in-service training builds teachers' and administrators' "assessment literacy," creating a community that sees assessment as a tool to improve outcomes for children. Families are part of this community, with regular communication, partnership, and involvement.

Program Evaluation and Accountability

Regularly evaluate early childhood programs in light of program goals, using varied, appropriate, conceptually and technically sound evidence to determine the extent to which programs meet the expected standards of quality and to examine intended as well as unintended results.

Indicators of Effectiveness

◆ *Evaluation is used for continuous improvement*—Programs undertake regular evaluation, including self-evaluation, to document the extent to which they are achieving desired results, with the goal of engaging in continuous improvement. Evaluations focus on processes and implementation as well as outcomes. Over time,

evidence is gathered that program evaluations do influence specific improvements.

◆ *Goals become guides for evaluation*—Evaluation designs and measures are guided by goals identified by the program, by families and other stakeholders, and by the developers of a program or curriculum, while also allowing the evaluation to reveal unintended consequences.

◆ *Comprehensive goals are used*—The program goals used to guide the evaluation are comprehensive, including goals related to families, teachers and other staff, and community as well as child-oriented goals that address a broad set of developmental and learning outcomes.

◆ *Evaluations use valid designs*—Programs are evaluated using scientifically valid designs, guided by a "logic model" that describes ways in which the program sees its interventions having both medium- and longer-term effects on children and, in some cases, families and communities.

◆ *Multiple sources of data are available*—An effective evaluation system should include multiple measures, including program data, child demographic data, information about staff qualifications, administrative practices, classroom quality assessments, implementation data, and other information that provides a context for interpreting the results of child assessments.

◆ *Sampling is used when assessing individual children as part of large-scale program evaluation*—When individually administered, norm-referenced tests of children's progress are used as part of program evaluation and accountability, matrix sampling is used (that is, administered only to a systematic sample of children) so as to diminish the burden of testing on children and to reduce the likelihood that data will be inappropriately used to make judgments about individual children.

◆ *Safeguards are in place if standardized tests are used as part of evaluations*—When individually administered, norm-referenced tests are used as part of program evaluation, they must be developmentally and culturally appropriate for the particular children in the program, conducted in the language children are most comfortable with, with other accommodations as appropriate, valid in terms of the curriculum, and technically sound (including reliability and validity). Quality checks on data are conducted regularly, and the system includes multiple data sources collected over time.

◆ *Children's gains over time are emphasized—* When child assessments are used as part of program evaluation, the primary focus is on children's gains or progress as documented in observations, samples of classroom work, and other assessments over the duration of the program. The focus is not just on children's scores upon exit from the program.

◆ *Well-trained individuals conduct evaluations—* Program evaluations, at whatever level or scope, are conducted by well-trained individuals who are able to evaluate programs in fair and unbiased ways. Self-assessment processes used as part of comprehensive program evaluation follow a valid model. Assessor training goes beyond single workshops and includes ongoing quality checks. Data are analyzed systematically and can be quantified or aggregated to provide evidence of the extent to which the program is meeting its goals.

◆ *Evaluation results are publicly shared—*Families, policy makers, and other stakeholders have the right to know the results of program evaluations. Data from program monitoring and evaluation, aggregated appropriately and based on reliable measures, should be made available and accessible to the public.

CREATING CHANGE THROUGH SUPPORT FOR PROGRAMS

Implementing the preceding recommendations for curriculum, child assessment, and program evaluation requires a solid foundation. Calls for better results and greater accountability from programs for children in preschool, kindergarten, and the primary grades have not been backed up by essential supports for teacher recruitment and compensation, professional preparation and ongoing professional development, and other ingredients of quality early education.

The overarching need is to create an integrated, well-financed system of early care and education that has the capacity to support learning and development in all children, including children living in poverty, children whose home language is not English, and children with disabilities. Unlike many other countries, the United States continues to have a fragmented system for educating children from birth through age eight, under multiple auspices, with greatly varying levels of support, and with inadequate communication and collaboration.

Many challenges face efforts to provide all young children with high-quality curriculum, assessment, and evaluation of their programs. Public commitment, along with investments in a well-financed system of early childhood education and in other components of services for young children and their families, will make it possible to implement these recommendations fully and effectively.

Glossary

accountability

Holding teachers, schools, and school districts responsible for student outcomes through various accounting systems, including large-scale student testing.

accreditation

Recognition of a program or school by a national or regional professional or governing organization whose quality standards and evaluation critiera have been met.

achievement standards

Descriptions of what knowledge and/or skills student are expected to achieve over a particular time period or academic year.

adequate yearly progress

A term used in the No Child Left Behind Act that refers to expected achievements in reading and math beginning in third grade and refers to a predetermined percentage of students scoring at or above "proficiency" on statewide standardized tests.

age appropriate

Behaviors and expectations for behavior or learning that can reasonably be expected at a given age.

age-equivalent score

A score derived by comparing a student's test performance with that of a representative sample of children at each age.

age norms

Normative information based on age, to which an individual's test score can be compared.

aggregated data

An assemblage of student (or class) products and other assessment information brought together to establish a holistic view of student progress toward stated goals.

antibias curricula and pedagogy

Curricula, materials, and teaching strategies that challenge prejudice and stereotyping biases and help all children regardless of race, gender, or ableness to construct positive identities and a sense of personal efficacy.

archival portfolio

A portfolio in which representative selections from and information about the student is maintained over time.

assessment

The use of multiple measures and techniques to obtain evidence of student development and learning.

assistive technologies

Defined by Federal Individuals with Disabilities Education Improvement Act of 2004 (P. L. 108-446) as "any item, piece of equipment, or product system, whether acquired commercially off the shelf, modified, or customized, that is used to increase, maintain, or improve the functional capabilities of a chld with a disability."

at risk

Children whose prenatal or early environments, experiences, or health conditions presuppose less than optimal physical/motor, psychosocial, cognitive, language development, or academic success.

authentic assessment

Assessment derived from learning processes and student products emerging from meaningful, relevant, and developmentally appropriate curricula.

average yearly progress (AYP)

That which schools must demonstrate under the No Child Left Behind Act. AYP is the annual level of improvement as measured on student assessments and other academic indicators, set by each state.

benchmark

a. A standard, based on research evidence, by which changes in children's development and learning are noted or marked, thereby providing teachers with direction in facilitating the next step in children's learning.

b. When referring to policies associated with accountability, defined more narrowly: "specific description of knowledge or skill that students should acquire by a particular point in their schooling" (Kendall/McREL, 2001).

bias

A particular preference, inclination, point of view, or philosophy that impedes impartial perspectives and judgment; a lack of objectivity.

bilingualism

Proficiency in two languages.

bridge class

A grade placement, usually between two grades, designed to provide an additional year for growth and development prior to a child's entry into a particular grade.

child well-being indicators

Aspects of a child's life that represent potential risk to optimal development.

cognitive-interactionist theory

A theory that emphasizes the interaction of heredity and environment in the cognitive development of the individual.

cognitive processes

The mental activities involved in thinking and making meaning.

construct validity

A test of validity based on the relationship between the test and a related theory; concerned with the psychological meaningfulness of the test.

content standards

Descriptions of what a student should know and be able to do within a particular subject matter or content area.

content validity

The extent to which the content of a test samples the type of behavior it is designed to measure.

context-responsive assessment

Assessment that takes into account the various influencing elements in a situation or event and responds appropriately based on this information.

contextualistic theory

Attends to the circumstances of time, place, people, activity, philosophical, physical, and psychological characteristics and conditions that surround an event.

cost-benefit analysis

A process of calculating the costs of a program or intervention relative to the benefits. By dividing the total cost of a program by the number of children served, a cost-to-benefit ratio can be obtained that reveals how much it costs to achieve each specific outcome.

criterion

A predetermined standard or level of performance to be achieved.

criterion-referenced test

Tests or other assessments that measure success or failure to meet a predetermined objective.

criterion-related validity

The extent to which scores on the test can be correlated with a stated criterion.

critical (or sensitive) period

A period of time when there is increased potential for development, learning, or consolidation of previously learned skills and knowledge.

cultural diversity

Refers to the amalgam of beliefs, value systems, attitudes, traditions, and family practices that are held by different groups of people.

culturally responsive pedagogy

Instruction adapted to take into account various cultural values, behaviors, and ways of learning.

developmental diversity

Refers to the possible range of growth and ability characteristics among individuals within the same range of chronological ages.

developmentally appropriate

Expectations and practices based on what is known about child growth and development.

developmentally inappropriate

Expectations and practices that fail to acknowledge the unique growth and developmental characteristics associated with age and individuality.

developmental screening

A process of large-scale assessment using standardized procedures to identify individuals who might benefit from further, more specific assessment.

diagnostic testing

A process that usually involves several tests and assessment procedures to compile and categorize physical/motor, psychological, social, and/or academic symptoms and characteristics for the purpose of identifying specific conditions and prescribing appropriate intervention or remediation. Diagnostic testing is usually performed by a medical doctor or licensed diagnostician.

dispositions

Various attitudes and personality traits, such as curiosity, creativity, resourcefulness, responsibility, initiative, interests, effort, challenge seeking, and so on, considered important for effective thinking and learning; sometimes referred to as *habits of mind* or *approaches to learning*.

downshifting

A psychophysiological response to perceived threat, which is accompanied by a sense of helplessness or lack of self-efficacy.

early learning standards

Expectations for learning and development of young children.

emergent curriculum
A dynamic instructional strategy that adjusts and enriches the curriculum as child development and interests emerge.

emergent development
The concept that growth, development, and learning are continually changing and progressing toward more mature or sophisticated forms.

English as a Second Language (ESL)
Refers to individuals whose first language is not English.

ethnicity
A particular group's shared heritage, which generally includes a common history with distinctive traditions and celebrations. Ethnic groups generally speak a common language and often share common religious beliefs.

evaluation
A systematic process of describing program components and outcomes.

expressive language
Oral communication; spoken language.

family systems theory
The theory purporting that each family includes members who are interconnected in individualistic ways, each influencing and also being influenced in individualistic ways by one another.

formal assessments
Assessments that utilize predeveloped tests that are related to specific developmental or curriculum content and are standardized and scored according to specific psychometric guidelines.

formative evaluation
Assessment of student learning that takes place as learning occurs and is used to inform current instructional practices.

functional assessment
An in-context performance assessment of how a child functions.

gifted and talented
Individuals who show exceptional ability or functioning in intellectual, creative, artistic, leadership, or specific academic fields.

grade-equivalent score
A score that is compared to an average score of a reference group of test-takers in the same grade.

grade norm
The average score for a representative sample of test-takers in the same grade to which a student's individual score is compared.

growth-based accountability model
An accountabiity model that grants schools credit for student improvement over time by tracking individual achievement year to year.

highly qualified teacher
A public school teacher who has a bachelor's degree, has full state certification, and has demonstrated subject-matter competency for each core academic subject taught. A stated goal of the No Child Left Behind Act of 2002 is that every child will be taught by a highly qualified teacher.

high-stakes tests
Tests for which significant (life-influencing) decisions, such as group or grade placement, assignment to special programs, promotion, and retention are made based on an individual's score. Sometimes scores on high-stakes tests are used to rank schools, teachers, and school districts, and allocation of public funds are tied to rankings.

HIPPY
Home Instruction Program for Preschool Youngsters, a home-based early childhood education program for parents of young children.

inclusion
Providing education for students with disabilities in general education settings.

individual education program (IEP)
A written plan for the education of a student with disabilities that follows procedures for development and implementation that have been set forth by federal legislation.

individual family service plan (IFSP)
A written plan of child and family needs, outcomes to be achieved, and the specific services that will be provided. Its development involves the family and must meet criteria established by federal law.

individually appropriate
Experiences and expectations that are responsive to and respectful of the uniqueness of the individual.

inference
A conclusion based on logic that suggests explanations, reasons, or causes for behaviors or events.

informal assessments
Assessments of child development and learning that are ongoing, in many contexts; usually designed and carried out by the classroom teacher.

interrater reliability
The degree to which two or more observers are in agreement with what was observed. The higher the agreement between observers' accounts, judgments, and inferences, the higher the interrater reliability.

intervention
Strategies or activities (such as medical or psychological treatment, speech-language therapy, providing adaptive equipment, modifying the physical environment, and accessing and advocating for appropriate resources and policies) designed to facilitate optimal development in children with special needs.

kid-watching
Informal, ongoing teacher observation of children in a variety of situations within the classroom and school, including the lunchroom, outdoor learning center, and transition times.

kindergarten prototype
A perceptual model of the characteristics typically thought to represent a child's readiness or unreadiness for the kindergarten experience.

learning disability
A disorder in one or more of the basic psychological procesesses involved in attending to, understanding, or using spoken or writen language; suspected when a student persistently displays inabilities to listen, think, speak, read, write, spell, or do mathematical calculations.

learning outcomes
A predetermined body of knowledge or skills expected to have been achieved over a certain period of time and as a result of a particular education strategy.

learning styles
Individual variations in preferred, or most efficient, modalities and contexts for learning.

least restrictive environment (LRE)
A learning environment in which children with disabilities are allowed to participate to the extent possible while still having their special needs met.

legal immigrants
Individuals who have been admitted into the United States with valid visa and have been approved for temporary or permanent residence.

licensing
A system for assuring that certain programs that serve children and families meet standards set by the state.

limited English proficiency (LEP)
Lack of facility with the English language.

long-term immigrant
An individual who has immigrated to the United States and remains with or without permanent residency status or having applied for citizenship. May be a first, second, or later generation immigrant.

mandated assessments
Assessments required by federal, state, local school district, or other policy-making body; used as accountability measures to determine if certain goals or standards are being met.

metacognition
The ability to think about and regulate one's own thinking.

metalinguisitic awareness
The ability to think about the forms and meanings of language.

microcultural group
Groups to which all individuals belong, such as gender, social class, race, ethnicity, ableness, religion, and region.

multilinguilism
Proficiency in three or more languages.

multiple intelligences
The theory that there are many more kinds of intelligences than typically emphasized in traditional school curricula and measures of performance.

neuron
A nerve cell and its connections; the basic functional unit of the nervous system.

neurotransmitters
Chemicals that carry messages from one cell to another across the synapse.

nonverbal behavior
Communicative style (both intentional and nonintentional), which includes gestures, facial expressions, physical distance, and posture.

normative group
The sample of test-takers whose scores are used to establish the "norms" with which subsequent test-takers' scores are compared.

norm-referenced test
A test in which the test-taker's score is compared with the scores of a normative group or reference population.

objectivity
Refers to the ability of the assessor to derive data and information about a student that is free of personal feelings or biases.

outcomes
How and to what extent participants in a program or intervention benefit (or fail to do so) at the end of the program or intervention.

percentile rank
A score that reflects an individual's position relative to others; one where the score is placed on a scale where the percentage of scores that are *at or below* it are shown; not the same as a percentage of correct answers.

performance assessment
A general term for assessment of students' processes, products, demonstrations, exhibitions, or other overt evidences of learning.

performance standard
An established level of achievement, quality of performance, or level of proficiency that specifies what a student is supposed to know and be able to do at given points in time.

predictive validity
A measure of the extent to which a current test score can be used to estimate later scores or performance.

preproductive language

Earliest attempts to communicate (vocalizations and imitations of speech sounds, pointing, gesturing, facial expressions and other body language).

prime times

Periods in growth and development when aspects of the environment and relational experiences have their greatest potential for help or harm (also referred to as *sensitive periods*).

process portfolio

A method of collecting products of and documenting the emerging processes of children's learning.

program standard

Expectations for the quality of education and child-care settings.

psychosocial theory

A theory that emphasizes social and cultural influences on personality development.

random sample

A sample (objects, events, people) drawn from a population in an unbiased manner that ensures that each member has an equal chance of being selected.

raw score

The actual number of correct answers on a test.

readiness

A developmental state in which the child is believed to be able to benefit from and succeed with a particular learning requirement.

readiness indicators

A set of characteristics or attributes thought to be indicative of a child's ability to benefit from and succeed with a particular learning requirement.

receptive language

Language that is comprehended but not necessarily produced.

redshirting

Holding back a child who is eligible for school entry in the hope that an extra year of growth and development will be of benefit.

reflective thinking

The act of thinking about and giving careful consideration to various aspects of an experience or event, which can lead to deeper understanding and sometimes changed perspectives.

reliability

The consistency with which various tests or assessment strategies produce the same or similar results for an individual from one administration to the next.

rubrics

A list of descriptions, characteristics, or performance expectations for each of the points on a fixed scale.

scaffolding

A process by which an adult or a more skilled child facilitates the acquisition of knowledge or skills in the learner through coaching or providing needed information.

screening

A first step in identifying, through tests, examinations, or other procedures, children who may need professional diagnostic evaluation and/or intervention.

self-efficacy

The feeling that what one does matters and that one's efforts are worthwhile and effective.

sensitive periods

Periods in growth and development when aspects of the environment and relational experiences have their greatest potential for help or harm (also referred to as *prime times*).

simultaneous bilingualism

The process of learning two languages at the same time, beginning at birth.

stakeholder

Individuals who have a substantial interest in the outcomes of school and student performance—students, teachers, administrators, parents, or policymakers.

standardized test

An instrument administered under prescribed conditions and scored in a predetermined manner; the scores are compared to those of a representative sample of a particular population, that is, a certain age, grade, geographic location, or other definable group.

standards

Outcome statements that specify what children should know and be able to do.

stanine score

A nine-point scale that indicates average, below-average, and above-average ranks.

successive (or sequential) bilingualism

The process of learning a second language after acquiring proficiency in a first language.

summative evaluation

Summary information concerned with broad outcomes attained over time and usually compiled three times during the school year for use in collaborating with students and parents and providing summary reports for school or district evaluations.

thematic units or projects

Learning experiences organized around a central idea or theme that reflects the integration of the subject-matter content of the curriculum or developmental domains.

Touch Points

A program develped by Dr. T. Berry Brazelton designed to train professionals from a variety of child and family services to work with families to enhance the competencies of parents and build strong family relationships.

transitional grade

A grade placement, usually between two grades, designed to provide an additional year for growth and development prior to a particular grade entry (also referred to as a *bridge class*).

triangulated

Refers to merging information from several assessment strategies to reach a conclusion or draw inferences; better than relying on one measure.

underachievement

The discrepancy between what a student is percieved to know and be able to do and his or her lower level of achievement.

undocumented immigrant

Individuals who have entered the United States illegally, overstayed a valid visa, such as a tourist or student visa, or otherwise violated the terms of their immigration status.

validity

The degree to which a procedure or test measures what it purports to measure.

zone of proximal development (ZPD)

The level of development in learning a particular concept or skill in which assistance from an adult or more skilled child is needed but may soon be unnecessary.

References

Abedi J., Hofstetter, C. H., & Lord, C. (2004). Assessment accommodations for English-language learners: Implications for policy-based empirical research. *Review of Educational Research, 74*(1), 1–28.

Akhavan, N. (2006). *Help! My kids don't all speak English: How to set up a language workshop in your linguistically diverse classroom.* Portsmouth, NH: Heinemann.

American Academy of Pediatrics. (2006, October). *Clinical report: The importance of play in promoting healthy child development and maintaining strong parent-child bonds.* (Available at: http://www.aap.org).

American Educational Research Association. (2000). *Ethical standards of the American Educational Research Association.* Washington, DC: Author.

American Educational Research Association, American Psychological Association, & National Council on Measurement in Education. (1985). *Standards for educational and psychological testing.* Washington, DC: Author.

American Educational Research Association, American Psychological Association, & National Council on Measurement in Education. (1999). *Standards for educational and psychological testing.* Washington, DC: Author.

American Psychological Association. (2003). Ethical principles of psychologists and code of conduct. Washington, DC: Author.

Amrein, A. L., & Berliner, D. C. (2002, March 28). High-stakes testing, uncertainty and student learning. *Education Policy Analysis Archives, 10*(18). (Retrieved 1-5-06 from: http://epaa.asu.edu/epaa/v10n18/).

Annie E. Casey Foundation. (2005). *Kids count data book: State profiles of child well-being.* Baltimore, MD: Author.

Arlington Human Service Planners. (2003). *Caring for our kids.* (Unpublished document). Arlington, TX: Author.

Arnett, J. (1989). Caregivers in day-care centers: Does training matter? *Journal of Applied Developmental Psychology, 10,* 541–552.

Atkins-Burnett, S., Rowan, B., & Correnti, R. (2001). *Administering standardized achievement tests to young children: How mode of administration affects the reliability of standardized measures of student achievement in kindergarten and first grade.* Paper presented at the annual meeting of the American Educational Research Association, April, 2001. (Retrieved from: www.sii.soe.umich.edu/papers.html).

Bailey, D. B., Bruer, J. T., Symons, F. J., & Lichtman, J. W. (Eds.). (2001). *Critical thinking about critical periods.* Baltimore: Paul H. Brookes.

Banks, J. A., & Banks, C. A. (Eds.). (2001). *Multicultural education: Issues and perspectives* (4th ed.). New York: Wiley.

Barnett, W. S. (1995). Long-term effects of early childhood programs on cognitive and school outcomes. *The Future of Children, 5*(3), 25–50. Los Altos, CA: Center for the Future of Children, The David and Lucile Packard Foundation.

Barnett, W. S. (2004, December). Better teachers, better preschools: Student achievement linked to teacher qualifications. *Preschool Policy Matters, Issue 2.* National Institute for Early Education Research. (Retrieved from http://nieer.org/resources/policybriefs/2.pdf).

Barnett, W. S., & Boocock, S. S. (1998). *Early care and education for children in poverty: Promises, programs and long-term results.* Albany, NY: State University of New York Press.

Barnett, W. S., Lamy, C. & Jung, K. (2005). *The effects of state prekindergarten programs on young children's school readiness in five states.* New Brunswick, NJ: The National Institute for Early Education Research, Rutgers University.

Barnett, W. S., Young, J. W., & Schweinhart, L. J. (1998). How preschool education influences long-term cognitive development and school success. In W. S. Barnett & S. S. Boocock (Eds.), *Early care and education for children in poverty,* (pp. 167–184). Albany, NY: State University of New York Press.

Barrera, I., & Corso, R. M., with D. MacPherson. (2003). *Skilled dialogue: Strategies for responding to cultural diversity in early childhood*. Baltimore, MD: Paul H. Brookes.

Beaty, J. J. (2006). *Observing development of the young child* (6th ed.). Upper Saddle River, NJ: Merrill/Prentice Hall.

Behrman, R. E. (Ed.). (1995). Long-term outcomes of early childhood programs (Theme issue). *The Future of Children, 5*(3). Los Altos, CA: Center for the Future of Children, The David and Lucile Packard Foundation.

Behrman, R. E. (Ed.). (2004, Summer). Children of immigrant families (Theme issue). *The Future of Children, 14*(2). Los Altos, CA: Center for the Future of Children, The David and Lucile Packard Foundation.

Bentzen, W. R. (1997). *Seeing young children: A guide to observing and recording behavior* (3rd ed.). Albany, NY: Delmar.

Berger, E. H. (1995). *Parents as partners in education* (4th ed.). Upper Saddle River, NJ: Merrill/Prentice Hall.

Berk, L. (1985). Relationship of educational attainment, child oriented attitude, job satisfaction, and career commitment to caregiver behavior toward children. *Child Care Quarterly, 14*, 103–129.

Bloom, B. S., Madaus, G. F., & Hastings, J. T. (1981). *Evaluation to improve learning*. New York: McGraw-Hill.

Bodrova, E., & Leong, D. J. (1996). *Tools of the mind: The Vygotskian approach to early childhood education*. Upper Saddle River, NJ: Merrill/Prentice Hall.

Bohler, S. K., Eichenlaub, K. L., Litteken, S. D., & Wallis, D. A. (1996). Identifying and supporting low-literate parents. *The Reading Teacher, 50*(1) 77–79.

Bowman, B., Donovan, M. S., & Burns, M. S. (Eds.). (2001). *Eager to learn: Educating our preschoolers*. Washington, DC: National Academy Press.

Boyer, E. L. (1991). *Ready to learn: A mandate for the nation*. Princeton, NJ: Carnegie Foundation for the Advancement of Teaching.

Bradbard, M. R., Endsley, R. C., & Mize, J. (1992). The ecology of parent-child communications about daily experiences in preschool and day care. *Journal of Research in Childhood Education, 6*, 131–141.

Brandt, R. (1992). On performance assessment: A conversation with Grant Wiggins. *Educational Leadership, 49*(8), 35–37.

Bransford, J. D., Brown, A. L., & Cocking, R. R. (Eds.). (2000). *How people learn: Brain, mind, experience, and school*. Washington, DC: National Academy Press.

Bredekamp, S. (Ed.). (1987). *Developmentally appropriate practice in early childhood programs serving children from birth through age eight* (Expanded ed.). Washington, DC: NAEYC.

Bredekamp, S. (1990). Achieving model early childhood programs through accreditation. In C. Seefeldt (Ed.), *Continuing issues in early childhood education*. Upper Saddle River, NJ: Merrill/Prentice Hall.

Bredekamp, S., & Copple, C. (1997). *Developmentally appropriate practice in early childhood programs*. Washington, DC: NAEYC.

Bredekamp, S., & Rosegrant, T. (Eds.). (1992). *Reaching potentials: Appropriate curriculum and assessment for young children, Vol. 1*. Washington, DC: NAEYC.

Bredekamp, S., & Rosegrant, T. (Eds.). (1995). *Reaching potentials: Transforming early childhood curriculum and assessment, Vol. 2*. Washington, DC: NAEYC.

Bronfenbrenner, U. (1979). *The ecology of human development*. Cambridge: Harvard University Press.

Bronfenbrenner, U. (1986). Ecology of the family as a context for human development: Research perspectives. *Developmental Psychology, 22*, 723–742.

Bronfenbrenner, U. (1989). Ecological systems theory. In R. Vasta (Ed.), *Six theories of child development: Revised formulations and current issues. Annals of Child Development, 6*, 187–249. Greenwich, CN: JAI.

Bronfenbrenner, U. (2004). *Making human beings human: Bioecological perspectives on human development*. Thousand Oaks, CA: Sage Publications.

Bronfenbrenner, U., & Ceci, S. J. (1994). Nature-nurture reconceptualized in developmental perspective: A bioecological model. *Psychological Review, 101*(4), 568–586.

Bronfenbrenner, U., & Morris, P. A. (1998). The ecology of developmental processes. In W. Damon (Series Ed.) & R. M. Lerner (Vol. 1 Ed.), *Handbook of child psychology: Vol. 1: Theoretical models of human development* (pp. 993–1028). New York: Wiley.

Brooks-Gunn, J., & Duncan, G. J. (1997, Summer/Fall). *The future of children: Children and poverty* (Theme issue). Los Altos, CA: Center for the Future of Children, The David and Lucile Packard Foundation.

Brown, W. H., & Conroy, M. A. (1997). *Including and supporting preschool children with developmental delays in the early childhood classroom*. Little Rock, AR: Southern Early Childhood Association.

Bruer, J. T. (1999). *The myth of the first three years*. New York: The Free Press.

Burchinal, J. R., Roberts, J. E., Nabors, L. A., & Bryant, D. M. (1996). Quality of center child care and infant cognitive and language development. *Child Development, 67*, 606–620.

Buros, O. K. (1999). *Tests in print*. Highland Park, NJ: Gryphon Press.

Bursuck, W. D., Polloway, E. A., Plante, L., Epstein, M. H., Jayanthi, M., & McConeghy, J. (1996). Report card grading adaptations: A national survey of classroom practices. *Exceptional Children, 62*(4), 301–318.

Burts, D. C., Hart, C. H., Charlesworth, R., Fleege, P. O., Mosley, J., & Thomasson, R. H. (1992). Observed activities and stress behaviors of children in developmentally appropriate and inappropriate kindergarten classrooms. *Early Childhood Research Quarterly, 7,* 297–318.

Burts, D. C., Hart, C. H., Charlesworth, R., DeWolf, D., Ray, J., Manuel, K., & Fleege, P. O. (1993). Observed activities and stress behaviors of children in developmentally appropriate and inappropriate kindergarten classrooms. *Early Childhood Research Quarterly, 7,* 297–318.

Bryant, D. M., Burchinal, M., Lau, L. B., & Sparling, J. J. (1994). Family and classroom correlates of Head Start children's developmental outcomes. *Early Childhood Research Quarterly, 9,* 289–309.

Caine, R. N., & Caine, G. (1994). *Making connections: Teaching and the human brain.* New York: Addison-Wesley.

Caine, R. N., & Caine, G. (1997). *Education on the edge of possibility.* Alexandria, VA: Association for Supervision and Curriculum Development.

Campbell, F. A., & Ramey, C. T. (1995). Cognitive and school outcomes for high-risk African American students at middle adolescence: Positive effects of early intervention. *American Educational Research Journal, 32*(4), 743–772.

Campbell, F. A., Ramey, C. T., Pungello, E., Sparling, J. S., & Miller-Johnson, S. (2002). Early childhood education: Young adult outcomes from the Abecedarian Project. *Applied Developmental Science, 6*(1) 42–67.

Campione, J. (1983). Cited in Cazden, C. B. (1988). *Classroom discourse: The language of teaching and learning.* Portsmouth, NH: Heinemann.

Capps, R., Fix, M., Ost, C. J., Reardon-Anderson, J, & Passel, J. S. (2005). *The health and well-being of young children of immigrants.* Washington, DC: The Urban Institute.

Capps, R., Fix, M., Murray, J., Ost, J., Passel, J. S., & Herwantoro, S. (2005). *The new demography of America's Schools: Immigration and the No Child Left Behind Act.* Washington, DC: The Urban Institute.

Cary, S. (2000). *Working with language learners: Answers to teachers' top ten questions.* Portsmouth, NH: Heinemann.

Cazden, C. B. (1988). *Classroom discourse: The language of teaching and learning.* Portsmouth, NH: Heinemann.

Charney, S. C. (2002). *Teaching children to care: Classroom management for ethical and academic growth, K–8.* Greenfield, MA: Northeast Foundation for Children.

Chase, B. (2001). *Adding fairness to the testing equation.* (Retrieved from Connect for Kids at http://www.connectforkids.org/benton_topics).

Child Trends. (2001). Child Trends Research Brief, 2001. *School readiness: Helping communities get children ready for school and schools ready for children.* Washington, DC: Author.

Children's Defense Fund. (2005). *The state of America's children: Yearbook 2005.* Washington, DC: Author.

Children's Defense Fund. (2006). *The state of America's children: Yearbook 2006.* Washington, DC: Author.

Christian, L. G. (2006). Understanding families: Applying family systems theory to early childhood practice. *Young Children, 61*(1), 12–20.

Clarke-Stewart, K. A., Gruber, C. P., & Fitzgerald, L. M. (1994). *Children at home and in day care.* Hillsdale, NJ: Erlbaum.

Clarke-Stewart, K. A., Vandell, D. L., Burchinal, M., O'Brien, M., & McCartney, K. (2000). Do features of child care homes affect children's development? *Early Childhood Research Quarterly, 17*(1), 52–86.

Cole, M., & Cole, S. (1993). *The development of children.* New York: Freeman.

Comer, J. P. (2006, January 5). It takes more than tests to prepare the young for success in life. In *Quality Counts* (Theme issue). *Education Week, 25*(17), 59–61.

Consortium of National Arts Education Associations. (1994). *National standards for arts education.* Reston, VA: Music Educators National Conference.

Copple, C., & S. Bredekamp. (2006). *Basics of developmentally appropriate practice: An introduction for teachers of children 3 to 6.* Washington, DC: NAEYC.

Couchenour, D., & Chrisman, K. (2004). *Families, schools, and communities: Together for young children.* Albany, NY: Delmar Learning.

Currie, J. (2005). Health disparities and gaps in school readiness. *The Future of Children, 15*(1), 117–138.

DeLoach, J. S., Miller, K. F., & Pierroutsakos, S. L. (1998). Reasoning and problem-solving. In D. Kuhn & R. S. Siegler (Eds.), *Handbook of Child Psychology* (Vol. 2) (pp. 801–850). New York: Wiley.

Derman-Sparks, L., & The ABC Task Force. (1989). *Antibias curriculum: Tools for empowering young children.* Washington, DC: NAEYC.

Developmental Studies Center. (1996). *Ways we want our class to be: Class meetings that build commitment to kindness and learning.* Oakland, CA: Author.

Dever, M. T., & Barta, J. J. (2001). Standardized entrance assessment in kindergarten: A qualitative analysis of the experiences of teachers, administrators, and parents. *Journal of Research in Childhood Education, 15*(2), 220–233.

Dichtelmiller, M. L., Jablon, J. R., Marsden, D. B., & Meisels, S. J. (2001). *The work sampling system.* New York: REBUS.

Diffily, D., & Sassman, C. (2002). *Project-based learning with young children*. Portsmouth, NH: Heinemann.

Dinnebeil, L. A., & Hale, L. (1999). *Parents' perspectives about service coordination. Final report to the Bureau of Early Intervention Services, Ohio Department of Health*. (Unpublished manuscript).

Dinnebeil, L. A., Hale, L. & Rule. S. (1994). A qualitative analysis of parents' and service coordinators' descriptions of variables that influence collaborative relationships. *Topics in Early Childhood Special Education, 16*, 322–347.

Division for Early Childhood of the Council for Exceptional Children. (2002, April). *Position statement on responsiveness to family cultures, values, and languages*. Denver, CO: Author.

Dragan, P. B. (2005). *A how-to guide for teaching English language learners in the primary classroom*. Portsmouth, NH: Heinemann.

Dunn, L., & Kontos, S. (1997). Research in Review: What have we learned about developmentally appropriate practice? *Young Children, 53*(3), 4–13.

Earl, L. M. (2003). *Assessment as learning: Using classroom assessment to maximize student learning*. Thousand Oaks, CA: Corbin Press.

Eggen, P. D., & Kauchak, D. (1992). *Educational psychology: Classroom connections*. Upper Saddle River, NJ: Merrill/Prentice Hall.

Ehrie, J., Adams, G., & Tout, K. (2001, January). *Who's caring for your youngest children? Child care patterns of infants and toddlers*. Washington, DC: Urban Institute.

Ellison, L. (1992). Using multiple intelligences to set goals. *Educational Leadership, 50*(2), 69–72.

Engel, B. (1990). An approach to assessment in early literacy. In C. Kamii (Ed.), *Achievement testing in the early grades: The games grown-ups play* (pp. 119–134). Washington, DC: NAEYC.

Erikson, E. H. (1963). *Childhood and society*. New York: Norton.

Fan, X., & Chen, M. (2001). Parental involvement and students' achievement: A meta-analysis. *Educational Psychology Review, 13*, 1–22.

Federal Interagency Forum on Child and Family Statistics. (2005). *America's children: Key national indicators of well-being, 2002*. Washington, DC: U.S. Government Printing Office.

Fenichel, E. (Ed.). (2001, February/March). Linking assessment and intervention (Theme issue). *Zero to Three, 21*(4), 1–63.

Ferguson, P. C. (1991). Longitudinal outcome differences among promoted and transitional at-risk kindergarten students. *Psychology in the Schools, 28*, 139–146.

Fingerman, K., & Bermann, E. (2000). Applications of family systems theory to the study of adulthood. *International Journal of Aging and Human Development, 51*(1), 5–29.

Fleege, P. O. (1990). *Stress begins in kindergarten: A look at behavior during standardized testing*. Unpublished doctoral dissertation, Louisiana State University, Baton Rouge.

Foundation for Child Development. (2006). *Child and Youth Well-being Index Project*. (Retrieved from info@fcd-us.org/CWBIndex2006.html).

Galinsky, E. (2006). *The economic benefits of high-quality early childhood programs: What makes the difference?* New York: Committee for Economic Development.

Garcia, E. E. (2005). *Teaching and learning in two languages: Bilingualism and schooling in the United States*. New York: Teachers College Press.

Gardner, H. (1983). *Frames of mind: The theory of multiple intelligences*. New York: Basic Books.

Gardner, H. (1991). Assessment in context: The alternative to standardized testing. In B. R. Gifford & M. C. O'Connor (Eds.), *Changing assessments: Alternative views of aptitude, achievement and instruction*. Norwell, MA: Kluwer.

Gardner, H. (1993a). *Creative minds: An anatomy of creativity seen through the lives of Freud, Einstein, Picasso, Stravinsky, Eliot, Graham, and Gandhi*. New York: Basic Books.

Gardner, H. (1993b). *Frames of mind: Theory of multiple intelligences: Tenth Anniversary Edition*. New York: Basic Books.

Gardner, H. (1997). The first seven . . . and the eighth. *Education Leadership, 55*(1), 8–13.

Gardner, H. (1998). Reflections on multiple intelligences: Myths and messages. In A. E. Woolfolk, *Readings in Educational Psychology* (2nd ed., pp. 61–67). Boston: Allyn and Bacon.

Gardner, H. (1999). *Intelligence reframed: Multiple intelligences for the 21st century*. New York: Basic Books.

Gay, G. (2000). *Culturally responsive teaching: Theory, research and practice*. New York: Teachers College Press.

Gesell, A. (1925). *Guidance of mental growth in infant and child*. New York: Macmillan.

Gesell, A., & Amatruda, C. S. (1941). *Developmental diagnosis: Normal and abnormal child development*. New York: Hoeber.

Gilliam, W. S., & Leiter, V. (2003). Evaluating early childhood programs: Improving quality and informing policy. *Zero to Three, 23*(6), 6–13.

Gleason, J. B. (1997). *The development of language*. Needham Heights, MA: Allyn & Bacon.

Goals 2000: Educate America Act. Public Law 103-227. (1994).

Goldman, A. I. (1994). Argument and social epistemology. *Journal of Philosophy, 91*, 27–49.

Gonzalez-Mena, J. (2007). *Fifty early childhood strategies for working and communicating with diverse families.* Upper Saddle River, NJ: Merrill/Prentice Hall.

Goodman, Y. (1978). Kid watching: An alternative to testing. *National Elementary Principal, 57*(4), 41–45.

Gormley, W. T., Jr., Gayer, T., Phillips, D., & Dawson, B. (2005). The effects of universal pre-K on cognitive development. *Developmental Psychology, 41*(6), 872–884.

Grace, C., & Shores, E. F. (1998). *The portfolio book: A step-by-step guide for teachers.* Beltsville, MD: Gryphon House.

Graham, S., & Golan, S. (1991). Motivational influences on cognition: Task involvement, ego involvement, and depth of information processing. *Journal of Educational Psychology, 83*, 187–194.

Graue, M. E. (1993). *Ready for what? Constructing meanings of readiness for kindergarten.* New York: State University of New York Press.

Graue, M. E., Kroeger, J., & Brown, C. (2003). The gift of time: Enactments of developmental thought in early childhood practice. *Early Childhood Research and Practice, 5*(1). (Retrieved May 15, 2006, from http://ecrp.uiuc.edu/v5n1/graue.html).

Graves, D. (1983). *Writing: Teachers and children at work.* Exeter, NH: Heinemann.

Gredler, M. E. (1996). *Program evaluation.* Upper Saddle River, NJ: Merrill/Prentice Hall.

Greenough, W., Gunnar, M., Emde, R. J., Massinga, R., & Shonkoff, J. P. (2001). The impact of the caregiving environment on young children's development: Different ways of knowing. *Zero to Three, 21*(5), 16–23.

Greenspan, S. I. (1997). *The growth of the mind and the endangered origins of intelligence.* Reading, MA: Addison-Wesley.

Guralnick, M. J. (2001). Connections between developmental science and intervention science. *Zero to Three, 21*(5), 24–29.

Hamre, B., & Pianta, R. (2001). Early teacher-child relationships and the trajectory of children's school outcomes through eighth grade. *Child Development, 7*(12), 625–638.

Halliburton, A., & Thornburg, K. (2004). School readiness: Children, families, schools, communities. *Dimensions of Early Childhood, 32*(1), 30–36.

Harms, T., & Clifford, R. M. (2006). *Family day care rating scale.* New York: Teachers College Press.

Harms, T., Clifford, R. M., & Cryer, D. (2005). *Early childhood environment rating scale* (Rev. ed.). New York: Teachers College Press.

Harms, T., Cryer, D., & Clifford, R. M. (2006). *Infant/toddler environment rating scale* (Rev. ed.). New York: Teachers College Press.

Harms, T., Jacobs, E. V., & White, D. R. (1996). *School-age care environment rating scale.* New York: Teachers College Press.

Hart, B., & Risley, T. R. (1995). *Meaningful differences in the everyday experience of young American children.* Baltimore, MD: Paul H. Brookes.

Hart, C. H., Burts, D. C., & Charlesworth, R. (1997). Integrated developmentally appropriate curriculum: From theory and research to practice. In C. Hart, D. Burts, & Charlesworth, R. (Eds.). *Integrated curriculum and developmentally appropriate practice* (pp. 1–27). Albany, NY: State University of New York Press.

Harter, S. (1978). Pleasure derived from challenge and the effects of receiving grades on children's difficulty level choices. *Child Development, 49*, 788–799.

Haskins, R., & Rouse, C. (2005). *The future of children policy brief: Closing achievement gaps.* Los Altos, CA: Center for the Future of Children, The David and Lucile Packard Foundation.

Hastings, C. (1992). Ending ability grouping: A moral imperative. *Educational Leadership, 50*(2), 14.

Hatch, J. A. (2002). Accountability shovedown: Resisting the standards movement in early childhood education. *Phi Delta Kappan, 83*, 457–62.

Hatcher, V. B. G. (2005). *Readiness beliefs of parents of kindergarten age–eligible children enrolled in NAEYC accredited programs.* Unpublished doctoral dissertation, University of North Texas, Denton, Texas.

Hausfather, A., Toharia, A., LaRoche, C., & Engelsmann, F. (1997). Effects of age of entry, day-care quality, and family characteristics on preschool behavior. *Journal of Child Psychology and Psychiatry and Allied Disciplines, 38*, 441–448.

Henderson, A. T., & Mapp, K. L. (2002). *A new wave of evidence: The impact of school, family and community connections on student achievement.* Austin, TX: Southwest Educational Development Laboratory.

Hepburn, K. S. (2004). *Building culturally and linguistically competent services to support young children, their families, and school readiness.* Baltimore, MD: Annie E. Casey Foundation. (Retrieved from www.aecf.org/publications/data/cctoolkit.pdf).

Herman, J. L., Aschbacher, P. R., & Winters, L. (1992). *A practical guide to alternative assessment.* Alexandria, VA: Association for Supervision and Curriculum Development.

High/Scope Research Foundation. (1998). *Program Quality Assessment* (PQA). Ypsilanti, MI: Author.

Hogue, L. M. (2005, Fall). Defining readiness: Theoretical views in defining readiness for school entry. *ACEI Focus on Pre-K & K, 10*(1), 1–4.

Howard, J., Langer, J. A., Levenson, M. R., Popham, W. J., & Sadowski, M. (2003). *High stakes testing*. Cambridge, MA: Harvard Education Publishing Group.

Howes, C. (1997). Children's experiences in center-based child care as a function of teacher background and adult:child ratio. *Merrill-Palmer Quarterly, 43*, 404–425.

Howes, C., Phillips, D., & Whitebrook, M. (1992). Thresholds of quality: Implications for the social development of children in center-based child care. *Child Development, 63*, 449–460.

Howes, C., & Smith, E. W. (1995). Determinants of toddlers' experience in day care: Age of entry and quality of setting. *Child Care Quarterly, 42*, 140–151.

Huffman, L. R., & Speer, P. W. (2000). Academic performance among at-risk children: The role of developmentally appropriate practices. *Early Childhood Research Quarterly, 15*(2), 167–184.

Hughes, F. P. (1999). *Children, play and development* (3rd ed.). Boston: Allyn & Bacon.

Hyson, M. (2002). Emotional development and school readiness. *Young Children, 57*(6), 76–78.

Individuals with Disabilities Education Act of 2004. (IDEA) Public Law No. 108-446.

International Reading Association and National Association for the Education of Young Children. (1998). Learning to read and write: Developmentally appropriate practices for young children: A joint position statement. *Young Children, 53*(4), 30–46.

Isenberg, J. P., & Quisenberry, N. (2002). *Play: Essential for all children* (A position paper). Olney, MD: Association for Childhood Education International.

Jencks, C., & Phillips, M. (1998). *The Black-White test score gap*. Washington, DC: Brookings Institute.

Jones, E., & Nimmo, J. (1994). *Emergent curriculum*. Washington, DC: NAEYC.

Kagan, S. L. (1999). Cracking the readiness mystique. *Young Children, 54*(5), 2–3.

Kamii, C. (Ed.). (1990). *Achievement testing in the early grades: The games grown-ups play*. Washington, DC: National Association for the Education of Young Children.

Karoly, L. A., Kilburn, M. R., & Cannon, J. S. (2006). *Early childhood interventions: Proven results, future promise*. Santa Monica, CA: Rand Corporation.

Katz, C., Hoene, C., & deKerver, D. N. (2003). *Strengthening families in America's cities: Early childhood development*. Washington, DC: National League of Cities.

Katz, L. G. (1995). *Talks with teachers*. Norwood, NJ: Ablex.

Katz, L. G. (1997). *Talks with teachers of young children: A collection*. Norwood, NJ: Ablex.

Katz, L. G. (2003). Building a good foundation for children. In J. H. Helm & S. Beneke (Eds.). *The power of projects* (pp. 10–18). New York: Teachers College Press.

Katz, L. G., & Chard, S. (2000). *Engaging* children's minds: The project approach, (2nd ed.). Stamford, CT: Ablex.

Kauerz, K., & McMaken, J. (2004, June). *No Child Left Behind Policy Brief: Implications for the early learning field*. Denver, CO: Education Commission of the States.

Kaufman Early Education Exchange. (2002). *Set for success: Building a strong foundation for school readiness based on the social-emotional development of young children*. Kansas City, MO: Ewing Marion Kaufman Foundation.

Kellogg, J. (1988). Focus of change. *Phi Delta Kappan, 70*, 199–204.

Kendall, J. S. (2001). *A technical guide for revising or developing standards and benchmarks*. Aurora, CO: Mid-continent Regional Educational Laboratory (McREL).

Kidd, J. K., Sanchez, S. Y., & Thorp, E. K. (2004). Innovative practices in education—gathering family stories: Facilitating preservice teachers' cultural awareness and responsiveness. *Action in Teacher Education, 26*(1), 64–74.

Kluger, A. N., & DeNisi, A. (1996). Effects of feedback interventions on performance: A historical review, a meta-analysis, and a preliminary feedback intervention theory. *Psychological Bulletin, 119*(2), 254–284.

Kohn, A. (1993). *Punished by rewards: The trouble with gold stars, incentive plans, A's, praise, and other bribes*. Boston: Houghton Mifflin.

Kohn, A. (1994). From degrading to de-grading. In *What does it mean to be well educated? And more essays on standards, grading, and other follies*. Boston: Beacon Press.

Kohn, A. (1999). *The schools our children deserve: Moving beyond traditional classrooms and "tougher standards"* Boston: Houghton Mifflin.

Kohn, A. (2000). *The case against standardized testing: Raising the scores, ruining the schools*. Portsmouth, NH: Heinemann.

Kohn, A. (2004). *What does it mean to be well educated?* Boston: Beacon Press.

Kontos, S. J. (1991). Child care quality, family background and children's development. *Early Childhood Research Quarterly, 6*, 249–262.

Kontos, S., & Wilcox-Herzog, A. (1997). Teachers' interactions with children: Why are they so important? *Young Children, 52*(2), 4–12.

Kraft-Sayre, M. E., & Pianta, R. C. (2001). *Enhancing the transition to kindergarten: Linking children, families, and schools*. Charlottesville, VA: University of Virginia.

Kuhn, D. (1991). *The skills of argument*. Cambridge, England: Cambridge University Press.

Lacina, J. (2006, Summer). Virtual record keeping: Should teachers keep online grade books? *Childhood Education, 82*(4), 252–254.

Lally, J. R., Lerner, C., & Lurie-Hurvitz, L. (2001). National survey reveals gaps in the public's and parents' knowledge about early childhood development. *Young Children, 56*(2), 49–53.

Lamb, M. E. (1998). Nonparental child care: Context, quality, correlates, and consequences. In W. Damon, I. E. Sigel, & K. A. Renninger (Eds.), *Handbook of child psychology, vol. 4: Child psychology in practice.* New York: Wiley.

Lansdown, G. (2005, May). *Can you hear me? The right of young children to participate in decisions affecting them.* (Working Paper). The Netherlands: Bernard van Leer Foundation.

Lareau, A. (1989). *Home advantage: Social class and parental intervention in elementary education.* Philadelphia: The Falmer Press.

Lathrop, J. C. (1912). The Children's Bureau. *The American Journal Sociology, 18*(3), 318–330.

Lazar, I., & R. Darlington., (1982). Lasting effects of early education. *Monographs of the Society for Research in Child Development (Serial No. 195), 47*(2/3), 1–151.

Lee, V. E., & Burkam, D. T. (2002). *Inequality at the starting gate: Social background differences in achievement as children begin school.* Washington, DC: Economic Policy Institute.

Lennon, M. C. (Ed.). (2002). *Welfare, work, and well-being.* New York: National Center for Children in Poverty, Mailman School of Public Health, Columbia University.

Leonard, A. M. (1997). *I spy something! A practical guide to classroom observations of young children.* Little Rock, AR: Southern Early Childhood Association.

Levine, M. (2002). *A mind at a time.* New York: Simon & Shuster.

Lewelling, V. W. (1992). *Linguistic diversity in the United States: English plus and official English.* Washington, DC: ERIC clearing house on Literacy Education for Limited-English-Proficient Adults.

Lewis, V. S. (June, 1966). Stephen Humphreys Gurteen and the American origins of charity organizations. *Social Service Review 40,* 190–201.

Lundberg, E. O. (1935). *Child dependency in the United States.* New York: Child Welfare League of America.

Lyman, P., & Varian, H. (2003, June). How much information 2003? (Retrieved from http://2.sims.berkeley.edu/research/projects/how-much-info2000/execsum.htm).

Lyon, G. R., & Rumsey, J. M. (1996). *Neuroimaging: A window to the neurological foundations of learning and behavior in children.* Baltimore: Paul H. Brookes.

Madaus, G., & Clark, M. (2001). The adverse impact of high stakes testing on minority students: Evidence of 100 years of test data. In G. Orfield & M. L. Kornhaber (Eds.), *Raising standards or raising barriers? Inequality and high stakes testing in public education.* New York: The Century Foundation Press.

Magnuson, K. A., & Waldfogel, J. (2005). Early childhood care and education: effects on ethnic and racial gaps in school readiness. In School readiness: Closing racial and ethnic gaps (Theme issue). *The Future of Children, 15*(1), 169–196. Los Altos, CA: Center for the Future of Children, The David and Lucile Packard Foundation.

Marcon, R. A. (1999). Positive relationships between parent-school involvement and public school inner-city preshoolers' development and academic performance. *School Psychology Review, 28*(3), 395–412.

Marsden, D. B., Meisels, S. J., Steele, D. M., & Jablon, J. R. (1993). *The Work Sampling System: The portfolio collection process for early childhood and early elementary classrooms.* Ann Arbor, MI: University of Michigan, Center for Human Growth and Development.

Matthews, H., & Ewen, D. (January, 2006). *Reaching all children? Understanding early care and education participation among immigrant families,* Washington, DC: Center for Law and Social Policy.

Maude, S. P., Catlett, C. Moore, S. M. Sanchez, S. Y., & Thorp, E. K. (2006). Educating and training students to work with culturally, linguistically, and ability-diverse young children and their families. *Zero to Three, 26*(3), 26–35.

McLanahan, S. (2005). School readiness: Closing racial and ethnic gaps (Theme issue). *The Future of Children, 15*(1). Los Altos, CA: Center for the Future of Children, The David and Lucile Packard Foundation.

McLean, M., Wolery, M., & Bailey, D. B., Jr. (2004). *Assessing infants and preschoolers with special needs* (3rd ed.). Upper Saddle River, NJ: Merrill/Prentice Hall.

Meisel, W. T., & Reynolds, A. J. (1999). Parent involvement in early intervention for disadvantaged young children: Does it matter? *Journal of Social Psychology, 37*(4), 379–402.

Meisels, S. J. (1986). Testing four- and five-year-olds. *Educational Leadership, 44,* 90–92.

Meisels, S. J. (1987). Uses and abuses of developmental screening and school readiness testing. *Young Children, 42*(2), 4–6.

Meisels, S. J. (1989, April). High-stakes testing. *Educational Leadership, 46*(7), 16–22.

Meisels, S. J. (1992). Doing harm by doing good: Iatrogenic effects of early childhood enrollment and promotion policies. *Early Childhood Research Quarterly, 7,* 155–174.

Meisels, S. J. (1993). Remaking classroom assessment with the Work Sampling System. *Young Children, 48*(5), 34–40.

Meisels, S. J. (1999). Assessing readiness. In R. C. Pianta & M. J. Cox (Eds.), *The transition to kindergarten.* (pp. 39–66). Baltimore, MD: Brookes Publishing.

Meisels, S. J. (2001). Fusing assessment and intervention: Changing parents' and providers' views of young children. *Zero to Three, 21*(4), 4–10.

Meisels, S. J., & Atkins-Burnett, S. (2005). *Developmental screening in early childhood: A guide* (5th ed.). Washington, DC: NAEYC.

Meisels, S. J., Jablon, J. R., Marsden, D. B., Dichtelmiller, M. L., Dorfman, A. B., & Steele, D. M. (1994). *The Work Sampling System: An overview.* Ann Arbor, MI: Rebus Planning Associates.

Meisels, S. J., Liaw, E., Dorfman, A., & Nelson, R. F. (1995). The Work Sampling System: Reliability and validity of a performance assessment for young children. *Early Childhood Research Quarterly, 10,* 277–296.

Meisels, S. J., Marsden, D. B., Dombro, A. L., Weston, D. R., & Jewkes, A. M. (2003). *The Ounce Scale.* New York: Pearson Early Learning.

Meisels, S. J., Xue, Y., Bickel, D., Nicholson, J., & Atkins-Burnett, S. (2001). Parental reactions to authentic performance assessment. *Educational Assessment, 7*(1), 61–65.

Meyer, C., Schumann, S., & Angello, N. (1990). *Northwest Evaluation Association white paper on aggregating portfolio data.* Lake Oswego, OR: Northwest Evaluation Association Press.

Millon, J. (2000). Get parents tuned into online grade books. Alexandria, VA: National Association of Elementary School Principals. Retrieved April 20, 2006 from: www.naesp.org/ContentLoad.do?contentId=320.

Ministry of Education. (1991). *Supporting learning: Understanding and assessing the progress of children in the primary program.* Victoria, British Columbia, Canada: Author.

Morrison, F. J., Griffith, E. M., & Alberts, D. M. (1997). Nature-nurture in the classroom: Entrance age, school readiness, and learning in children. *Developmental Psychology, 33*(2), 254–262.

Munk, D. D., & Bursuck, W. D. (1998). Can grades be helpful *and* fair? *Educational Leadership, 55*(4), 44–47.

National Association of Early Childhood Specialists in State Departments of Education (NAECS/SDE) and National Association for the Education of Young Children (NAEYC). (2002). *Early learning standards: Creating the conditions for success.* Washington, DC: NAEYC.

National Academy of Science. (2004). *Assessment in support of instruction and learning: Bridging the gap between large scale and classroom assessment.* Washington, DC: National Academy Press.

National Association for the Education of Young Children. (1995). *School readiness: A position statement.* Washington, DC: Author.

National Association for the Education of Young Children (2005a). NAEYC code of ethical conduct (Position statement). Endorsed by the Association for Childhood Education International. Washington, DC: Author. (Retrieved from www.naeyc.org/about/positions/).

National Association for the Education of Young Children. (2005b). *NAEYC early childhood program standards and accreditation criteria.* Washington, DC: Author.

National Association for the Education of Young Children. (2005c). *Screening and assessment of young English-language learners.* (Supplement to the NAEYC position statement on Early Childhood Curriculum, Assessment, and Program Evaluation). Washington, DC: Author.

National Association for the Education of Young Children. (2005d). *Statement of commitment and code of ethical conduct.* Washington, DC: Author.

National Association for the Education of Young Children & National Association of Early Childhood Specialists in State Departments of Education. (2000). *Still! Unacceptable trends in kindergarten entry and placement* (Position statement). Washington, DC: NAEYC.

National Association for the Education of Young Children & National Association of Early Childhood Specialists in State Departments of Education (NAECS/SDE). (2003). *Early childhood curriculum, assessment, and program evaluation: Building an effective, accountable system in programs for children birth through age 8* (Joint position statement with expanded resources). Washington, DC: NAEYC.

National Association of School Psychologists. (1997). *Principles for professional ethics. School Psychology Review, 26,* 651–676.

National Association of State Boards of Education. (1988). *Right from the start: The report of the NASBE task force on early childhood education.* Alexandria, VA: Author.

National Center for Children in Poverty. (2002). *Promoting the emotional well-being of children and families: Using mental health strategies to move the early childhood agenda and promote school readiness.* New York: Author.

National Center for History in the Schools. (1996). *National standards for history.* Los Angeles: Author.

National Commission on Excellence in Education. (1983, April). *A nation at risk: The imperative for educational reform.* Washington, DC: U.S. Department of Education.

National Conference of State Legislatures. (2005). *Task force on No Child Left Behind: Final report.* Washington, DC: Author.

National Council of Teachers of English and the International Reading Association. (2003). *Standards for the English language arts.* Washington, DC: Author.

National Council of Teachers of Mathematics. (1989; 1991). *Curriculum and evaluation standards for school mathematics.* Reston, VA: Author.

National Council of Teachers of Mathematics. (1994). *Assessment standards for school mathematics*. Reston, VA: Author.

National Council of Teachers of Mathematics. (2000). *Principles and standards for school mathematics*. Reston, VA: Author. (Retrieved from http://standards.nctm.org).

National Education Association (1929; 1975). *Code of Ethics for the Education Profession*. Washington, DC: Author.

National Education Goals Panel. (1991). *The national education goals report: Building a nation of learners*. Washington, DC: Author.

National Education Goals Panel. (1995). *Reconsidering children's early development and learning: Toward common views and vocabulary*. Washington, DC: Author.

National Education Goals Panel. (1997). *Special early childhood report*. Washington, DC: Author.

National Forum on Assessment. (1995). *Principles and indicators for student assessment systems*. Cambridge, MA: National Center for Fair and Open Testing.

National Governors Association. (2005a). *Building the foundation for bright futures: A governor's guide to school readiness*. Washington, DC: Author.

National Governors Association. (2005b). *Final report of the NGA task force on school readiness*. Washington, DC: Author.

National Institute of Child Health and Development. (2002). Early child care and children's development prior to school entry: Results from NICHD study of early child care. *American Educational Research Journal, 39*, 133–164.

National Institute of Child Health and Development Early Child Care Research Network. (1996). Characteristics of infant child care: Factors contributing to positive caregiving. *Early Childhood Research Quarterly, 11*, 269–306.

National Institute of Child Health and Development Early Child Care Research Network. (2002). Child care structure, process, outcomes: Direct and indirect effects of child care quality on young children's development. *Psychological Science, 13*, 199–206.

National Institute for Early Education Research. (2006). *The state of preschool: 2006 State preschool yearbook*. New Brunswick, NJ: Author.

National Research Council. (1996). *National science education standards: Observe, interact, change, learn*. Washington, DC: National Academy Press.

National School Readiness Indicator Initiative. (2005). (Retrieved from http://www.gettingready.org).

National Scientific Council on the Developing Child. (2004). *Young children develop in an environment of relationships*. (Working Paper #1). Waltham, MA: The Heller School for Social Policy and Management. (Retrieved from http://www.developingchild.net).

Nelson, C. A., Thomas, K., & deHaan, M. (2006). *Neuroscience of cognitive development: The role of experience and the developing brain*. Indianapolis, IN: Wiley.

Noble, K. G., Tottenham, N., & Casey, B. J. (2005). Neuroscience perspectives on disparities in school readiness and cognitive achievement. *The Future of Children, 15*(1), 71–89. Los Altos, CA: Center for the Future of Children, The David and Lucile Packard Foundation.

No Child Left Behind Act of 2002. Public Law No.107-110-Jan.8, 2002, 115 STAT.1425. Retrieved from http://www.ed.gov/policy/elsec/leg/esea02/107-110.pdf).

Obegi, A. D., & Ritblatt, S. N. (2005). Cultural competence in infant/toddler caregivers: Application of a tri-dimensional model. *Journal of Research in Childhood Education, 19*(3), 199–213.

Okagaki, L., & Frensch, P. A. (1998). Parenting and children's school achievement: A multiethnic perspective. *American Educational Research Journal, 35*(1), 123–144.

Otto, B. (2006). *Language development in early childhood* (2nd ed.). Upper Saddle River, NJ: Merrill/Prentice Hall.

Parents as Teachers. (2006). *Parents as Teachers Information*. (Retrieved from http://www.parentsasteachers.org).

Peisner-Feinberg, E. S., & Burchinal, M. R. (1997). Relations between preschool children's child-care experiences and concurrent development: The cost, quality, and outcomes study. *Merrill-Palmer Quarterly 43*, 451–477.

Peisner-Feinberg, E. S., Burchinal, M. R., Clifford, R. M., Culkin, M. L., Howes, C., Kagan, S. L., et al. (2001). The relation of preschool child-care quality to children's cognitive and social developmental trajectories through second grade. *Child Development, 72*(5), 1534–1553.

Pellegrino, J. W., Chudowsky, N., & Glaser, R. (Eds.). (2001). *Knowing what students know: The science and design of educational assessment*. Washington, DC: National Academy Press.

Pena, D. (2000). Parent involvement: influencing factors and implications. *Journal of Educational Research, 94*, 42–54.

Perlmutter, J., Bloom, L., Rose, T., & Rogers, A. (1997). Who uses math? Primary children's perceptions of the uses of mathematics. *Journal of Research in Childhood Education, 12*(1), 58–70.

Perry, B. D. (1999). Early life social-emotional experiences affect brain development. *American Academy of Pediatric News, 15*(6), 18–19.

Perry, B. D., Pollard, R. A., Blakley, T. L., Baker, W. L., & Vigilante, D. (1995). Childhood trauma, the neurobiology of adaptation, and "use-dependent" development of the brain. How "states" become "traits." *Infant Mental Health Journal, 16*(4), 271–291.

Peth-Pierce, R. (2001). A good beginning: Sending America's children to school with the social and emotional competence they need to succeed. Chapel Hill: University of North Carolina. Monograph based on two papers commissioned by the Child Mental Health Foundations and Agencies Network. (Retrieved from www.nimh.nih.gov/childhp/monograph.pdf).

Phillips, D. (1995, March 1). Testimony before the Senate Committee on Labor and Human Resources. Washington, DC.

Phillips, M., Crouse, J., & Ralph, J. (1998). Does the Black-White test score gap widen after children enter school? In C. Jencks & M. Phillips (Eds.). *The Black-White test score gap.* Washington, D.C.: Brookings.

Phillipsen, L. C., Burchinal, M. R., Howes, C., & Cryer, D. (1997). The prediction of process quality from structural features of child care. *Early Childhood Research Quarterly, 12,* 281–303.

Piaget, J. (1926). *The language and thought of the child.* New York: Harcourt, Brace & World.

Piaget, J. (1952). *The origins of intelligence in children.* New York: Norton.

Piaget, J. (1963). *The psychology of intelligence.* Patterson, NJ: Littlefield, Adams.

Pianta, R. C., Cox, M. J., Early, D., & Taylor, L. (1999). Kindergarten teachers' practices related to the transition to school: Results of a national survey. *Elementary School Journal, 100*(1), 71–86.

Pianta, R. C., Rimm-Kaufman, S. E., & Cox, M. J. (1999). An ecological approach to kindergarten transition. In R. C. Pianta & M. J. Cox (Eds.), *The transition to kindergarten.* Baltimore, MD: Brookes.

Plyer v. Doe, 457 U.S. 202 (1982).

Public Education Network (2006). Open to the public: The public speaks out on No Child Left Behind: A summary of nine hearings (September, 2005–January, 2006). (Retrieved from www.publiceducation.org.).

Puckett, M. B., & Black, J. K. (2005). *The young child: Development from prebirth through age eight* (4th ed.). Upper Saddle River, NJ: Merrill/Prentice Hall.

Puckett, M. B., & Diffily, D. (2004). *Teaching young children: An introduction to the early childhood profession* (2nd ed.). Albany, NY: Thompson/Delmar Learning.

Quindlen, A. (2005, June 13). The last word: Testing: One, two, three. *Newsweek,* p. 88.

Ramey, C. T., & Ramey, S. L. (2004). Early learning and school readiness: Can early intervention make a difference? *Merrill-Palmer Quarterly: Journal of Developmental Psychology 50*(4) 471–491.

Raver, C. C. (2002). Emotions matter: Making the case for the role of young children's emotional development for early school readiness. *SRDC Social Policy Report 16*(3). Society for Research in Child Development. (Retrieved from www.srcd.org/spr.html).

Raver, C. C., & Knitzer, J. (2002). *Ready to enter: What research tells policymakers about strategies to promote social and emotional school readiness among three- and four-year-old children.* New York: National Center for Children in Poverty.

Restak, R. (2001). *The secret life of the brain.* Washington, DC: Dana Foundation Press and Joseph Henry Press.

Rimm-Kaufman, S. E., & Pianta, R. C. (2001). An ecological perspective on the transition to kindergarten: A theoretical framework to guide empirical research. *Journal of Applied Developmental Psychology, 21*(5), 491–511.

Roach, V., Ascroft, J., Stamp, A., & Kysilko, D. (Eds.). (1995, May). *Winning ways: Creating inclusive schools, classrooms and communities,* Alexandria, VA: National Association of State Boards of Education.

Rock, D. A., & Stenner, A. J. (2005). Assessment issues in the testing of children at school entry. *The Future of Children: School readiness: Closing racial and ethnic gaps 15*(1), 15–34. Los Altos, CA: Center for the Future of Children, The David and Lucile Packard Foundation.

Rosegrant, T. (1989). Cited in NAEYC & NAECS/SDE. (1990). Guidelines for appropriate curriculum content and assessment in programs serving children ages five through eight. *Young Children, 46*(3), 21–38.

Sacks, J. (2001, April 29). *Standardized minds: The high price of America's testing culture and what we can do to change it.* Cambridge, MA: Perseus Books.

Saft, E., & Pianta, R. (2001). Teachers' perceptions of their relationships with students: Effects of child age, gender, and ethnicity of teachers and children. *School Psychology Quarterly, 12*(2), 125–141.

Salmon, M. H., & Zeitz, C. M. (1995). Analyzing conversational reasoning. *Informal Logic, 17,* 1–23.

Saluja, G., Scott-Little, C., & Clifford, R. M. (2000, Fall). Readiness for school: A survey of state policies and definitions. *Early Childhood Research and Practice 2*(3). (Retrieved August 4, 2001, from http://ecrp.uiuc.edu/v2n2/saluja.html).

Salvia, J., & Ysseldyke, J. E. (1998). *Assessment* (7th ed.). Boston: Houghton Mifflin.

Santos, R. M. (2004). Ensuring culturally and linguistically appropriate assessment of young children. *Young Children, 59*(1), 48–50.

Santos, R. M., Fowler, S. A., Corso, R. M., & Bruns, D. (2000). Acceptance, acknowledgement, and adaptability: Selecting culturally and linguistically appropriate early childhood materials. *Teaching Exceptional Children, 32*(3), 14–22.

Schweinhart, L. J. (1997). The High/Scope preschool curriculum comparison study through age 23. *Early Childhood Research Quarterly, 12*(2), 117–143.

Schweinhart, L. J., Monte, J., Xiang, Z., Barnett, W. S., Belfield, C. R., & Nores, M. (2005). *The High/Scope Perry preschool study through age 40: Summary, conclusions, and frequently asked questions.* Ypsilanti, MI: High/Scope Educational Research Foundation.

Schweinhart, L. J., & Weikart, D. P. (1998). Why curriculum matters in early childhood education. *Education Leadership, 55*(6), 57–60.

Seefeldt, C., & Wasik, B. (2002). *Kindergarten: Fours and fives go to school.* Upper Saddle River, NJ: Merrill/Prentice Hall.

Shepard, L. A., & Smith, M. L. (1986). Synthesis of research on school readiness and kindergarten retention. *Educational Leadership, 44*(3), 78–86.

Shepard, L. A., & Smith, M. L. (1987). Effects of kindergarten retention at the end of first grade. *Psychology in the Schools, 24,* 346–357.

Shepard, L. A., & Smith, M. L. (1988). Escalating academic demand in kindergarten: Counterproductive policies. *The Elementary School Journal, 89*(2), 135–145.

Shepard, L. A., & Smith, M. L. (1989). *Flunking grades: Research and policies on retention.* Philadelphia: The Falmer Press.

Sherman, A. (1997). *Poverty matters: The cost of child poverty in America.* Washington, DC: Children's Defense Fund.

Shonkoff, J. P., & Meisels, S. J. (Eds.). (2000). *Handbook of early childhood intervention* (2nd ed.). New York: Cambridge University Press.

Shonkoff, J. P., & Phillips, D. A. (Eds.). (2000). *From neurons to neighborhoods: The science of early childhood development.* Washington, DC: National Academy Press.

Shore, R. (1997). *Rethinking the brain: New insights into early development.* New York: Families and Work Institute.

Siegel, D. J. (1999). *The developing mind: Toward a neurobiology of interpersonal experience.* New York: Guilford Press.

Sigel, I. (1990). What teachers need to know about human development. In D. Dill & Associates (Eds.), *What teachers need to know* (pp. 76–93). San Francisco, CA: Jossey-Bass.

Sigel, I., & Saunders, R. (1979). An inquiry into inquiry: Questions asked as an instructional model. In L. Katz (Ed.), *Current topics in early childhood education* (Vol. 2, pp. 169–193). Norwood, NJ: Ablex.

Slavin, R. E. (1991). Synthesis of research on cooperative learning. *Educational Leadership, 48*(5), 71–81.

Society for Research in Child Development, Committee on Ethical Standards for Research with Children. (1990). *Ethical standards for research with children.* Ann Arbor, MI: Author.

Southern Early Childhood Association. (2000). *Developmentally appropriate assessment* (Position statement). Little Rock, AR: Author.

Steglin, D. A. (2005). Making the case for play policy: Research-based reasons to support play-based environments. *Young Children, 60*(2), 76–85.

Stiggins, R. J. (1997a). *Student-Centered Classroom Assessment.* (2nd ed.). Upper Saddle River, NJ: Merrill/Prentice Hall.

Stiggins, R. J. (1997b). Quoted in: Using assessment to motivate students. *Education Update, 39*(8), 6.

Stiggins, R. J. (2002). Assessment crisis: The absence of assessment FOR learning. *Phi Delta Kappa, 83*(10), 758.

Stipek, D., Feiler, R., Daniels, D., & Milburn, S. (1995). Effects of different instructional approaches on young children's achievement and motivation. *Child Development, 66,* 209–223.

Swope, K., & Miner, B. (Eds.). (2002). *Failing our kids: Why the testing craze won't fix our schools.* Milwaukee, WI: Rethinking Schools, Ltd.

Sylwester, R. (1995). *A celebration of neurons: An educator's guide to the human brain.* Alexandria, VA: Association for Supervision and Curriculum Development.

Sylwester, R. (1997). The neurobiology of self-esteem and aggression. *Educational Leadership, 54*(5), 75–79.

Sylwester, R. (1998). Art for the brain's sake. *Educational Leadership, 56*(3), 31–35.

Takanishi, R. (2004). Leveling the playing field: Supporting immigrant children from birth to eight. *The Future of Children, 14*(2), 61–79. (Retrieved from http://www.futureofchildren.org/usr_doc/takanishi.pdf).

Thomas, A. (1989). Reviews of research: Ability and achievement: Implications of research for classroom practice. *Childhood Education, 65,* 235–241.

Thompson, R. A. (2001). Development in the first years of life. *The Future of Children, 11*(1), 21–33. Los Altos, CA: Center for the Future of Children, The David and Lucile Packard Foundation.

U.S. Administration for Children and Families, Health and Human Services, Head Start Bureau (2003, July). *The National Reporting System and English Language Learners. Head Start Bulletin, 76,* 20.

U.S. Department of Education, National Center for Education Statistics, Office of Educational Research and Improvement. (2000). *Findings from the early childhood longitudinal study, kindergarten class of 1998–1999.* Washington, DC: Author.

U.S. Department of Education, Office of Special Education and Rehabilitative Services. (2006). *Special Education Services Data Analysis System.* Washington, DC: Author.

U.S. Department of Health & Human Services, Administration for Children & Families, & U.S. Department of

Education/Early Childhood—Head Start Task Force. (2002–2006). *The Head Start Child Outcomes Framework.* Washington, DC: Author.

Valencia, S. (1990). A portfolio approach to classroom reading assessment: The whys, whats, and hows. *The Reading Teacher, 43*, 338–340.

Van Ausdale, D., & Feagin, J. R. (2001). *The first R: How children learn race and racism.* Washington, DC: Teaching for Change.

Vandell, D. L., & Wolfe, B. (2000). *Child care quality: Does it matter and does it need to be improved?* Washington, DC: Office of the Assistant Secretary for Planning and Evaluation, U.S. Department of Health and Human Services.

Vandivere, S., Pitzer, L., Halle, T. G., & Hair, E. C. (2004, October). Indicators of early school success and child well-being. *Child Trends Data Bank: Cross Currents*, Issue 3 (Publication No. 2004-24), 1–14.

Volger, K. E. (2002, September 22). The impact of high-stakes, state-mandated student performance assessment on teacher's instructional practices. *Education, 123*(1), 39.

Volling, B. L., & Feagans, L. V. (1995). Infant day care and children's social competence. *Infant Behavior and Development, 18*, 177–188.

Vygotsky, L. (1934/1962). *Thought and language* (E. Hanfmann & G. Zakar, Trans.). Cambridge, MA: MIT Press.

Vygotsky, L. S. (1930–1935/1978). *Mind in society* (M. Cole, S. Schribner, V. John-Steiner, & E. Souberman, Trans.). Cambridge, MA: Harvard University Press.

White, K., Hohn, R., & Tollefson, N. (1997). Encouraging elementary students to set realistic goals. *Journal of Research in Childhood Education, 12*(1), 48–57.

Wieder, S., & Greenspan, S. (2001). The DIR (Developmental, individual-difference, relationship-based) approach to assessment and intervention planning. *Zero to Three, 21*(4), 11–19.

Wien, C. A. (2004). *Negotiating standards in the primary classroom: The teacher's dilemma.* New York: Teachers College Press.

Zigler, E., & Bishop-Josef, S. J. (2004, Winter). Play under siege. *Schools of the 21st Century Newsletter.* New Haven, CT: Yale University.

Zigler, E. F., Singer, D. G., & Bishop-Josef, S. J. (2004). *Children's play: The roots of reading.* Washington, DC: Zero to Three Press.

Zigler, E. F., Finn-Stevenson, M., & Hall, N. W. (2002). *The first three years and beyond.* New Haven, CT: Yale University Press.

Zigler, E., & Styfco, S. C. (1997). A "Head Start" in what pursuit? IQ versus social competence as the objective of early intervention. In B. Devlin, S. F. Feinberg, D. Resnick, & K. Roeder (Eds.). *Intelligence, genes, and success: Scientists' response to "the bell curve,"* pp. 283–314. New York: Springer Verlag.

Zill, N., & West, J. (2001). *Entering kindergarten: Findings from the Condition of Education 2000.* [NCES 2001-035]. Washington, DC: U.S. Department of Education, Office of Educational Research and Development.

Name Index

Subject Index